"In this book Dr Johnson makes the case that competition law should be used to enforce banking cartels by comparing the actions taken in the UK, EU and US following the LIBOR and FX benchmark manipulation crises. Concise and engaging, and tackling a fascinating and timely issue, it is a must-read for readers interested in market manipulation and competition law".

Dan Joyner, Elton B. Stephens Professor of Law, *University of Alabama School of Law*

"Dr Johnson's monograph delves into the intricate world of benchmark interest rate manipulation by competing banks. By meticulously comparing enforcement approaches across the UK, EU, and US through the lens of competition law, the book provides valuable insights for policymakers, regulators, and academics".

Professor Richard Whish, *Kings College London*

"This is a must read for anyone interested in financial crimes and market law. The book offers an excellent overview and in-depth analysis of the UK, EU and the US regulatory regimes for fighting market manipulation. For those interested in the EU financial crimes framework, the book will be particularly interesting to read because of the intriguing chapters on the tangled relationship between the EU's anti market abuse measures and that of competition law enforcement, which is scrutinized in the book. I very much recommend this book".

Professor Ester Herlin-Karnell, *University of Gothenburg*

"Diana Johnson has produced a well-researched and extremely readable monograph on the intersection between financial crime and competition law. It examines the banking cartels seen in the LIBOR and FX manipulation crises through the lens of competition law. Dr Johnson compares the enforcement approaches taken by the UK, the EU and the US, concluding that competition law should be applied to future banking cartels and providing recommendations for future legislative and policy reform".

Professor Peter Whelan, *University of Leeds*

"The monograph takes an innovative approach to a key topic in white-collar crime. The book investigates the benchmark market manipulation hypothesis from a competition law standpoint. By examining LIBOR and FX cases across three different jurisdictions (the UK, the United States, and Europe), it provides insightful conclusions not only on the UK legal system, but also on the global dimension of the matter".

Enrico Basile, Ph.D., Assistant Professor of Criminal Law and White-Collar Crime, *Università "Luigi Bocconi", Milano, Italy*

"This book provides a comprehensive analysis of some of the different international responses that have emerged to tackle market manipulation. For anyone interested in this area this book provides essential reading on what can be done to better counter market manipulation and related problems and they will learn a great deal from it".

Professor Mark Button, *University of Portsmouth*

"This is a go-to book for understanding how competition law can be effectively used to tackle benchmark manipulation. Dr Johnson uses an in-depth comparative analysis of responses to the LIBOR and FX benchmark manipulation scandal in the United Kingdom, European Union and United States, providing fascinating insights into an area that is under-researched".

Associate Professor Branislav Hock, *University of Portsmouth*

"This monograph is particularly useful to those researching or working in enforcement of financial crime, because Dr Johnson has identified a gap in the literature of benchmark manipulation. She argues for the UK regulators using its full range of enforcement powers, especially competition law, to enforce benchmark manipulation. Her monograph is thought-provoking and adds to the scholarship of financial regulation".

Dr Alison Lui, Reader in Corporate and Financial Law, Associate Dean Global Engagement at *Liverpool John Moores University*

Competition Law and Financial Crime

Financial crime is a significant drain on economies across the world. This book looks at one aspect of financial crime, that of benchmark interest rate manipulation by competing banks, with the aim of identifying the best approach for the United Kingdom to take to the enforcement of laws against future benchmark manipulation.

The manipulation of any benchmark interest rate by bankers, colluding for their own gain, is likely to negatively affect a large proportion of the population, as many people have loans pegged to a benchmark interest rate. This monograph investigates the approach the UK took to enforcing action against the benchmark manipulation which took place in the London Interbank Offered Rate and the Foreign Exchange benchmark manipulation scandals. As part of this investigation, the approaches taken in the European Union and the United States of America are examined and compared to the approach taken in the UK for the same crime to draw conclusions and make recommendations to improve the UK approach for future instances of benchmark manipulation. The work fills an important gap in the literature by comparing and evaluating the laws and enforcement policies pertaining to the use of competition law in counteracting benchmark manipulation in the UK, EU and US. It argues that competition law is an effective enforcement tool when used in the financial services sector and that it provides regulators with a wide range of enforcement options when a breach of competition law is established.

The book will be a valuable resource for academics, researchers and policymakers working in the areas of financial crime, competition law, comparative law and criminal justice.

Diana Johnson is Solicitor and Senior Lecturer in Law at the University of the West of England, Bristol. Her research is on financial crime and competition law, with a particular focus on corporate criminal liability, deferred prosecution agreements, fraud and money laundering. Diana has written several publications on these topics and has submitted evidence to policymakers and influential organisations including the Law Commission, the FCA and the Treasury. Diana is a Board Member for the South West Fraud Forum and has experience of contributing to an Innovate UK funded project, which examines the submission of suspicious activity reports to the National Crime Agency for the regulated sectors.

The Law of Financial Crime

Series Editors:

Nicholas Ryder *Professor of Law, Cardiff University, School of Law and Politics, UK.*
Dr. Lachmi Singh *Associate Lecturer, Bristol Law School, University of the West of England, UK.*
Sam Bourton *Lecturer in Law, the University of the West of England, UK.*

While a growing number of high profile financial crime cases have hit the headlines recently the topic of financial crime is also generating much attention amongst academics and practitioners. This series will be the first to be dedicated to the law of financial, or economic, crime and offers a platform for important and original research in this area.

Books in the series will cover traditional subjects of financial crime including money laundering, terrorist financing, fraud, market abuse, insider dealing, market manipulation, tax evasion, bribery and corruption. But broader legal and regulatory issues will also be covered as well as emerging areas of concern such as the risks to stability of the financial system posed by financial crime. Emphasis will be placed on comparative approaches to the subject considering legislation across a number of jurisdictions as well as international regulations where appropriate, giving the series a truly global outlook.

The titles in the series are primarily aimed at an audience of researchers, scholars and practitioners in the area but should also be of interest to policy makers, law enforcement agencies, financial regulatory agencies, as well as people employed within the financial services sector.

Available titles in this series include:

Anti-Money Laundering and the Law
Comparative Approaches to Countering Predicate Crimes
Engin Erken and Umut Turksen

Global Anti-Money Laundering Regulation
Developing Countries Compliance Challenges
Edited by Nicholas Ryder, Nkechikwu Valerie Azinge-Egbiri and Ehi Eric Esoimeme Esq

Financial Investigation and Financial Intelligence
A Critical Analysis
Craig Hughes and David Hicks

Competition Law and Financial Crime
A Comparative Analysis of International Responses to Market Manipulation
Diana Johnson

For more information about this series, please visit: www.routledge.com/The-Law-of-Financial-Crime/book-series/FINCRIME

Competition Law and Financial Crime

A Comparative Analysis of International Responses to Market Manipulation

Diana Johnson

Routledge
Taylor & Francis Group
LONDON AND NEW YORK

First published 2025
by Routledge
4 Park Square, Milton Park, Abingdon, Oxon OX14 4RN

and by Routledge
605 Third Avenue, New York, NY 10158

Routledge is an imprint of the Taylor & Francis Group, an informa business

British Library Cataloguing-in-Publication Data
A catalogue record for this book is available from the British Library

Library of Congress Cataloging-in-Publication Data
Names: Johnson, Diana (Law teacher), author.
Title: Competition Law and Financial Crime: a Comparative Analysis of International Responses to Market Manipulation / Diana Johnson.
Description: New York: Routledge, 2025. | The Law of Financial Crime | Includes bibliographical references. |
Identifiers: LCCN 2024045397 (print) | LCCN 2024045398 (ebook) | ISBN 9781032540313 (hardback) | ISBN 9781032544793 (paperback) | ISBN 9781003425106 (ebook) Subjects: LCSH: Commercial crimes–Law and legislation. | Competition, Unfair. Classification: LCC K5215.J66 2025 (print) | LCC K5215 (ebook) | DDC 345/.0268–dc23/eng/20241009
LC record available at https://lccn.loc.gov/2024045397
LC ebook record available at https://lccn.loc.gov/2024045398

ISBN: 978-1-032-54031-3 (hbk)
ISBN: 978-1-032-54479-3 (pbk)
ISBN: 978-1-003-42510-6 (ebk)

DOI: 10.4324/9781003425106

Typeset in Galliard
by Deanta Global Publishing Services, Chennai, India

Contents

Foreword

The factors that contributed toward the 2007–2008 global financial crisis have been debated, researched and written about for nearly 20 years. There is not one main factor that contributed toward the biggest financial crisis since the Wall Street Crash and subsequent Great Depression in 1929. A large proportion of academic literature on the link between financial crime and the 2007–2008 global financial crisis focused on fraud and the responses by financial regulatory agencies in numerous jurisdictions. Financial regulators used a wide range of enforcement powers ranging from imposing record-breaking financial penalties on financial institutions in the United States of America, the United Kingdom and the European continent. The legal basis of these financial penalties came under the guise of breaches of either financial crime laws or financial regulation laws. The largest fines were imposed for the London Interbank Offered Rate (LIBOR) and the Foreign Exchange (FX) benchmark manipulation scandals. Despite the imposition of these record financial penalties, many of the senior managers involved in this conduct were not and are still not accountable under the existing legal and regulatory frameworks. One of the major problems faced in the imposition of corporate criminal liability within the United Kingdom has been the common law rules since the decision of the House of Lords in *Tesco Supermarkets v Nattrass* and the *Serious Fraud Office v Barclays*. In order to address this problem, successive governments have relied on the introduction of the failure to prevent model in the Bribery Act 2010, the Criminal Finances Act 2017 and the Economic Crime and Corporate Transparency Act 2023. Successive UK governments have claimed that the failure to prevent model and the use of deferred prosecution agreements have resulted in the United Kingdom having one of the most aggressive enforcement strategies toward corporate criminal liability. However, it is important to point out that the United Kingdom's financial services regulator, the Financial Conduct Authority, is not permitted to use deferred prosecution agreements due to the restrictions imposed by the Crime and Courts Act 2013. Therefore, there is a sense of frustration regarding the limited levels of accountability for corporate malpractice.

In this monograph, Dr Diana Johnson advocates an alternative approach that relies on the use of competition law in the enforcement of benchmark manipulation in the United Kingdom, the European Union and the United States of America. Dr Johnson has undertaken and performed an excellent monograph that will be very important to both the practitioner and the academic community by producing a monograph that compares and critically evaluates the laws and enforcement policies pertaining to the use of competition law in the enforcement of benchmark manipulation. The conclusions are authoritative, and policymakers and key stakeholders should take note of the recommendations that she puts forward. I commend this excellent work.

Dr Nic Ryder
Professor in Financial Crime, Cardiff University

1 Introduction

1.1 Introduction

Financial crime[1] is a significant drain on economies across the world, and it has been estimated that financial crime in the United Kingdom (UK) is a multibillion pound problem.[2] This book will look at one aspect of financial crime, that of market manipulation. The type of market manipulation examined in this book is the manipulation of benchmark interest rates (benchmark rates) carried out by competing banks, as seen in the London Interbank Offered Rate (LIBOR) and Foreign Exchange benchmark (FX) manipulation scandals of 2012–2013, litigation from which has only recently concluded in the United States (US)[3] and the UK.[4] The manipulation of any benchmark interest rate by bankers, colluding for their own gain, will negatively affect a large proportion of the population, as many people and businesses have loans pegged to a benchmark interest rate.

1 Financial crime includes money laundering, fraud, terrorist financing, bribery and corruption and market manipulation.

2 HM Government, 'Economic Crime Plan 2023-2026' (GOV.UK, 2023) 8 <https://assets.publishing.service.gov.uk/media/642561b02fa848001 3ec0f97/6.8300_HO_Economic_Crime_Plan_2_v6_Web.pdf> accessed 13 July 2024; and O Bennett and A Shalchi, 'Economic Crime in the UK: A Multi-Billion Pound Problem' (House of Commons Library, 6 April 2022) 4 <https://commonslibrary.parliament.uk/research-briefings/cbp-9013/> accessed 23 July 2024.

3 See: Criminal Division, US Department of Justice, 'United States v The Royal Bank of Scotland PLC (and RBS Securities Japan Limited)' (Criminal Division, US Department of Justice, 27 September 2023) <https://www.justice.gov/criminal/criminal-vns/case/united-states-v-royal-bank-scotland-plc-and-rbs-securities-japan-limited> accessed 26 July 2024; and J Godoy, 'U.S. Jury Finds Credit Swisse Did Not Rig Forex Market' (*Reuters*, 20 October 2022) <https://www.reuters.com/markets/us/us-jury-finds-credit-suisse-did-not-rig-forex-market-2022-10-20/> accessed 20 July 2024.

4 S Tobin, 'UK Libor Trader Hayes Given Route to Appeal Rate-Rigging Conviction at Supreme Court' (*Reuters*, 21 May 2024) <https://www.reuters.com/world/uk/uk-libor-trader-hayes-given-route-appeal-rate-rigging-conviction-supreme-court-2024-05-21/> accessed 15 July 2024.

DOI: 10.4324/9781003425106-1

This book will undertake a novel examination of the approaches to the enforcement of the LIBOR and FX benchmark rate manipulation taken in the European Union (EU) and the US, and each will be compared to the approach taken in the UK in order to draw conclusions and make recommendations to improve the UK approach for future instances of benchmark manipulation. In particular, the use of competition law in the enforcement of the LIBOR and FX benchmark rate manipulation in each jurisdiction will be examined, with consideration being given to the advantages that the use of competition law engendered in the EU and US. An important reason that competition law should be considered in the enforcement of financial crime is because of the extensive and significant enforcement options available to regulators once a breach of competition law has been established.

Competition law was used by the EU and US to enforce the LIBOR and FX benchmark manipulation scandals, and it will be seen in each of the case study chapters (Chapters 3, 4 and 5) that the penalties imposed on banks in the US and EU dwarfed those imposed by UK regulators on the same banks.[5] Also, the UK charged 13 individual traders with the criminal charge of conspiracy to defraud in connection with the LIBOR and FX cartels rather than using the criminal cartel offence, and in Chapter 3, it will be seen that the majority of these individuals were acquitted upon appeal.[6] This book, therefore, looks at whether the legislative framework in the UK provides sufficient enforcement powers to enable UK regulators to enforce a further incidence of benchmark manipulation using competition law in future. The book also examines the deterrent effect of financial crime enforcement in each of the UK, EU and US with the aim of drawing conclusions about the deterrent effect of sanctions and to determine whether any improvements are needed to individual regimes in order to deter banks and traders from engaging in benchmark manipulation in the future.

Following the comparison between the ways in which these selected jurisdictions enforced the LIBOR and FX benchmark manipulation, this book goes on to consider how the Financial Conduct Authority (FCA) has used its competition law powers in the enforcement of benchmark manipulation since it became a concurrent competition law regulator with the Competition and Markets Authority (CMA) in 2015.[7] A recent UK government report noted that there have been very few competition enforcement cases in regulated

5 H Hillman, 'Are the Current Laws and Potential Enforcement Measures Effective in Achieving the Accountability of Bank Directors for Their Actions, or the Actions of the Banks they Manage? A Comparison of UK and US Approaches' in N Ryder and others (eds), *Fighting Financial Crime in the Global Economic Crisis* (Routledge 2016) 202.

6 Serious Fraud Office, 'SFO Concludes Investigation into LIBOR Manipulation' (Serious Fraud Office, 18 October 2019) <https://www.sfo.gov.uk/2019/10/18/sfo-concludes-investigation-into-libor-manipulation/#:~:text=The%20SFO's%20investigation%20into%20LIBOR,LIBOR%20offence%20in%20the%20UK.> accessed 30 July 2024.

7 Financial Services (Banking Reform) Act 2013, Schedule 8.

sectors, including the financial services sector, of which the financial services sector is one, since competition powers were given to the FCA.[8] The reasons for this are considered and analysed in Chapters 6, 6 and 7.

The comparison made between the approach to the enforcement of benchmark manipulation taken by the UK, EU and US will inform the discussion of whether competition law is a suitable tool with which to enforce the financial crime of market manipulation. The LIBOR benchmark rate has now been phased out, due in part to its involvement in the financial crisis and the LIBOR manipulation scandal[9] however, this research is as relevant to the LIBOR and the FX as to any other benchmark rate used by banks.

This book fills an important gap in academic literature by carrying out the first in-depth comparison and evaluation of the laws and enforcement policies used in the enforcement of the LIBOR and FX benchmark manipulation in the UK, EU and US. This book is also the first to carry out a detailed analysis of the use of competition law in enforcing benchmark manipulation in these three jurisdictions. This book argues that competition law is an effective enforcement tool when used in the financial services sector and that it provides regulators with a wide range of enforcement options when a breach of competition law is established. It will be seen that significant insights can be gained from the EU and US in the use of competition law to enforce benchmark manipulation.

1.2 Aim of the Book

The central aim of this book is to demonstrate that the use of competition law to enforce the financial crime of benchmark manipulation will provide regulators with a wide range of significant enforcement powers, which, if used, would create a much greater deterrent effect to the crime of benchmark manipulation than the sanctions imposed in the UK following the LIBOR and FX benchmark manipulation crisis. Demonstrating that competition law is effective in the enforcement of benchmark manipulation will help the UK to tackle benchmark manipulation more successfully than it did in the LIBOR and FX crisis and will help prevent future benchmark manipulation by attracting more whistleblowers, incentivising banks to use compliance programmes and raising awareness of the significant sanctions for breach of competition law.

8 Department for Business, Energy & Industrial Strategy, 'Competition Law Review: Post Implementation Review of Statutory Changes in the Enterprise and Regulatory Reform Act 2013' (GOV.UK, 31 March 2019) <https://www.legislation.gov.uk/ukpga/2013/24/pdfs/ukpgaod_20130024_en.pdf> accessed 1 July 2024.

9 S Klingler and O Syrstad, 'Life after LIBOR' (2021) 141(2) *Journal of Financial Economics* 783–801.

This book will build upon existing academic literature in the key fields of financial crime[10] and competition law.[11] Financial crime is an umbrella term covering many individual crimes, such as market manipulation,[12] money laundering,[13] terrorism financing[14] and bribery.[15] The aspects of financial crime relevant to this book include market manipulation and the analysis of the LIBOR and FX benchmark manipulation, which has attracted a lot of academic commentary, together with subsequent benchmark manipulation cases.[16]

10 Including N Ryder, *The Financial Crisis and White Collar Crime: The Perfect Storm?* (Edward Elgar 2014); KHS Pickett and JM Pickett, *Financial Crime Investigation and Control* (Wiley New York 2002); and J Markham, *Law Enforcement and the History of Financial Market Manipulation* (Routledge 2015).

11 Including R Whish & D Bailey, *Competition Law* (10th edn, Oxford University Press 2021); P Whelan, *The Criminalisation of European Cartel Enforcement: Theoretical, Legal and Practical Challenges* (Oxford University Press 2014); I Lianos and others, *Competition Law* (Oxford University Press 2019); and Gerber DJ, *Competition Law and Antitrust* (Oxford University Press 2020).

12 See E Herlin-Karnell and N Ryder, *Market Manipulation and Insider Trading* (Hart 2019) 14; J. Austin, *Insider Trading and Market Manipulation: Investigating and Prosecuting Across Borders* (Edward Elgar: Cheltenham, 2017); and J. Markham *Law Enforcement and the History of Financial Market Manipulation* (Routledge: London, 2015).

13 See SC Brown and B Hertstein, 'Failure to Prevent Money Laundering and the Supervisory Principle' (2022) 8 *Criminal Law Review* 648; E Herlin-Karnell and N Ryder, 'The Robustness of EU Financial Crimes Legislation: A Critical Review of the EU and UK Anti-Fraud and Money Laundering Scheme' (2017) 27(4) *European Business Law Review* 427; D Chaikin and J Sharman, *Corruption and Money Laundering: A Symbiotic Relationship* (Palgrave New York, 2009); P Alldridge, *Money Laundering Law: Forfeiture, Confiscation, Civil Recovery, Criminal Laundering and Taxation of the Proceeds of Crime* (Hart 2003); and M. Galland, *Money Laundering and the Proceeds of Crime: Economic Crime and Civil Remedies* (Edward Elgar 2005).

14 See J Gurule, *Unfunding Terror: The Legal Response to the Financing of Global Terrorism* (Edward Elgar 2010); and N Ryder, *The Financial War on Terror: A Review of Counter-Terrorist Financing Strategies Since 2001* (Routledge 2015).

15 See D Hall, 'Financial Crises and Fraud: A Pattern Emerges' in L Pasculli and N Ryder (eds), *Corruption in the Global Era: Causes, Sources and Forms of Manifestation* (Routlege 2019); RD Luz and G Spagnolo, 'Leniency, Collusion, Corruption and Whistleblowing' (2017) 13(4) *Journal of Competition Law & Economics* 729; A Palmer *Countering Economic Crime: A Comparative Analysis* (Routledge 2017); D Chaikin and J Sharman *Corruption and Money Laundering: A Symbiotic Relationship* (Palgrave: New York 2009); and J Fisher, 'Who Should Prosecute Fraud, Corruption and Financial Markets Crime?' (London School of Economics and Political Science, December 2013) <https://www.lse.ac.uk/law/Assets/Documents/law-and-financial-markets-project/fisher-who-should-prosecute.pdf> accessed 8 July 2024.

16 See RM Abrantes-Metz and others, 'Libor Manipulation?' (2012) 36(1) *Journal of Banking and Finance*; A Akhigbe and others, 'Foreign Exchange Manipulation and the Equity Returns of Global Banks' (2020) 57(2) *Journal of Financial Services Research* 207; JA Batten, 'Financial Market Manipulation, Whistleblowing, and the Common Good: Evidence from the LIBOR Scandal' (2022) 58(1) *ABACUS* 1; R Calo, 'Digital Market Manipulation' (2014) 82(4) *George Washington Law Review* 995.

SE Foster, 'LIBOR Manipulation and Antitrust Allegations' (2013) 11(29) *DePaul Business & Commercial Law Journal* 291; J Fouquau and PK Spieser, 'Statistical Evidence about LIBOR Manipulation: A "Sherlock Holmes" Investigation' (2015) 50(1) *Journal of Banking and Finance* 632.

Market manipulation has many harmful effects, including damage to market integrity, the undermining of investor confidence and making markets subject to systemic crises.[17] The EU recognises the damage market manipulation can inflict, stating in its market abuse regulation[18] that the reason for criminalising market manipulation is to protect market integrity and public confidence in financial markets.[19] Many commentators have written about the laws governing market manipulation in the financial services sector in the UK, EU and US.[20] However, there is very little literature when it comes to a discussion of how competition law could be used to enforce market manipulation the financial sector in the UK,[21] although some academics have written about its use in the US and EU for market manipulation in the financial services sector.[22] This is a gap in the literature that this book intends to fill by formulating proposals about the use of competition law in future market manipulation cases in the UK.

Much has been written about the LIBOR crisis,[23] with academics such as Yeoh[24] arguing that the reforms to financial regulation may not have gone

17 See E Lomnicka, 'Preventing and Controlling the Manipulation of Financial Markets: Towards a Definition of "Market Manipulation"' (2001) 8(4) *Journal of Financial Crime* 297; K Sergakis, *The Law of Capital Markets in the EU: Disclosure and Enforcement* (Palgrave Corporate and Financial Law 2017); TCW Lin, 'The New Market Manipulation' (2017) 66(6) *Emory Law Journal* 1253; and E Herlin-Karnell and N Ryder, *Market Manipulation and Insider Trading* (Hart 2019).

18 Regulation (EU) No 596/2014 of the European Parliament and of the Council of 16 April 2014 on Market Abuse (Market Abuse Regulation) [2014] OJ 2 173/1.

19 Ibid., Preamble (2).

20 For instance, see J Grey, 'Financial Services and Markets Tribunal Orders that Costs of Successful Challenge to Enforcement Action for Market Abuse Be Paid by FSA' (2007) 15(2) *Journal of Financial Regulation and Compliance* 217; and E Herlin-Karnell and N Ryder *Market Manipulation and Insider Trading* (Hart 2019).

21 See B McGrath, 'Banking and Antitrust: The View from the UK' (2010) 127 *Banking Law Journal* 563; D Harrison, *Competition Law and Financial Services* (Routledge 2014) – NB this book only briefly mentions banking cartels and makes one passing reference to the LIBOR manipulation; and R Ball, 'Competition Law and LIBOR in Three Jurisdictions: US, UK and EU' in Ryder N (ed), *White Collar Crime and Risk – A Critical Reflection* (Routledge 2018).

22 For instance, see SD Ledgerwood and JA Verlinda, 'The Intersection of Antitrust and Market Manipulation Law' (2017) <https://ssrn.com/abstract=2908878> accessed 26 July 2024; J Hamburger, 'Crowding the Market: Is There Room for Antitrust in Market Manipulation Cases?' (2015) 21(4) *International Trade Law and Regulation* 120; and D Scheld and others, 'Managing Antitrust Risks in the Banking Industry (2016) 12(1) European Competition Journal 113.

23 For example see P Yeoh, 'Libor Benchmark: Practice, Crime and Reforms' (2016) 23(4) *The Journal of Financial Crime* 1140; RM. Abrantes-Metz and others, 'Libor Manipulation?' (2012) 36(1) *Journal of Banking and Finance*; R Poskitt and W Dassanayake, 'Modelling the Lowballing of the LIBOR Fixing' (2015) 42(1) *International Review of Financial Analysis* 270; Samantha Strimling and Eric Talley, 'Who Put The "Lie" in LIBOR (And Who Should Take It Out)? Civil LIBOR Litigation in the US' (2014) 8(2) *Law and Financial Markets Review* 145; and T Angeletti, 'The Differential Management of Financial Illegalisms: Assigning Responsibilities in the Libor Scandal' (2019) 53(4) *Law and Society Review* 1233.

24 P Yeoh 'Libor Benchmark: Practice, Crime and Reforms' (2016) 23(4) *The Journal of Financial Crime* 1140.

far enough and that continued vigilance from all stakeholders in the banking industry is required to prevent further misconduct. Other academics, such as Ryder and Hall,[25] have undertaken a comparative analysis of related jurisdictions (US and UK) to tackling corporate financial crime in light of the LIBOR crisis, although there is no research comparing the enforcement of market manipulation in the UK to the enforcement actions taken by the EU and the US.[26] This book intends to conduct a novel in-depth analysis of the different ways in which the UK, EU and US approached the enforcement of the LIBOR and FX benchmark manipulation crisis and the extent to which each jurisdiction used its competition law powers in this enforcement.

In each chapter of this book, four distinct but connected themes will be considered as part of the research. The themes are first, the role of competition law whistleblowing and leniency regimes in the identification and prosecution of cartels; second, a consideration of civil vs criminal sanctions for breaches of competition law and financial crime; third, an evaluation of corporate criminal liability in the different jurisdictions; and fourth, the role of Deferred Prosecution Agreements for companies who have breached criminal law. These themes will be outlined and discussed in Chapter 2 and then examined in detail in each later chapter of this book. In relation to the third theme, corporate criminal liability has been written about extensively, not just in the context of financial crime.[27] Academics have written about the use of corporate criminal responsibility in the field of financial crime, exploring themes such as the lack of criminal prosecutions after the 2008 financial crisis,[28] the UK's

25 N Ryder, 'Too Scared to Prosecute and Too Scared to Jail?' A Critical and Comparative Analysis of Enforcement of Financial Crime Legislation Against Corporations in the USA and the UK' (2018) 82(3) *The Journal of Financial Crime* 245; and C Hall, 'Anything for You Big Boy: A Comparative Analysis of Banking Regulation in the United States and the United Kingdom in Light of the LIBOR Scandal' (2013) 34(1) *Northwestern Journal of International Law and Business* 153.

26 N Ryder, 'Too Scared to Prosecute and Too Scared to Jail?' A Critical and Comparative Analysis of Enforcement of Financial Crime Legislation Against Corporations in the USA and the UK' (2018) 82(3) *The Journal of Financial Crime* 245.

27 For example see Law Commission, 'Corporate Criminal Liability: An Options Paper' (Law Commission, 10 June 2022) <https://s3-eu-west-2.amazonaws.com/lawcom-prod-storage-11jsxou24uy7q/uploads/2022/06/Corporate-Criminal-Liability-Options-Paper_LC.pdf/> accessed 10 July 2024; N Werle, 'Prosecuting Corporate Crime When Firms Are Too Big to Jail: Investigation, Deterrence, and Judicial Review' (2019) 128(5) *Yale L J* 1366; Peter J Henning, 'Corporate Criminal Liability and the Potential for Rehabilitation' (2009) 46(4) *American Criminal Law Review* 1417; Barry J Pollack, Annie W Reisinger, 'Lone Wolf or The Start of A New Pack: Should the FCPA Guidance Represent a New Paradigm in Evaluating Corporate Criminal Liability Risks?' (2014) 51(1) *American Criminal Law Review* 121; and Sarah Field and Lucy Jones, 'Is the Net of Corporate Criminal Liability under the Corporate Homicide and Corporate Manslaughter Act 2007 Expanding?' (2015) 36(6) *Business Law Review* 216.

28 For example, see N Ryder, 'Too Scared to Prosecute and Too Scared to Jail? A Critical and Comparative Analysis of Enforcement of Financial Crime Legislation Against Corporations

recent approach to criminalising the 'failure to prevent' certain crimes such as bribery, tax evasion and fraud, categorised by Campbell as 'an indirect form of omissions liability'[29] and the introduction of political–economic constraints into corporate liability, whereby prosecutors are unable to credibly threaten criminal sanctions to large companies, such as banks, for fear that their collapse would threaten the economy and investor confidence in the markets.[30] This is known as the 'too big to jail' argument,[31] and this will be explored further in this book. This book will continue the discussion about the paucity of corporate criminal prosecutions in the UK compared to the US, the UK's recent approach to corporate criminal liability and the 'too big to jail' argument in relation to large corporations such as banks.[32] The book will build on each of these arguments and will focus on the specific financial crime of benchmark manipulation and the different ways in which corporate criminal liability has been and could be used to deter this crime in the future.

To summarise, the gaps identified in the literature that this book will fill include how market manipulation can be enforced by competition law in the UK, the completion of the first in-depth comparative analysis of how the UK, EU and US enforced the LIBOR and FX crisis and a comparative analysis of how banking cartels can be enforced using competition law in the the UK, EU and US. This book will build on existing financial crime and competition law research, and its findings will be used to form proposals for further competition law reform in the UK, with the aim of enabling regulators to improve their enforcement of future banking benchmark manipulation cartels.

1.3 Competition Law and Benchmark Interest Rates

Definitions of competition law and benchmark manipulation, which are used throughout this book, will be briefly introduced below.

---

in the USA and the UK' (2018) 82(3) *The Journal of Financial Crime* 245; and Henry N Pontell and others, 'Too Big To Fail, Too Powerful To Jail? On The Absence of Criminal Prosecutions after the 2008 Financial Meltdown' (2014) 61 *Crime Law Soc Change* 1.

29 L Campbell, 'Corporate Liability and the Criminalisation of Failure' (2018) 12(2) *Law and Financial Markets Review* 57.

30 N Werle, 'Prosecuting Corporate Crime When Firms Are Too Big to Jail: Investigation, Deterrence and Judicial Review' (2019) 128(5) *The Yale Law Journal* 1366.

31 Ibid.

32 See N Werle, 'Prosecuting Corporate Crime When Firms Are Too Big to Jail: Investigation, Deterrence, and Judicial Review' (2019) 128 *Yale L J* 1366; N Ryder, 'Too Scared to Prosecute and Too Scared to Jail? A Critical and Comparative Analysis of Enforcement of Financial Crime Legislation Against Corporations in the USA and the UK' (2018) 82(3) *The Journal of Criminal Law* 243; and H Pontell and others, 'Too Big To Fail, Too Powerful To Jail? On the Absence of Criminal Prosecutions after the 2008 Financial Meltdown' (2014) 61(1) *Crime Law Soc Change* 1.

1.3.1 Competition Law

Competition law has been defined as 'the laws that are intended to make sure that there is fair competition between businesses'.[33] A central aim of competition law is the enhancement of consumer welfare by prohibiting agreements that harm competition and preventing abusive behaviour by companies holding a dominant market position.[34] Competition law prohibits the collusion of competitors, such as the collusion between competing banks seen in the LIBOR and FX benchmark manipulation cartels, due to the harmful effects such collusion has on consumers. In the context of this book, competition law refers to those specific competition laws in force in the UK, EU and US before and after the LIBOR and FX crisis. These competition laws are outlined in Chapter 2 and then set out in detail in each of the case study chapters – Chapters 3 (UK), 4 (EU) and 5 (US).

Historically, the enforcement of competition law has been restricted in the financial services market in the UK, in which regulators have instead elected to use detailed prescriptive rules governing the conduct of financial services firms.[35] This is consistent with the approach adopted by the Financial Services Authority (FSA) and the FCA toward the enforcement of the LIBOR and FX benchmark manipulation, which ignored the concerns raised by the then competition law regulator, the Office of Fair Trading (OFT), about a breach of competition law.[36]

A benefit of utilising competition law instead of financial regulation to enforce benchmark manipulation is that the UK competition regulator, following a breach of competition law, has the power to impose significant fines of up to 10% of a company's worldwide turnover, impose structural or behavioural directions on a company, accept commitments from infringing companies and disqualify directors for up to 15 years for a breach of competition law by their company.[37] There is also a criminal cartel offence available to regulators for collusion between bankers at competing banks, such as the collusion seen in the LIBOR and FX manipulation scandal.[38] These powers were in place

33 Cambridge University Press, 'Competition Law' (Cambridge Business English Dictionary, 2024) <https://dictionary.cambridge.org/dictionary/english/competition-law> accessed 16 July 2024.

34 House of Commons Library, 'The UK Competition Regime' (UK Parliament, 25 May 2021) <https://commonslibrary.parliament.uk/research-briefings/sn04814/> accessed 24 July 2024; and WF Shughart, 'On the Virginia School of Antitrust: Competition Policy, Law & Economics and Public Choice' (2022) 191(102) *Public Choice* 1, 3.

35 D Harrison, *Competition Law and Financial Services* (Routledge 2016) 61.

36 Financial Services Authority, 'Internal Audit Report a Review of the Extent of Awareness within the FSA of Inappropriate LIBOR Submissions' (FCA, March 2013) 80, 81 <https://www.fca.org.uk/publication/corporate/fsa-ia-libor.pdf> accessed 30 July 2024.

37 R Whish and D Bailey, *Competition Law* (10th edn, Oxford University Press 2021) 424–460, Competition Act 1998 ss. 36, 32, 31 and Company Directors Disqualification Act 1986 s. 9A.

38 Enterprise Act 2002, s.188.

at the time of the benchmark manipulation scandal of 2012–2013 but were not used in the UK. If they had been used, the penalties imposed on banks and individuals are likely to have been substantially greater and would have created a more significant deterrent effect on both the banks and the individuals involved in the benchmark manipulation than the regulatory fines imposed by the financial services regulator.

The second key definition used in this book, that of benchmark interest rate manipulation, is introduced below.

1.3.2 Benchmark Interest Rates

A benchmark interest rate (benchmark rate) is a financial marker that is used as a reference point for many widely used financial instruments, including loans, mortgages and hire purchase agreements.[39] Therefore, any manipulation of a benchmark rate will adversely affect a large proportion of the population because many individuals and businesses have loans, such as mortgages, personal or commercial loans that will be pegged to a benchmark rate. Some of the key benchmark interest rates that are examined this book are the LIBOR, the FX and the Euro Interbank Offered Rate (EURIBOR), which was manipulated at the same time as the LIBOR and FX benchmarks. In the UK, financial penalties were imposed by the FSA and FCA for the manipulation of the LIBOR and FX benchmark rates, but none of these fines were made using competition law powers, although competition law was in force in the UK at this time.[40] This is examined in detail in Chapter 3. However, in the EU and US competition law powers were used to enforce some or all of the LIBOR and FX benchmark manipulation, and higher fines were levied in those jurisdictions against the offending banks as a result.[41] Therefore, this book considers whether using competition law powers in the enforcement of future benchmark manipulation will provide the UK's financial services regulator with a wider range of enforcement options in future than if they simply use their financial regulation powers.

1.4 Rationale for the Book

The backdrop to this book is the rising cost of financial crime to the UK economy, estimated to run into tens or hundreds of billions of pounds per year, which gives rise to a need for regulators to make the most effective use of their

39 A Theodosopoulou, 'Interest Rate Benchmarks Regulation: Work in Progress' (2014) 29(9) *Journal of International Banking Law and Regulation* 536.

40 Competition Law Act 1998, Chapter I Agreements, s.2.

41 R Ball, 'Competition Law and LIBOR in Three Jurisdictions: The United States of America, the United Kingdom and the European Union' in N Ryder (ed), *White Collar Crime and Risk – Financial Crime, Corruption and the Financial Crisis* (Palgrave 2018) 174–175, 179.

enforcement powers.[42] In particular, the enforcement powers that are available to regulators when a breach of competition law is established are extensive and significant in each of the three selected jurisdictions, the UK, the EU and the US. However, in the UK there is a lack of awareness of competition law by businesses, as highlighted by research carried out on behalf of the CMA.[43] A review by the government into how competition law powers have been used by sector regulators[44] found that sector regulators, such as the FCA, had been reluctant to use their competition enforcement powers since competition law powers were granted to them for use in their market sectors.[45] The report speculated that the reason for this was that:

> Regulators believe that their ex-ante regulatory tools are a quicker, more cost-effective and less resource-intensive way of improving outcomes for consumers than enforcement action under Competition Act 1998.[46]

The government concluded that 'regulators preferred to use their regulatory powers rather than their competition powers, as they had more experience of using the regulatory powers'.[47] For this reason, in the Financial Services (Banking Reform) Act 2013, the FCA was given an explicit duty to consider, *before* using its regulatory powers, whether it would be more appropriate to use its competition law enforcement powers instead.[48] This provision, known

42 HM Government, 'Economic Crime Plan 2023-2026' (GOV.UK, 2023) 8 <https://assets.publishing.service.gov.uk/media/642561b02fa8480013ec0f97/6.8300_HO_Economic_Crime_Plan_2_v6_Web.pdf> accessed 13 July 2024; and O Bennett and A Shalchi, 'Economic Crime in the UK: A Multi-Billion Pound Problem' (House of Commons Library, 6 April 2022) 4 <https://commonslibrary.parliament.uk/research-briefings/cbp-9013/> accessed 13 July 2024.

43 IFF Research, 'Competition Law Business Tracking Research Competition & Markets Authority' (GOV.UK, May 2021) 3, 44 <https://assets.publishing.service.gov.uk/media/60ee9fbdd3bf7f5688e5d96d/CMA_Competition_Law_Business_Survey_2021_Final_Report_.pdf> accessed 13 July 2024.

44 Sector regulators in UK competition law include the regulators of various market sectors, including the FCA, the Civil Aviation Authority, the Office of Communications and the Gas and Electricity Markets Authority. For a full list of sector regulators, see Competition and Markets Authority, 'CMA Call for Views: How Regulators Work Together to Protect Consumers' (GOV.UK, 24 August 2023) Notes to Editors point 4 <https://www.gov.uk/government/news/cma-call-for-views-how-regulators-work-together-to-protect-consumers#:~:text=The%20sector%20regulators%20with%20concurrent,Ofgem)%3B%20the%20Payment%20Systems> accessed 24 July 2024.

45 Department for Business, Energy & Industrial Strategy, 'Competition Law Review: Post Implementation Review of Statutory Changes in the Enterprise and Regulatory Reform Act 2013' (GOV.UK, 31 March 2019) 42 <https://www.legislation.gov.uk/ukpga/2013/24/pdfs/ukpgaod_20130024_en.pdf> accessed 14 July 2024.

46 Ibid 42.

47 Ibid 43.

48 Financial Services (Banking Reform) Act 2013 Schedule 8, Part 1, s3 as it amends the Financial Services and Markets Act 2000, s.234K(1).

as the 'primacy provision', came into force in April 2015, which is after the majority of the LIBOR and FX enforcement had taken place in the UK.[49]

The government's report demonstrated that there is a need for the FCA to start making more frequent use of its competition law powers in the financial services sector, as intended by the legislative changes made by the government following the 2007/2008 financial crisis.[50] However, it will be seen in Chapter 3 of this book that the FCA is not making full use of their competition law powers, so businesses in the financial sector are not aware of competition law or how it is enforced. Presumably because of this lack of sufficient use of competition law powers by the FCA, it has been identified that there is a lack of awareness of competition law by UK businesses generally.[51] Andrew Tyrie, the former chair of the CMA and the Parliamentary Banking Commission, stated that major regulatory reform is urgently needed in order to raise the profile of competition law with businesses in the UK.[52] Tyrie stated that two-thirds of businesses do not know that the CMA enforces competition law and that one in ten businesses openly admit to discussing prices with competitors, similar to the actions taken by the bank traders in the LIBOR and FX cartels, unaware that this is a breach of competition law.[53]

The research set out in this book is needed because each incidence of misconduct and manipulation by a bank and/or its employees of a financial benchmark rate has wide ranging consequences on global financial markets, market confidence and on the public's perception of banks.[54] The benchmark rates examined in this book are used in the global financial markets, so manipulation of one or more benchmark rates will have an effect on worldwide markets as well as those in each of the selected jurisdictions. For instance, financial instruments such as mortgages, student loans, financial derivatives, and other financial products often rely on a particular named benchmark rate as a reference rate, so any manipulation of submissions used to calculate those rates can have significant negative effects on consumers and financial markets world-

49 D Jones, 'The FCA's New Competition Powers: What Do They Mean for the Financial Services Industry?' (Financial Conduct Authority, 21 November 2014) <https://www.fca.org.uk/news/speeches/fca%E2%80%99s-new-competition-powers-what-do-they-mean-financial-services-industry> accessed 13 July 2024.

50 See Schedule 8, Part 2, Paragraph 9 of the Financial Services (Banking Reform) Act 2013, which added the FCA to the list of sector regulators in s.54 of the Competition Act 1998, giving the FCA its competition law powers.

51 A Tyrie, 'The UK Competition Regulator Is Not Fit for Purpose' *Financial Times* (London, 24 February 2021) <https://www.ft.com/content/4d0e284c-c29c-4879-a408-1163386b0128> accessed 24 July 2024.

52 Ibid.

53 Ibid.

54 Commodity Futures Trading Commission, 'CFTC Orders Barclays to Pay $200 Million Penalty for Attempted Manipulation of and False Reporting Concerning LIBOR and Euribor Benchmark Interest Rates' (Commodity Futures Trading Commission, 27 June 2012) <https://www.cftc.gov/PressRoom/PressReleases/6289-12> accessed 24 July 2024.

wide.[55] Therefore, it is important to ensure that each jurisdiction has in place robust and comprehensive investigation, regulation and enforcement powers to deter and punish banks and individuals who consider benchmark rate fixing.

Further analysis of the use of competition law in the regulation and enforcement of benchmark rate manipulation in the EU and US could persuade the UK competition regulators to use their wide range of competition law powers in a future benchmark manipulation scandal involving one of the other benchmark interest rates such as the ISDAfix, oil and gold benchmarks. The use of the stronger and more extensive competition law enforcement powers will have a greater deterrent effect on the banks and traders than the use of financial regulatory powers has had to date. In the last financial crisis there were few people left unaffected as the fall out of the LIBOR and FX manipulation had a significant impact on individuals, businesses and governments in the UK, EU and US.[56]

It is important to examine the advantages of using competition law to enforce benchmark manipulation because further benchmark manipulation cartels are highly likely to occur in the future, due to the temptation of substantial profits for the banks involved. For instance, since the LIBOR and FX scandals, the European Commission has accused four banks of participating in a sovereign bond cartel to rig prices for sovereign bonds and related debt in breach of competition law.[57] If further banking cartels do take place, they are likely to have a global reach, as banks such as Deutsche Bank and Credit Suisse are multinational investment banks that maintain offices in key financial centres around the world. Therefore, it is important to ensure that financial crime regulators have the best powers available to them. Competition law is very well-suited for the enforcement of financial crime, which can be demonstrated by comparing the financial penalties issued in the UK and those issued by the EU and the US for the same LIBOR and FX rigging offences. The key difference between the fines was that the EU and US fines were significantly higher than those imposed by UK regulators on the banks involved. The EU and US used competition laws to enforce the benchmark manipulation, and the UK used financial regulation in its enforcement. These points are examined in detail in each of the three case study chapters (Chapters 3, 4 and 5), and comparisons are made between the three approaches in Chapter 6.

The rationale of this book is, therefore, to demonstrate to regulators, legislators and policymakers that competition law is more suitable for dealing with

55 S Klingler and O Syrstad, 'Life after LIBOR' (2021) 141 *Journal of Financial Economics* 783, 783.

56 P Yeoh, 'Libor Benchmark: Practice, Crime and Reforms' (2016) 23(4) *Journal of Financial Crime* 1140, 1149.

57 European Commission, 'Antitrust: Commission Sends Statement of Objections in US Dollar Supra Sovereign, Sovereign and Agency Bond Trading Cartel' (European Commission, 20 December 2018) <https://ec.europa.eu/commission/presscorner/detail/en/IP_18_6895> accessed 14 July 2024.

the financial crime of benchmark manipulation than financial regulation. To demonstrate this, the book will examine the responses of each of the UK, EU and US to the LIBOR and FX scandal in order to see how much (if at all) each jurisdiction used its competition law powers to enforce the benchmark manipulation and to examine the result of the enforcement action taken. As part of this examination, the type of sanctions, civil or criminal, used in each jurisdiction will be assessed. In relation to criminal sanctions, the issue of corporate criminal liability is considered in each of the case study chapters (Chapters 3, 4 and 5), due to its use in the US, alongside the use by regulators of deferred prosecution agreements (DPAs).[58] The issues of corporate criminal liability and DPAs are relevant to consider a due to their use by US regulators in the enforcement of LIBOR and FX benchmark manipulation against corporate entities such as the banks involved.

As part of this research, this book will examine how the competition law whistleblowing/leniency regimes operate in the financial services sector in each jurisdiction. Having a competition law whistleblowing and/or leniency programme is essential to the identification of and the enforcement of the law against cartels because cartels are typically secret, verbal agreements, that make them hard to identify and extremely difficult for regulators to gather sufficient evidence on in order to prosecute.[59]

This novel detailed comparison of the use of competition law to enforce the LIBOR and FX benchmark manipulation in the UK, EU and US, together with the examination of the type of sanctions imposed and how the competition leniency regimes operate, will provide important information and analysis to legislators, regulators, policymakers and researchers.

1.5 Methodology Employed in the Book

As stated above, the aim of this book is to undertake a comparative analysis of the role that competition law plays in regulating and enforcing benchmark manipulation in the UK, EU and the US. To fulfil this aim, this book employs a comparative methodology of research, supported by a doctrinal analysis of the law. A comparative methodology involves the comparison of laws, with the aim of finding similarities or differences.[60] In this book, the laws from each of the three selected jurisdiction will be examined, with similarities and differences between them identified and the success or failure of the laws in practice analysed. Comparative legal research is recognised as a method of determining how different legal systems have addressed similar problems, perhaps in

58 L Campbell, 'Trying Corporations: Why Not Prosecute?' (2019) 31(2) *Current Issues in Criminal Justice* 269, 270.

59 P Dijkstra and J Seifert, 'Cartel Leniency and Settlements: A Joint Perspective' (2023) 63 *Review of Industrial Organisation* 239, 240.

60 E Orucu, 'Developing Comparative Law' in E Orucu, D Nelken (eds), *Comparative Law: A Handbook* (Hart 2007) 44.

a different way and with different degrees of perceived success or failure.[61] Comparative research includes providing a critical perspective into different legal practices, facilitating the harmonisation of laws and assisting with law reform and policy development.[62] The common components of the competition and financial crime legislative and regulatory regimes of the UK, EU and US will be analysed and evaluated in this book to consider how well they have worked to regulate financial crime in each jurisdiction since the LIBOR and FX crisis.

Together with the comparative methodology outlined above, a doctrinal analysis of the relevant laws in the UK, EU and US will also be employed. Using a doctrinal analysis of laws is essential to ascertain the laws relating to benchmark manipulation in each of the three selected jurisdictions before deciding whether any legislative reform is needed. The legal doctrine relevant to this research is competition law and its interaction with the legislative frameworks of financial crime in each of the three identified jurisdictions. This doctrinal analysis will draw upon domestic legislation in the UK, EU and US, international treaties, reports published by governmental bodies and regulators, journal articles and academic books. Websites of the key competition and financial services regulators in each jurisdiction are also used as relevant sources.

The use of a comparative methodology supported by doctrinal analysis of relevant laws will support the key aim of this book, which is to understand the operation of competition law when it is used to enforce the financial crime of benchmark manipulation and to propose changes, if considered appropriate, to legislation and/or policy based on the comparative analysis.

1.6 Reasons for Comparing the UK, EU and US

There are three key reasons for selecting the jurisdictions of the UK, the EU and the US as case studies to compare in this book. First, the three jurisdictions have been selected because all three experienced the LIBOR and FX benchmark manipulation due to the interconnected nature of banking.[63] Second, all three have similar laws and cultures and work together to dominate international trade and global diplomacy.[64] In particular, these three jurisdic-

61 R Schlesinger, 'The Past and Future of Comparative Law' (1995) 43 AJCL, 477.

62 E Orucu, 'Developing Comparative Law' in E Orucu, D Nelken (eds), *Comparative Law: A Handbook* (Hart 2007) 44.

63 A Roncoroni et al., 'Working Paper Series: Interconnected Banks and Systemically Important Exposures' (European Central Bank, November 2019) <https://www.ecb.europa.eu/pub/pdf/scpwps/ecb.wp2331~ab59126ee2.en.pdf> accessed 26 July 2024.

64 For instance, see K Donovan and others, 'The US, EU and UK Need a Shared Approach to Economic Statecraft. Here's Where to Start' (Atlantic Council, 20 September 2023 <https://www.atlanticcouncil.org/in-depth-research-reports/report/us-eu-uk-need-shared-approach-to-economic-statecraft/> accessed 24 July 2024; White & Case LLP, 'Operational Resil-

tions all have similar competition laws, the oldest of which are those of the US, which originally conceived of competition law as a discipline designed to control anticompetitive acts of businesses.[65] US competition laws are known to have strongly influenced the creation of the EU and UK competition laws.[66] In fact, as Mario Monti, the former European Commissioner for Competition Policy stated:

> The influence of US antitrust law was profound during the early years of the development of competition policy in Europe and has continued ever since. This influence has helped to ensure that today, after almost 50 years of application and development of antitrust rules in Europe, we can confidently say that we share the same goals and pursue the same results on both sides of the Atlantic.[67]

This demonstrates the strong link between US and EU competition laws. UK competition laws are virtually identical to those of the EU because, due to the UK's previous membership of the EU, UK competition laws were directly taken from the supranational EU competition laws.[68] The close link between EU and UK competition law is unlikely to change significantly in the near future as, since Brexit took place on 31 January 2020, UK competition law has remained substantially the same. It is stated in the EU–UK Trade and Cooperation Agreement that the UK will continue to respect the shared competition law principles and allow businesses in the EU and UK to compete on a level playing field, although some divergence will be allowed in less significant areas of competition law.[69]

---

ience in the UK, EU and US: A Comparison' (White & Case, 1 December 2022) <https://www.whitecase.com/insight-our-thinking/financial-regulatory-observer-2022-operational-resilience-uk-eu-and-us> accessed 24 July 2024; and V James, 'The "Special Relationship" Between the US and the UK' (University of Cambridge, 11 April 2022) <https://magazine.alumni.cam.ac.uk/special-relationship-between-us-and-uk/> accessed 26 July 2024.

65 EM Fox and D Healey, 'When the State Harms Competition – The Role for Competition Law' (2014) 79(3) *Antitrust Law Journal* 769, 770.

66 AD Chirita, 'A Legal-Historical Review of the EU Competition Rules' (2014) 63(2) *International and Comparative Law Quarterly* 281, 289.

67 M Monti, 'Antitrust in the US and Europe: A History of Convergence' (American Bar Association, 14 November 2001 <https://ec.europa.eu/commission/presscorner/api/files/document/print/en/speech_01_540/SPEECH_01_540_EN.pdf> accessed 18 July 2024.

68 M Smith, 'Competition after Brexit: Divergence For Differentiation Or Parallelism For Consensus' (Symposium on Competition Law, 13 February 2023) <https://www.catribunal.org.uk/sites/cat/files/2023-02/2023-02-12_Glasgow%20Conference_Competition%20Law%20after%20Brexit_0.pdf> 1 accessed 26 July 2024; and European Union (Withdrawal Agreement) Act 2018.

69 European Commission, 'The EU-UK Trade and Cooperation Agreement' (European Commission, 30 April 2021) Article 355 <https://ec.europa.eu/info/strategy/relations-non-eu-countries/relations-united-kingdom/eu-uk-trade-and-cooperation-agreement_en> accessed 24 July 2024.

The third reason for comparing the three selected jurisdictions is that, in addition to sharing similar competition laws, the three selected jurisdictions also share similar democratic ideals and principles and cooperate on political, security and economic issues.[70] For instance, the majority of EU member states, as well as the US and the UK are members of the North Atlantic Treaty Organisation, whose purpose is to guarantee the freedom and security of its members.[71] These similar competition laws and close political relationships provide a stable and consistent basis for the comparisons of the LIBOR and FX benchmark manipulation enforcement, which will be made between the three jurisdictions in this book.

1.7 Structure and Layout of the Book

This book has been split into seven chapters. Following on from this introduction, Chapter 2 explains the LIBOR and FX crises and the relevant competition laws and financial regulation in each jurisdiction. In particular this chapter explains how competition law applies to the LIBOR and FX benchmark manipulation cartels and identifies the relevant competition laws in each jurisdiction: the UK (Chapter I of the Competition Act 1998[72]), the EU (Article 101 of the Treaty on the Functioning of the EU[73]) and the US (Section 1 of the Sherman Act 1890[74]). The chapter also sets out the available sanctions for breach of competition law in each jurisdiction.

The third chapter is the first of three case studies and looks at the UK to examine the approach taken to the enforcement of the LIBOR and FX benchmark manipulation cartels. It analyses the legal and regulatory framework and considers why the UK chose to use financial regulation and the criminal offence of conspiracy to defraud rather than its competition laws, including the criminal cartel offence.[75]

The fourth chapter focuses on the EU and scrutinises its approach to the enforcement of the LIBOR and FX banking cartels. The EU used its civil competition laws to investigate and enforce the LIBOR and FX benchmark manipulation. The legislative changes that the EU has made since the LIBOR

70 US Department of State, 'US Relations with United Kingdom' (US Department of State, 2 June 2022) <https://www.state.gov/u-s-relations-with-united-kingdom/#:~:text=The%20strong%20relationship%20between%20the,%2C%20security%2C%20and%20economic%20issues.> accessed 24 July 2024.

71 NATO, 'NATO Member Countries' (North Atlantic Treaty Organisation, 24 January 2024) <https://www.nato.int/cps/en/natohq/nato_countries.htm> accessed 31 July 2024.

72 Competition Act 1998 s.2.

73 Consolidated version of the Treaty on the Functioning of the European Union OJ *C 326*, Article 101.

74 Sherman Act 1890 15 U.S.C., s.1.

75 Enterprise Act 2002, s.188.

and FX crisis will be examined, in particular the Market Abuse Regulation[76] and Directive[77] of 2014 will be assessed, together with the criminal offence for market manipulation that these laws contain. The EU's competition leniency regime, including the competition law whistleblower incentives and protection, will be assessed to determine any perceived benefits of the regime.

The final case study chapter focuses on the US. It starts by examining the way in which the US approached the enforcement of the LIBOR and FX benchmark manipulation cartels. As the US is the only one of the three case studies that used criminal competition law powers in the enforcement of these scandals, it provides an excellent example to assess the success of the use of criminal competition law enforcement. The US leniency regime for competition law (known as antitrust) breaches is examined, as is the use of DPAs by US antitrust regulators when a criminal breach of the Sherman Act 1890 by a company was established in connection with the benchmark manipulation cartels.

The sixth chapter compares the approach of each jurisdiction to the enforcement of the LIBOR and FX manipulation cartels. It compares the competition law leniency/whistleblower regimes of each jurisdiction to determine which regimes worked best to assist the regulators and whether the availability of these regimes is adequately publicised in the financial markets sector. This chapter analyses and compares the use of civil and criminal sanctions and considers the advantages and disadvantages of criminal sanctions against both individuals and corporate bodies. The use of DPAs when a company is found guilty of a criminal offence (such as the breach of the US antitrust laws) is examined and evaluated.

The final chapter provides an overall conclusion, emphasising the central argument of this book, that the UK should fully utilise its competition law enforcement powers in its enforcement of financial crime. Having identified the approaches of the EU and US in Chapters 4 and 5, it is recommended that the UK takes a tougher approach to the enforcement of financial crime in order to provide a strong deterrent to both companies and individuals.

76 Regulation (EU) No 596/2014 of the European Parliament and of the Council of 16 April 2014 on Market Abuse (Market Abuse Regulation) OJ L173/1.

77 Directive 2014/57/EU of the European Parliament and of the Council of 16 April 2014 on Criminal Sanctions for Market Abuse (Market Abuse Directive) [2014] OJ 2 173/179.

2 Background to the LIBOR and FX Benchmark Manipulation Crisis

2.1 Introduction

This chapter will set the scene for the book by examining the significance of the London Interbank Offered Rate (LIBOR) and Foreign Exchange (FX) benchmark manipulation scandal of 2012–2013[1] and its impact in the United Kingdom (UK), European Union (EU) and United States of America (US). It will investigate the background of the LIBOR and FX crisis and the reasons why the different regulators in each jurisdiction took different approaches to their enforcement of the same crisis.[2] The differences between the use of financial regulation and competition law to penalise those companies and individuals involved in the LIBOR and FX scandal in each jurisdiction are introduced. This chapter will outline key definitions and will introduce and explain the themes that run through the book. These themes include the value of whistleblowing and leniency regimes in the detection of cartels, such as the banking cartels that were at the heart of the LIBOR and FX benchmark manipulation, and the evaluation of the use of civil vs criminal penalties for benchmark manipulation. The final two themes are a consideration of how corporate criminal liability is attributed for financial crime and/or competition law and the use of deferred prosecution agreements (DPAs) in each jurisdiction when a company has been found guilty of a crime. Finally, this chapter will explain the significance of this topic and the contribution of this research to the wider debate on financial crime, market manipulation and competition law.

1 A Stenfors and L Muchimba, 'The Anatomy of Three Scandals: Conspiracies, Beauty Contests, and Sabotage in OTC Markets' (2023) 57(2) *Journal of Economic Issues* 539, 539.

2 Regulators for financial crime and competition law in the UK are the Financial Conduct Authority and the Competition and Markets Authority, in the EU it is the European Commission and in the US regulators include the Department of Justice, the Federal Trade Commission, the Securities and Exchange Commission and the Commodities Futures Trading Commission.

DOI: 10.4324/9781003425106-2

2.2 Key Definitions

This section will discuss some of the key definitions used throughout this book: financial crime, benchmark manipulation, market manipulation, competition law and cartels. It will conclude by introducing the competition law enforcement powers and competition regulators in each of the UK, EU and US.

2.2.1 Financial Crime

One of the earliest definitions of white-collar crime was offered by Edwin Sutherland, who described it as a crime committed by 'respectable or at least respected business and professional men'.[3] There is no single internationally recognised definition of 'financial crime', although Interpol's definition is a useful starting point:

> Financial crime ranges from basic theft or fraud committed by ill-intentioned individuals to large-scale operations masterminded by organized criminals with a foot on every continent.[4]

Gottschalk adds to the above definition of financial crime by stating that white collar criminals find crime a more convenient opportunity to generate revenue or solve a problem than other legitimate means.[5] The terms 'financial crime', 'corporate crime' and 'white-collar crime' have become synonymous with the 2008 financial crisis and the LIBOR and FX benchmark manipulation crisis.[6] However the different terms used to describe financial crime are contentious amongst academic scholars and there is no accepted definition.[7]

In the US, the Federal Bureau of Investigation (FBI) gives white-collar crime a wide definition:

> These crimes are not violent, but they are not victimless. White-collar crimes can destroy a company, wipe out a person's life savings, cost investors billions of dollars, and erode the public's trust in institutions.[8]

3 EH Sutherland, 'White-Collar Criminality' (1940) 5(1) *American Sociological Review* 1, 1.

4 Interpol 'Financial Crime' (Interpol, 2022) <https://www.interpol.int/en/Crimes/Financial-crime> accessed 21 July 2024.

5 T Dearden and P Gottschalk, 'Convenience Theory and Cybercrime Opportunity: An Analysis of Online Cyber Offending' (2023) 45(3) *Deviant Behaviour* 348, 348.

6 See K Harrison and N Ryder, *The Law Relating to Financial Crime in the United Kingdom* (Routledge 2022) 100, 101.

7 For contrasting views see S Green, 'The Concept of White Collar Crime in Law and Legal Theory' (2004) *Buffalo Criminal Law Review* 8, 1; KHS Pickett and JM Pickett, *Financial Crime Investigation and Control*, (Wiley, New York 2002); N Ryder, *The Financial Crisis and White Collar Crime: The Perfect Storm?* (Edward Elgar 2014) and P Gottschalk, 'Categories of Financial Crime' (2010) 17(4) *Journal of Financial Crime* 441.

8 Federal Bureau of Investigation, 'White Collar Crime' (FBI, 2024) <https://www.fbi.gov/investigate/white-collar-crime> accessed 21 July 2024.

The definition of white-collar crime by the FBI includes the examples of health care fraud, corporate fraud, money laundering, securities and commodities fraud, mortgage and financial institution fraud and intellectual property theft/ piracy.[9]

EUROPOL, the law enforcement agency of the EU for serious and organised crime,[10] defines economic crime as being 'illegal acts committed by an individual or a group of individuals to obtain a financial or professional advantage'.[11] The European Commission states that 'The fight against financial crime, which includes anti-money laundering and countering the financing of terrorism (AML/CTF), is vital for financial stability and security in Europe and the integrity of financial markets'.

The UK has defined financial crime as being:

> Any offence involving fraud or dishonesty; misconduct in, or misuse of information relating to, a financial market; or handling the proceeds of crime; or the financing of terrorism.[12]

More recently, the UK in its Economic Crime Plan 2 (2022–2026) has defined financial or economic crime as:

> A broad category of activity involving money, finance or assets, the purpose of which is to unlawfully obtain a profit or advantage for the perpetrator or cause loss to others. This poses a threat to the UK's economy and its institutions and causes serious harm to society and individuals.[13]

Even without an internationally accepted definition of financial crime, it can be seen that, due to the global nature of financial markets and the international nature of the UK's trading partners, the UK is exposed to the impact of international banks who engage in financial crime. This is particularly relevant to the LIBOR and FX benchmark manipulation scandal. The precise scale of financial crime in the UK is unknown but is estimated to cost tens or hundreds of billions of pounds a year.[14] The Government's Economic Crime Plan 2

9 Ibid.

10 EUROPOL, 'About Europol' (EUROPLL, 2022) <https://www.europol.europa.eu/about-europol> accessed 29 June 2024.

11 EUROPOL, 'Economic Crime' (EUROPOL, 1 January 2020) <https://www.europol.europa.eu/crime-areas-and-trends/crime-areas/economic-crime> accessed 21 June 2024.

12 Financial Service and Markets Act 2000, s.1H(3).

13 HM Government, 'Economic Crime Plan 2 2023-2026' (OGL, 30 March 2023) <https://assets.publishing.service.gov.uk/media/642561b02fa848001 3ec0f97/6.8300_HO_Economic_Crime_Plan_2_v6_Web.pdf> accessed 29 June 2024.

14 O Bennett and A Shalchi, 'Economic Crime in the UK: A Multi-Billion Pound Problem' (House of Commons Library, 6 April 2022) <https://researchbriefings.files.parliament.uk/documents/CBP-9013/CBP-9013.pdf> accessed 5 July 2022.

2023–2026 recognises the need to tackle financial crime due to its impact on the UK's economy and its competitiveness, citizens, legitimate businesses and international reputation.[15] A review of the literature carried out in Chapter 1[16] illustrated previous instances of market manipulation and reckless banking practices, both types of financial crime.[17] For example, market manipulation, such as that seen in the LIBOR and FX benchmark manipulation crisis, has also been heavily associated with the Wall Street Crash of 1929,[18] the Savings and Loans Crisis,[19] the collapse of numbers of US corporations (including Enron, Arthur Andersen and WorldCom) and the infamous Ponzi fraud scheme of Bernard Madoff,[20] all of which affected the three jurisdictions considered in this book.

The consideration of financial crime in this book will focus on the financial crime of market manipulation, which is the crime carried out during the LIBOR and FX benchmark interest rate manipulation. Both the terms 'market manipulation' and 'benchmark manipulation' will be outlined below.

2.2.2 Benchmark Manipulation

Benchmark interest rate manipulation (benchmark manipulation) is a type of financial crime that comes within the definition of market manipulation, which will be examined below. Benchmark manipulation was at the heart of the LIBOR and FX scandal and will be discussed throughout this book. A benchmark interest rate can be defined as a financial marker, which is used as a reference point for many financial instruments, including loans, pension funds, mortgages, credit card debt and hire purchase agreements.[21] Any manipulation of a benchmark interest rate, therefore, is likely to negatively affect a large proportion of the population by raising interest rates on anything from personal loans to mortgages.[22] The LIBOR benchmark interest rate was one

15 HM Government, 'Economic Crime Plan 2 2023-2026' (OGL, 30 March 2023) <https://assets.publishing.service.gov.uk/media/642561b02fa8480013ec0f97/6.8300_HO_Economic_Crime_Plan_2_v6_Web.pdf> accessed 29 July 2024.

16 See Section 1.2 of Chapter 1.

17 N Ryder, 'The Financial Crisis and Financial Crime in the UK: A Critical Analysis of the Response By Financial Regulatory Agencies' (2016) 39(1) *The Company Lawyer* 4.

18 United States Senate, 'Subcommittee on Senate Resolutions 84 and 234 (The Pecora Committee)' (United States Senate, 16 June 1934) <https://www.senate.gov/artandhistory/history/common/investigations/Pecora.htm> accessed 8 March 2024.

19 WK Black, *The Best Way to Rob a Bank Is to Own One: How Corporate Executives and Politicians Looted the S & L Industry* (University of Texas Press 2014).

20 N Ryder, 'The Financial Crisis and Financial Crime in the UK: A Critical Analysis of the Response By Financial Regulatory Agencies' (2016) 39(1) *The Company Lawyer* 4.

21 J Horn, 'Accident, Scandal, Disaster: The Media Framing of Corporate Crime' (2023) 81(1) *Crime, Law and Social Change* 203, 221.

22 A Stenfors and L Muchimba, 'The Anatomy of Three Scandals: Conspiracies, Beauty Contests, and Sabotage in OTC Markets' (2023) 57(2) *Journal of Economic Issues* 539, 544,

of the main interest rate benchmarks used in financial markets at the time of the benchmark manipulation crisis,[23] meaning that the manipulation of the LIBOR benchmark rate by the banking cartels affected millions of people and businesses around the world. This is due to the fact that hundreds of trillions of dollars in securities and loans have been linked to LIBOR, including government debt, student loans and mortgages.[24] The FX market is the largest financial market in the world,[25] so the manipulation of both the LIBORand FX benchmark rates had a significant affect on the financial markets and all those businesses and individuals who used them. For instance, when the LIBOR rose due to the illegal arrangements put in place by the banking cartels, payments dues on variable rate mortgages that were fixed to the LIBOR also rose, costing millions of consumers more each month.[26] In the LIBOR and FX crises, there were few people left unaffected, as the fall out of the LIBOR and FX manipulation had a significant impact on individuals, businesses and governments in the UK, EU and US.[27] LIBOR has now been phased out, due in part to its involvement in the financial crisis and the LIBOR manipulation scandal;[28] however, other benchmarks exist and may be subject to the same sort of manipulation in the future.[29] A recent example of another instance of benchmark manipulation involved the ISDAfix benchmark, which was manipulated by multiple banks in the same way as the LIBOR and FX benchmarks were manipulated.[30] The ISDAfix benchmark, like the LIBOR, affects more than $300 trillion in interest-rate-related derivatives and securities, so the impact of any artificial manipulation is significant.[31]

The key benchmark interest rates that will be examined as part of this book are the LIBOR, the FX and the Euro Interbank Offered Rate (EURIBOR), all of which were manipulated by bankers from competing banks. In the UK,

23 Bank of England, 'Transition from LIBOR to Risk Free Rates' (Bank of England, 1 June 2024) <https://www.bankofengland.co.uk/markets/transition-to-sterling-risk-free-rates-from-libor> accessed 25 June 2024.

24 P Yeoh, 'Libor Benchmark: Practice, Crime and Reforms' (2016) 23(4) *Journal of Financial Crime* 1140.

25 M Cutkovic, 'Foreign Exchange Market Participants: Who Controls the Forex Market?' (Axi Financial Services Ltd, 2021) <https://www.axi.com/uk/blog/education/forex/forex-market-participants> accessed 25 June 2024.

26 P Yeoh, 'Libor Benchmark: Practice, Crime and Reforms' (2016) 23(4) *Journal of Financial Crime* 1140.

27 D Hau and D Skeie, 'LIBOR: Origins, Economics, Crisis, Scandal and Reform' (Federal Reserve Bank of New York Staff Reports, Staff Reports, March 2014) <https://www.newyorkfed.org/medialibrary/media/research/staff_reports/sr667.pdf> accessed 8 March 2024.

28 Bank of England, 'Transition from LIBOR to Risk Free Rates' (Bank of England, 1 June 2024) <https://www.bankofengland.co.uk/markets/transition-to-sterling-risk-free-rates-from-libor> accessed 25 June 2024.

29 E Fuller and Others, 'The End of LIBOR' (2018) 135(3) *Banking Law Journal* 183.

30 J Chen, 'LIBOR's Poker' (2021) 55(1) *Journal of Financial Markets* 100586.

31 AK Pascall, 'Tail Wagging the Dog: The Manipulation of Benchmark Rates - A Competitive Bone of Contention' (2016) 39(2) *World Competition* 161.

numerous financial penalties, described in detail in Chapter 3, were imposed by the Financial Conduct Authority (FCA) for manipulation of various benchmark interest rates, but none of these fines were made using the FCA's competition law powers.[32] Conversely, in the EU and US competition law powers were used for these global incidents of benchmark manipulation and higher fines were levied as a result, as described in Chapters 4 and 5. Therefore, this book considers whether using competition law powers in the enforcement of future benchmark manipulation will provide the UK's financial services regulator with greater powers than if they simply use their financial regulation powers in future instances of benchmark manipulation.

2.2.3 Market Manipulation

As stated above, the term 'market manipulation' is often used to describe benchmark manipulation.[33] Market manipulation has been defined as 'unwarranted interference in the operation of ordinary market forces of supply and demand; an interference in the market's normal price-forming mechanism'.[34] The UK's National Fraud and Cyber Crime Reporting Centre states that 'market manipulation could include making false or misleading statements and completing transactions that have the purpose of giving a false impression about supply or demand'.[35] The US Securities and Exchange Commission defines market manipulation as 'intentional conduct designed to deceive investors by controlling or artificially affecting the market'.[36] Both of these definitions describe what sounds like a type of fraud, talking about deception and misleading others. The EU includes the term market manipulation in the 2014 Market Abuse Regulation (MAR 2014)[37] when it defined market abuse as consisting of the offences of 'insider dealing, the unlawful disclosure of inside information and market manipulation'.[38] The 2014 Market Abuse

32 Financial Conduct Authority, 'Benchmark Enforcement' (Financial Conduct Authority, 13 September 2018) <https://www.fca.org.uk/markets/benchmarks/enforcement> accessed 21 June 2024.

33 K Sergakis, *The Law of Capital Markets in the EU: Disclosure and Enforcement* (Palgrave 2018) 173.

34 E Lomnicka, 'Preventing and Controlling the Manipulation of Financial Markets: Towards a Definition of "Market Manipulation"' (2001) 8(4) *Journal of Financial Crime* 297.

35 National Fraud and Cyber Crime Reporting Centre, 'Market Manipulation' (Action Fraud) <https://www.actionfraud.police.uk/a-z-of-fraud/market-manipulation> accessed 8 June 2024.

36 Securities and Exchange Commission, 'Manipulation' (US Securities and Exchange Commission, March 28 2008) <https://www.sec.gov/fast-answers/answerstmanipulhtm.html> accessed 3 July 2024.

37 Regulation (EU) No596/2014 of the European Parliament and of the Council of 16 April 2014 on Market Abuse (Market Abuse Regulation) OJ L173/1.

38 Ibid, Article 1.

Directive (MAD 2014) uses the same definition of market abuse[39] and explains that: 'Market abuse harms the integrity of financial markets and public confidence in securities, derivatives and benchmarks'.[40] For the purposes of the EU market abuse regime (MAR), market manipulation is defined as, *inter alia*, the transmission of false or misleading information that manipulates the calculation of a benchmark.[41] This part of the definition of market manipulation was a new addition for MAR 2014 and MAD 2014, following the LIBOR crisis and did not feature in the definition of market manipulation in the EU's 2003 market abuse directive (MAD 2003),[42] which may explain, at least in part, why the EU used its competition law powers rather than its market abuse regime in its enforcement of the LIBOR crisis. The European Commission now has criminal powers to enforce market manipulation, including benchmark manipulation, which will be discussed in detail in Chapter 4.

2.2.4 Competition Law

One of the key areas being examined in this book is competition law and its purpose. In particular, the role that competition law did or did not play in the enforcement of the LIBOR and FX crisis in the UK, EU and US will be examined in detail. Competition law exists to promote 'greater efficiency and productivity' for the benefit of all rather than the few.[43] Competition laws in the UK, EU and US exist to protect consumers and businesses, so competition law is normally seen as a force for good and has an impact on everyone in society when properly applied.[44] However, competition law was not used by the UK regulators to prosecute those institutions and individuals involved in the LIBOR and FX crisis, unlike the regulators in the US and the EU, who used competition law. There is a need to examine the potential benefits of enforcing benchmark manipulation cartels with competition law in the UK with a view to persuading UK regulators of the value the competition rules have in the enforcement of financial crime. One of the key benefits of enforcing benchmark manipulation cartels using competition law is the wide range and strength of the sanctions available to regulators for breach of competition law. Greater sanctions levied against both individuals and banks (or other companies) involved in benchmark manipulation are likely to act as a greater deterrent against future instances of manipulation.

39 Ibid.
40 Ibid, Preamble (1).
41 Ibid. Article 12(1)(d).
42 Directive 2003/6/EC of the European Parliament and of the Council of 28 January 2003 on Insider Dealing and Market Manipulation ((Market Abuse) [2003] OJ 2 96/01).
43 ME Stuck, 'Is Competition Always Good?' (2013) Volume 1(1) *Journal of Antitrust Enforcement* 162.
44 RM Steuer, 'The Simplicity of Antitrust Law' (2012) 14(2) *University of Pennsylvania Journal of Business Law* 543.

In each of the selected jurisdictions of this book, there are different rules to regulate competition, although the reasons that the three jurisdictions have been selected is because there are significant similarities between the three competition law regimes. The US antitrust rules were established before the EU competition law rules and formed the inspiration for the development of the EU rules.[45] The UK competition laws are almost identical to those of the EU, by virtue of the UK's membership of the EU for 47 years, until it left in January 2021. The areas of competition law in the US, EU and UK that are the most relevant to the enforcement of the LIBOR and FX benchmark manipulation cartels are discussed below.

The US competition law (known as antitrust) that is relevant to benchmark manipulation cartels is contained in the Sherman Act 1890 (the Sherman Act). Section 1 provides:

> Every contract, combination in the form of trust or otherwise, or conspiracy, in restraint of trade or commerce along the several States, or with foreign nations, is declared to be illegal.[46]

The requirements of this section can be broken down into three separate components. The first is for there to be a contract, trust or conspiracy between businesses. Second, that agreement must restrict competition (restrain trade or commerce) in some manner. Third, the effect of the agreement must be experienced amongst more than one state of the US or with foreign nations. Therefore, if the effects of the agreement are solely experienced within one state, the Section 1 offence will not be made out.

These three components can clearly be seen in the EU's Article 101 of the Treaty on the Functioning of the European Union (Article 101),[47] which is the area of competition law most relevant to this book. These components are, first, that there must be an agreement, decision by association of undertakings or concerted practice between undertakings; second, that this agreement may affect trade between member states; and third, that the agreement has its object or effect the prevention, restriction or distortion of competition within the internal market.[48] As with Section 1 of the Sherman Act, there is a requirement for there to be an agreement between businesses, for that agreement to restrict competition and for the effects of the agreement to be felt amongst more than one state of the EU.

45 M Monti, 'Antitrust in the US and Europe: A History of Convergence' (American Bar Association, 14 November2001) <https://ec.europa.eu/commission/presscorner/api/files/document/print/en/speech_01_540/SPEECH_01_540_EN.pdf> accessed 18 February 2024.

46 Sherman Act 1890 15 U.S.C.

47 Consolidated Version of the Treaty on the Functioning of the European Union OJ C326, Article 101.

48 Ibid.

The most relevant UK competition law to this book is the Chapter I prohibition of the Competition Act 1998 (Chapter I), which also has three components. First, there must be an agreement, a decision by associations of undertakings or a concerted practice. Second, that agreement must have as its object or effect the restriction of competition, and third, the agreement must affect trade in the UK.[49] Each of these competition laws – Section 1 of the Sherman Act, Article 101 and the Chapter I prohibition – apply to cartels, such as those seen in the LIBOR and FX benchmark manipulation crisis. Cartels are examined further and defined below.

The competition law provisions for each of the UK, EU and US will be discussed in more detail in later chapters, but it can be seen that the competition laws in each of the three jurisdictions are similar, which will prove useful for comparisons concerning the use of competition law in the enforcement of the LIBOR and FX crises.

2.2.5 Cartels

A cartel consists of a group of competitors, such as banks, who typically join together to fix prices, limit production, or to share markets or customers between them.[50] Cartel agreements, concerted practices or arrangements by competitors to restrict competition in the marketplace mean that these companies no longer need to compete with each other, as they can rely on the terms of the agreement reached with fellow cartel members.[51] The LIBOR and FX benchmark manipulation was carried out by traders at competing banks, who were found by the European Commission, using almost identical competition law provisions to those of the UK, to have colluded in the manipulation of the benchmarks for their own gain, which fulfils the definition of a cartel.

Cartels are viewed as the most harmful breach of competition law in all three jurisdictions. In the UK, cartels are also subject to a criminal offence in the Enterprise Act 2002, which provides that it is a criminal offence for individuals to engage in hard-core cartel activity.[52]

For many years, the banking sector in the UK, EU and US has been vulnerable to abuse by cartels. This vulnerability of the banking sector to cartel behaviour is due to the small number of large banks, all of which operate across multiple jurisdictions. This is a classic situation in which cartels are likely to develop and to exist undetected for a long period.[53] As stated above, bank-

49 Competition Act 1998, s2.

50 P Whelan, 'Cartel Criminalization and the Challenge of "Moral Wrongfulness"' (2013) 33(3) *Oxford Journal of Legal Studies* 535.

51 L Danagher, 'Strict Liability and the Mens Rea of Cartel Crime' (2020) 9(1) *Criminal Law Review* 789.

52 Enterprise Act 2002, s 188.

53 Organisation for Economic Co-operation and Development, 'Bank Competition and Financial Stability' (OECD, 5 October 2011) <https://www.oecd-ilibrary.org/finance-and-invest-

ing cartels were at the heart of the LIBOR and FX crisis.[54] In the LIBOR and FX crisis, traders from different competing banks communicated via chat rooms and phone calls and worked to raise or lower the banks' LIBOR and FX submissions in order to suit the traders' individual trading positions with the aim of increasing their profit from transactions.[55] This type of conduct is caught by competition law, as it would be classified as a 'hard-core' cartel between competitors. This is relevant to the actions carried out by the banks and individual traders during the LIBOR and FX scandal, as the exchange of insider information with a competitor bank, together with aligning exposure positions and planning transactions with one or more competitor, is certainly likely to come within the definition of a price-fixing cartel.[56]

Cartels, such as those in the LIBOR and FX crises, are notoriously difficult to prosecute because their members operate in conditions of extreme secrecy.[57] This means that cartels are hard to detect and that it is extremely difficult for regulators to gather sufficient evidence of the cartel's existence to allow for a successful prosecution.[58] Cartel conduct is viewed by regulators as the most harmful form of anticompetitive behaviour, and commentators argue that cartels are an anathema to free market competition.[59] Regulators are often forced to rely on whistleblowers and leniency regimes, discussed below, in order to obtain enough evidence to prosecute a suspected cartel. Once a cartel has been detected and sufficient evidence has been obtained, regulators should be encouraged to use the most appropriate legislation to enforce it, which this book will argue is likely to be competition law.

The US cartel laws have been in existence since the Sherman Act of 1890.[60] The primary enforcer of the cartel provisions of the Sherman Act is the Antitrust Division of the Department of Justice (DoJ), which is empowered to bring criminal charges against both individuals and companies who engage

---

ment/bank-competition-and-financial-stability/competition-in-retail-banking-and-financial-stability_9789264120563-4-en> accessed 20 July 2024.

54 C Lim, 'Libor, Strategy, and International Cartel Investigations' (2013) 4(1) *Journal of European Competition Law and Practice* 87.

55 European Commission, 'Commission Fines Barclays, RBS, Citigroup, JPMorgan and MUFG E107 Billion for Participating in Foreign Exchange Spot Trading Cartel' (European Commission, 16 May 2019) <https://ec.europa.eu/commission/presscorner/detail/en/IP_19_2568> accessed 8 July 2024.

56 C Lim, 'Libor, Strategy, and International Cartel Investigations' (2013) 4(1) *Journal of European Competition Law and Practice* 87.

57 H Van de Bunt, 'Walls of Secrecy and Silence: The Madoff Case and Cartels in the Construction Industry' (2010) 9(3) *Criminology and Public Policy* 435.

58 DJ Gerber, *Competition Law and Antitrust, A Global Guide* (Oxford University Press 2020) 54.

59 J Clarke, 'The Increasing Criminalization of Economic Law - A Competition Law Perspective' (2012) 19(1) *Journal of Financial Crime* 76.

60 Sherman Act 1890, 15 U.S.C. s.1.

in cartel behaviour.[61] This provision has enabled the DoJ to collect extremely high fines for breach of the cartel provisions in the Sherman Act. To date, the highest individual fine levied against a company for a Sherman Act violation is $925m, which was imposed on CitiCorp in 2017 for its participation in the FX benchmark manipulation cartel.[62] More detail about the fines imposed by US regulators for the LIBOR and FX benchmark manipulation cartels is presented in Chapter 6.

The UK laws governing cartels are contained in the Chapter I prohibition of the Competition Act 1998. In addition to this civil prohibition, there is also a criminal cartel offence for hard-core cartels in the Enterprise Act 2002, which provides for the imprisonment of individuals for up to five years.[63] Despite the introduction of the cartel offence in the Enterprise Act 2002, as mentioned above, in 2011, a government consultation found that the deterrent effect of the new cartel offence had been weaker than it had intended.[64] There had only been one successful prosecution of the cartel offence[65] by the date of the consultation,[66] which was seen by the government to be due to the requirement to prove the dishonesty of individual cartel members in order to reach a conviction.[67] As a result, the government concluded that the requirement to prove the dishonesty of an individual cartel member should be removed from the offence in order to make it easier to successfully prosecute cartels.[68] This decision was eventually legislated in the Enterprise and Regulatory Reform Act 2013, in which three key changes were made to the cartel offence; the dishonesty requirement was removed, the scope of the offence was reduced and three defences were introduced.[69] However, the amendments to the cartel offence

61 US Department of Justice, 'Criminal Enforcement' (US Department of Justice, 22 May 2020) <https://www.justice.gov/atr/criminal-enforcement> accessed 4 July 2024.

62 US Department of Justice, 'Sherman Act Violations Resulting in Criminal Fines & Penalties of $10 Million or More' (US Department of Justice, 24 July 2020) <https://www.justice.gov/atr/sherman-act-violations-yielding-corporate-fine-10-million-or-more> accessed 8 April 2024.

63 Enterprise Act 2002, s.188.

64 Department for Business, Innovation and Skills, 'A Competition Regime for Growth: A Consultation on Options for Reform' (GOV.UK, March 2011) <https://assets.publishing.service.gov.uk/government/uploads/system/uploads/attachment_data/file/31411/11-657-competition-regime-for-growth-consultation.pdf> accessed 14 June 2024

65 Ibid, para. 6.5.

66 Competition and Markets Authority, 'Marine Hose: Criminal Cartel Investigation' (GOV.UK, 14 November 2008) <https://www.gov.uk/cma-cases/marine-hose-criminal-cartel-investigation> accessed 18 July 2024.

67 Department for Business, Innovation and Skills, 'Growth, Competition and the Competition Regime: Government Response to Consultation' (GOV.UK, March 2012) <https://assets.publishing.service.gov.uk/government/uploads/system/uploads/attachment_data/file/192722/12-512-growth-and-competition-regime-government-response.pdf> accessed 14 July 2024.

68 Ibid.

69 Enterprise and Regulatory Reform Act 2013, s47(8).

have not been successful in increasing prosecutions; there have only been four criminal prosecutions of the cartel offence from the date of its introduction in the Enterprise Act 2002.[70] Some commentators suggest that, contrary to the government's intentions, the removal of the dishonesty element of the cartel offence and the introduction of defences has led to cartel conduct being harder, rather than easier, to prosecute.[71] This book recommends a further reform of the criminal cartel offence to make it easier for prosecutors to use, as the government intended by its amendments of the offence and to allow for criminal corporate liability for cartel involvement.

The laws in the EU applicable to cartels are set out in Article 101, which was used as the basis for the European Commission's enforcement of the LIBOR and FX benchmark manipulation cartels.[72] The fines imposed by the European Commission were significantly higher than those imposed by UK authorities for the same benchmark manipulation and were based on competition law rather than the financial regulation the UK regulators used as a basis for their fines. For example, in the EU, Deutsche Bank was fined €725.4m by the European Commission for participating in the illegal cartel to rig the rate of the LIBOR and EURIBOR benchmark interest rates[73] however, the fine imposed by the FCA on Deutsche Bank for its participation in the same benchmark manipulation cartel was just £227m.[74] Further detail about the fines imposed by the European Commission are discussed in Chapter 5. It is argued in this book that competition law is well suited to enforcing the financial crime of benchmark manipulation, laws which the UK could have used but chose not to. The next section takes a look at the competition law enforcement powers available to regulators when enforcing a breach of competition law, which will include a cartel, which is a clear breach of competition law in each of the UK, EU and US.

70 Competition and Markets Authority, 'Competition and Markets Authority Cases' (Competition and Markets Authority, 2022) <https://www.gov.uk/cma-cases?case_type%5B%5D=criminal-cartels> accessed 10 March 2024.

71 P Gilbert, 'Changes to the UK Cartel Offence—Be Careful What You Wish For' (2015) 6(3) *Journal of European Competition Law & Practice* 192.

72 European Commission, 'Commission Fines Barclays, RBS, Citigroup, JPMorgan and MUFG E107 Billion for Participating in Foreign Exchange Spot Trading Cartel' (European Commission, 2 December 2021) <https://ec.europa.eu/commission/presscorner/detail/en/ip_21_6548> accessed 11 July 2024.

73 M Thompson, 'EU Fines Banks Record $2.3b over Libor' (CNN Business, 4 December 2013) <https://money.cnn.com/2013/12/04/news/companies/libor-europe-fines/?iid=EL> accessed 8 July 2024.

74 Financial Conduct Authority, 'Deutsche Bank Fined £227 Million by Financial Conduct Authority for LIBOR and EURIBOR Failings and for Misleading the Regulator' (Financial Services Authority, 23 April 2015) <https://www.fca.org.uk/news/press-releases/deutsche-bank-fined-%C2%A3227-million-financial-conduct-authority-libor-and-euribor> accessed 17 June 2024.

2.2.6 *Competition Enforcement Powers and Regulators*

An important reason why competition law should be considered in the enforcement of financial crime is because of the extensive and significant enforcement options available to regulators once a breach of competition law has been established. Of the three jurisdictions considered in this book not all treat cartels, such as those involved in the LIBOR and FX benchmark manipulation, in the same manner. The UK and US each have criminal penalties for cartel participants. However, the EU does not have the power to treat participation in a cartel as a criminal offence, having only civil competition laws available.[75] The UK has both civil competition law and additional criminal penalties available to regulators to enforce a cartel.[76] A brief overview of competition enforcement powers and competition law regulators for each jurisdiction is discussed below.

The main competition regulatory authority in the UK is the Competition and Markets Authority (CMA), which was set up by the Enterprise and Regulatory Reform Act 2013.[77] Its powers of investigation and enforcement come from the Competition Act 1998, the Enterprise Act 2002 and the Enterprise and Regulatory Reform Act 2013. The CMA works alongside 'sector regulators', including the FCA, who also have competition enforcement powers, which they use with their sector knowledge to ensure that competition is upheld in all markets in the UK and that businesses operate within the law.[78]

The UK's civil penalties for breach of competition law are extensive and are set out in the Competition Act 1998, the Enterprise Act 2002 and the Company Directors Disqualification Act 1986. The most significant civil penalty for breach of competition law is the power to impose fines of up to 10% of a company's worldwide turnover in the business year preceding the CMA's decision.[79] Regulators can also impose directions on infringing undertakings in order to bring an infringement to an end.[80] Interim measures can be adopted by a regulator in a matter of urgency in order to bring an infringement to an end, also legally binding commitments can be entered into between the

75 C Tonna-Barthet and L O'Carroll, 'Procedural Justice in the Age of Tech Giants – Justifying the EU Commission's Approach to Competition Law Enforcement' (2020) 16(2) *European Competition Journal* 264.

76 Competition Act 1998, s36 and Enterprise Act 2002, s.190.

77 Enterprise and Regulatory Reform Act 2013, Part 3.

78 R Whish, 'The United Kingdom's "Enhanced Concurrency Regime"' (2018) 17(2) *Competition Law Journal* 63; and Competition and Markets Authority, 'Annual Concurrency Report 2022' (Competition and Markets Authority, 27 April 2022) <https://www.gov.uk/government/publications/annual-report-on-concurrency-2022/promoting-competition-in-services-we-rely-on-the-annual-concurrency-report-2022> accessed 10 July 2024.

79 Competition Act 1998 (Determination of Turnover for Penalties) Order 2000, SI 2000/309.

80 Competition Act 1998, s32(1).

regulator and infringing undertakings.[81] Commitments may be both structural and behavioural, for example, they may involve a business agreeing to cease or modify its conduct, terminating an arrangement, removing a particular clause from an agreement, withdrawing from a particular activity, licensing specific assets, or even divesting itself of part of its business. Commitments are, therefore, a powerful tool for regulators to use in order to end a competition investigation by agreement between regulator and infringing company.[82] In addition to these powers, the Enterprise Act 2002[83] gave competition regulators the power to disqualify directors for up to 15 years when the director knew or ought to have known that their company has breached competition law, a power that the CMA has been making more use of in recent years.[84]

The UK's criminal penalties for hard-core cartels are the toughest of any country in the EU and include the imprisonment for up to five years and/or a fine for any person guilty of participating in a cartel.[85] A 'hard-core' cartel is the most harmful type of cartel and consists of an agreement (which does not have to be formal or legal) between competitors in which they agree to do any of the following: fix prices, limit or prevent production of a service or product, divide between at least two businesses the supply in the UK of a product or service, or make bid-rigging arrangements.[86] However, there are problems associated with the prosecution of individuals under the criminal cartel offence, which are discussed below. An important omission for UK regulators is that there is no criminal corporate offence to punish the companies who employ cartel participants, even though the company itself will often benefit from the cartel. This lack of criminal corporate liability in UK competition law will be discussed further below and in Chapter 4.

Finally, the UK competition regime allows regulators to instigate market investigations[87] which give the CMA or a sectoral regulator, such as the FCA, the power to impose a wide range of remedies if there is a finding of a pre-

81 BKKJ Rodger, 'Application of the Domestic and EU Antitrust Prohibitions: An Analysis of the UK Competition Authority's Enforcement Practice' (2020) 8(1) *Journal of Antitrust Enforcement* 86.

82 Competition and Markets Authority, 'Guidance on the CMA's Investigation Procedures in Competition Act 1998 Cases: CMA8' (GOV.UK, 21 January 2022) para 10.16 <https://www.gov.uk/government/publications/guidance-on-the-cmas-investigation-procedures-in-competition-act-1998-cases/guidance-on-the-cmas-investigation-procedures-in-competition-act-1998-cases#investigation-outcomes> accessed 21 July 2024.

83 Enterprise Act 2002, s204.

84 C Chijioke-Oforji, 'Director Accountability for Breach Of Competition Law: Practical Lessons From the CMA's Increased Use of Disqualification Powers' (2020) 42(1) *European Competition Law Review* 24.

85 EJ Morgan, 'Criminal Cartel Sanctions Under the UK Enterprise Act: An Assessment' (2010) 17(1) *International Journal of the Economics of Business* 67.

86 Enterprise Act 2002 s.188(2).

87 Enterprise Act 2002, s.131(1) as amended by the Enterprise and Regulatory Reform Act 2013.

vention, restriction or distortion of competition in that market.[88] Remedies include the requirement for far-reaching structural or behavioural changes to the market and recommendations by the regulator to the government for legislative changes for a change in policy or regulation in relation to the market.[89]

The competition, or antitrust, law regulators in the US consist of the DoJ and the Federal Trade Commission (FTC). The DoJ is the primary enforcer of antitrust law in the US and is empowered to handle all criminal prosecutions and civil suits in which the US has an interest.[90] The DoJ has undertaken a number of high profile international cartel prosecutions in a variety of markets.[91] Companies found to have participated in an illegal cartel are made to pay substantial fines, such as those imposed for participation in the FX benchmark manipulation cartels described in Chapter 6.[92] Additionally, the DoJ has the power to prosecute individuals involved in a cartel and to compel firms to compensate affected customers.[93] For individuals convicted for their involvement in a criminal cartel, there is a maximum period of imprisonment for a breach of the Sherman Act of 10 years as well as, or instead of, a fine of up to $1m.[94] For companies though, the maximum criminal fine is $100m, which can be increased substantially under the Alternative Fines Act, which permits prosecutors to ignore this statutory maximum and fine defendants up to 'twice the gross gain or twice the gross loss' for the offence.[95] The FTC has shared jurisdiction with the DoJ to investigate non-hard-core, or less harmful, cartels under the Federal Trade Commission Act 1914.[96] The FTC has only civil rather than criminal enforcement powers; only the DoJ has the power to carry out criminal antitrust enforcement actions.

In the EU, the competition regulator is the European Commission, which is responsible for investigating and taking action against infringements of Articles 101 and 102.[97] The European Commission works with the

88 A Coscelli and A Horrocks, 'Making Markets Work Well: The UK Market Investigations Regime' (2014) 10(1) *Competition Policy International* 881.
89 See Enterprise Act 2002, s.138, as amended by the Enterprise and Regulatory Reform Act 2013 and A Chrysovalantis and others, 'A Waste of Energy? A Critical Assessment of the Investigation of the UK Energy Market by the Competition And Markets Authority' (2017) 21(1) *Competition & Change* 45.
90 Ibid.
91 JB Baker, 'The Case for Antitrust Enforcement' (2003) 17(4) *Journal of Economic Perspectives* 27.
92 Sherman Act 1890 15 U.S.C., s.1.
93 Sherman Act 1890 15 U.S.C., s.1.
94 Sherman Act 1890, 15 U.S.C. s.1.
95 J Green, 'Cartels Laws and Regulations' (Global Legal Insights, 21 May 2020) <https://www.globallegalinsights.com/practice-areas/cartels-laws-and-regulations/usa> accessed 26 July 2024.
96 Federal Trade Commission Act 1914, 15 U.S.C., s.5.
97 Consolidated version of the Treaty on the Functioning of the European Union OJ *C 326*, Articles 101 and 102.

National Competition Authorities, which are the competition regulators in each Member State, to enforce breaches of competition law.[98] The European Commission typically takes on investigations into pan-European breaches of competition law.[99] Remedies which can be imposed for breach of EU competition law are similar to those of the UK listed above, which stem from the UK's membership of the EU and the harmonisation of competition law regimes. Remedies for breaches of competition law are fines of up to 10% of an undertaking's worldwide turnover the preceding business year, the power to agree structural and/or behavioural commitments with infringing undertakings, the imposition of structural and/or behavioural decisions and the power to take interim measures to stop an infringement of competition law.[100] In cartel cases, the Commission has imposed fines totalling €3.8t on the financial services sector between 2013 and 2021, demonstrating how seriously it takes its responsibility for prosecuting cartels.[101]

In addition to the above competition enforcement powers in the UK, US and EU, the ability for individuals to bring private enforcement actions, known as 'class actions', exists in all jurisdictions studied. The class actions brought following the LIBOR and FX manipulation will be discussed in Chapters 4, 5 and 6.

Now that the key definitions used in this book have been provided, the next section of this chapter will examine the recent history of the financial sector in the UK, EU and US. It will be seen that the banking sector has a long history of market manipulation and financial crime, which led up to the LIBOR and FX benchmark manipulation cartels being examined in this book.

2.3 Background to the LIBOR and FX Crisis

Prior to the LIBOR and FX crisis, there have been significant financial crises over the last century.[102] This section investigates each of them in order to identify common trends and a pattern of events leading up to the LIBOR and FX crisis and market manipulation in the banking sector since then. The three

98 European Commission, 'European Competition Network Overview' (European Commission, 23 March 2020) <https://ec.europa.eu/competition/ecn/index_en.html> accessed 27 June 2024.

99 M Ioannidou, '"Responsive" Remodelling of Competition Law Enforcement' (2020) 10(4) *Oxford Journal of Legal Studies* 846.

100 Council Regulation (EC) No 1/2003 of 16 December 2002 on the Implementation of the Rules on Competition Laid Down in Articles 81 and 82 of the Treaty.

101 European Commission, 'Statistics on Cartel Cases' (European Commission, 10 December 2021) <https://ec.europa.eu/competition-policy/cartels/statistics_en> accessed 21 July 2024.

102 D Hall, 'Financial Crises and Fraud: A Pattern Emerges' in L Pasculli and N Ryder (eds), *Corruption in the Global Era: Causes, Sources and Forms of Manifestation* (Routledge 2019).

significant financial crises are the Great Depression of 1929,[103] the Savings and Loans crisis[104] of the 1980s and 1990s and the 2008 financial crisis.[105] These three financial crises have been selected as all involved market manipulation in the financial sector, as the LIBOR and FX crisis did, and they are examined in turn below.

2.3.1 The Great Depression

The Great Depression is the term coined for the worldwide economic downturn that began in the US in October 1929.[106] It caused drastic declines in output, severe unemployment and acute deflation in almost every country in the world.[107] Most economists believe that the start of the Great Depression was the stock market crash of 1929, but some dispute this and see the stock market crash as a symptom rather than a cause of the Great Depression.[108] The Great Depression differed from ordinary economic slumps in many ways: its severity (economic output in the US dropped about 30% between 1929 and 1933), its length (unemployment in 1939 was still just 17%) and its international character (almost all industrialised countries suffered).[109]

It is likely that the Great Depression had many causes, but most commentators agree that the lack of market regulation, including the lack of prohibition of insider trading and other forms of market manipulation, exacerbated the downturn.[110] The government attempted to address this lack of regulation in the years following the stock market crash of 1929 by introducing a

103 The Pecora Report concluded that 'the exposure of the extent and effect of manipulative practices' by the banks in the run up to the Wall Street crash 'was one of the most salutary and important accomplishments of the investigation', see Committee on Banking and Currency, 'Stock Exchange Practices' (United States Government: Washington DC, June 1934) at 30 <https://www.senate.gov/about/resources/pdf/pecora-final-report.pdf> accessed 21 July 2024.

104 For discussion of the factors, including fraud and insider abuse, that contributed to the Savings and Loans crisis, see N Ryder, *The Financial Crisis and White Collar Crime: The Perfect Storm?* (Edward Elgar 2014).

105 For discussion of the role of market manipulation in the financial crisis, see N Ryder, *The Financial Crisis and White Collar Crime: The Perfect Storm?* (Edward Elgar 2014); and K Engel and P McCoy, 'A Tale of Three Markets: The Law and Economics of Predatory Lending' (2002) *Texas Law Review*, 80(6), 1255.

106 Committee on Banking and Currency, 'Stock Exchange Practices' (United States Government: Washington DC, June 1934) at 30 <https://www.senate.gov/about/resources/pdf/pecora-final-report.pdf> accessed 21 July 2024.

107 LE Ohanianab, 'What – or Who – Started the Great Depression?' (2009) 144(6) *Journal of Economic Theory* 2310.

108 Ibid.

109 RJ Samuelson, 'Don't Blame Wall Street' *The New York Times* (New York, 9 December 2001) <https://www.nytimes.com/2001/12/09/books/don-t-blame-wall-street.html> accessed 6 July 2024.

110 J Crotty, 'Structural Causes of the Global Financial Crisis: A Critical Assessment of the "New Financial Architecture"' (2009) 33(4) *Cambridge Journal of Economics* 563.

raft of laws designed to regulate the financial markets. These laws included the Glass-Steagal Act of 1933.[111] The main objective of this Act was to prevent commercial banks from engaging in investment speculation activities, an activity perceived to have been a key component in the stock market crash.[112] Two other key acts introduced by President Roosevelt shortly after the Glass-Steagal Act were the 1933 Securities Act[113] and the 1934 Securities Exchange Act.[114] The Securities Exchange Act set up a new regulatory authority, the Securities and Exchange Commission (SEC) to regulate the US securities markets.[115] The SEC became the central body to make and enforce the rules for securities markets. One of the key objectives of the 1933 Securities Act was to 'prohibit deceit, misrepresentation, and other fraud in the sale of securities'.[116] This is particularly relevant to this book, as these acts laid the groundwork for the regulation of the financial crime of market manipulation, which was seen in the LIBOR and FX crisis.[117] These acts were the first important government intervention in the financial markets and the beginning of a significant increase in regulation in the financial markets.[118]

No part of Europe was left untouched by the effects of the Great Depression, although Poland, Germany and Austria were the worst affected with high unemployment and business collapses.[119] Part of the problem for Europe was the end of the significant amount of US loans that had been made to European countries following the end of the First World War.[120] Furthermore, the tying of European countries' economies to that of the US by their participation in the 'Gold Standard', in order to stabilise their economies, helped to enhance

111 Glass-Steagal Act of 1933.

112 B Nikolić, 'Rise and Fall of Regulatory State in Financial Markets' (2013) 28(1) *Journal of International Banking Law and Regulation* 1.

113 Securities Act of 1933.

114 Securities Exchange Act of 1934 15 U.S.C.

115 Ibid, s.4(a).

116 Securities and Exchange Commission, 'The Laws that Govern the Securities Industry' (US Securities and Exchange Commission, 2022) <https://www.investor.gov/introduction-investing/investing-basics/role-sec/laws-govern-securities-industry#sox2002> accessed 26 July 2024.

117 The Pecora Commission's Report provided several examples of the link between the Great Depression, mentioned above, and financial crime, see Committee on Banking and Currency, 'Stock Exchange Practices' (United States Government: Washington DC, June 1934) at 30 <https://www.senate.gov/about/resources/pdf/pecora-final-report.pdf> accessed 21 July 2024.

118 B Nikolić, 'Rise and Fall of Regulatory State in Financial Markets' (2013) 28(1) *Journal of International Banking Law and Regulation* 1.

119 P Clavin, 'The Great Depression in Europe, 1929-39' (History Today, 1 September 2000) <https://www.historytoday.com/archive/great-depression-europe-1929-39> accessed 1 July 2024.

120 Encyclopedia.com, 'Great Depression in Europe' (Encyclopedia.com, 3 May 2020) <https://www.encyclopedia.com/economics/encyclopedias-almanacs-transcripts-and-maps/europe-great-depression> accessed 28 June 2024.

the economic problems in Europe at the time of the Great Depression in the US. Over the summer of 1931, banking crises took place, first in Austria and then many other European countries. In the UK, in September 1931 a different banking crisis took place following the widespread collapse of confidence in Europe's financial markets. Interest rates rose, many companies ran into financial difficulties and the UK's national deficit was rising. The UK decided to leave the Gold Standard on 20 September 1931 and, from then until the start of the Second World War in 1939, some signs of economic recovery were made in the UK.[121]

As explained above, one of the components of the Great Depression was the lack of market regulation in the run up to the stock market crash, which allowed financial crime, in particular insider trading and other types of market manipulation, to flourish. This lack of governmental market regulation in financial markets is one of the common themes across the three financial crises which form the background to the LIBOR and FX crisis and the market manipulation that was carried out by the banking cartels. The next financial crisis that took place after the Great Depression also started in the US and was known as the Savings and Loans crisis.

2.3.2 Savings and Loans Crisis

In the 1980s in the US, the financial sector suffered through a period of distress that was focused on the US savings and loan industry. The savings and loan industry has a long history in the US, with the first savings and loan institution being established in Pennsylvania in 1831.[122] Savings and loan institutions were originally organised by groups of people who wanted to buy their own homes but did not have sufficient savings to purchase them.[123] Members of a group would pool their savings and lend them to a few of the group members in order to finance home purchases. As the loans were repaid, funds were then lent to other members. The savings and loan institutions in the US ran into trouble in the late 1970s and early 1980s when inflation and interest rates rose sharply, resulting in heavy losses for the institutions.[124] Virtually every savings and loan institution was insolvent on a market-value basis by 1981; however the government was reluctant to see the industry fail, so it became

121 Ibid.

122 NM Riccucci, 'Unsung Heroes: Federal Execucrats Making a Difference' (Georgetown University Press 1995).

123 SB Bailey, 'Chopping at the Roots: A Proposal to Change the Focus of Criminal Laws Dealing with Savings and Loan Fraud' (1997) 24(2) *American Journal of Criminal Law* 401.

124 ES Kao, 'Moral Hazard During the Savings and Loan Crisis and the Financial Crisis of 2008-09: Implication for Reform and the Regulation of Systemic Risk Through Disincentive Structures to Manage Firm Size and Interconnectedness' (2012) 67(4) *New York University Annual Survey of American Law* 817.

involved in a conspiracy, which set the scene for the fraudulent accounting by the banks.[125]

US regulators responded to the problems being experienced by the savings and loans institutions by a long period of financial deregulation, which began with the Depository Institutions Deregulation and Monetary Control Act of 1980.[126] This, together with later deregulatory acts,[127] compounded the problem by making it easier for the institutions to enter into highly speculative investment strategies and to commit the fraudulent accounting that was taking place by the savings and loans institutions.[128] The Act called upon the financial regulatory agencies to limit regulation in the financial sector, with the aim of minimising the compliance costs and paperwork associated with the regulation and to eliminate conflicts, duplication and inconsistencies in regulations whenever possible. The legislative changes made did appear to help the savings and loans institutions in the short term; from 1982 to 1985 these institutions experienced a rapid growth; however, this growth did not solve the problems associated with the still largely insolvent industry and by the end of the 1980s, hundreds of savings and loans institutions were closed, with their losses estimated to have cost US taxpayers as much as $124b[129] and 1,100 people were prosecuted, including top executives at many of the largest failed banks,[130] with a 92% conviction rate.[131] However, the major reform legislation passed to resolve the savings and loans crisis in the US resulted in a period of stability and profitability for the next 20 years, until the financial crisis of 2008.

In the UK in the 1980s, there was also a significant deregulation of financial markets under Margaret Thatcher's conservative government, known as the 'Big Bang'.[132] This deregulation involved various rule changes for the London Stock Exchange, which came into effect on 27 October 1986, together with

125 WK Black, *The Best Way to Rob a Bank Is to Own One: How Corporate Executives and Politicians Looted the S & L Industry* (University of Texas Press 2014).

126 B Nikolić, 'Rise and Fall of Regulatory State in Financial Markets' (2013) 28(1) *Journal of International Banking Law and Regulation* 1; and the Depository Institutions Deregulation and Monetary Control Act of 1980 PL 96-221.

127 Including the Garn-St Germain Depository Institutions Act of 1982 12 *U.S.C.* 226.

128 WK Black, *The Best Way to Rob a Bank Is to Own One: How Corporate Executives and Politicians Looted the S & L Industry* (University of Texas Press 2014).

129 KJ Robinson, 'Savings and Loans Crisis 1980-1989' (Federal Reserve History, 22 November 2013) <https://www.federalreservehistory.org/essays/savings_and_loan_crisis> accessed 27 June 2024.

130 J Elsinger, 'Why Only One Top Banker Went to Jail for the Financial Crisis' *New York Times* (New York, 30 April 2014) <https://www.nytimes.com/2014/05/04/magazine/only-one-top-banker-jail-financial-crisis.html> accessed 30 June 2024.

131 JJ McDonald, 'Similarities between the Savings and Loan Crisis and Today's Current Financial Crisis: What the Past Can Tell Us about the Future' (2009) 76(4) *Defense Counsel Journal* 470.

132 J Robertson, 'How the Big Bang Changed the City of London for Ever' (*BBC News*, 27 October 2016) <https://www.bbc.co.uk/news/business-37751599> accessed 29 July 2024.

the introduction of the Financial Services Act 1986, which used a mixture of government regulation and self-regulation for the financial services industry.[133] The Big Bang had a significant effect on the UK's financial markets, with many older trading firms being taken over by large domestic and international banks. Some have argued that as a result of deregulation, the UK became a playground for criminals.[134] In an internal memo to Margaret Thatcher from David Willets, who worked in the No. 10 Policy Unit, the merits of the Big Bang were considered. In the memo, Willets said that sudden financial deregulation was likely to lead to 'unethical behaviour' and ultimately to 'boom and bust' as banks became more competitive with each other.[135] This memo appears to have accurately forecast both the 2008 financial crisis and the market manipulation that was behind the LIBOR and FX crisis. From memos transferred to the National Archives after 30 years behind closed doors, it is apparent that ministers in Thatcher's government were aware of the potential downsides of a sudden deregulation of the financial services sector but decided that the City needed to change in order to remain competitive.[136]

At the time of the Savings and Loans crisis in the US, the EU was also pursuing a path to financial deregulation. In the late 1980s and early 1990s, many European countries lifted capital controls, deregulated interest rates and harmonised rules and regulation of financial instruments.[137] This process of deregulation in the EU was formalised by the adoption of a five-year financial harmonisation programme, the Financial Services Action Plan in 1999.[138] This plan had three main objectives, to establish a single market in financial services across the EU, to make retail markets open and secure and to strengthen the rules on prudential supervision.[139]

As with the Great Depression of the 1930s, it can be seen that one of the key components of the Savings and Loans crisis was the period of deregulation that led to the fraudulent accounting by many of the savings and loans institutions. Deregulation in financial markets is shown to have provided the perfect environment for financial criminals to disguise their fraudulent activities. It encourages large financial institutions, such as banks, to compete more

133 A Lidbetter, 'Judicial Control of Financial Services Legislation' (1995) 11 *Journal of Business Law* 590.

134 R Bosworth-Davies, 'Investigating Financial Crime: The Continuing Evolution of The Public Fraud Investigation Role – A Personal Perspective' (2009) Company Lawyer, 30(7) 195.

135 J Pickard, 'Archives 1985 & 1986: Thatcher Policy Fight over "Big Bang" Laid Bare' (*The Financial Times,* London, 30 December 2014) <https://www.ft.com/content/f3c0d500-8537-11e4-bb63-00144feabdc0> accessed 29 June 2024.

136 Ibid.

137 E Pérez-Caldentey and M Vernengo, 'The Euro Imbalances and Financial Deregulation: A Post-Keynesian Interpretation of the European Debt Crisis' (Levy Economics Institute, January 2012) <http://www.levyinstitute.org/pubs/wp_702.pdf> accessed 16 June 2024.

138 European Commission, 'Commission Communication of 11 May 1999 entitled "Implementing the Framework for Financial Markets: Action Plan"' *COM* (1999) 232 final.

139 Ibid.

aggressively and to increase their exposure to risk,[140] one of the key problems of each of the three financial crisis examined in this section and equally relevant for the LIBOR and FX crisis. This deregulation of financial markets in the US, EU and UK formed the backdrop for the next financial crisis, which took place approximately 20 years after the US savings and loans crisis and the UK's Big Bang. The 2008 financial crisis is examined below.

2.3.3 2008 Financial Crisis

The LIBOR and FX benchmark manipulation took place before, during and after the 2008 financial crisis, with the first LIBOR manipulation cartel estimated to have started before 2007,[141] and the first FX cartel dating from 2009.[142] Whilst this benchmark manipulation was taking place, the 2008 financial crisis occurred. The 2008 financial crisis was heavily influenced by the 'subprime' crisis,[143] a banking crisis caused a global economic recession,[144] which is considered by many economists to have been the most serious financial crisis since the Great Depression of the 1930s.[145] Subprime lending is an expression given by mortgage lenders to high-risk, or subprime, debtors with poor credit histories.[146] A combination of low US interest rates at the time and an extension of credit to those with poor credit histories played a significant role in the crisis.[147] The economic problems began in the years before 2008 with the lending practices in the US subprime mortgage markets.[148] Subprime mortgage lending was a method of spreading the risk of high-defaulting risk

140 C Kirkland, 'Thatcherism and the Origins of the 2007 Crisis' (2015) 10(4) *British Politics* 514.

141 Financial Services Authority, 'Internal Audit Report: A Review of The Extent of Awareness within the FSA of Inappropriate LIBOR Submissions' (Financial Conduct Authority, March 2013) <https://www.fca.org.uk/publication/corporate/fsa-ia-libor.pdf> accessed 21 July 2024.

142 European Commission, 'Antitrust: Commission Fines UBS, Barclays, RBS, HSBC and Credit Suisse €344 Million For Participating in a Foreign Exchange Spot Trading Cartel' (European Commission, 2 December 2021) <https://ec.europa.eu/commission/presscorner/detail/en/ip_21_6548> accessed 21 July 2024.

143 S Rossi, 'Can It Happen Again? Structural Policies to Avert Further Systemic Crisis' (2011) 40(2) *International Journal of Political Economy* 61.

144 A Arora, 'The 2007-09 Banking Crisis and the EU's Regulatory Response' (2010) 21(5) *European Business Law Review* 603.

145 J Crotty, 'Structural Causes of the Global Financial Crisis: A Critical Assessment of the "New Financial Architecture"' (2009) 33(4) *Cambridge Journal of Economics* 563.

146 A Francis and N Ryder, 'Preventing and Intervening in White Collar Crimes: The Role of Regulatory Agencies' in ML Rorie (ed), *The Handbook of White-Collar Crime* (John Wiley & Sons Inc 2020).

147 A Arora, 'The Global Financial Crisis: A New Global Regulatory Order? (2010) 8 *Journal of Business Law* 670.

148 N Ryder and others eds., *Fighting Financial Crime in the Global Economic Crisis* (Routledge 2016).

mortgages across different financial institutions. This model of lending, which became popular in the US in the years prior to 2008, was known as originate-to-distribute, and it involved the originator of the subprime mortgage selling those mortgages to other banks.[149] An unusually large fraction of subprime mortgages, which originated in 2006 and 2007, became delinquent or in foreclosure only months later, which heralded the start of the subprime crisis.[150] As the subprime mortgage crisis began to unfold, it became apparent that many of the mortgages that had a very high risk of borrower default had been bundled with mortgages with a much lower risk of borrower default and so many banks had not sufficiently assessed the credit risks of default on the mortgages they had taken on.[151]

The crisis first became apparent in August 2007 when the short-term funding market and interbank lending abruptly stalled.[152] This significant event followed the news on the same day that French bank BNP Paribas intended to close three of its subsidiaries who invested in US subprime mortgage assets using short-term borrowed money.[153] This was rapidly followed by the dramatic collapse of UK mortgage bank Northern Rock in September 2007.[154] Images of bank account holder's queueing to withdraw their money from the bank were shown worldwide. From this point, the financial markets looked increasingly unstable, culminating in the collapse of the Lehman Brothers bank, the fourth largest bank in the US, on 15 September 2008, which sent all the markets into a panic.[155] Prior to this, the US economy had appeared to be booming – industrial production, exports and retail sales were positive, with no significant downturn in them until after the September announcement about the Lehman Brothers bank, which became the start of the global banking crisis.[156]

A number of factors such as fraud, greed and predatory lending by banks such as Lehman Brothers contributed to the global crisis, which followed the collapse of the Lehman Brothers.[157] By the time Lehman Brothers collapsed,

149 A Purnanandam, 'Originate-to-Distribute Model and the Subprime Mortgage Crisis' (2011) 24(6) *The Review of Financial Studies* 1881; and TG Reeday, *The Law Relating to Banking* (5th edn. Butterworths 1985).

150 Y Demyanyk and O Van Hemert, 'Understanding the Subprime Mortgage Crisis' (2011) 24(6) *The Review of Financial Studies* 1848.

151 Ibid.

152 HS Shin, 'Reflections on Northern Rock: The Bank Run that Heralded the Global Financial Crisis' (2009) 23(1) *Journal of Economic Perspectives* 101.

153 Ibid.

154 Ibid.

155 M Dooley, M Hutchison, 'Transmission of the U.S. Subprime Crisis to Emerging Markets: Evidence on the Decoupling-Recoupling Hypothesis' (2009) 28(8) *Journal of International money and Finance* 1331.

156 Ibid.

157 S Rossi, 'Can It Happen Again? Structural Policies to Avert Further Systemic Crisis' (2011) 40(2) *International Journal of Political Economy* 61.

which has been described as 'the biggest corporate failure in history',[158] a variety of other US and International Investment banks declared themselves in trouble. This includes for example Merrill Lynch,[159] American Insurance Group,[160] Freddie Mac,[161] Fannie Mae,[162] HBOS,[163] Royal Bank of Scotland,[164] Fortis[165] and Alliance and Leicester.[166] These banks were rescued by a variety of measures put into place in the US, the most notable of which was a $700m bank bailout announced by President George Bush on 3 October 2008.[167] This bailout became the Emergency Economic Stabilisation Act of 2008[168] and was designed to buy from the US banks mortgage-backed securities that were failing in order to save the US and global financial system from collapse. The bailout of the US banking system continued in 2009 when President Obama introduced the Fraud Enforcement and Recovery Act 2009 to combat the fraud and white-collar crime seen in the financial crisis[169] and the American Recovery and Reinvestment Act 2009,[170] which were followed by the Dodd-Frank Wall Street Reform and Consumer Protection Act of 2010

158 S Farrell, 'Lehman Brothers Collapse: Where Are the Key Figures Now?' *The Guardian* (London, 11 September 2018) <https://www.theguardian.com/business/2018/sep/11/lehman-brothers-collapse-where-are-the-key-figures-now> accessed 24 July 2024.

159 D Erkens and others, 'Corporate Governance in the 2007–2008 Financial Crisis: Evidence from Financial Institutions Worldwide' (2012) 18(2) *Journal of Corporate Finance.*

160 A Francis and N Ryder, 'Preventing and Intervening in White Collar Crimes: The Role of Regulatory Agencies' in ML Rorie (ed), *The Handbook of White-Collar Crime* (John Wiley & Sons Inc 2020).

161 H Thompson, 'The Political Origins of the Financial Crisis: The Domestic and International Politics of Fannie Mae and Freddie Mac "Corporate Governance in the 2007–2008 Financial Crisis: Evidence from Financial Institutions Worldwide"' (2009) 80(1) *The Political Quarterly* 17.

162 Ibid.

163 A Francis and N Ryder, 'Preventing and Intervening in White Collar Crimes: The Role of Regulatory Agencies' in ML Rorie (ed), *The Handbook of White-Collar Crime* (John Wiley & Sons Inc 2020).

164 D Erkens and others, 'Corporate Governance in the 2007–2008 Financial Crisis: Evidence from Financial Institutions Worldwide' (2012) 18(2) *Journal of Corporate Finance.*

165 Y Fassin and D Gosselin, 'The Collapse of a European Bank in the Financial Crisis: An Analysis from Stakeholder and Ethical Perspectives' (2011) 102(1) *Journal of Business Ethics* 169.

166 N Mathiason, 'Three Weeks that Changed the World' *The Guardian* (London, 28 December 2008) <https://www.theguardian.com/business/2008/dec/28/markets-credit-crunch-banking-2008> accessed 15 July 2024.

167 M Collins, 'The Big Bank Bailout' *Forbes* (New Jersey, 14 July 2015) <https://www.forbes.com/sites/mikecollins/2015/07/14/the-big-bank-bailout/#250404d62d83> accessed 13 July 2024.

168 Emergency Economic Stabilization Act of 2008 12 U.S.C. 5201.

169 N Ryder, *The Financial Crisis and White Collar Crime: The Perfect Storm?* (Edward Elgar 2014).

170 Fraud Enforcement and Recovery Act 2009 and American Recovery and Reinvestment Act of 2009 PL 111-5.

(the Dodd-Frank Act).[171] The aim of the Dodd-Frank Act was: 'to promote the financial stability of the United States by improving accountability and transparency in the financial system, to end "too big to fail", to protect the American taxpayer by ending bailouts, to protect consumers from abusive financial services practices, and for other purposes'.[172] However, the Dodd-Frank Act was not able to prevent the abusive financial services practice of benchmark manipulation, which took place in the LIBOR and FX crisis.

Following the 2008 financial crisis, various legislative measures were introduced in the UK. These included the Banking (Special Provisions) Act 2008, which nationalised the Northern Rock bank. This was followed by the Special Resolution Regime to prop up failing banks.[173] Two years later, the Financial Services Act 2010 gave new powers to the UK financial regulator of the time, the Financial Services Authority (FSA), increasing its enforcement powers to promote financial stability.[174] This was followed by two key legislative acts, the Banking Act 2009 and the Financial Services Act 2012, which, respectively, changed the UK financial services regulator and introduced a comprehensive bank resolution regime. The FSA was replaced by two regulators: Prudential Regulatory Authority (PRA) and the FCA[175] introducing the new 'twin peaks' financial regulatory structure.[176] The FCA was the financial regulator at the time of the LIBOR crisis. The Banking Act 2009 introduced a comprehensive bank resolution regime, known as the 'special resolution regime',[177] which provides the authorities with tools to manage the failure of any financial sector businesses.[178]

The EU also reacted to the 2008 financial crisis by introducing new legislation. This included new rules to strengthen financial supervision of banks, new tools for bank recovery and resolution and an improved regulatory framework for banks, insurance, securities markets and other sectors.[179] Furthermore, laws were also adopted in the EU to tackle excessive volatility in financial markets, including new rules on hedge funds, short selling, credit rating agencies and

171 N Ryder, U Turksen, S Hassler, 'Introduction' in N Ryder and others (eds), *Fighting Financial Crime in the Global Economic Crisis* (Routledge 2015).

172 Preamble to the Dodd-Frank Wall Street Reform and Consumer Protection Act of 2010 12 U.S.C. 5301.

173 N Ryder, *The Financial Crisis and White Collar Crime: The Perfect Storm?* (Edward Elgar 2014).

174 N Ryder, U Turksen, S Hassler, 'Introduction' in N Ryder and others (eds), *Fighting Financial Crime in the Global Economic Crisis* (Routledge 2015).

175 Financial Services Act 2012 s 6.

176 M Killick, '"Twin Peaks" - A New Series or a New Chimera? An Analysis of the Proposed New Regulatory Structure in the UK' (2012) *Company Lawyer* 33(12) 366.

177 Banking Act 2009, s 1.

178 Ibid.

179 European Commission, 'Financial Services Policy' (European Commission, 2022) <https://ec.europa.eu/info/business-economy-euro/banking-and-finance/financial-reforms-and-their-progress/financial-services-policy_en> accessed 15 July 2024.

derivatives.[180] In particular, the EU started its regulatory response to the financial crisis by allowing Member States to rescue their banking sectors by recapitalisation and state buyouts. It did this by letting Member States know that it would apply EU State Aid rules flexibly.[181] The EU also enacted a regulation on credit reference agencies in 2009.[182] Its aim in enacting this regulation, which became law in every Member State, was to tackle the perceived failure of credit rating agencies in the financial crisis to properly appreciate the risks associated with complex financial instruments such as the securities backed by subprime debt which had played a key role in the financial crisis.[183] An illustration of this was given by the European Commission which said this problem was seen when structured finance products were backed by risky subprime mortgages and then issued with incorrect ratings that were far too high.[184] A further legislative action taken by the EU in relation to the financial markets was to strengthen the Capital Requirements Directive.[185] This revision of the EU rules on capital requirements for banks was designed to tighten up, amongst other things, the way in which banks assess the risks connected with their trading book and to require banks to have sound remuneration practices that do not encourage or reward excessive risk-taking.[186] However, as with the legislative measures introduced in the US and UK following the 2008 financial crisis, the changes made in the EU to combat risky and speculative behaviour by banks were also not sufficient to prevent the LIBOR and FX benchmark manipulation, which will be discussed further below.

It is clear from the reaction of the lawmakers in the US, EU and UK following the 2008 financial crisis that the removal of legislation and supervision from financial markets, known as deregulation, had caused significant damage to both global economies and customer confidence.[187] Zagaris states that a key component facilitating international white collar or economic crime is trade

180 A Arora 'The 2007-09 Banking Crisis and the EU's Regulatory Response' (2010) 21(5) *European Business Law Review* 603.

181 Ibid.

182 Regulation (EC) No 1060/2009 of the European Parliament and of the Council of 16 September 2009 on Credit Rating Agencies, OJ 2009 L 302/2.

183 E Parker and M Bake, 'Regulation of Credit Rating Agencies in Europe' (2009) Journal of International Banking and Financial Law 401.

184 European Commission, 'Regulating Credit Rating Agencies' (European Commission, 1 May 2019) <https://ec.europa.eu/info/business-economy-euro/banking-and-finance/financial-supervision-and-risk-management/managing-risks-banks-and-financial-institutions/regulating-credit-rating-agencies_en> accessed 29 July 2024.

185 Directive 2006/49/EC of the European Parliament and the Council of 14 June 2006 on the Capital Adequacy of Investment Firms and Credit Institutions, OJ 2006 L177/201.

186 A Arora 'The 2007-09 Banking Crisis and the EU's Regulatory Response' (2010) 21(5) *European Business Law Review* 603.

187 A Arora, 'The Global Financial Crisis: A New Global Regulatory Order? (2010) 8 *Journal of Business Law* 670.

liberalisation[188] and other commentators agree, recognising that deregulation and decreased enforcement are instrumental to the escalation of financial crimes in the financial services industry.[189] It can be seen that in the UK, the deregulation that took place with the Big Bang resulted in a dramatic increase in takeovers and other corporate restructuring programmes, which, in turn, provided the opportunity to hide accounting manipulation and fraud, turning the UK into a playground for financial criminals, playing a significant role in the next crisis.[190] However, before the newly minted legislative acts had had time to take effect, the next banking crisis had taken hold, with the discovery in 2012 of significant market manipulation of the LIBOR and FX benchmark interest rates involving many international banks.

2.4 The LIBOR and FX Scandals Explained

The previous section described the backdrop to the LIBOR and FX benchmark manipulation crisis. This section will now examine the crisis itself and the two benchmark interest rates at the heart of the manipulation.

LIBOR was created in 1986 and was an important benchmark interest rate used in many financial contracts for more than 40 years.[191] As mentioned above, the LIBOR benchmark interest rate has now been phased out, and from September 2024 will no longer be quoted.[192] The LIBOR benchmark has been abandoned due to its involvement in the 2008 financial crisis as well as the LIBOR and FX manipulation scandal.[193] New benchmarks, including SONIA for pound sterling and SOFR for US dollars have replaced LIBOR.[194] At the time of the LIBOR manipulation crisis, however, the benchmark was prepared by reference to the average of submissions provided by 16 of the world's largest banks and was regulated by the British Bankers' Association

188 B Zagaris, *International White Collar Crime* (Cambridge University Press 2010).

189 G Dagan, 'The Criminalization of the Financial Services Industry through Deregulation and Decreased Enforcement' (ProQuest Dissertations Publishing, January 2015) <https://search-proquest-com.ezproxy.uwe.ac.uk/docview/1654999449?pq-origsite=summon> accessed 28 June 2024.

190 S Toms, 'Financial Scandals: A Historical Overview' (2019) 49(5) *Accounting and Business Research* 477.

191 M Marquit, B Curry, 'What Is Libor and Why Is It Being Abandoned?' *Forbes Advisor* (New Jersey, 21 December 2021) <https://www.forbes.com/advisor/investing/what-is-libor/> accessed 22 July 2024.

192 Bank of England, 'Transition from LIBOR to Risk-Free Rates' (Bank of England, 3 July 2023) <https://www.bankofengland.co.uk/markets/transition-to-sterling-risk-free-rates-from-libor> accessed 1 April 2024.

193 E Fuller and others, 'The End of LIBOR' (2018) 135(3) *Banking Law Journal* 183.

194 M Marquit, 'What Is Libor and Why Is It Being Abandoned?' *Forbes Advisor* (New Jersey, 21 December 2021) <https://www.forbes.com/advisor/investing/what-is-libor/> accessed 1 July 2024.

(now UK Finance).[195] Each daily submission indicated what each bank estimated to be the interest rate that banks can charge each other on commercial loans in the London market.[196] LIBOR was considered a good indicator of liquidity in the financial system and underpinned $300t worth of financial contracts worldwide.[197] The British Bankers' Association officials had previously insisted that LIBOR could not be manipulated, thus demonstrating that self-regulation by the banking industry has not been a success.[198] Self-regulation had also been shown to fail in the banking scandals of the 1990s involving BCCI and Barings Bank, mentioned above.[199] The significance to consumers and businesses of any benchmark manipulation is hard to assess, yet it has been estimated that for transactions and contracts that utilised LIBOR as a benchmark for establishing borrowing costs, even a slight understatement of the rate may have generated sizable wealth transfers from lenders to borrowers.[200] Because the LIBOR benchmark was used as the basis for settlement of interest rate contracts on many of the world's major futures and options exchanges as well as most over the counter and lending transactions (commercial and individual), the impact and reach of the LIBOR manipulation is unquantifiable but hugely significant.[201] In 2012, an international investigation led by the US into the LIBOR benchmark interest rate uncovered collusion by various international banks to manipulate LIBOR for their own purposes, namely to make profit.[202]

At the same time that the LIBOR benchmark manipulation was uncovered, manipulation of the FX benchmark manipulation rate was also discovered. The FX market is a systemically important market, being one of the largest and most liquid markets in the world with a daily average turnover of $5.3t,

195 British Banking Association, 'BBA to Hand over Administration of LIBOR to Intercontinental Exchange Benchmark Administration Ltd' (BBA, 17 January 2014) <https://www.bba.org.uk/news/press-releases/bba-to-hand-over-administration-of-libor-to-intercontinental-exchange-benchmark-administration-ltd/#.XtN0hS-ZNhE> accessed 10 July 2024.

196 *R v Tom Alexander William Hayes* [2015] EWCA Crim 1944.

197 Ibid.

198 I Kaminska and others, 'Bankers Embark on Libor Rate-Setting Rethink For LIBOR' *Financial Times* (London, 6 March 2012) <https://www.ft.com/content/cefbc2a6-677c-11e1-b6a1-00144feabdc0> accessed 8 July 2024.

199 TC Baxter, 'Breaking the Billion Dollar Barrier – Learning the Lessons of BNL, Daiwa, Barings and BCCI' (1997) 9(1) *Journal of Money Laundering Control* 15; and Ryder N, *The Financial Crisis and White Collar Crime: The Perfect Storm?* (Edward Elgar 2014).

200 R Abrantes-Metz and others, 'Libor Manipulation?' (2012) 36(1) *Journal of Banking and Finance* 136.

201 Ibid.

202 L Vaughan and G Finch, 'Libor Scandal: The Bankers Who Fixed the World's Most Important Number' *The Guardian* (London, 18 January 2017) <https://www.theguardian.com/business/2017/jan/18/libor-scandal-the-bankers-who-fixed-the-worlds-most-important-number> accessed 4 July 2024.

40% of which takes place in London.[203] Investigations in the UK, US and EU revealed that banking cartels made up of some individual traders in charge of FX trading of the Group of Ten (G10) currencies exchanged sensitive information and trading plans and occasionally coordinated their trading strategies through various online professional chat rooms to manipulate the FX benchmark interest rate. Commissioner Margrethe Vestager said in relation to the European Commission's enforcement of the FX benchmark manipulation:

> Companies and people depend on banks to exchange money to carry out transactions in foreign countries…these cartel decisions send a clear message that the Commission will not tolerate collusive behaviour in any sector of the financial markets.[204]

In addition to the LIBOR and FX benchmark interest rates, there are other financial benchmark interest rates used by banks, such as the Isdafix,[205] the EURIBOR[206] and oil and gold benchmarks, many of which have been subject to allegations of manipulation.[207] For instance, a recent example of the manipulation of a different benchmark interest rate relates to the Isdafix benchmark in which several international banks were involved, including Barclays Bank, Citibank, Goldman Sachs and the Royal Bank of Scotland.[208] By February 2017, the US Commodity Futures Trading Commission (CFTC) had imposed $570m in penalties for this attempted manipulation of the Isdafix benchmark,[209] but these figures have kept growing with each successive case brought by the CFTC. In the latest Isdafix benchmark manipulation case,

203 Financial Conduct Authority, 'FCA Fines Five Banks £1.1 Billion For FX Failings and Announces Industry-Wide Remediation Programme' (Financial Conduct Authority, 12 November 2014) <https://www.fca.org.uk/news/press-releases/fca-fines-five-banks-%C2%A311-billion-fx-failings-and-announces-industry-wide-remediation-programme> accessed 26 July 2024.

204 European Commission, 'Commission Fines Barclays, RBS, Citigroup, JPMorgan and MUFG E107 Billion for Participating in Foreign Exchange Spot Trading Cartel' (European Commission, 16 May 2019) <https://ec.europa.eu/commission/presscorner/detail/sl/IP_19_2568> accessed 14 July 2024.

205 C Jiakai, 'LIBOR's Poker' (2021) 55(1) *Journal of Financial Markets* (Amsterdam, Netherlands) 100586.

206 A Rodriguez-Lopez and others, 'Evaluating Euribor Manipulation: Effects on Mortgage Borrowers' (2021) 40(1) *Finance Research Letters* 101795.

207 A Frino and others 'The Impact of Commodity Benchmarks on Derivatives Markets: The Case of the Dated Brent Assessment and Brent Futures' (2018) 95(1) *Journal of Banking and Finance*.

208 Commodity Futures Trading Commission, 'CFTC Orders the Royal Bank of Scotland to Pay $85 Million Penalty for Attempted Manipulation of US Dollar ISDAFIX Benchmark Swap Rates' (Commodity Futures Trading Commission, 3 February 2017) <https://www.cftc.gov/PressRoom/PressReleases/7527-17> accessed 8 July 2024.

209 Ibid.

Bank of America NA was ordered to pay a fine of $30m.[210] These cases of benchmark manipulation show that the LIBOR scandal of 2012 was not a one-off and that the rewards of rate-fixing for banks and individual employees within banks are too great a temptation for them. This highlights the importance of this examination of the benefits of the use of competition law to enforce future benchmark manipulation cartels.

In the LIBOR scandal of 2012, some of the contributor banks fraudulently reported artificially low or high interest rates as their LIBOR submissions so that their traders could make profits on derivatives pegged to the base rate.[211] There was a further incentive for banks to report LIBORs higher than they were in practice because LIBOR is also viewed by the market as an indicator of a bank's health, so some banks were able to make themselves appear healthier than they actually were by reporting fictitious rates. The banks found to have been involved with the fraudulent LIBOR reporting included Barclays Bank,[212] JP Morgan Chase,[213] HSBC,[214] Bank of America,[215] Citigroup,[216] UBS,[217] Royal Bank of Scotland[218] and Deutsche Bank.[219] Evidence suggests that this collusion between the banks preceded the 2008 financial crisis and before the resulting re-regulation of the financial markets.[220]

The LIBOR and FX scandals were significant because of the central role that the LIBOR and FX benchmarks played in global finance at the time. The LIBOR was, at the time of the benchmark manipulation scandal, one of the most important interest rates in finance, and trillions of business and consumer

210 Ibid.

211 Financial Conduct Authority 'Barclays Fined £59.5 Million for Significant Failings in Relation to LIBOR and EURIBOR' (Financial Conduct Authority, 22 March 2012) <https://www.fca.org.uk/news/press-releases/barclays-fined-%C2%A3595-million-significant-failings-relation-libor-and-euribor> accessed 24 July 2024.

212 Financial Services Authority, 'Final Notice to Barclays Bank Plc' (Financial Services Authority, 27 June 2012) <https://www.fca.org.uk/publication/final-notices/barclays-jun12.pdf> accessed 24 July 2024.

213 BBC News, 'JP Morgan Fined £26m over Interest Rate Cartel' (*BBC News*, 21 December 2016) <https://www.bbc.co.uk/news/business-38389576> accessed 31 July 2024.

214 J Treanor, 'Bleak Day For British Banking as Libor Arrests Follow Record Fine For HSBC' (*The Guardian* London, 11 December 2012) <https://www.theguardian.com/business/2012/dec/11/banking-libor-fine-hsbc> accessed 31 July 2024.

215 P Crowe, 'LIBOR Rigging Criminal Charge and Fines' *Insider* (New York, 20 May 2015) <https://www.businessinsider.com/libor-rigging-criminal-charges-and-fines-2015-5?r=US&IR=T> accessed 31 July 2024.

216 Ibid.

217 Ibid.

218 Ibid.

219 J Treanor, 'Deutsche Bank Hit by Record $25bn Libor-Rigging Fine' *The Guardian* (London, 23 April 2015) <https://www.theguardian.com/business/2015/apr/23/deutsche-bank-hit-by-record-25bn-libor-rigging-fine> accessed 22 July 2024.

220 R Stokes, 'LIBOR Manipulations: The Limits and Potential of Corporate Criminal Liability' in Ryder and others (eds), *Fighting Financial Crime in the Global Economic Crisis* (Routledge 2015).

financial contracts were based on it.[221] Numerous investigations into alleged manipulation of the LIBOR and FX benchmarks took place in the UK, EU and US after the scandal was exposed.[222] These investigations, lawsuits and the enforcement measures imposed have contributed to a loss of public confidence in the global financial markets and in banks and bankers in particular.[223]

This book examines the different ways in which the manipulation of the LIBOR and FX benchmark interest rates has been enforced by regulators in the UK, EU and US. It considers how different penalties have been used in each jurisdiction with the aim of making recommendations for legislative and policy changes to improve the enforcement and prevention of financial crime. The UK authorities, out of the three selected jurisdictions, imposed the lowest total fines for LIBOR and FX related offences to date.[224] The UK was also the only jurisdiction of the three not to use competition law in the investigation or enforcement of LIBOR or FX related offences. The reasons for this will be examined in detail, together with legislation passed since the LIBOR crisis, to identify the pros and cons to the UK of using its competition law enforcement powers in any future benchmark manipulation crisis. This book argues that if regulators in the UK use their competition law powers to enforce future benchmark manipulation, a range of significant penalties can be imposed to penalise offences, thus preventing further misconduct. The use of more substantial competition law penalties is likely to have a significant positive effect on society at large, ensuring that banks compete with each other rather than working together for their own benefit at the cost of consumers and businesses.

In the next part of this chapter, key themes that are covered in the book will be introduced and the rationale for including each of them will be explained. These themes are first, the role of competition law whistleblowing and leniency regimes in the detection of cartels in the three jurisdictions being examined. Second, the benefits and drawbacks of both criminal and civil penalties available to regulators for the enforcement of benchmark rate manipulation. Third, corporate criminal liability, or the different ways in which companies can be held liable for the actions of their employees, will be considered, and

221 BBC News, 'Libor: What Is It and Why Does It Matter? (BBC News, 3 August 2015) <https://www.bbc.co.uk/news/business-19199683> accessed 22 July 2024.

222 For instance *R v Tom Alexander William Hayes* [2015] EWCA Crim 1944, *Icap plc, Icap Management Services Ltd, Icap New Zealand Ltd v European Commission* 2017 Case T-180/15; and see Serious Fraud Office, 'Senior Bankers Sentenced to 9 Years for Rigging EURIBOR Rate' (Serious Fraud Office, 1 April 2019) <https://www.sfo.gov.uk/2019/04/01/senior-bankers-sentenced-to-9-years-for-rigging-euribor-rate/> accessed 22 July 2024.

223 TL David, 'Reforming the Culture of Banking: Restoring Trust and Confidence in Banking' (2014) 4(2) *Journal of Financial Management, Markets and Institutions* 221.

224 R Ball, 'Competition Law and LIBOR in Three Jurisdictions: US, UK and EU' in Ryder N (ed), *White Collar Crime and Risk – A Critical Reflection* (Routledge, 2018).

the final theme to be discussed is the use in the different jurisdictions of DPAs as an enforcement tool.

2.5 Key Themes

2.5.1 The Role of Whistleblowing and Leniency Regimes in the Detection of Cartels

This section will examine the role that competition law whistleblowing and leniency regimes play in the discovery of a benchmark manipulation cartel. A leniency programme is an essential tool in the arsenal of competition law regulators because a leniency programme is designed to incentivise cartel members to inform on the other cartel members to the regulator. Even the knowledge that a leniency, or whistleblowing, programme exists can result in a type of 'Russian roulette' for cartel participants, in which cartel members never know which of them will be the first to blow the whistle and break up the cartel. If the competition law whistleblowing provisions are set at the right level, this can increase the pressure on individual cartel members to be the first one out of the cartel, to reap the rewards and to be free from penalty. According to the European Commission, this situation seeds distrust and suspicion amongst cartel members.[225] It is clear that having a leniency and/or a whistleblowing, policy is critical for regulators in their fight to crack down on cartels. Businesses, such as banks, that participate in a cartel are normally aware that their behaviour is illegal and, as a result, go to great lengths to keep the cartel secret.[226] As a result, the detection of cartels is harder than the detection of other types of illegal behaviour. To address this problem, each of the EU, UK and US has a leniency policy. These will be considered in turn below.

The EU has a policy that grants immunity from a fine to the first business in a cartel to submit information to the Commission, providing that the information is sufficient to either find an infringement of Article 101 by the cartel or to carry out an investigation.[227] However, no immunity will be granted if the Commission already had sufficient evidence to proceed with an inspection or infringement decision.[228]

225 European Commission, 'About the Cartel Leniency Policy' (European Commission, 11 March 2019) <https://ec.europa.eu/competition/cartels/leniency/leniency.html> accessed 16 July 2024.

226 European Commission, 'Cartels Overview' (European Commission, 15 March 2017) <https://ec.europa.eu/competition/cartels/overview/index_en.html>accessed 17 July 2024.

227 European Commission, 'Commission Notice on Immunity from Fines and Reduction of Fines in Cartel Cases' OJ [2006] C 298/17, para 8.

228 Ibid, paras 10 and 11.

In addition to the Commission's leniency policy for cartels, which forms part of its competition legislation, under the EU market abuse regime,[229] there are further provisions to incentivise whistleblowing. Under the MAR 2014,[230] Member States are able to provide financial incentives for whistleblowers in some circumstances.[231] The MAR 2014 states that measures regarding whistleblowing are necessary to facilitate detection of market abuse and to ensure the protection and the respect of the rights of the whistleblower and the accused person.[232] There is also the requirement in the MAR 2014 for Member States to require financial services businesses to have in place internal procedures for their employees to be able to report infringements of the market abuse laws.[233] These measures increase the likelihood of regulators finding out about potential breaches of the market abuse regime.

An EU Directive to protect whistleblowers[234] has also recently been passed, which will further bolster the market abuse regime by incentivising individuals to provide financial regulators with information and evidence of market abuse, including information about banking cartels formed to manipulate benchmark interest rates. These whistleblowing powers, taken in conjunction with the wide-reaching criminal and civil powers for financial regulators have created a strong framework for the EU's market abuse and competition law enforcement regime.[235]

The UK has a cartel leniency policy that offers total or partial immunity from fines or prosecution to the first business or individual respectively, who comes forward with information about the cartel.[236] This immunity is subject to certain conditions, including that the CMA is not already investigating the cartel and does not otherwise have sufficient information to establish the existence of the cartel.[237] As well as receiving immunity from fines, a business

229 Regulation (EU) No 596/2014 of the European Parliament and of the Council of 16 April 2014 on Market Abuse (Market Abuse Regulation) [2014] OJ 2 173/1 and Directive 2014/57/EU of the European Parliament and of the Council of 16 April 2014 on Criminal Sanctions for Market Abuse (Market Abuse Directive) [2014] OJ 2 173/179.

230 Regulation (EU) No 596/2014 of the European Parliament and of the Council of 16 April 2014 on Market Abuse (Market Abuse Regulation) [2014] OJ 2 173/1

231 Ibid.

232 Regulation (EU) No 596/2014 of the European Parliament and of the Council of 16 April 2014 on Market Abuse (Market Abuse Regulation) [2014] OJ 2 173/1, Preamble 74.

233 Ibid, Article 32(3).

234 Directive (EU) 2019/1937 of the European Parliament and of the Council of 23 October 2019 on the Protection of Persons Who Report Breaches of Union Law, OJ L 305/17 26/11/2019.

235 A Jochema and others, 'The Impact of the 2002 Reform of the EU Leniency Program on Cartel Outcomes' (2020) 71(1) *International Journal of Industrial Organization* 1.

236 Competition and Markets Authority, 'Leniency and No-Action Applications in Cartel Cases' (GOV.UK, 1 July 2013) <https://www.gov.uk/government/publications/leniency-and-no-action-applications-in-cartel-cases> accessed 24 July 2024.

237 Competition and Markets Authority, 'Guidance: Cartels: Come Forward and Apply for Leniency' (GOV.UK, 11 March 2019) <https://www.gov.uk/guidance/cartels-confess-and-apply-for-leniency> accessed 1 July 2024.

applying for leniency will receive immunity from criminal prosecutions for any of its cooperating current or former employees or directors and protection from director disqualification proceedings for all directors who cooperate with the investigation.[238]

In addition to the leniency policy, between 2017 and 2023 the CMA offered a financial reward of up to £100,000 for information about cartel activity[239] and anonymity for whistleblowers.[240] The financial reward for whistleblowers was increased in June 2023 to an amount up to £250,000[241] however, when the average salaries of bankers working in London at the banks who were involved in the LIBOR and FX crisis are considered (between £174,000 and £306,000 in 2023),[242] even the new reward of up to £250,000 appears to be an insufficient incentive to blow the whistle on a cartel that is making that individual and his/her bank large sums of money.

There has been much debate about the provision of any financial reward to individuals or businesses who have broken the law by participating in a cartel. However, the CMA have attempted to justify their stance on this by stating that because cartels are generally conducted in secret, they are hard to detect and prove, so for this reason, the CMA believes that offering financial rewards will lead to the detection and prosecution of cartels.[243] In providing incentives to whistleblowers, the CMA is pursuing a different strategy to that of the FCA, which has expressed its concern that incentivising whistleblowers 'could create a number of moral and other hazards'.[244] The FCA has also observed that offering financial incentives to whistleblowers might undermine internal whistleblowing procedures introduced and maintained by

238 R Whish & D Bailey, *Competition Law* (10th edn, Oxford University Press 2021).

239 Competition and Markets Authority, 'CMA Launches Campaign to Crack Down on Cartels' (GOV.UK, 31 March 2014) <https://www.gov.uk/government/news/cma-launches-campaign-to-crack-down-on-cartels> accessed 1 June 2024.

240 Competition and Markets Authority, 'Rewards for Information About Cartels' (Competition and Markets Authority, 2024) <https://www.gov.uk/government/publications/cartels-informant-rewards-policy/rewards-for-information-about-cartels#:~:text=If%20you%20have%20information%20on,for%20information%20about%20cartel%20activity.> accessed 27 June 2024.

241 Competition and Markets Authority, 'Blowing the Whistle on Cartels' (GOV.UK, 6 June 2023) <https://www.gov.uk/government/news/blowing-the-whistle-on-cartels#:~:text=The%20Competition%20and%20Markets%20Authority,cartel%20activity%20they%20have%20witnessed.> accessed 20 June 2024.

242 Z Tulon, 'London's Investment Banking Salaries and Bonuses' (efinancialcareers, 19 October 2023) <https://www.efinancialcareers.co.uk/news/2023/10/london-investment-bank-pay> accessed 27 June 2024.

243 Ibid.

244 Financial Conduct Authority, 'Financial Incentives for Whistleblowers' (Financial Conduct Authority, July 2014) <https://www.fca.org.uk/publication/financial-incentives-for-whistleblowers.pdf> accessed 3 July 2024.

firms.[245] Since the CMA started offering financial rewards to whistleblowers in exchange for information about cartels, calls to the CMA's cartels hotline rose 18% in 2018 to 556, up from 471 in the previous year.[246] This demonstrates that the financial reward scheme has incentivised people who would not otherwise have contacted the CMA with information about a cartel.

The DoJ has a leniency programme, which it describes as being its most important investigative tool for detecting cartel activity.[247] The DoJ's leniency program offers a reduction in fines for cartel members that bring evidence to the antitrust authority. It also offers the complete exemption from fines and criminal prosecution. The leniency program aims at attracting leniency applications by encouraging subjects of ongoing investigations to consider whether they qualify for leniency in other than the currently inspected markets where they engage in cartel activities.[248] There are three different types of leniency that a company or individual can apply for in the DoJ's leniency programme; Type A and Type B Corporate Leniency and individual leniency.[249] It is often promoted as a tool that has the potential to bring a series of cartels tumbling down like a house of cards. [250]

In addition to the DoJ's leniency programme, there are additional incentives to whistleblowers. In the Dodd-Frank Act,[251] whistleblowers who provide original information that leads to a successful enforcement action can be rewarded with a 10%–30% share of the financial penalty collected by the regulator.[252] One of the key regulators for this legislation is the SEC,[253] whose mission is to protect investors, maintain fair, orderly and efficient markets and facilitate capital formation.[254] As part of the incentive for whistleblowers

245 D Hall and N Ryder, 'The Protection of Whistle-Blowers in the United Kingdom - A Critical and Comparative Commentary' in Grasso, C (ed), *Whistleblowers: Voices of Justice* (Springer 2020).

246 B Thompson, 'Number of Whistleblowing Reports on UK Cartels up 18% Last Year' (*Financial Times* London, 28 May 2019) <https://www.ft.com/content/bd41277c-7d54-11e9-81d2-f785092ab560> accessed 3 July 2024.

247 US Department of Justice, 'Leniency Program' (US Department of Justice, 4 April 2022) <https://www.justice.gov/atr/leniency-program> accessed 3 July 2024.

248 Y Lefouili and C Roux, 'Leniency Programs for Multimarket Firms: The Effect of Amnesty Plus on Cartel Formation' (2008) 30(6) *International Journal of Industrial Organization* 624.

249 Department of Justice, 'Antitrust Division Leniency Policy and Procedures' (US Department of Justice, April 2022) <https://www.justice.gov/atr/page/file/1490246/download> accessed 21 July 2024.

250 M Martyniszyn, 'Leniency (Amnesty) Plus: A Building Block or a Trojan Horse?' (2015) 3(2) *Journal of Antitrust Enforcement* 391.

251 The Dodd-Frank Wall Street Reform and Consumer Protection Act, 12 USC 5301.

252 Ibid., S. 922

253 Ibid., S. 2(12)(b).

254 US Securities and Exchange Commission, 'What We Do' (Sec.Gov, 10 June 2013) <https://www.sec.gov/Article/whatwedo.html> accessed 8 June 2022.

to come forward, the Dodd-Frank Act expressly prohibits retaliation against whistleblowers by employers and allows whistleblowers a cause of action if they are discriminated against or discharged by their employers as a result of their whistleblowing.[255] The US whistleblower incentivisation policy has been extremely successful as, since 2011, the SEC has awarded over $1b to whistleblowers.[256] These whistleblowers have resulted in more than $6b paid to the SEC in enforcement actions, demonstrating the value to the regulator of the information provided to it by whistleblowers.[257]

From the above, it can be seen that in the three jurisdictions being examined, there are a variety of approaches to incentivise whistleblowers in order to facilitate the detection of cartels. However, following recent changes in the UK and EU, each jurisdiction now offers financial incentives to whistleblowers in the hope that more cartels can be brought to justice. This will be considered further in later chapters that examine the UK, EU and US legislative and policy regimes for tackling future banking cartels. Once a cartel has been brought to the attention of the authorities, the enforcement powers available to them can then be examined.

2.5.2 Criminal and Civil Penalties Available to Regulators for Benchmark Manipulation

When considering the best way to penalise the financial crime of benchmark manipulation, the range of both civil and criminal penalties available to regulators must be examined. In the case study Chapters 3, 4 and 5 the sanctions available to UK, EU and US regulators will be assessed and a critical analysis of the civil and criminal sanctions used will be carried out for each jurisdiction. It is generally held that criminal law is meant to punish and civil sanctions to compensate.[258] However, commentators have pointed to civil sanctions that appear to be more criminal or penal in nature, such as the extremely high fines that can be imposed by the European Commission under its competition laws – up to 10% of a company's worldwide turnover – have been described as punitive and capable of being classified as a criminal sanction.[259] Therefore, in

255 US Securities and Exchange Commission, 'Whistleblower Program' (US Securities and Exchange Commission, 8 December 2011) <https://www.sec.gov/spotlight/dodd-frank/whistleblower.shtml> accessed 8 July 2024.

256 US Securities and Exchange Commission, 'Whistleblower Awards over $1 Billion' (US Securities and Exchange Commission, 4 June 2020) <https://www.sec.gov/page/whistleblower-100million> accessed 8 July 2024.

257 Ibid.

258 K Mann, 'Punitive Civil Sanctions: The Middleground between Criminal and Civil Law' (1992) 101(8) *The Yale Law Journal* 1795.

259 V Franssen, 'The EU's Fight against Corporate Financial Crime: State of Affairs and Future Potential' (2018) 19(5) *German Law Journal* 1221.

the assessment of whether sanctions available to regulators are civil or criminal, the deterrent effect of each sanction is considered.

The starting point for any discussion on attaching criminal corporate liability to international institutions is 'too big to fail'. This was clearly explained when the then US Attorney General, Eric Holder, told a Senate Judiciary Committee hearing that some financial institutions have become 'so large' that it makes it 'difficult for us to prosecute them'.[260] Holder's remarks were made during a discussion about why the DoJ had failed to bring criminal charges against HSBS for allegedly laundering money for Mexican drug cartels.[261] Holder explained to the Senate Judiciary Committee that criminal charges against large companies will have a 'negative impact on the national economy, perhaps world economy', due to the fact that for the companies themselves such a hard-line approach is likely to have a devastating effect in terms of collateral consequences, which can include significant financial losses, reputational repercussions and criminal convictions.[262] Instead of prosecuting HSBC for money laundering in 2012, the bank agreed to enter into a DPA with the DoJ and to pay a fine of $1.256m.[263] Committee member Charles E. Grassley commented: 'After hearing today's testimony, big bankers know that if they commit financial crimes, they can expect a passive response from the Justice Department'.[264] This is a valid response to the avowed declaration that the DoJ will not prosecute businesses that are 'too large', but there are good reasons for this pragmatic approach to the imposition of criminal charges on businesses that so many thousands, sometimes millions, of people depend on.

The DoJ have learnt from their experiences of successfully prosecuting large companies and are scared of a repeat of the significant repercussions that can result. In March 2002, one of the first examples of the effects that criminal charges can have on a large company was that Arthur Andersen LLP, which was successfully prosecuted for obstruction of justice in connection with the

260 D Douglas, 'Holder Concerned Megabanks Too Big to Jail' *The Washington Post* (Washington, 6 March 2013) <https://www.washingtonpost.com/business/economy/holder-concerned-megabanks-too-big-to-jail/2013/03/06/6fa2b07a-869e-11e2-999e-5f8e0410cb9d_story.html> accessed 8 July 2024.

261 US Department of Justice, 'HSBC Holdings Plc and HSBC Bank USA NA Admit to Anti-Money Laundering and Sanctions Violations, Forfeit $1256 Billion in Deferred Prosecution Agreement' (United States Department of Justice, 11 December 2012) <https://www.justice.gov/opa/pr/hsbc-holdings-plc-and-hsbc-bank-usa-na-admit-anti-money-laundering-and-sanctions-violations>accessed 16 July 2024.

262 N Ryder, '"Too Scared to Prosecute and Too Scared to Jail?" A Critical and Comparative Analysis of Enforcement of Financial Crime Legislation against Corporations in the USA and the UK' (2018) 82(3) *The Journal of Criminal Law* 245.

263 Ibid.

264 D Douglas, 'Holder Concerned Megabanks Too Big To Jail' (*The Washington Post* Washington, 6 March 2013) <https://www.washingtonpost.com/business/economy/holder-concerned-megabanks-too-big-to-jail/2013/03/06/6fa2b07a-869e-11e2-999e-5f8e0410cb9d_story.html> accessed 8 July 2024.

Enron affair in the United States.[265] In this case, Arthur Andersen who audited Enron Corp, an energy company, was charged with the destruction of documents and the obstruction of justice in order to obscure accounting malpractices that had taken place. The initial successful criminal conviction (which was overturned on appeal)[266] resulted in Arthur Andersen agreeing to surrender its practising licence, which, in turn, led to its dissolution within a matter of months.[267] The decision to prosecute the whole firm rather than the individuals involved in the criminal behaviour led to extreme damage to the firm's reputation, which then led to the loss of clients in large numbers. The ramifications of the criminal charges happened in a very short space of time; from the date of the criminal conviction on 15 June until the dissolution of Arthur Andersen on 31 August 2002 was just under two months.[268] The firm had gone from being a $9b global professional services firm, employing 85,000 people in 84 countries, to dissolution in a frighteningly fast period of time.[269] The collateral damage that is done when ending the life of a large company, including in Arthur Anderson's case the loss of approximately 30,000 jobs, has given regulators around the world pause for thought.[270] For banks, collateral damage following a removal of their licence to operate could also result in severe disruption to the global financial markets and a loss of investor confidence.

At the time of the criminal conviction of Arthur Andersen, it became clear that the reputational damage of bringing criminal charges against a global company were immeasurable. In particular, for a business that bases its reputation on trust the reputational damage is more likely to be irreparable, converting a criminal conviction into a corporate death penalty. This was demonstrated again later the same year when regulators considered bringing criminal charges against another global organisation, WorldCom, and its key executives implicated in the fraud. WorldCom was one of the world's largest telecommunication companies when US regulators discovered fraudulent accounting practices at the business.[271] The SEC charged WorldCom on 26

265 CNN Money, 'WorldCom Criminal Charges Weighed' (*CNN Money*, 25 July 2002) <https://money.cnn.com/2002/07/25/news/companies/worldcom/index.htm> accessed 28 July 2024.

266 G Markoff, 'Arthur Andersen and the Myth of the Corporate Death Penalty: Corporate Criminal Convictions in the Twenty-First Century' (2013) 15(3) *University of Pennsylvania Journal of Business Law* 797.

267 PM Torbert, 'What Felled Arthur Andersen? It Depends...' (2015) 3(1) *Peking University Law Journal* 227.

268 Ibid.

269 Ibid.

270 N Ryder, '"Too Scared to Prosecute and Too Scared to Jail?" A Critical and Comparative Analysis of Enforcement of Financial Crime Legislation against Corporations in the USA and the UK' (2018) 82(3) *The Journal of Criminal Law* 245.

271 US Securities and Exchange Commission, 'Form 10-K' (Sec.Gov, 31 December 2002) <https://www.sec.gov/Archives/edgar/data/723527/000119312504039709/d10k.htm> accessed 28 July 2024.

June 2002 with defrauding investors by improper accounting.[272] In addition to charging the company, WorldCom's CEO, Bernard Ebbers, and its Chief Financial Officer, Scott Sullivan, were both charged shortly afterward[273] and were both sentenced to 25[274] and five[275] years, respectively, in jail for their roles in the fraudulent accounting for which WorldCom was convicted. The criminal charges against both WorldCom and four other of its directors[276] led to the demise of the entire corporation, as it went bankrupt in July 2002,[277] reporting the largest bankruptcy in US history[278] before the 2008 financial crisis.

From one perspective, it can be argued that both the case of Arthur Anderson and that of WorldCom were successes for US regulators; both of these global giants had been removed from their positions of power, and the effect of the criminal charges against each company had a significant deterrent effect on other companies.[279] However, it must be noted that the criminal charges against Arthur Andersen were subsequently reversed on appeal to the Supreme Court in 2005.[280] The collateral damage from the initial criminal corporate liability charges consisted of job losses that ran into the thousands for both WorldCom[281] and Arthur Andersen,[282] and both this and the bankruptcy and dissolution of the companies ultimately had a negative impact on the US economy due to the job losses, reputational damage and the loss in quick succession of two major players in the US economy. Criminal prosecutions of

272 G Giroux, 'What Went Wrong?: Accounting Fraud and Lessons from the Recent Scandals' (2008) 74(4) *Social Research: An International Quarterly* 1205.

273 Ibid.

274 US Department of Justice, 'United States v Bernard Ebbers' (US Department of Justice, 17 December 2019) <https://www.justice.gov/usao-sdny/united-states-v-bernard-ebbers> accessed 28 July 2024.

275 J Bayot, 'Ex-WorldCom Officer Sentenced to 5 Years in Accounting Fraud' *The New York Times* (New York, 12 August 2005) <https://www.nytimes.com/2005/08/12/business/exworldcom-officer-sentenced-to-5-years-in-accounting-fraud.html> accessed 28 July 2024.

276 G Giroux, 'What Went Wrong?: Accounting Fraud and Lessons from the Recent Scandals' (2008) 74(4) *Social Research: An International Quarterly* 1205.

277 US Securities and Exchange Commission, 'Form 10-K' (Sec.Gov, 31 December 2002) <https://www.sec.gov/Archives/edgar/data/723527/000119312504039709/d10k.htm> accessed 28 July 2024.

278 S Romero, 'WorldCom's Collapse: The Overview; WorldCom Files for Bankruptcy; Largest US Case' *The New York Times* (New York, 22 July 2002) <https://www.nytimes.com/2002/07/22/us/worldcom-s-collapse-the-overview-worldcom-files-for-bankruptcy-largest-us-case.html> accessed 28 July 2024.

279 G Markoff, 'Arthur Andersen and the Myth of the Corporate Death Penalty: Corporate Criminal Convictions in the Twenty-First Century' (2013) 15(3) *University of Pennsylvania Journal of Business Law* 797.

280 Ibid.

281 G Giroux, 'What Went Wrong?: Accounting Fraud and Lessons from the Recent Scandals' (2008) 74(4) *Social Research: An International Quarterly* 1205.

282 N Ryder, '"Too Scared to Prosecute and Too Scared to Jail?" A Critical and Comparative Analysis of Enforcement of Financial Crime Legislation against Corporations in the USA and the UK' (2018) 82(3) *The Journal of Criminal Law* 245.

companies are now relatively rare because regulators weigh up the collateral damage to employees and creditors of a company, who are innocent of the charges but who will be disproportionately harmed if a successful criminal prosecution leads to the dissolution, or death, of a company.

In the UK the FCA has the power to prosecute corporate entities for a wide variety of criminal activities.[283] However to date, this power has only been used once against a bank.[284] Notably, following the LIBOR and FX crisis, the FSA, the UK's financial regulator at that time, was criticised by the HM Treasury Select Committee for its decision not initiate criminal proceedings in relation to LIBOR.[285] In the EU, powers to prosecute companies for financial crime exist but, as with the UK, have yet to be used by regulators against a financial institution.[286]

As explained above, there may be a reluctance by regulators in each of the three jurisdictions being examined in this book to use criminal penalties against large, international financial institutions, that can be perceived as 'too large' to be prosecuted. This reluctance to use criminal penalties that may result in a corporate 'death sentence' for a financial institution will be considered in later chapters, as it means that alternative penalties, such as civil penalties (predominately fines) and DPAs, are more likely to be used by regulators.

In the next section, a detailed look at the ability of regulators in each of the UK, EU and US to make companies criminally liable for financial crime, including benchmark rate manipulation, will be carried out.

2.5.3 Corporate Criminal Liability

A key theme that will be considered in this book is that of corporate criminal liability and the criminal prosecution of corporations.[287] In particular, the different ways in which a bank can be held liable for the actions of its employees will be examined. In the LIBOR and FX crisis, the LIBOR and FX benchmark

283 Financial Services and Markets Act 2000 ss 401 and 402 and the Financial Services Act 2012 ss 89 – 91.

284 Financial Conduct Authority, 'NatWest Fined £264.8 Million for Anti-Money Laundering Failures' (Financial Conduct Authority, 13 December 2021) <https://www.fca.org.uk/news/press-releases/natwest-fined-264.8million-anti-money-laundering-failures> accessed 28 July 2024.

285 House of Commons Treasury Committee, 'Fixing LIBOR: Some Preliminary Findings' (HC 2012-13 HC481-I) 103.

286 Regulation (EU) No 596/2014 of the European Parliament and of the Council of 16 April 2014 on Market Abuse (Market Abuse Regulation) [2014] OJ 2 173/1 Article 30 and Directive 2014/57/EU of the European Parliament and of the Council of 16 April 2014 on Criminal Sanctions for Market Abuse (Market Abuse Directive) [2014] OJ 2 173/179 Article 9.

287 G Markoff, 'Arthur Andersen and the Myth of the Corporate Death Penalty: Corporate Criminal Convictions in the Twenty-First Century' (2013) 15(3) *University of Pennsylvania Journal of Business Law* 797.

interest rates were manipulated by traders from different banks who formed cartels in which they discussed whether and how much to raise or lower their bank's LIBOR and FX submissions for a particular period. The problems that each jurisdiction faced in bringing the traders and their employers, the banks, to justice following the exposure of the benchmark manipulation will be examined. There are various ways in which a company can be held liable for the actions of its employees in each of the jurisdictions being examined in this book.

In the US, the principle of '*respondeat superior*' underlies corporate criminal liability.[288] This has been applied broadly by courts and means that a business is responsible for all its employees' actions undertaken in the course and scope of their employment and, at least in part, for the benefit of the business.[289] This principle enables prosecutors to assign criminal liability to companies with relative ease, even when employees act contrary to corporate policy or even instructions.[290] A further means of assigning criminal liability to a company in the US is the doctrine of 'collective knowledge'.[291] Prosecutors relying on this doctrine do not have to demonstrate that a single individual had the knowledge to satisfy the intent element of a crime.[292] Instead, that knowledge may be attribute to many employees of the company to form an overall corporate knowledge of the offence. This, again, increases the chances of US prosecutors establishing corporate criminal liability when a financial crime has been committed.

In the UK, the position is similar, but prosecutors have a harder job to assign liability to companies. There are two primary methods of establishing corporate criminal liability: vicarious and nonvicarious liability.[293] Vicarious liability has only limited application for criminal law, in areas such as health and safety and environmental offences.[294] Therefore, prosecutors for financial crime offences must look to nonvicarious liability in order to establish corporate liability for a crime. The main way of doing this in the UK has, for many years, been the 'identification doctrine'. The identification doctrine involves identifying the most senior officers of the company, who represent

288 *Perdue v. Mitchell*, 373 So. 2d 650 (1979).

289 Bryan Cave, 'Corporate Criminal Liability – Perspectives from the US, UK and France' (Bryan Cave Leighton Paisner LLP, 13 April 2018) <https://www.lexology.com/library/detail.aspx?g=a87d8ace-7b5e-482b-a907-9a69e20f02cdl> accessed 14 July 2024.

290 ME Roszkowski and CL Roszkowski, 'Making Sense of Respondent Superior: An Integrated Approach for Both Negligent and Intentional Conduct' (2005) 14(2) *Southern California Review of Law and Women's Studies* 235.

291 C Jezierski, 'Corporate Liability in United States' (*Global Compliance News*, 11 July 2019) <https://globalcompliancenews.com/white-collar-crime/corporate-liability-united-states/> accessed 14 July 2024.

292 *United States v. Bank of New England*, 821 F.2d 844 (1st Cir. 1987).

293 CPS, 'Corporate Prosecutions' (The Crown Prosecution Service, 1 May 2019) <https://www.cps.gov.uk/legal-guidance/corporate-prosecutions> accessed 14 July 2024.

294 Ibid.

the 'directing mind and will' of the company and then proving corporate criminal liability through his/her conduct and state of mind.[295] The identification doctrine is widely accepted to have frustrated the prosecution of large companies for economic crimes in England and Wales.[296] This is because, while the identification of the 'directing mind and will' of the company and the attribution of criminal intent may be straightforward for small companies, prosecutors are often unable to perform this task when dealing with large, complex organisations.[297] The identification doctrine applies to all types of offences, including those that require *mens rea*.[298] This requirement to prove criminal responsibility of some or all of the Board of Directors has proved difficult from an evidential point of view, leading some commentators to describe the identification doctrine as 'an impossibly high bar to achieve anything'.[299] A recent change to the law, however, has expanded the identification doctrine to apply to the 'senior managers'[300] of a company for certain specified financial crimes.[301] These crimes include fraud, false accounting, conspiracy to defraud, money laundering, terrorist financing and bribery.[302] This expansion of the identification doctrine is welcome and will provide prosecutors with further powers to attribute criminal liability to companies in the UK using the principle of vicarious liability when their senior managers undertake specified economic crimes during the course of their employment, whether or not for the benefit of the company.[303]

The difficulties experienced by prosecutors over the past 52 years in assigning criminal liability for financial crime to companies using the identification doctrine have been addressed, to a certain extent, by the Bribery Act 2010, which introduced a 'failure to prevent' offence, specifically, the offence of failing to prevent bribery.[304] This strict liability offence applies to any person associated with the company who pays a bribe to attract or retain business. In addition to this, the Criminal Finances Act 2017 enhanced regulators' enforcement powers for corruption, money laundering and tax evasion offences. It introduced

295 *Tesco Supermarkets Ltd v Nattrass* [1972] AC 153 as updated by *Serious Fraud Office v Barclays* [2018] EWHC 3055 (QB), [2020] 1 Cr App R 28.

296 M Dsouza, 'The Corporate Agent in Criminal Law - An Argument for Comprehensive Identification' (2020) *Cambridge Law Journal* 79 (1), 91, 118; and Law Commission, 'Corporate Criminal Liability: An Options Paper' (10 June 2022) at 39, 40 <https://lawcom.gov.uk/project/corporate-criminal-liability/> accessed 26 July 2024.

297 See for example the case of *SFO v Barclays* [2018] EWHC 3055 (QB).

298 *St Regis Paper Co. Ltd. v. R.* [2012] 1 Cr App R 14.

299 H Spector, 'SFO v Barclays: Elusive Corporate Liability in the UK' (2020) 10, Arch Rev, 6-10, at 7.

300 Ibid, s. 196(4).

301 Economic Crime and Corporate Transparency Act 2023, s. 196(1).

302 Ibid, Schedule 12.

303 Economic Crime and Corporate Transparency Act 2023, s. 196(1).

304 Bribery Act 2010, S. 7.

new 'failure to prevent' offences for UK and foreign tax evasion.[305] A further 'failure to prevent' offence has also now been created in the Economic Crime and Corporate Transparency Act 2023, which introduced a 'failure to prevent fraud' offence, along the same lines as the offences in the Bribery Act 2010 and the Criminal Finances Act 2017. Under this offence, a large organisation will be held accountable if they profit from a fraud committed by a person associated with the organisation.[306]

The EU has the concept of corporate criminal liability in its legislation for some financial crimes, but it also recognises the diversity in the Member States when it comes to the imposition of criminal liability on legal persons. For this reason it uses the word 'sanctions' rather than 'penalties' in its legislation.[307] The financial crimes of market manipulation, money laundering and the unlawful disclosure of inside information attract criminal sanctions against both legal and natural persons in the EU's market abuse regime.[308] However the EU follows the identification principle in the assignment of liability to companies; for instance, it specifies that for the market manipulation offence to apply to a company, it will apply 'to the natural persons who participate in the decision to carry out activities for the account of the legal person concerned'.[309]

Therefore, it can be seen that the US leads the way on corporate criminal liability, followed by the UK and EU, whose prosecutors find it harder to successfully assign liability for financial crime to companies. Once laws on corporate criminal liability can be more successfully used by prosecutors, the option of entering into a DPA with an offending company will then be available, in order to lessen the impact or risk of a corporate death for the corporation in breach of criminal law. DPAs are discussed further below.

2.5.4 Deferred Prosecution Agreements

The last theme to be considered in this chapter is that of DPAs. A DPA is an alternative to prosecuting a company in a criminal court, and a DPA is typically not available to a company as of right, but may be offered to a company by a regulator whether or not the company has self-reported for its crime.[310] Settlement tools such as Corporate Non-Prosecution Agreements and DPAs were first used in the US in the early 1990s following the 1994 *Prudential*

305 Criminal Finances Act 2017, Ss. 45 and 46.

306 Economic Crime and Corporate Transparency Act 2023, s. 199(1).

307 G Vermeulen and others, *Liability of Legal Persons for Offences in the EU* (Maklu-Publishers 2012).

308 Regulation (EU) No 596/2014 of the European Parliament and of the Council of 16 April 2014 on Market Abuse (Market Abuse Regulation) [2014] OJ 2 173/1, Articles 8(5), 12(4) and 10(1).

309 Ibid., Article 12(4).

310 B Hertstein, M Berry and SC. Brown, 'Deferred Prosecution Agreements in Jersey: Ways to Buttress the Castle' (2024) 3(1) *Journal of Economic Criminology* 100046, 7.

Securities[311] trial, which saw the first DPA involving a public company.[312] DPAs, which are entered into between the company or companies under investigation and the relevant regulator, operate by allowing companies to escape criminal liability if they agree to pay a fine instead of facing criminal prosecution.[313] DPAs often also involve some form of behaviour regulation to manage the offending behaviour such as undertaking to cooperate in the future prosecution of individuals and the payment of compensation to victims.[314] There has been a marked increase of use of DPAs in the US since 2003.[315] They are a popular settlement option for companies under investigation who, by entering into a DPA, are able to avoid having to enter a guilty plea or to face the substantial costs of defending a criminal trial, with all the associated reputational damage that would cause. However whether DPAs can be viewed as a useful tool from the regulator's point of view depends on whether their success is viewed in purely financial terms or whether the entry into a DPA instead of taking a company to trial is seen as a 'soft option', allowing companies to absolve themselves of responsibility and avoid the risks of potential prosecution.[316] Many commentators cautiously welcome DPAs as a pragmatic response to corporate crime,[317] whilst others lament the fact that justice does not appear to be done when a DPA is entered into in lieu of a criminal trial.[318] These differences in opinion will be considered in further detail in Chapters 3, 4, 5 and 6.

Since 2014, DPAs have been in use in the UK, enacted by the Crime and Courts Act 2013, for offences set out in that Act, including conspiracy to defraud.[319] The only regulators with power to issue DPAs in the UK are the Serious Fraud Office (SFO) and the Crown Prosecution Service.[320] Their first use was in the case of Standard Bank in 2015, which was accused of failure

311 *In re Prudential Securities Inc.*, 158 F.R.D. 562 (1994).

312 CR Alexander and MA Cohen, 'The Evolution of Corporate Criminal Settlements: An Empirical Perspective on Non-Prosecution, Deferred Prosecution, and Plea Agreements' (2015) 52(1) *The American Criminal Law Review* 537.

313 C King and N Lord, 'Deferred Prosecution Agreements in England & Wales: Castles Made of Sand?' (2020) 1(1) *Public Law* 307.

314 A Palmer, 'Justice Deferred Is Justice Denied?' in N Ryder and L Pasculli (eds), *Corruption, Integrity and the Law* (Routledge 2020) 108.

315 CR Alexander and MA Cohen, 'The Evolution of Corporate Criminal Settlements: An Empirical Perspective on Non-Prosecution, Deferred Prosecution, and Plea Agreements' (2015) 52(1) *The American Criminal Law Review* 537.

316 C King and N Lord, 'Deferred Prosecution Agreements in England & Wales: Castles Made of Sand?' (2020) 1(1) *Public Law* 307.

317 Ibid.

318 R Cheung, 'Deferred Prosecution Agreements: Cooperation and Confession' (2018) 12(1) *Cambridge Law Journal*; and A Palmer, 'Justice Deferred Is Justice Denied?' in N Ryder and L Pasculli (eds), *Corruption, Integrity and the Law* (Routledge 2020) 108.

319 A Palmer, 'Justice Deferred Is Justice Denied?' in N Ryder and L Pasculli (eds), *Corruption, Integrity and the Law* (Routledge 2020) 92.

320 Ibid 92.

to prevent bribery contrary to Section 7 of the Bribery Act 2010.[321] The DPA was granted for a three year period, which expired in November 2018, bringing to an end the criminal charges against the bank. In exchange for the dropping of criminal charges after the term of the DPA, Standard Bank had to pay multimillion dollar sums as fines and compensation to victims. In addition to the financial penalties, Standard Bank agreed to cooperate with the SFO and to be subject to a review of its antibribery and corruption controls. It was also required to implement recommendations made by Price Waterhouse Coopers LLP, who acted as an independent reviewer in the case.[322] It has been argued that the use of DPAs are an illustration of restorative justice in action; participating offenders such as Standard Bank work with regulators to manage their offending behaviour and are helped, as part of the DPA, to find both moral- and financial-based opportunities to repair the harm done by them to their victims.[323] Whether UK regulators should consider the use of DPAs to tackle the financial crime of benchmark manipulation will be considered in Chapter 3.

Currently, the EU has not used DPAs as a form of settlement of criminal proceedings in financial crime. To date only two Member States (one now former Member State) have used DPAs, one being the UK, the other France. It appears likely, however, that the EU will have to consider the use of DPAs in the near future if the European Commission forms a strong case for the criminal prosecution of a large company, such as an international bank, the prosecution of which could have a negative impact on the national or world economy. It is likely that the EU's relatively new criminal penalty powers in its market abuse directive and regulation will present the opportunity for a DPA to be considered by European regulators.[324]

In the next section of this chapter, an examination of possible changes in competition law policy for the UK stemming from its exit from the EU will be assessed. The consideration and analysis of possible deviation by the UK in the future from the competition law policy and law of the EU is important in the context of this research, which is predicated on the three jurisdictions of the UK, EU and US being based on the same or similar competition law.

321 C King and N Lord, 'Deferred Prosecution Agreements in England & Wales: Castles Made of Sand?' (2020) 1(1) *Public Law* 307.

322 Serious Fraud Office Case Information, 'Standard Bank PLC' (Serious Fraud Office, 3 September 2019) <https://www.sfo.gov.uk/cases/standard-bank-plc/> accessed 14 July 2024.

323 D McStravick, 'Deferred Prosecution Agreements and the Restorative Justice Paradigm' in N Ryder and L Pasculli (eds), *Corruption, Integrity and the Law* (Routledge 2020) 113.

324 Regulation (EU) No 596/2014 of the European Parliament and of the Council of 16 April 2014 on Market Abuse (Market Abuse Regulation) [2014] OJ 2 173/1; and Directive 2014/57/EU of the European Parliament and of the Council of 16 April 2014 on Criminal Sanctions for Market Abuse (Market Abuse Directive) [2014] OJ 2 173/179.

2.6 Post-Brexit

Following the departure of the UK from the EU on 31 January 2020, the UK entered into a transition period until the end of December 2020, after which EU competition law stopped having direct effect in the UK.[325] As part of its exit from the EU, the UK moved to become a standalone competition regime that had a significant effect on the CMA's caseload as the UK's principal competition regulator.[326] Most commentators agreed prior to Brexit that there was unlikely to be any significant change to competition in the UK in the short term because the competition rules contained in the Competition Act 1998 would remain *in situ* and because these rules are substantively the same as the EU competition rules.[327] This has been and still is the case; however, a new law has since been passed that is designed to amend and improve the UK competition law system separate from that of the EU.[328] This new law came into being following the government's proposals for reform of the competition regime.[329] The stated aim of the reforms was, in the words of the Secretary of State for Business, Energy and Industrial Strategy:

> Now that we have left the EU, we have an opportunity to implement regulations that work better for the UK. We are moving in a more agile way than the EU, whilst maintaining high standards. We can forge our own path to deliver growth, innovation, and competition while minimising burdens on business.[330]

The reforms included in the new law, the Digital Markets, Competition and Consumers Act, include changes to the UK merger control regime, a duty for the CMA to take action as soon reasonably practicable when exercising its competition powers and increased penalties for failure to comply with CMA information requests, penalties for businesses that breach commitments,

325 J Tomlinson and LL Gormsen, 'Stumbling Towards the UK's New Administrative Settlement: A Study of Competition Law Enforcement After Brexit' (2018) 20(1) *Cambridge Yearbook of European Legal Studies* 233; and European Union (Withdrawal) Act 2018.

326 Competition and Markets Authority, 'The UK's Withdrawal from the EU - The CMA's Role Post Brexit' (GOV.UK, 28 January 2020) <https://www.gov.uk/government/news/the-uk-s-withdrawal-from-the-eu-the-cma-s-role-post-brexit> accessed 14 July 2024.

327 J Fingleton and others, 'The Implications of Brexit for UK Competition Law and Policy' (2017) 13(3) *Journal of Competition Law & Economics* 389.

328 See the Digital Markets, Competition and Consumers Act 2024, which received Royal Assent in May 2024.

329 Department for Business, Energy & Industrial Strategy, 'Reforming Competition and Consumer Policy: Government Response' (GOV.UK, 20 April 2022) <https://www.gov.uk/government/consultations/reforming-competition-and-consumer-policy/outcome/reforming-competition-and-consumer-policy-government-response> accessed 1 July 2024.

330 Ibid.

undertakings, directions or interim measures imposed by the CMA.[331] Other changes made include the extension of the CMA's reach in enforcing UK competition law to agreements implemented outside the UK if they have a substantial effect in the UK.[332]

One of the key changes to UK competition law that was made as a result of Brexit was the removal of the requirement for UK courts and regulators to make decisions that are consistent with the principles of the EU treaties and the decisions and principles laid down by the Court of Justice of the EU (CJEU) in relation to Articles 101 and 102 of the Treaty for the Functioning of the EU.[333] This requirement for a consistent application of UK and EU competition laws was previously located in Section 60 of the Competition Act, but this has now been replaced with Section 60A, which gives the CMA and UK courts discretion to depart from EU case law in specified circumstances.[334] These circumstances include consideration of the differences between markets in the UK and markets in the EU or developments in the form of economic activity since the time the case law was made and generally accepted principles of competition analysis were established.[335] It was seen as unlikely by commentators before Brexit that well-established case law, which is grounded in EU competition principles, would be reversed by UK courts without a very compelling reason.[336] However other commentators have anticipated that a gradual loosening or separation of the elements that made up the EU–UK competition relationship pre-Brexit will occur.[337]

The EU–UK Trade and Cooperation Agreement entered into in 2020 included a commitment by both parties to maintain fair competition laws to address anticompetitive agreements and abuses of a dominant position.[338] The agreement also contained provisions for developing arrangements for

331 Ashurst, 'DMCC Act: Key Changes to the CMA's Investigatory Powers' (Ashurst, 24 June 2024) <https://www.ashurst.com/en/insights/dmcc-act-key-changes-to-the-cmas-investigatory-powers/> accessed 27 June 2024.

332 Cooley LLP, 'UK Competition and Markets Authority Receives Enhanced Merger Control and Enforcement Powers' (Cooley LLP, 25 June 2024) <https://uklitigation.cooley.com/uk-competition-and-markets-authority-receives-enhanced-merger-control-and-enforcement-powers/#page=1> accessed 27 June 2024.

333 Competition (Amendment etc.) (EU exit) Regulations 2019 No.93.

334 J Ellison, 'Implications of Brexit on UK Competition Law' (Mayer Brown LLP, 2022) <https://www.mayerbrown.com/en/perspectives-events/publications/2021/04/implications-of-brexit-for-uk-competition-law> accessed 16 July 2024.

335 J Vickers, 'Consequences of Brexit for Competition Law and Policy' (2017) 33(1) *Oxford Review of Economic Policy* 70.

336 A Andreangeli, 'EU Competition Law Put to the Brexit Test: What Impact Might the Exit of the UK from the Union Have on the Enforcement of the Competition Rules?' (2018) 11(17) *Yearbook of Antitrust and Regulatory Studies* 7.

337 LM Davison, 'Envisaging the Post-Brexit Landscape: An Articulation of the Likely Changes to the EU–UK Competition Policy Relationship' (2018) 39(1) *Liverpool Law Review* 99.

338 European Commission, 'The EU-UK Trade and Cooperation Agreement' (European Commission, 30 April 2021) <https://ec.europa.eu/info/strategy/relations-non-eu-countries

future cooperation between the EU and the UK authorities, which should hopefully guard against the UK losing the pre-Brexit cooperation between the CMA and other national competition regulators and its access to the National Competition Authorities database, a fear expressed by some pre-Brexit commentators.[339] Since its creation, the CMA has worked closely with the European Commission and the competition regulators in each of the EU Member States (known as the European Competition Network),[340] and it continues to do so, despite the absence of any formal cooperation agreement. [341] The CMA is also a member of the International Competition Network, an organisation that seeks to facilitate effective international cooperation between its member competition agencies.[342] In 2025, the CMA will host the International Competition Network Conference in Edinburgh, where it will play host to 141 competition authorities from 129 member countries.[343] These networks enable information about competition infringements and enforcement to be shared between different competition regulators across the world when necessary. For example, when it is necessary to identify and enforce a future benchmark fixing cartel operating across multiple countries and jurisdictions, this network may be of assistance to the CMA.

Since Brexit, the CMA has relied more heavily on the sector regulators, such as the FCA, in order to manage its increased case load, which now includes larger, more complex cases, which pre-Brexit, the European Commission would have dealt with.[344] In its Annual Plan for 2024–2025 the CMA states that 2024 marks ten years since the promotion of competition and the application of certain competition powers have been shared with sector regulators.[345]

/relations-united-kingdom/eu-uk-trade-and-cooperation-agreement_en> accessed 16 July 2024.

339 R Whish, 'Brexit and EU Competition Policy' (2016) 7(5) *Journal of European Competition Law & Practice* 297.

340 European Commission, 'European Competition Network (ECN)' (European Commission, 2024) <https://competition-policy.ec.europa.eu/antitrust-and-cartels/european-competition-network_en> accessed 25 June 2024.

341 I Maher, M Hosseini, 'Cooperation between National Competition Authorities: An Overview of EU and National Case Law (Concurrences, 18 January 2024) 116089, 1 <https://www.concurrences.com/en/bulletin/special-issues/cooperation-between-national-competition-authorities/cooperation-between-national-competition-authorities-an-overview-of-eu-and> accessed 25 July 2024.

342 International Competition Network, 'International Competition Network: All Competition, All the Time' (International Competition Network, 2024) <https://www.internationalcompetitionnetwork.org/> accessed 25 July 2024.

343 Competition and Markets Authority, 'CMA to Host 2025 International Competition Network Conference' (GOV.UK, 17 May 2024) <https://www.gov.uk/government/news/cma-to-host-2025-international-competition-network-conference> accessed 25 June 2024.

344 J Fingleton and others, 'The Implications of Brexit for UK Competition Law and Policy' (2017) 13(3) *Journal of Competition Law & Economics* 389.

345 Competition and Markets Authority, 'Competition and Markets Authority Annual Plan 2022/23' (Parliament Publications, 24 March 2022) 26 <https://assets.publishing.ser-

This sharing of competition enforcement powers with sector regulators in the regulated sector is designed to free up the CMA to focus on the more complex, international competition cases in order to ensure that there would be no significant reduction in competition enforcement in the UK post-Brexit.[346]

It can be seen from the above that there have not been any substantive changes to the UK's competition regime since Brexit, so it appears that the commentators who predicted no substantive changes in the short term following Brexit were correct.[347]

2.7 Conclusion

This chapter has set the scene for later chapters by defining key terms used throughout the book, such as financial crime, benchmark manipulation, competition law and cartels. It has also introduced the key themes that will be revisited during the book, including the value of competition law whistleblowing and leniency regimes in the detection of banking cartels, consideration of whether civil or criminal enforcement powers are of most use to regulators in the enforcement of benchmark manipulation, the attribution of corporate criminal liability and the availability and value of DPAs. The relevant competition law for the enforcement of benchmark manipulation has also been identified, along with the relevant regulators in each jurisdiction. The starting point of this book, the LIBOR and FX crisis, has been introduced, along with the key financial crises that led up to it and consideration of its significance and the likelihood of a similar crisis happening again in the future. Finally, the impact of Brexit on the topic of this book has been considered. What follows next is the first of three case studies, in which the UK's approach to the enforcement of the LIBOR and FX crisis is examined in detail.

vice.gov.uk/government/uploads/system/uploads/attachment_data/file/1062414/Final_Annual_Plan_for_2022_23.pdf> accessed 1 July 2024.

346 Ibid.

347 For example, see J Vickers, 'Consequences of Brexit for Competition Law and Policy' (2017) 33(1) *Oxford Review of Economic Policy* 70; J Fingleton and others, 'The Implications of Brexit for UK Competition Law and Policy' (2017) 13(3) *Journal of Competition Law & Economics* 389; and A Andreangeli, 'EU Competition Law Put to the Brexit Test: What Impact Might the Exit of the UK from the Union Have on the Enforcement of the Competition Rules?' (2018) 11(17) *Yearbook of Antitrust and Regulatory Studies* 7.

3 UK Competition Law and Financial Crime

3.1 Introduction

This chapter examines the role that competition law should play in the United Kingdom (UK) in relation to the enforcement of benchmark interest rate manipulation (benchmark manipulation). Since the 2008 financial crisis, the UK banking sector has shown itself to be vulnerable to infringements of competition law due, in part, to the small number of large banks, each of which has a significant market share, known as an oligopoly.[1] The oligopolistic structure of banking was identified by the Organisation for Economic Co-operation and Development, which stated that it contributed to the financial crisis.[2] An oligopolistic market is an ideal situation for a criminal cartel to emerge, as illustrated in the London Interbank Offered Rate (LIBOR) and Foreign Exchange (FX) benchmark manipulation scandal. Here, bankers from competing banks colluded to raise or lower the LIBOR and FX benchmark interest rates in order to benefit their own trading positions.[3] However, although the LIBOR and FX benchmark interest rate scandal involved bankers from competing banks operating cartels, which are illegal under competition law, no competition law was used to enforce this crime in the UK. In fact, there is a paucity of competition law cases in the financial sector, with the application

1 See M Dong, S Huangfu, H Sun and C Zhou, 'A Macroeconomic Theory of Banking Oligopoly' (2021) 138 *European Economic Review* 103864; and Unknown, 'Cracking the Oligopoly: British Banks' *The Economist* (London, 14 September 2013) 63.

2 Organisation for Economic Co-operation and Development, 'Bank Competition and Financial Stability' (OECD, 5 October 2011) 19 <https://www.oecd-ilibrary.org/finance-and-investment/bank-competition-and-financial-stability/competition-in-retail-banking-and-financial-stability_9789264120563-4-en> accessed 20 July 2024.

3 L Vaughan and G Finch, 'Libor Scandal: The Bankers Who Fixed the World's Most Important Number' *The Guardian* (London, 18 January 2017) <https://www.theguardian.com/business/2017/jan/18/libor-scandal-the-bankers-who-fixed-the-worlds-most-important-number> accessed 4 June 2024.

DOI: 10.4324/9781003425106-3

of competition law to the financial sector being an overlooked and somewhat obscure subject in the UK.[4]

As its starting point, this chapter will consider why competition law was not used to enforce any of the LIBOR or FX benchmark manipulation cartels, despite the fact that the competition laws to prohibit cartels were in place at that time. In Chapters 4 and 5, the actions of the European Union (EU) and the United States (US), who, at that time, had similar competition laws to those of the UK, will be examined, as both the US and EU investigated and fined offending banks for LIBOR and FX offences using competition law.[5] Because mortgages, student loans, commercial loans, financial derivatives and other financial products often relied on LIBOR as a reference rate, the manipulation of submissions used to calculate those rates will have had significant negative effects on consumers and financial markets.[6] It has been estimated that LIBOR was used to price trillions of pounds worth of mortgages, loans and other financial transactions, which demonstrates the impact and reach of the benchmark interest rate at the time the benchmark manipulation took place.[7]

This chapter considers the LIBOR and FX scandals through the lens of competition law. Previous commentators have focused on the financial regulation framework used in the UK to enforce LIBOR and FX offences rather than considering the competition laws used in the EU and US for the same benchmark manipulation.[8] This chapter will argue that the UK regulators could have achieved successful criminal prosecutions of individual traders and imposed significantly higher fines together with other civil enforcement measures on banks, such as commitments and director disqualifications, if the regulators had used competition law to enforce the LIBOR and FX manipulation cartels. It will be argued that the Financial Conduct Authority (FCA) and Competition and Markets Authority (CMA) must use competition law to enforce future instances of benchmark manipulation to ensure the competitiveness of the banking industry. It appears that the CMA agrees with

4 AK Pascall, 'Tail Wagging the Dog: The Manipulation of Benchmark Rates - A Competitive Bone of Contention' (2016) 39(2) *World Competition* 161.

5 R Ball, 'Competition Law and Libor in Three Jurisdictions: US, UK and EU' in N Ryder (ed), *White Collar Crime and Risk – A Critical Reflection* (Palgrave 2018).

6 K Gibbons, 'Business as Usual for LIBOR?' (2014) *Journal of International Banking and Financial Law* 3 194.

7 *USA v. Connolly*, No. 19-3806 (L) (2d Cir. 2022); and BBC News, 'Libor: What Is It and Why Does It Matter?' (*BBC News*, 3 August 2015) <https://www.bbc.co.uk/news/business-19199683> accessed 31 July 2024.

8 For example, see JA Batten, 'Financial Market Manipulation, Whistleblowing, and the Common Good: Evidence from the LIBOR Scandal' (2022) 58(1) *ABACUS* 1; A Akhigbe and others, 'Foreign Exchange Manipulation and the Equity Returns of Global Banks' (2020) 57(2) *Journal of Financial Services Research* 207; and V Callaghan and Z Ullah, 'The LIBOR Scandal – the UK's Legislative Approach' (2013) 28(4) *Journal of International Banking Law and Regulation* 160.

this viewpoint, as illustrated by its provisional finding in 2023 that five major banks, Citi, Deutsche Bank, HSBC, Morgan Stanley and Bank of Canada, broke competition law by unlawfully sharing commercial information relating to UK government bonds with each other using internet chat rooms.[9] This case has many parallels with the LIBOR and FX cartels, in which traders also operated using internet chat rooms to share commercially sensitive information, and it appears that the CMA is investigating this behaviour as a cartel and a breach of competition law, unlike the previous UK approach seen in the enforcement of the LIBOR and FX crisis, which is discussed below.

This book argues that if a wider range of penalties had been imposed on banks for the LIBOR and FX benchmark manipulation under competition law, this would have increased the deterrent effect for the crime of benchmark manipulation. It has been argued that fines alone are seen as a cost of business for many large organisations such as international banks,[10] so combining significant fines with other sanctions, such as director disqualifications and commitments, is likely to make more of an impact than the imposition of fines alone. It is imperative that the UK government ensures that a robust system of competition law is in place and that the relevant competition law regulators are encouraged to use competition law to prevent future instances of benchmark manipulation and to ensure the competitiveness of the banking industry.

The legislative changes that came into force after the LIBOR and FX crisis, many of which involved competition law, will be closely examined. In particular this chapter analyses the relatively recent sharing of competition law regulation powers between the CMA and the FCA in relation to the regulation of competition law in the financial sector. Since April 2015, the FCA has had competition law enforcement powers;[11] however, its primary function has historically been to regulate the financial sector using financial regulation rather than to enforce competition law in relation to financial crime.[12] This may be one of the reasons the FCA appears to be reluctant to use its new competition law powers in the financial services market.

The LIBOR and FX benchmark manipulation scandal has attracted a great deal of literature and academic commentary.[13] Market manipulation such

9 Competition and Markets Authority, 'UK Government Bonds: Suspected Anti-Competitive Arrangements' (GOV.UK, 24 May 2023) <https://www.gov.uk/cma-cases/financial-services-sector-suspected-anti-competitive-practices> accessed 22 July 2024.

10 H Macartney and P Calcagno, 'All Bark and No Bite: The Political Economy of Bank Fines in Anglo-America' (2019) 26(4) *Review of International Political Economy*.

11 Enterprise and Regulatory Reform Act 2013 s 51.

12 For instance, the fines issued by the regulator to banks following the LIBOR crisis were made pursuant to s91 (Misleading statements in relation to benchmarks) of the Financial Services Act 2012 and s206(1) (Financial Penalties) of the Financial Services and Markets Act 2000.

13 See RM Abrantes-Metz and others, 'Libor Manipulation?' (2012) 36(1) *Journal of Banking and Finance* 136; A Akhigbe and others, 'Foreign Exchange Manipulation and the Equity Returns of Global Banks' (2020) 57(2) *Journal of Financial Services Research* 207; JA Batten, 'Financial Market Manipulation, Whistleblowing, and the Common Good: Evidence from the

as that seen in the LIBOR and FX manipulation damages market integrity, undermines investor confidence and makes markets subject to systemic crises.[14] However, little has been written about the role that competition law could have, or could have had, in regulating the manipulation of benchmark interest rates,[15] although some academics have written about its use in the US and EU for market manipulation in the financial services sector.[16] There is a clear need for the role of competition law in the enforcement of benchmark manipulation to be examined, as it could lead to more effective enforcement by UK regulators in future instances of benchmark manipulation. In considering the role of competition law in the regulation of benchmark manipulation, this chapter assesses whether more can or should be done to provide competition law enforcement powers in the financial sector to the current UK competition law regulators. Furthermore, this chapter also determines whether competition law is more likely to be used now to prosecute individuals if benchmark manipulation happens again. The conclusion will consider whether the measures taken after the LIBOR and FX benchmark manipulation scandal of 2012–2013 have put into place a system that will enable competition law to regulate financial crime in the future, or whether further reform measures are needed to improve the current system. By way of background to the LIBOR and FX manipulation scandal of 2012–2013, a brief outline of the recent history of banking regulation and of competition law in the UK is provided below.

LIBOR Scandal' (2022) 58(1) *ABACUS* 1; R Calo, 'Digital Market Manipulation' (2014) 82(4) *George Washington Law Review* 995; SE Foster, 'LIBOR Manipulation and Antitrust Allegations' (2013) 11(29) *DePaul Business & Commercial Law Journal* 291; J Fouquau and PK Spieser, 'Statistical Evidence about LIBOR Manipulation: A "Sherlock Holmes" Investigation' (2015) 50(1) *Journal of Banking and Finance* 632.

14 See E Lomnicka, 'Preventing and Controlling the Manipulation of Financial Markets: Towards a Definition of "Market Manipulation"' (2001) 8(4) *Journal of Financial Crime* 297; K Sergakis, *The Law of Capital Markets in the EU: Disclosure and Enforcement* (Palgrave 2017); TCW Lin, 'The New Market Manipulation' (2017) 66(6) *Emory Law Journal* 1253; and E Herlin-Karnell and N Ryder, *Market Manipulation and Insider Trading* (Hart 2019).

15 See B McGrath, 'Banking and Antitrust: The View from the UK' (2010) 127 *Banking Law Journal* 563; D Harrison, *Competition Law and Financial Services* (Routledge 2016) 14; and R Ball, 'Competition Law and LIBOR in Three Jurisdictions: US, UK and EU' in N Ryder (ed), *White Collar Crime and Risk – A Critical Reflection* (Routledge 2018).

16 For instance, see J Hamburger, 'Crowding the Market: Is There Room for Antitrust in Market Manipulation Cases?' (2015) 21(4) *International Trade Law and Regulation* 120; D Scheld and others, 'Managing Antitrust Risks in the Banking Industry (2016) 12(1) *European Competition Journal* 113; and SD Ledgerwood and JA Verlinda, 'The Intersection of Antitrust and Market Manipulation Law' (2017) <https://ssrn.com/abstract=2908878> accessed 10 July 2023.

3.2 Development of Financial Services Regulation in the UK

This section will outline the recent history of the financial services sector in the UK in the run up to the LIBOR and FX crisis. This outline will provide context for the crisis and for the legislative action that was taken after it. Since the 'Big Bang' in 1986, referred to in Chapter 2, the UK financial services sector has experienced turbulent times.[17] The significant banking failures in the 1990s of the Bank of Credit and Commerce International in 1991 and of Barings Bank in 1995 were each linked to poor regulation and financial crime.[18] The failure of these banks led to the enactment of the Financial Services and Markets Act 2000 (FSMA). FSMA contained a statutory objective for the UK's financial services regulator, then the Financial Services Authority (FSA), to reduce financial crime.[19] The FSA was able to impose financial penalties, as well as to initiate criminal proceedings for any offence under FSMA.[20] These powers meant that the FSA was the first UK financial regulatory agency with the ability to impose both financial penalties and to instigate criminal proceedings for financial crime.[21]

However, it was not long after the enactment of FSMA that further turbulence was experienced in the UK's banking sector. Barclays Bank was found to have 'acted inappropriately' by manipulating its US dollar LIBOR submissions following requests by its interest rate derivatives traders dating from 2005.[22] Barclays aimed to improve its trading positions and to maximise its profit by the manipulation of the benchmark interest rate. The start of the 2008 financial crisis then became evident from August 2007, when the first indications of problems with US subprime mortgages,[23] which had been packaged into collateralised debt obligations[24] in order to cushion and disguise banks' exposure to such a high-risk debt, were uncovered.[25] From this point, matters went from bad to worse in the UK, with the liquidity crisis faced by

17 LCB Gower, '"Big Bang" and City Regulation' (1988) 51 MLR 7.

18 L Drennan, 'Ethics, Governance and Risk Management: Lessons From Mirror Group Newspapers and Barings Bank' (2004) 52(3) *Journal of Business Ethics* 257.

19 The Financial Services and Markets Act 2000, s6.

20 The Financial Services and Markets Act 2000, s206(1) and s402.

21 A Francis and N Ryder, 'Preventing and Intervening in White Collar Crimes: The Role of Regulatory Agencies' in N Ryder (ed) in *White Collar Crime and Risk – A Critical Reflection* (Palgrave 2018).

22 Financial Services Authority 'Final Notice to Barclays Bank Plc' (Financial Services Authority, 27 June 2012) para 8 <https://www.fca.org.uk/publication/final-notices/barclays-jun12.pdf> accessed 9 July 2024.

23 i.e. Mortgages granted to 'subprime' borrowers who have a lower credit-rating than mortgages granted to 'prime' borrowers.

24 CDOs are complex financial instruments and, in the run-up to the financial crisis, they contained both subprime and prime mortgages, which disguised the amount of risk exposure an investor (such as a bank) was taking.

25 H Pontell and others, 'Too Big To Fail, Too Powerful To Jail? On the Absence of Criminal Prosecutions after the 2008 Financial Meltdown' (2014) 61(1) *Crime Law Soc Change* 1.

the Northern Rock bank in 2007.[26] The subsequent run on the Northern Rock bank[27] shook the confidence of consumers in the banking industry and was to have wide-reaching ramifications. Northern Rock had to be bailed out by a government loan and, ultimately, in February 2008, was nationalised for a four-year period.[28]

In the US, several financial institutions exposed to the subprime crisis were either subject to take over bids[29] or were bailed out by the US government.[30] This was closely followed by the collapse of Lehman Brothers on 15 September 2008, which triggered panic amongst consumers across the world.[31] In October 2008, Iceland saw its three largest banks collapse, leading to the UK government using its counterterrorist financing laws to freeze the assets of their UK subsidiary banks to protect UK customers.[32] This was followed by the bail-out of several UK banks, including the Royal Bank of Scotland (RBS), Lloyds TSB and Halilfax Bank of Scotland (HBOS), by the government between September 2007 and December 2009.[33] These bail-outs initially cost £137b of public money, however the majority of this has since been recouped with the net loss to public money being estimated at £23b.[34]

In the aftermath of the 2008 financial crisis, it became apparent that the FSA had failed in its regulation of the financial services sector.[35] The light-touch approach[36] to supervision of banks and other financial firms taken by the FSA had failed to question or prevent the sectoral practices that led to the

26 A Campbell, 'The Run on the Rock and its Consequences' (2008) 9(2) *Journal of Banking Regulation* 61.
27 i.e., When large groups of depositors tried to withdraw their money from the Northern Rock bank due to fears about its financial stability.
28 HS Shin, 'Reflections on Northern Rock: The Bank Run That Heralded the Global Financial Crisis' (2009) 23(1) *Journal of Economic Perspectives* 101.
29 Bear Sterns was taken over by JP Morgan on 14 March 2008 and see National Commission on the Causes of the Financial and Economic Crisis in the US, 'The Financial Crisis Inquiry Report' (Financial Crisis Inquiry Commission, January 2011) <https://www.govinfo.gov/content/pkg/GPO-FCIC/pdf/GPO-FCIC.pdf> accessed 21 July 2024.
30 Fannie Mae and Freddie Mac banks were bailed out by the US government on 7 September 2008.
31 N Dumontaux, A Pop, 'Understanding the Market Reaction to Shockwaves: Evidence from the Failure of Lehman Brothers' (2013) 9(3) *Journal of Financial Stability* 269.
32 Anti-Terrorism, Crime and Security Act 2001, s 1.
33 House of Commons Library, 'Bank Rescues of 2007-09: Outcomes and Cost' (UK Parliament, 8 October 2018) <https://commonslibrary.parliament.uk/research-briefings/sn05748/> accessed 20 May 2024.
34 Ibid.
35 A Arora, 'The Global Financial Crisis: A New Global Regulatory Order?' (2010) 8(1) *Journal of Business Law* 670, 673; and G Wilson and S Wilson, 'The FSA, "Credible Deterrence" and Criminal Enforcement – A "Haphazard Pursuit"?' (2014) 21(1) *Journal of Financial Crime* 4.
36 G Wilson and S Wilson, 'The FSA, "Credible Deterrence" and Criminal Enforcement – A "Haphazard Pursuit"? (2014) 21(1) *Journal of Financial Crime* 4.

2008 financial crisis.[37] The decision by the FSA to focus only on market abuse enforcement, without horizon-scanning to identify threats to systemic stability was identified as a key failure of the FSA, with the FSA being blamed for the collapse of Northern Rock.[38] This perceived failure of the FSA ultimately led to the government replacing the FSA with new tougher authorities.[39]

The 2008 financial crisis led to a plethora of banking regulations and reforms,[40] including the Banking Act 2008, then the Banking Act 2009 and the Financial Services Act 2010. Following on from these legislative reforms, the Turner Report[41] and the Walker Report[42] all outlined possible culprits said to have played a part in causing the financial crisis.[43] Following this extensive list of reports and legislative changes, the response of the then coalition government was to set up the wide-ranging Independent Commission on Banking.[44] The Independent Commission on Banking was asked to consider structural and related nonstructural reforms to the UK banking sector to promote financial stability and competition.[45] The Commission recommended a ring-fencing of retail banking from investment banking and found that there were issues relating to competition in the UK retail banking sector. One of the recommendations from the Independent Commission on Banking's was to ensure that the primary duties of the future FCA include the promotion of competition within the UK banking sector and to consider whether to make a market investigation reference (referred to below) in the next few years. The Banking Commission's report was followed by a series of statutes, implementing its recommendations, which affected both the financial services sector and UK competition law.[46] It is positive that the Banking Commission identified

37 Ibid.

38 For example see S Ghosh and S Patnaik, 'The Independent Banking Commission (Vickers) Report: Squaring the Circle?' (2012) 54(2) *International Journal of Law and Management* 141.

39 G Wilson and S Wilson, 'The FSA, "Credible Deterrence" and Criminal Enforcement – A "Haphazard Pursuit"?' (2014) 21(1) *Journal of Financial Crime* 4.

40 House of Commons Treasury Committee, 'The Run on the Rock' (HC 56-1).

41 Financial Services Authority, 'The Turner Review A Regulatory Response to the Global Banking Crisis' (Financial Services Authority, March 2009) <http://www.actuaries.org/CTTEES_TFRISKCRISIS/Documents/turner_review.pdf> accessed 13 July 2024.

42 D Walker, 'A Review of Corporate Governance in UK Banks and Other Financial Industry Entities Final Recommendations' (National Archives, 26 November 2009) <https://webarchive.nationalarchives.gov.uk/ukgwa/+/www.hm-treasury.gov.uk/d/walker_review_261109.pdf> accessed 12 July 2024.

43 C Chambers-Jones, 'The Vickers Report' (2011) 32(11) *Business Law Review* 280.

44 Ibid.

45 Independent Commission on Banking, 'Independent Commission on Banking: Final Report, Recommendations' (GOV.UK, 12 September 2011) <https://webarchive.nationalarchives.gov.uk/ukgwa/20120827143059/http://bankingcommission.independent.gov.uk///> accessed 10 July 2024.

46 The Financial Services Act 2012, the Enterprise and Regulatory Reform Act 2013 and The Financial Services (Banking Reform) Act 2013.

the benefits of increasing the use of competition law in the banking sector, but it would have been better if the competition law existing at the time had been used in the LIBOR and FX crisis instead of financial regulation.

These legislative changes affected both the financial services sector and competition law. They were enacted following the LIBOR and FX crises of 2012–2013 and are examined below.

It can be seen from this brief history of the financial services sector prior to the LIBOR and FX crisis that self-regulation had not worked for the banking sector and that independent reports recommended the use of competition law in the financial services market. The next section of this chapter will look at the recent history of competition law in the run up to the LIBOR and FX crisis. This, as with the recent history of the financial services sector, will provide context for the crisis and for the legislation enacted in its immediate aftermath.

3.3 The Development of UK Competition Law and Policy

In the enforcement of the 2008 financial crisis and the LIBOR and FX benchmark manipulation scandals, competition law was not used by UK regulators. However, the primary purpose of competition law is to ensure the regulation of market economies,[47] and in the House of Lords debate during the passage of the Competition Act 1998, Lord St. John of Bletso stated that 'Competition law provides the framework for competitive activity…As such it is of vital importance'.[48] It is important to note that competition law is another tool available to regulators to enforce the crime of benchmark manipulation; therefore, a summary of how competition law has developed in parallel with the UK's financial services regulation is set out below.

Competition law in the UK is predominantly statute-based. There has been significant change in both policy and the powers given to the competition enforcement bodies over the last 50 years. Before the UK joined the EU,[49] its competition law was contained in the Monopolies and Restrictive Trade Practices (Inquiry and Control) Act 1948.[50] This Act established a competition regulator, the Monopolies and Restrictive Practices Commission in order to investigate anticompetitive behaviour.[51] This was followed by the Restrictive Trade Practices Act 1956, which moved regulation of anticompetitive practices to a new Restrictive Practices Court.[52] Further competition legislation followed, in the form of the Resale Prices Act 1964 and then the Monopolies

47 A Bradford and A Chilton, 'Competition Law Around the World from 1889 to 2010: The Competition Law Index' (2018) 14(3) *Journal of Competition Law & Economics* 393.
48 HL Deb 30 October 1997, vol 582, cc1144-95.
49 European Communities Act 1972.
50 R Whish and D Bailey, *Competition Law* (10th edn, Oxford University Press 2021).
51 Monopolies and Restrictive Trade Practices (Inquiry and Control) Act 1948.
52 S Wilks, *In the Public Interest: Competition Policy and the Monopolies and Mergers Commission* (Manchester University Press 1999).

and Mergers Act 1965, which extended the remit of the Restrictive Practices Commission to cover mergers and takeovers. It has been observed that the UK competition regime 'really does not have an anti-monopoly policy…', but that, instead, the Monopolies Commission subjected businesses to occasional, *ad hoc*, scrutiny.[53] This weak competition regulator was only changed in response to pressure on the government following the UK's entry into the EU. The EU required all member states to make their competition laws consistent with the EU competition regime, consisting of Article 101,[54] which deals with restrictive practices between businesses, including cartels, and Article 102,[55] which deals with the abuse of a dominant market position. In order to do this, the Fair Trading Act 1973 came into force, creating the post of Director General of Fair Trading, who would oversee a new governmental body known as the Office of Fair Trading (OFT).[56] The OFT took over from the Monopolies and Restrictive Practices Commission and was the primary UK competition regulator, along with a Competition Commission (CC).[57] Criticisms were regularly levied at the OFT because it was ineffective, particularly in relation to the amount of time its competition investigations took and in relation to how many of the investigations led to no enforcement action being taken.[58] Significant changes to the UK competition regime were not made until the Competition Act 1998, which contains the majority of the UK's current competition law and is analysed below. The changes made by the Competition Act 1998 more closely aligned UK competition law with EU competition law.[59] The Competition Act also created the CC[60] and provided a transition period for businesses to prepare for the new prohibition-based competition policy to come into force.[61]

The next significant change to competition law in the UK came when the Enterprise and Regulatory Reform Act 2013 abolished both the OFT and the CC and established the current competition regulator, the CMA.[62] The removal of the OFT and CC was carried out in order to address two key

53 T Sharpe, 'Privatisation, Regulation and Competition' (1984) 5(1) *Fiscal Studies* 47.

54 Consolidated Version of the Treaty on the Functioning of the European Union [2007] OJ C326/88 Article 101.

55 Ibid.

56 P Freeman, 'The Competition and Markets Authority: Can the Whole Be Greater Than the Sum of Its Parts?' (2013) 1(1) *Journal of Antitrust Enforcement* 4.

57 R Whish and D Bailey, *Competition Law* (10th edn, Oxford University Press 2021).

58 National Audit Office, 'Progress Report on Maintaining Competition In Markets' (National Audit Office, 5 March 2009) <https://www.nao.org.uk/report/progress-report-on-maintaining-competition-in-markets/> accessed 19 July 2024.

59 P Roth, 'The Continual Evolution of Competition Law' (2019) 7(1) *Journal of Antitrust Enforcement* 6.

60 Competition Act 1998, s45.

61 D Parker, 'Reforming Competition Law in the UK: The Competition Act 1998' (2000) *CRI Occasional Paper* 14.

62 Enterprise and Regulatory Reform Act 2013, s26(2) and s25.

concerns identified by the government following a 2011 consultation on how to reform the competition regime.[63] The government's concerns were, first, that there had been too few competition law cases initiated by the OFT and, second, that of the cases that had been brought, they took too long to prosecute.[64] The government said in its 2012 response to the consultation that it intended that the creation of the CMA, in place of the OFT, would provide the impetus to use competition powers and processes in the most flexible and dynamic way, enable more efficient use of scarce public resources and create a single powerful advocate for competition in the UK, in Europe and internationally.[65] This aim expressed by the government shows the importance it attached to the use of competition law, including its use in the 'regulated sectors', one of which is the financial services sector.[66] However, although the legislative changes that were enacted came into place at the same time as the LIBOR and FX benchmark manipulation, no competition law was used by the UK in the enforcement of these crimes.

Commentators have observed that there has been a lack of application of competition law to the financial services sector, despite the fact that, over the past two decades, the government has commissioned reports that have identified concerns about the lack of competition law in the banking market, and these reports have raised concerns over the lack of competition in parts of the banking industry.[67] In 1998, the then Chancellor Gordon Brown invited Sir Donald Cruickshank to review the functioning of the retail banking sector in the UK. The Cruickshank report concluded that 'competition problems were found in all markets investigated' after examining the levels of innovation, competition and efficiency both within the industry and in comparison to international standards.[68] The Cruickshank report was preceded by a 2011

63 Department for Business, Innovation and Skills, 'A Competition Regime for Growth: A Consultation on Options for Reform' (GOV.UK, March 2011) <https://assets.publishing.service.gov.uk/government/uploads/system/uploads/attachment_data/file/31411/11-657-competition-regime-for-growth-consultation.pdf> accessed 14 July 2024.

64 P Freeman, 'The Competition and Markets Authority: Can the Whole Be Greater Than the Sum of Its Parts?' (2013) 1(1) *Journal of Antitrust Enforcement* 4.

65 Department for Business, Innovation and Skills, 'Growth, Competition and the Competition Regime: Government Response to Consultation' (GOV.UK, March 2012) <https://assets.publishing.service.gov.uk/government/uploads/system/uploads/attachment_data/file/192722/12-512-growth-and-competition-regime-government-response.pdf> accessed 14 July 2024.

66 Ibid.

67 B McGrath, 'Banking and Antitrust: The View From The UK' (2010) 127 *Banking Law Journal* 563; and D Harrison, *Competition Law and Financial Services* (Routledge 2016).

68 HM Treasury, 'Competition in UK Banking: A Report to the Chancellor of the Exchequer' (National Archives, 20 March 2000) <https://webarchive.nationalarchives.gov.uk/ukgwa/20050301221631/http://www.hm-treasury.gov.uk/documents/financial_services/banking/bankreview/fin_bank_reviewfinal.cfm> accessed 13 July 2024.

Treasury Select Committee report into competition and choice in the retail banking sector, which stated that:

> We believe effective competition cannot take place in an environment where firms which are perceived as 'too important to fail' are both protected from the discipline of the market place and derive tangible benefits from this status.[69]

The reference to 'too important to fail' refers to the perception that certain banks would cause catastrophic effects to a country's economy should they fail, which, therefore, prevents regulators from penalising them for breaches of the law in the same way that other firms would be penalised for the same crimes. However, the Cruickshank report also concluded that:

> Competition cannot be divorced from wider regulatory issues, including the 'too important to fail' problem.[70]

Other inquiries and investigations indicate a long-standing and widespread concern about the effectiveness and nature of competition in the banking sector.[71] Following the 2008 financial crisis, the government took legislative action, outlined below, to ensure that the financial services regulator is compelled to consider the use of competition law in the enforcement of financial crime. These legislative changes introduced following the LIBOR and FX crisis are outlined and critiqued below.

It is notable that, even though the UK had competition law legislation at the time, no prosecutions of individuals involved in the LIBOR or FX manipulation cartels were brought by UK regulators using competition law and no action was taken against the banks involved using competition law either. The advantages that the use of competition law would bring to the enforcement of benchmark rate manipulation cartels are outlined below, together with an explanation of the relevant law and how it is applicable to the LIBOR and FX scandal. UK competition law is contained in the Competition Act 1998 and

69 House of Commons Treasury Committee, 'Competition and Choice in Retail Banking' (HC612-I).

70 Ibid.

71 For example see Competition and Markets Authority, 'Retail Banking Market Investigation' (Competition and Markets Authority, 14 July 2015) <https://assets.publishing.service.gov.uk/media/55a4eb9040f0b61560000005/Barriers_to_entry_and_expansion_-_capital_requirements__IT_and_payment_systems.pdf> accessed 13 May 2024; and Office of Fair Trading, 'OFT Review of Barriers to Entry, Expansion and Exit in Retail Banking' (Office of Fair Trading, 4 November 2010) <https://uk.practicallaw.thomsonreuters.com/1-503-8196?transitionType=Default&contextData=(sc.Default)&firstPage=true> accessed 13 July 2024; and European Commission, 'Report on the Retail Banking Sector Inquiry' (European Commission, 31 January 2007) <https://ec.europa.eu/competition/sectors/financial_services/inquiries/sec_2007_106.pdf> accessed 12 July 2024.

the Enterprise Act 2002, although related provisions can be found in other statutes.[72] These statutes fundamentally changed both the substantive provisions of the previous competition law and the existing regulatory architecture, removing a raft of old legislation at the same time.[73] The Competition Act contains two prohibitions, known as the Chapter I and Chapter II prohibitions.[74] Both Chapter I and the cartel offence in the Enterprise Act prohibit cartels such as those seen in the LIBOR and FX benchmark manipulation scandals mentioned in Chapter 2.[75] The powers available to regulators for breach of competition law were detailed in Chapter 2 and include the power to impose fines of up to 10% of a business' worldwide turnover, the power to accept behavioural or structural commitments from a business, the power to impose interim measures to stop a breach of competition law and the power to disqualify directors for up to 15 years for a breach of competition law.[76] Additionally, the Enterprise Act 2002 gives regulators the power to impose a prison sentence of up to five years for individuals involved in a cartel, although these powers have not yet been used by the CMA in a contested case ,and there have only been a handful of convictions following guilty pleas.[77]

In the LIBOR and FX benchmark manipulation, the European Commission found, using almost identical competition law provisions to those of the UK, that traders from competing banks had colluded, using internet chat rooms and phone calls to each other, in the manipulation of the benchmarks for their own gain, which fulfils the definition of a cartel.[78] The Enterprise Act 2002 provides that it is a criminal offence for individuals to engage in hard-core cartel activity, which is fulfilled by the price-fixing carried out in the benchmark manipulation cartels.[79] However, no prosecutions of individuals involved in the LIBOR or FX manipulation were brought by UK regulators using competition law. This was not the case in the US and EU, so the question must be asked; why did the UK not use its considerable enforcement powers under competition law?[80]

72 For instance, the Enterprise and Regulatory Reform Act 2013, which created the CMA.
73 R Whish and D Bailey, *Competition Law* (10th edn, Oxford University Press 2021).
74 Further detail on these prohibitions is discussed in Chapter 2 of this book.
75 Enterprise Act 2002, s.188(1).
76 Competition Act 1998 and Company Director Disqualification Act 1986, s9A.
77 P Reddy, 'The Future of the Criminal Cartel Offence in the UK' (Norton Rose Fulbright, January 2021) <https://www.nortonrosefulbright.com/en/knowledge/publications/51dd9da8/the-future-of-the-criminal-cartel-offence-in-the-uk> accessed 8 July 2024.
78 European Commission, 'Commission Fines Barclays, RBS, Citigroup, JPMorgan and MUFG E107 Billion for Participating in Foreign Exchange Spot Trading Cartel' (European Commission, 16 May 2019) <https://ec.europa.eu/commission/presscorner/detail/en/IP_19_2568> accessed 10 July 2024.
79 Enterprise Act 2002, s.188(1).
80 For example, see the European Commission press release: 'Antitrust: Commission Fines Banks €1.49 Billion for Participating in Cartels in the Interest Rate Derivatives Industry', (European Commission, 4 December 2013) <https://europa.eu/rapid/press-release_IP

One possible reason for the UK not using competition law against the banks and traders responsible for the LIBOR and FX benchmark manipulation was the perception or fear by the government and regulatory bodies that the banks were too big/important to be allowed to fail, as noted in the Cruickshank report.[81] This concern was also raised by the Parliamentary Commission on Banking Standards (Banking Commission), in which certain reasons were identified to explain why it is difficult to allow banks to fail.[82] The reasons included the provision by banks of essential services, the destruction of value that insolvency brings to a business, which can magnify creditor losses and the risk that disorderly failure can 'cause contagion':[83]

> Allowing one bank to fail in a disorderly way could spread panic among creditors of other similar institutions and cause a wider financial crisis.[84]

These fears have led to resistance to reform in the banking sector in the UK as well as a resistance to the application of competition law to the financial services sector.[85] The Banking Commission identified three key areas that have prevented reform in the banking sector, including a pervasive attitude that 'it's all under control', perception that reform would result in 'risks to the competitiveness of the UK banking sector'; and reluctance to participate in 'biting the hand that feeds us'.[86] Therefore, there appears to be an uphill battle to persuade the UK regulators to use their substantial competition law powers against banks and traders, although this has not held back the US and EU from using similar powers against the same banks. The next two sections of this chapter will first look at the enforcement of the LIBOR benchmark manipulation and, second, at how the FX manipulation was enforced.

3.4 The LIBOR Scandal and Enforcement in the UK

This section will look at how the LIBOR benchmark manipulation was enforced in the UK and will identify areas where competition law could have been used, together with the benefits that competition enforcement would

-13-1208_en.htm> accessed 8 June 2024; and the US Department of Justice press release: 'Five Major Banks Agree to Parent-Level Guilty Pleas' (US Department of Justice, 20 May 2015) <https://www.justice.gov.opa/pr/five-major-banks-agree-parent-level-guilty-pleas> accessed 4 July 2024.

81 H Pontell and others, 'Too Big To Fail, Too Powerful to Jail? On the Absence of Criminal Prosecutions after the 2008 Financial Meltdown' (2014) 61 *Crime, Law and Social Change* 1.

82 Parliamentary Commission on Banking Standards, 'Changing Banking for Good' (HL 2013-14 HL 27-II, HC 171-II).

83 Ibid.

84 Ibid, para 68.

85 D Harrison, *Competition Law and Financial Services* (Routledge 2014).

86 Parliamentary Commission on Banking Standards, 'Changing Banking for Good' (HL 2013-14 HL 27-II, HC 171-II) 166.

bring. In the UK, the banks and individuals involved with LIBOR, FX and the Euro Interbank Offered Rate (EURIBOR) benchmark manipulation fared significantly better than they did when prosecuted under antitrust and competition law by US and EU regulators.[87] As previously stated, no competition law was used by UK authorities to enforce the LIBOR and FX manipulation, although the competition regulator of the time, the OFT, did raise competition concerns about benchmark manipulation with the FSA. However, the FSA warned the OFT against investigating possible LIBOR benchmark manipulation. Transcripts from a meeting between the FSA's Chief Executive Officer (CEO) and the OFT's CEO as early as November 2008 (during the 2008 financial crisis) state that the OFT was 'contemplating looking at... LIBOR'.[88] An exchange of emails took place between the FSA and OFT in which the OFT made it clear it was concerned about the potential for collusion amongst the LIBOR submitting banks to the detriment of consumers or other banks.[89] The exchange ended in a letter sent from the FSA CEO to the OFT saying that:

> At the present time, the FSA would not encourage a further investigation into LIBOR as the BBA [British Bankers' Association] has recently conducted its own review of the process and made some changes.[90]

The letter also stated:

> More importantly, we believe there may be financial stability implications of announcing an investigation at the present time, due to the LIBOR-OIS [Overnight Indexed Swap] spread being such a key indicator of funding costs'[91]

This exchange clearly shows that the competition regulator wanted to investigate the LIBOR manipulation as a potential cartel between the banks but was warned off by the financial services regulator due to fears of political instability. The competition regulator did not take matters further, to the detriment of the enforcement of the LIBOR manipulation, taking the UK out of step with the EU enforcement of LIBOR, which was entirely carried out using

87 R Ball, 'Competition Law and LIBOR in Three Jurisdictions: US, UK and EU' in N Ryder (Ed), *White Collar Crime and Risk – A Critical Reflection* (2018).

88 Financial Services Authority, 'Internal Audit Report: A Review of the Extent of Awareness within the FSA of Inappropriate LIBOR Submissions' (Financial Services Authority, March 2013) Section 3.4.1 <https://www.fca.org.uk/publication/corporate/fsa-ia-libor.pdf> accessed 18 July 2024.

89 Ibid.

90 Ibid.

91 Ibid.

competition law and resulted in significantly higher fines than those imposed in the UK for the same financial crimes.

In the UK, six banks were fined by the FSA and the FCA for breaches to the FSA's Principles for Businesses in relation to LIBOR benchmark manipulation.[92] Barclays Bank Plc was fined £59.5m in 2012, discounted by 30% from £85m due to Barclays' agreement to settle at an early stage of the FSA's investigation.[93] By comparison, Barclays was fined $160m by the US Department of Justice (DoJ)[94] and $200m by the Commodity Futures Trading Commission.[95] Barclays did not receive a fine from the European Commission because it received full immunity for acting as a whistleblower and revealing the existence of the cartel to the European Commission. Barclays thereby avoided a fine of around €690m for its participation in the LIBOR benchmark manipulation.[96] The UK fine represented approximately 1% of Barclays Bank's profit of £5,879m before tax in 2010–2011, which the House of Commons Treasury Select Committee noted did not appropriately reflect the gravity of the misconduct.[97] This discrepancy in the level of fines issued for the same instances of benchmark manipulation in the UK, compared to the fines issued in the EU and US, highlights a serious concern about the level of enforcement and of deterrence against financial crime in the UK. The use of competition law in the imposition of these fines would have allowed the competition regulator to issue fines of up to 10% of Barclay's turnover (not profit) for breach of competition law.[98]

92 Financial Services Authority, 'Final Notice to Barclays Bank Plc' (Financial Services Authority, 27 June 2012) <https://www.fca.org.uk/publication/final-notices/barclays-jun12.pdf> accessed 8 July 2024; Financial Services Authority, 'Final Notice to UBS AG' (Financial Services Authority, 19 December 2012) <https://www.fca.org.uk/publication/final-notices/ubs.pdf> accessed 24 July 2024 and

Financial Services Authority, 'Final Notice to the Royal Bank of Scotland plc' (Financial Services Authority, 6 February 2013) <https://www.fca.org.uk/publication/final-notices/rbs.pdf> accessed 8 July 2024.

93 Ibid.

94 Department of Justice, 'Barclays Bank PLC Admits Misconduct Related to Submissions for the London Interbank Offered Rate and the Euro Interbank Offered Rate and Agrees to Pay $160 Million Penalty' (US Department of Justice, 27 June 2012) <https://www.justice.gov/opa/pr/barclays-bank-plc-admits-misconduct-related-submissions-london-interbank-offered-rate-and> accessed 24 July 2024.

95 Commodity Futures Trading Commission, 'CFTC Orders Barclays to pay $200 Million Penalty for Attempted Manipulation of and False Reporting Concerning LIBOR and Euribor Benchmark Interest Rates' (CFTC, 27 June 2012) <https://www.cftc.gov/PressRoom/PressReleases/6289-12> accessed 4 July 2024.

96 European Commission, 'AMENDED - Antitrust: Commission Fines Banks € 149 Billion For Participating In Cartels In The Interest Rate Derivatives Industry' (European Commission, 3 December 2013) <https://ec.europa.eu/commission/presscorner/detail/en/IP_13_1208> accessed 16 July 2024.

97 House of Commons Treasury Committee, 'Fixing LIBOR: Some Preliminary Findings' (HC 2012-13 HC481-I).

98 Competition Act 1998, s36(8).

A further illustration of the different level of fines handed out for the same instances of LIBOR manipulation is the fines given to the RBS by the UK, EU and US regulators. In the UK, RBS was fined £87.5m;[99] however, it was fined £207m by the Commodity Futures Trading Commission[100] and £150m by the DoJ.[101] RBS was fined €260m by the European Commission for the same LIBOR manipulation, with a further settlement penalty of €131m for its participation in the manipulation of the EURIBOR benchmark interest rate.[102] The fines imposed in the UK are smaller than those imposed in the EU and US. The size of the sanctions imposed by regulators should be comparable to the offence committed and, in the case of the LIBOR manipulation, the offence was the same in each jurisdiction, so the fines should have been comparable.[103] Therefore, it is clear that the fines imposed by UK regulators had significantly less of a deterrent effect than those imposed by the EU or US for the same offences.

Other banks that were fined by UK authorities in connection with LIBOR rate fixing were the Swiss bank UBS AG (£160m),[104] Lloyds Bank plc and the Bank of Scotland plc were together fined £105m,[105] and Deutsche Bank was fined the largest amount: £227m in 2015.[106] There were no criminal

99 Financial Services Authority, 'Final Notice Issued to the Royal Bank of Scotland Plc' (Financial Conduct Authority, 6 February 2013) para. 1 <https://www.fca.org.uk/publication/final-notices/rbs.pdf> accessed 20 July 2024.

100 Commodity Futures Trading Commission, 'CFTC Orders the Royal Bank of Scotland plc and RBS Securities Japan Limited to Pay $325 Million Penalty to Settle Charges of Manipulation, Attempted Manipulation, and False Reporting of Yen and Swiss Franc LIBOR' (Commodity Futures Trading Commission, 6 February 2013) <https://www.cftc.gov/PressRoom/PressReleases/6510-13> accessed 16 July 2024.

101 US Department of Justice, 'RBS Securities Japan Limited Agrees to Plead Guilty in Connection with Long-Running Manipulation of Libor Benchmark Interest Rates' (Department of Justice, 6 February 2013) <https://www.justice.gov/opa/pr/rbs-securities-japan-limited-agrees-plead-guilty-connection-long-running-manipulation-libor> accessed 16 July 2024.

102 European Commission, 'AMENDED - Antitrust: Commission Fines Banks €149 Billion for Participating in Cartels in the Interest Rate Derivatives Industry' (European Commission, 3 December 2013) <https://ec.europa.eu/commission/presscorner/detail/en/IP_13_1208> accessed 16 July 2024.

103 H Hillman, 'Current Laws and Potential Enforcement Measures' in *Fighting Financial Crime in the Global Economic Crisis* N Ryder, U Turksen and S Hassler (Eds) (Routledge 2015).

104 Financial Services Authority, 'Final Notice Issued to UBS AG' (Financial Conduct Authority, 19 December 2012) para. 1 <https://www.fca.org.uk/publication/final-notices/ubs.pdf> accessed 20 July 2024.

105 Financial Conduct Authority, 'Lloyds Banking Group Fined £105m for Serious LIBOR and Other Benchmark Failings' (Financial Conduct Authority, 28 July 2014) <https://www.fca.org.uk/news/press-releases/lloyds-banking-group-fined-%C2%A3105m-serious-libor-and-other-benchmark-failings> accessed 16 July 2024.

106 Financial Conduct Authority, 'Deutsche Bank Fined £227 Million by Financial Conduct Authority for LIBOR and EURIBOR Failings and for Misleading the Regulator' (Financial Conduct Authority, 23 April 2015) <https://www.fca.org.uk/news/press-releases/

prosecutions of banks in the UK, unlike in the US,[107] in relation to the LIBOR fixing accusations due to the difficulties associated with the identification doctrine, which is discussed further below.

Although no criminal prosecutions were instigated in the UK against banks in relation to the LIBOR fixing accusations, unlike in the US,[108] criminal proceedings were taken against some of the individual traders involved in benchmark manipulation using the common law offence of conspiracy to defraud. This offence has been used in the past to prosecute cartel members but has not been successful due to the difficulty in proving the fraud element of the offence.[109] The regulators did not use the criminal cartel offence against the traders who were involved in the LIBOR manipulation. This will be discussed further below. In 2012, the Serious Fraud Office (SFO) launched a criminal investigation into LIBOR manipulation, which ran for seven years before it was closed in 2019.[110] The investigation resulted in charges being brought against 13 individuals, the highest profile of whom, Tom Hayes, a former derivatives trader at both UBS and Citigroup in Tokyo, was the last to be found guilty.[111] Hayes was convicted on eight counts of conspiracy to defraud in relation to the manipulation of the Japanese Yen LIBOR between 2006 and 2010.[112] He was sentenced to 14 years imprisonment in 2015,[113] which was reduced to 11 years on appeal.[114] Hayes was freed from prison in January 2021 after serving five and a half years.[115] Hayes recently lost an appeal against his conviction for conspiracy to defraud in the Court of Appeal and has stated that he intends to apply to have the case heard by the Supreme Court, so this litigation may continue.[116] Four other bankers were also jailed for their part in the LIBOR

---

deutsche-bank-fined-%C2%A3227-million-financial-conduct-authority-libor-and-euribor> accessed 8 July 2024.

107 US Department of Justice, 'Five Major Banks Agree to Parent-Level Guilty Pleas' (US Department of Justice, 20 May 2015) <https://www.justice.gov/opa/pr/five-major-banks-agree-parent-level-guilty-pleas> accessed 4 July 2024.

108 Ibid.

109 M Lester, 'Prosecuting Cartels for Conspiracy to Defraud' (2008) 7(1) *Competition Law Journal* 134.

110 Serious Fraud Office, 'SFO Concludes Investigation into LIBOR Manipulation' (Serious Fraud Office, 18 October 2019) <https://www.sfo.gov.uk/2019/10/18/sfo-concludes-investigation-into-libor-manipulation/#:~:text=The%20SFO's%20investigation%20into%20LIBOR,LIBOR%20offence%20in%20the%20UK.> accessed 2 July 2024.

111 Ibid.

112 Judgment in *R v Tom Alexander William Hayes* [2015] EWCA Crim 1944, paras 1 & 2

113 Serious Fraud Office, 'LIBOR Yen (Hayes)' (Serious Fraud Office, 15 January 2015) <https://www.sfo.gov.uk/cases/libor-hayes/> accessed 26 July 2024.

114 Judgment in *R v Tom Alexander William Hayes* [2015] *EWCA Crim* 1944, para. 108.

115 J Partridge, 'City Trader Jailed for Libor Rigging Freed After Five Years' *The Guardian* (London, 29 January 2021) <https://www.theguardian.com/business/2021/jan/29/city-trader-jailed-for-libor-rigging-freed-after-five-years> accessed 16 July 2024.

116 B Castro, 'Former Traders Tom Hayes and Carlo Palombo's Convictions Upheld by Court of Appeal' (Law Society Gazette, 27 March 2024) <https://www.lawgazette.co.uk/news

manipulation, with jail terms ranging from two to six years.[117] However, the high level of acquittals, six in total, and low level of convictions suggests that the common law offence was not the best option for prosecutors. Change is needed in order to make it easier for prosecutors to secure more convictions in similar circumstances.[118] If the criminal cartel offence had been used by the OFT to prosecute the individuals involved in the benchmark manipulation, prosecutors may have had a greater chance of success, although the criminal cartel offence, despite looking relevant to the LIBOR manipulation, has not been entirely successful in practice. There have only been seven criminal cartel cases commenced by the CMA, with only five successful criminal prosecutions of the cartel offence,[119] with the last criminal conviction having been secured in 2017.[120] Some commentators have argued that offence should be reformed by the introduction of a *mens rea* of intention in order for it to operate effectively and fairly.[121] The first iteration of the cartel offence contained a *mens rea* of dishonesty,[122] which the OFT felt created too much uncertainty in jury trials.[123] This led to the reform of the cartel offence in 2013 in which the requirement for dishonesty to be proved was removed, with three defences being introduced to ensure fairness.[124] Whelan argues that the amendments to the offence made in 2013 have created a fundamentally flawed offence which

---

/former-traders-convictions-upheld-by-court-of-appeal/5119208.article> accessed 2 July 2024.

117 Editorial, 'Libor-Rigging Trial: Ex-Barclays Traders Jailed for Two To Six Years' *The Guardian* (London, 7 July 2016) <https://www.theguardian.com/business/2016/jul/07/libor-rigging-trial-ex-barclays-traders-jailed-merchant-pabon-mathew-johnson> accessed 16 July 2024.

118 See N Ryder, '"Too Scared to Prosecute and Too Scared to Jail?" A Critical and Comparative Analysis of Enforcement of Financial Crime Legislation Against Corporations in the USA and the UK' (2018) 82(3) *The Journal of Criminal Law* 243, for discussion about the effect of criminal proceedings against financial institutions and the likely deterrent effect to reduce future misconduct.

119 Competition and Markets Authority, 'Competition and Markets Authority Cases' (Competition and Markets Authority, 2024) <https://www.gov.uk/cma-cases?case_type%5B%5D=criminal-cartels> accessed 10 July 2024.

120 Pinsent Masons, 'UK Anti-Cartel Laws and Their Enforcement' (Pinsent Masons, 5 March 2020) <https://www.pinsentmasons.com/out-law/guides/uk-anti-cartel-laws-and-their-enforcement> accessed 16 July 2024.

121 L Danagher, 'Strict Liability and the Mens Rea of Cartel Crime' (2020) 9(1) *Criminal Law Review* 789.

122 The test for determining dishonesty for the purposes of the Cartel Offence was set out by the Court of Appeal in *R v Ghosh* [1982) QB 1053.

123 Office of Fair Trading, 'OFT's Response to the Government's Consultation: A Competition Regime for Growth: A Consultation on Options for Reform' (National Archives, June 2011) <https://assets.publishing.service.gov.uk/government/uploads/system/uploads/attachment_data/file/312068/L-O-competition-regime-for-growth.pdf> accessed 16 July 2024.

124 Enterprise and Regulatory Reform Act 2013, s47.

is unworkable in practice.[125] This book recommends the reform of the cartel offence to make it easier for prosecutors to secure convictions in cartel cases, such as those seen in the LIBOR and FX benchmark manipulation crises in order to provide a deterrent from engaging in benchmark manipulation cartels. It is also recommended that the cartel offence is amended to make it apply to companies as well as to individuals, to enable employers to be vicariously liable for the actions of their employees in forming a cartel, from which the employer banks benefit financially. This will be discussed further below.

In addition to the public enforcement of the LIBOR benchmark manipulation outlined above, there have been various private enforcement claims against the banks involved in LIBOR manipulation in the UK. One case was brought by Leeds City Council and others against Barclays Bank plc in relation to alleged LIBOR manipulation between 2006 and 2008 that affected long term loans entered into between Barclays and Leeds City Council and other local authorities.[126] All the loans referenced LIBOR in order to calculate interest rates or break fees. The claim was based on an allegation by the claimants that they entered into various loan agreements with Barclays on the basis of fraudulent misrepresentations to the effect that Barclays would not engage in LIBOR manipulation.[127] Another case was brought by the Property Alliance Group Ltd against RBS.[128] Neither of these cases was successful for the claimants. The private enforcement actions taken against the banks found guilty of LIBOR manipulation by regulators have introduced an element of uncertainty for the banks, which regulatory fines do not. Private enforcement claims can, therefore, be seen as another type of deterrent against the commission of this type of financial crime. In the US, class actions have been successfully brought against some of the banks involved in manipulating LIBOR being fined for $20m, which on top of the regulators civil and criminal fines, is a significant amount.[129] There are two ongoing class actions in relation to the FX manipulation cartels, which came to light just after the LIBOR manipulation. These class actions are described below, and it is significant to note that both have been undertaken using competition law, based on a decision made by the

125 P Whelan, 'Section 47 of the Enterprise and Regulatory Reform Act 2013: A Flawed Reform of the UK Cartel Offence' (2015) 78(3) *Modern Law Review* 493.

126 *Leeds City Council & London Borough of Newham v Barclays Bank Plc & Barclays Bank UK Plc* [2021] EWHC 363 (Comm).

127 L Freeman and others, 'English Court Judgment Increases the Challenges for LIBOR Claimants' (Covington & Burling LLP, 9 March 2021) <https://www.cov.com/en/news-and-insights/insights/2021/03/english-court-judgment-increases-the-challenges-for-libor-claimants> accessed 16 July 2024.

128 *Property Alliance Group Limited v The Royal Bank of Scotland PLC* [2018] EWCA Civ 355.

129 M McSherry, 'Barclays Pays $20m to Settle US Class-Action Lawsuit over Libor Fixing' *The Independent* (London, 9 October 2014) <https://www.independent.co.uk/news/business/news/barclays-pays-20m-to-settle-us-classaction-lawsuit-over-libor-fixing-9783555.html> accessed 16 July 2024.

European Commission, which found a breach of competition law had taken place.

3.5 The FX Scandal and Enforcement in the UK

This section will now examine the FX benchmark manipulation, which took place at the same time as the LIBOR manipulation, and its enforcement in the UK. Unlike the LIBOR, the FX benchmark consists of a market in which currencies are bought and sold.[130] It is one of the largest and most liquid markets in the world with a daily average turnover of $5.3 trillion, 40% of which takes place in London.[131] Between 2007 and 2012, a series of cartels, consisting of traders from competitor banks, operated to manipulate the FX benchmark interest rate to suit their trading positions. The cartels called themselves ‘the players’, ‘the 3 musketeers’, ‘1 team, 1 dream’, ‘a co-operative’ and ‘the A-team’.[132] The SFO opened a criminal investigation into the FX benchmark manipulation in 2014; however, the investigation was closed due to insufficient evidence for a reasonable prospect of conviction.[133] Commentators at the time attributed the closure of the investigation to the difficulty in making a corporate prosecution pursuant to the identification principle, outlined in Chapter 2, and called for a change in the law on corporate criminal responsibility to enable corporate criminal prosecutions rather than the imposition of regulatory fines against firms.[134] Although no criminal penalties were imposed on banks involved with the FX benchmark manipulation, the FCA did impose regulatory fines.[135] The banks fined were Citibank NA, HSBC Bank Plc,

130 A Michael, ’Forex Trading for Non-experts’ *Forbes Advisor* (New Jersey, 12 April 2022) <https://www.forbes.com/uk/advisor/investing/what-is-forex-trading/> accessed 15 July 2024.

131 Financial Conduct Authority, ’FCA Fines Barclays £284,432,000 for Forex Failings’ (Financial Conduct Authority, 19 May 2015) <https://www.fca.org.uk/news/press-releases/fca-fines-barclays-%C2%A3284432000-forex-failings#:~:text=The%20Financial%20Conduct%20Authority%20(FCA,(FX)%20business%20in%20London.> accessed 8 July 2024.

132 Financial Conduct Authority, ‘FCA Fines Five Banks £1.1 Billion for FX Failings and Announces Industry-Wide Remediation Programme’ (Financial Conduct Authority, 12 November 2014) <https://www.fca.org.uk/news/press-releases/fca-fines-five-banks-%C2%A311-billion-fx-failings-and-announces-industry-wide-remediation-programme> accessed 15 July 2024.

133 Serious Fraud Office, ‘SFO Closes Forex Investigation’ (Serious Fraud Office, 15 March 2016) <https://www.sfo.gov.uk/2016/03/15/sfo-closes-forex-investigation/> accessed 13 July 2024.

134 J Quinn, ‘SFO Ends Foreign Exchange Probe but Admits Wrongdoing Occurred in City of London’ *The Telegraph* (London, 15 March 2016) <https://www.telegraph.co.uk/business/2016/03/15/serious-fraud-office-ends-foreign-exchange-probe-but-admits-wron/> accessed 13 July 2024.

135 Transparency International UK, ‘Corporate Liability for Economic Crime’ (Transparency International UK, 30 June 2017) <https://issuu.com/transparencyuk/docs/ti-uk_submission_-_corporate_liabil> accessed 5 July 2024.

JPMorgan Chase Bank NA, RBS and UBS AG, who were collectively fined £1.1b.[136] These fines were the largest ever imposed by the FCA or the FSA, and the FCA's then director of supervision said that:

> The supervisory measures that we are announcing today will help make sure that real cultural change is delivered across the industry, and that senior management take responsibility for ensuring that the highest standards of integrity operate across all of their trading businesses.[137]

However, with the imposition of regulatory fines rather than the finding of a criminal offence against the banks, the deterrent effect of such enforcement is questionable – fines are easily absorbed into the operating costs of a bank and often will not even exceed the profit made from the illegal activity.[138] Following the fines to the above five banks, Barclays was fined £284.4m by the FCA in 2015 for failing to adequately control its FX business.[139]

In 2019, a competition-law-based class action was commenced in the Competition Appeals Tribunal against the banks on behalf of asset managers, pension funds, hedge funds and companies that suffered losses as a result of the FX market manipulation.[140] Because there was no finding by a UK regulator of a breach of competition law, the class action is based on a decision made by the European Commission that fined banks for participating in two cartels that manipulated the FX benchmark, in breach of competition law.[141] There is another class action that relates to the same FX manipulation by the same banks.[142] The Competition Appeals Tribunal has recently ruled to stay both FX class applications, and the applicants have been given permission to resubmit a

136 Financial Conduct Authority, 'FCA Fines Five Banks £1.1 Billion for FX Failings and Announces Industry-Wide Remediation Programme' (Financial Conduct Authority, 12 November 2014) <https://www.fca.org.uk/news/press-releases/fca-fines-five-banks-%C2%A311-billion-fx-failings-and-announces-industry-wide-remediation-programme> accessed 15 July 2024.

137 Ibid.

138 H Macartney and P Calcagno, 'All Bark and No Bite: The Political Economy of Bank Fines in Anglo-America' (2019) 26(4) *Review of International Political Economy*.

139 Financial Conduct Authority, 'FCA Fines Barclays £284,432,000 for Forex Failings' (Financial Conduct Authority, 19 May 2015) <https://www.fca.org.uk/news/press-releases/fca-fines-barclays-%C2%A3284432000-forex-failings#:~:text=The%20Financial%20Conduct%20Authority%20(FCA,(FX)%20business%20in%20London.> accessed 8 July 2024.

140 *Michael O'Higgins FX Class Representative Limited v Barclays Bank PLC and Others* [2022] CAT 16; and UK Foreign Exchange Cartel Claim, 'Michael O'Higgins FX Class Representative Limited' (UK FX Cartel Claim, 13 April 2022) <https://www.ukfxcartelclaim.com/Home/About> accessed 13 July 2024.

141 European Commission, 'Antitrust: Commission Fines UBS, Barclays, RBS, HSBC and Credit Suisse €344 Million for Participating in a Foreign Exchange Spot Trading Cartel' (European Commission, 2 December 2021) <https://ec.europa.eu/commission/presscorner/detail/en/ip_21_6548> accessed 15 May 2024.

142 *Mr Phillip Evans v Barclays Bank PLC and Others* [2020] CAT 9.

revised application for certification on an opt-in basis rather than on the opt-out class action basis that the original applications were based on.[143]

The lack of competition law enforcement by UK regulators for the FX benchmark manipulation cartels is striking. The FX benchmark manipulation cartels were identified by the FCA as: 'traders at different Banks [who] formed tight knit groups in which information was shared about client activity',[144] but these same 'tight knit groups' of competitors were identified as 'cartels' that breached competition law by the European Commission using substantially the same competition law provisions as those of the UK. The enforcement of the FX benchmark manipulation cartels came after new legislation came into force, described below, which gave the FCA concurrent powers with the CMA to enforce competition law in the financial services sector, however no competition law was used for the FX benchmark manipulation cartels. The use of competition law to enforce these cartels would have given regulators the power to impose even more significant fines (up to 10% of each bank's worldwide turnover), to agree behavioural or structural commitments with each bank and the power to disqualify directors found to have breached competition law. Given that competition, or antitrust, law was used for these same benchmark manipulation cartels in both the US and EU, there is no obvious reason why the UK did not use competition law, with the associated significant penalties for breach, for these cartels. This appears to be a missed opportunity to have deterred future benchmark manipulation cartels, to the detriment of the UK financial services market.

3.6 Legislation Introduced Following the LIBOR and FX Scandal

This part of the chapter focuses on the legislative changes made to the competition law regime in the aftermath of the LIBOR and FX benchmark manipulation crisis. The main post-LIBOR changes were made following the government's 2011 consultation entitled *A Competition Regime for Growth*, in which it invited opinions on how to reform the competition law regime.[145] The government's response to its consultation, published in 2012, set out proposals to increase the use of competition law in the financial services sector,

143 *Michael O'Higgins FX Class Representative Limited v Barclays Bank PLC and Others* [2022] CAT 16.

144 Financial Conduct Authority, 'FCA Fines Barclays £284,432,000 for Forex Failings' (Financial Conduct Authority, 19 May 2015) <https://www.fca.org.uk/news/press-releases/fca-fines-barclays-%C2%A3284432000-forex-failings#:~:text=The%20Financial%20Conduct%20Authority%20(FCA,(FX)%20business%20in%20London.> accessed 15 July 2024.

145 Department for Business, Innovation and Skills, 'A Competition Regime for Growth: A Consultation on Options for Reform' (GOV.UK, March 2011) <https://assets.publishing.service.gov.uk/government/uploads/system/uploads/attachment_data/file/31411/11-657-competition-regime-for-growth-consultation.pdf> accessed 14 July 2024.

many of which were included in the Enterprise and Regulatory Reform Act 2013.[146] The government stated that its case for reforming the competition regime in the UK included the difficulties in successfully prosecuting infringements of the Competition Act 1998 at reasonable cost and in reasonable time and the duplication and inefficiencies caused by the division of responsibility for competition enforcement between two competition authorities. These perceived difficulties led to the changes introduced in the three key Acts analysed below.

The government was also influenced in its legislative changes by the report of the Banking Commission, which was set up to establish an inquiry into professional standards in the banking industry following the exposure of the scandal of the LIBOR manipulation in late June 2012.[147] The Banking Commission produced a report entitled 'Changing Banking for Good',[148] which contained a number of interesting observations about the reasons for the lack of competition law enforcement in the wake of the LIBOR crisis, such as the significant comment that: 'regulators tend to regulate and they do not think about competition as a tool that they can use'.[149] This certainly appears to have been the case in the UK's response to the LIBOR benchmark manipulation, as the financial services regulator did not work with the competition law regulator, the OFT at the time, to consider the competition law implications of the LIBOR and FX crisis, whilst other countries affected by the benchmark manipulation successfully used their competition law powers to investigate and then prosecute the traders and banks involved.[150] The Banking Commission's report does appear to have influenced the thinking of the UK government as, following its publication, a raft of competition legislation relating to the regulation of financial crime was introduced in the UK. This is looked at in more detail below.

In total, three Acts, each of which increased the use of competition law in the financial services sector were passed by the UK government following the financial crisis. The Financial Services (Banking Reform) Act 2013 conferred competition powers on the FCA.[151] In particular, the Act inserted

146 Department for Business, Innovation and Skills, 'Enterprise and Regulatory Reform Bill: Updated Policy Paper' (Parliament Publications, January 2013) <https://assets.publishing.service.gov.uk/government/uploads/system/uploads/attachment_data/file/87928/bis-13-654-enterprise-and-regulatory-reform-bill-policy-paper-jan-2013.pdf> accessed 17 July 2024.

147 Parliamentary Commission on Banking Standards, 'Changing Banking for Good' (HL 2013-14 HL 27-II, HC 171-II).

148 Ibid.

149 Ibid.

150 In particular, the US, which used its antitrust powers, and the EU, which used competition law to enforce the LIBOR rate fixing.

151 Financial Services (Banking Reform) Act 2013, s129 and Schedule 8.

a new provision[152] into FSMA that places a 'primacy' obligation on the FCA to consider, before using certain of its powers as financial regulator, whether its competition powers are more appropriate and, if so, to use them instead.[153] This is a significant change of direction and policy, especially given that no competition law was used in the prosecution of any of the LIBOR or FX benchmark manipulation perpetrators. The FCA's new competition powers can be used concurrently with those of the previously sole competition regulator in the UK: the CMA.[154] However, since the introduction of these extensive new powers for the FCA, the above-cited concern that 'regulators tend to regulate and they do not think about competition as a tool that they can use', [155] appears to have been a valid one, given that only two competition law cases have been brought by the FCA since it received its new competition powers in 2015.[156] The two cases decided by the FCA using its competition law powers are discussed below.

The second legislative Act that affected competition law in the financial services sector following the LIBOR and FX benchmark manipulation crisis was the Financial Services Act 2012, which changed the UK financial services regulator. The FSA, the financial services regulator at the time of the LIBOR and FX scandal, was replaced by the Prudential Regulatory Authority and the FCA.[157] The key regulator of the financial services industry is now the FCA, with power to prosecute financial crime. The Financial Services Act inserted into FSMA[158] a new competition objective for the FSA, which is to promote competition in the interests of consumers in the markets for regulated financial services, which is now one of the FCA's three operational objectives.[159] This competition objective, alongside the other objectives of the protection of consumers from bad conduct and the protection of the integrity of the UK financial system makes the FCA one of the few financial regulators in the world

152 The Financial Services (Banking Reform) Act 2013, Schedule 8 Part 1(3) inserted a new s234K into the Financial Services and Markets Act 2000, Part 16A.

153 Financial Services Act 2012, s.1E.

154 Financial Conduct Authority, 'Competition Law' (Financial Conduct Authority, 21 April 2016) <https://www.fca.org.uk/about/promoting-competition/powers> accessed 20 July 2024.

155 Parliamentary Commission on Banking Standards, 'Changing Banking for Good' (HL 2013-14 HL 27-II, HC 171-II).

156 Financial Conduct Authority, 'FCA Issues its First Decision under Competition Law' (Financial Conduct Authority, 21 February 2019) <https://www.fca.org.uk/news/press-releases/fca-issues-its-first-decision-under-competition-law> accessed 2 July 2024 and Financial Conduct Authority, 'FCA Fines Three Money Transfer Firms For Breaking Competition Law' (Financial Conduct Authority, 30 November 2023) <https://www.fca.org.uk/news/press-releases/fca-fines-three-money-transfer-firms-breaking-competition-law> accessed 2 July 2024.

157 Financial Services Act 2012 s 6.

158 As a new section 1B(3)(c) in Part 1A Financial Services and Markets Act 2000.

159 Financial Services Act 2012, s6(1).

with a core objective to promote competition.[160] The Financial Services Act 2012 also created a new criminal offence for knowingly or deliberately making false or misleading statements relating to benchmark-setting.[161] This criminal offence has not yet been used by a regulator but is a significant addition to the armoury any regulator will have available in any future benchmark manipulation. The introduction of this new criminal offence, in addition to the existing criminal cartel offence in the Enterprise Act 2002, gives the FCA two alternative options for criminal prosecutions against individuals and presumably will at least increase the regulator's chances of securing criminal convictions in any future benchmark manipulation cartel. However, it is important to note that there is no mention of corporate criminal liability for either cartels or benchmark manipulation. This is an omission that needs to be remedied so that banks are incentivised to prevent this financial crime from taking place in the future.

A third UK legislative change affecting the UK competition law regime following the LIBOR and FX crisis was the Enterprise and Regulatory Reform Act 2013. This Act amended the concurrency provisions found in the Competition Act 1998 and abolished the OFT and the CC, creating a single new regulator for competition.[162] The CMA is jointly responsible with the FCA for competition law enforcement in the financial services sector. Both of these relatively new regulators have had to learn how to work together in an efficient manner over the past few years in order to combat financial crime. The government set out its reasoning for keeping the independence of both the CMA and the sectoral regulators, rather than merging them into one regulator, as:

> This will continue to allow the integrated application of sectoral and competition law powers, the application of the sector regulators' industry expertise and ongoing sector surveillance to competition cases.[163]

In addition to the three Acts, the government has also given a 'strategic steer' to the CMA at its launch on 1 October 2013, stating that the CMA:

> Should work with sector regulators, including the Financial Conduct Authority for the financial services sector, to build up its sector capabilities

160 Financial Conduct Authority, 'FCA Mission: Our Approach to Competition' (Financial Conduct Authority, October 2018) <https://www.fca.org.uk/publication/corporate/our-approach-competition-final-report-feedback-statement.pdf> accessed 8 July 2024.

161 Financial Services Act 2012, s 91 and 92.

162 Enterprise and Regulatory Reform Act 2013 s54.

163 Department for Business, Innovation and Skills, 'Growth, Competition and the Competition Regime: Government Response to Consultation' (GOV.UK, March 2012) Part B para. 38 <https://assets.publishing.service.gov.uk/government/uploads/system/uploads/attachment_data/file/192722/12-512-growth-and-competition-regime-government-response.pdf> accessed 14 July 2024.

> and continuing to share competition expertise, including through joint enforcement work (within the legal framework), training and research.[164]

Then, in December 2015, the government issued a revised nonbinding 'strategic steer' to the CMA setting out the government's view that, in relation to the regulated sectors, the CMA should continue to focus on:

> Playing a leadership role with regulators that have competition powers, especially those that are new to the concurrency regime. The CMA should encourage those regulators to make greater use of their competition powers and to tackle anti-competitive actions in regulated markets.[165]

The concurrency of regulation between the CMA and the various sector regulators now allows each sector regulator, including the FCA, to apply competition law and to conduct market studies in order to identify areas where the sector market is not working competitively for the benefit of consumers.[166] However, it does not appear that these legislative changes have had the effect they were designed to produce – the FCA has only issued two decisions in the financial sector using its competition law powers.[167] Of the wide range of enforcement powers available to it, the FCA only imposed fines in both cases, and in the first case, those fines were only equivalent to 1% of the turnover

164 Department for Business, Innovation and Skills, 'Competition Regime: Response to Consultation on Statement of Strategic Priorities for the CMA' para. 9, Annex 1 (Parliament Publications, 1 October 2013) <https://assets.publishing.service.gov.uk/government/uploads/system/uploads/attachment_data/file/245607/bis-13-1210-competition-regime-response-to-consultation-on-statement-of-strategic-priorities-for-the-cma.pdf> accessed 19 July 2024.

165 Department for Business, Innovation and Skills, 'Competition Regime: Government's Response to the Consultation on the Strategic Steer to the Competition and Markets Authority' (Parliament Publications, December 2015) <https://assets.publishing.service.gov.uk/government/uploads/system/uploads/attachment_data/file/481040/BIS-15-659-government-response-governments-strategic-steer-to-the-competition-and-markets-authority.pdf> accessed 8 July 2024.

166 Competition and Markets Authority, 'Competition and Markets Authority Annual Plan 2023/24' (GOV.UK, 23 March 2023) 17 <https://assets.publishing.service.gov.uk/media/64240e7e60a35e00120cb06f/A_CMA_ANNUAL_PLAN_2023-2024_.pdf> accessed 24 July 2024.

167 Financial Conduct Authority, 'FCA Issues Its First Decision Under Competition Law' (Financial Conduct Authority, 21 February 2019) <https://www.fca.org.uk/news/press-releases/fca-issues-its-first-decision-under-competition-law> accessed 2 July 2024; and Financial Conduct Authority, 'FCA Fines Three Money Transfer Firms for Breaking Competition Law' (Financial Conduct Authority, 30 November 2023) <https://www.fca.org.uk/news/press-releases/fca-fines-three-money-transfer-firms-breaking-competition-law> accessed 2 July 2024.

of the three asset management firms involved in the first case.[168] However, because the FCA had the power to fine up to 10% of the turnover of each firm using its competition powers, the fines imposed look small by comparison. The competition law investigation in the first case took an unusually long time to reach the decision stage, with 15 months elapsing since the Statement of Objections was issued by the FCA to the infringing parties. This is a long time compared to the more usual five months that the CMA takes from the Statement of Objection stage to the issuance of a fine.[169] The second competition decision reached by the FCA involved behaviour more similar to that seen in the LIBOR and FX benchmark manipulation. There was a cartel that operated between three competing money transfer businesses in Glasgow that colluded to fix exchange rates on the conversion of UK pounds to Pakistan rupees when transferring money from the UK to Pakistan.[170] The firms also agreed to fix transaction prices for certain money transfers from the UK to Pakistan.[171] This case is encouraging, as it demonstrates that the FCA is able to use its competition law powers in relation to a price fixing cartel, similar to the ones seen in the LIBOR and FX manipulation. It is disappointing, however, that fines were the only punishment and that the criminal cartel offence was not used to prosecute the individuals involved. The fines themselves appear relatively small – ranging from £3,600 for one business to the highest fine of £139,500.[172] This was an uncontested case though, with a discount for cooperation during the investigation being reflected in the fines issued. If the FCA is to use its competition law powers in order to deter future crime, they must use more than just the power to fine companies in breach. The power to disqualify a director, for instance, is available to the regulator if a company is in breach of competition law.[173] This is a powerful sanction and would have a strong deterrent effect against future breaches of competition law when used in conjunction with a fine of up to 10% of a company's worldwide turnover.[174] The FCA has opened eight competition law cases in the financial sector since the FCA gained its competition law powers in 2015; only two of these cases have reached the stage of an infringement decision. Three of the six cases were closed without a decision, and three remain open.[175] It is clear that the FCA

168 Cleary Gottlieb, 'FCA Issues First Penalties for Competition Infringements' (Cleary Gottlieb, 26 February 2019) <https://www.clearygottlieb.com/-/media/files/alert-memos-2019/fca-issues-first-penalties-for-competition-infringements.pdf> accessed 8 July 2024.

169 Ibid.

170 Financial Conduct Authority, 'FCA Fines Three Money Transfer Firms For Breaking Competition Law' (FCA, 30 November 2023) <https://www.fca.org.uk/news/press-releases/fca-fines-three-money-transfer-firms-breaking-competition-law> accessed 4 July 2024.

171 Ibid.

172 Ibid.

173 Company Directors Disqualification Act 1986, s9A.

174 Competition Act 1998, s36.

175 Competition and Markets Authority, 'Competition Act 1998 Cases in the Regulated Sectors' (GOV.UK, 20 December 2023) <https://www.gov.uk/government/publications/compe-

has not fully embraced its competition law powers since its concurrent competition powers in the financial services sector came into force in April 2015.[176]

In its report of 2023, the CMA states that the concurrency arrangements have been working well, with high levels of collaboration between sector regulators.[177] However, with the FCA having made just two Competition Act decisions since 2015, it is apparent that the concurrency arrangements are not working well in the financial services sector. An independent report commissioned by the government in 2020 and published a year later, the Penrose Report, stated that the UK competition regime is ranked behind that of the US, France, Germany, the EU and Austria and concludes that reform is needed to update, improve and refresh.[178] Following this report, the government launched a consultation into how to reform competition and consumer policy.[179] The government proposed a further set of legislative changes to the competition regime in its consultation response, published in April 2022.[180] Many of the proposals were aimed at strengthening powers for the CMA and sector regulators, such as the FCA under the Competition Act 1998, including the ability to take interim measures to ensure competition authorities can intervene to prevent harm while investigations are still ongoing and powers to obtain information and sanction businesses that refuse to cooperate or comply with the CMA or regulators' Competition Act 1998 investigations and remedies.[181] The government has now passed the Digital Markets, Competition and Consumers Act 2024 (Digital Markets Act), which received Royal Assent in May 2024.[182] The Digital Markets Act is the biggest reform to the UK

tition-act-1998-cases-in-the-sectors-regulated-by-ukcn-members/competition-act-1998-cases-in-the-regulated-sectors> accessed 4 July 2024.

176 Competition and Markets Authority, 'Promoting Competition in Services We Rely On: The Annual Concurrency Report 2023' (GOV.UK, 10 May 2023) <https://www.gov.uk/government/publications/annual-report-on-concurrency-2023/promoting-competition-in-services-we-rely-on-the-annual-concurrency-report-2023> accessed 4 July 2024.

177 Ibid.

178 Penrose Report, 'Power to the People: Stronger Consumer Choice and Competition So that Markets Work for People, Not the Other Way Around' (Parliament Publications, February 2021) <https://assets.publishing.service.gov.uk/government/uploads/system/uploads/attachment_data/file/961665/penrose-report-final.pdf> accessed 17 July 2024.

179 Department for Business, Energy & Industrial Strategy, 'Reforming Competition and Consumer Policy: Consultation' (GOV.UK, 20 July 2021) <https://www.gov.uk/government/consultations/reforming-competition-and-consumer-policy> accessed 2 July 2024.

180 Department for Business and Trade, Department for Science, Innovation and Technology, 'Competition Reform: Policy Summary Briefing' (GOV.UK, 21 December 2023) <https://www.gov.uk/government/publications/digital-markets-competition-and-consumers-bill-supporting-documentation/competition-reform-policy-summary-briefing> accessed 4 July 2024.

181 Ibid.

182 Digital Markets, Competition and Consumers Act 2024.

competition and consumer law since the creation of the CMA in 2014,[183] and it significantly expands the CMA's existing investigation and enforcement powers in relation to competition law matters.[184] Key changes made by the Digital Markets Act are that the extraterritorial reach of UK competition law has been expanded – agreements, concerted practices and decisions that are implemented outside the UK but that have an immediate substantial and foreseeable effect on the trade within the UK will now be prohibited by UK competition law.[185] The previous requirement was that such agreements had to be implemented in the UK for the Chapter I prohibition to apply.[186] A further key change made in the Digital Markets Act is the increase in the CMA's powers of evidence gathering in relation to investigations of a breach of competition law and an increase to the CMA's powers of seizure in dawn raids – these powers of seizure have now been expanded to include domestic premises.[187] These powers could be used in the investigation of a future benchmark manipulation cartel, so any increase in the powers of investigation given to the CMA is welcome. It is to be hoped that giving the CMA and sector regulators increased enforcement and investigative powers will encourage the regulators to start more Competition Act cases in the regulated sectors. The FCA has had its competition powers for a substantial amount of time now but does not seem ready to use these powers in place of its financial regulatory powers in the foreseeable future.

Now that the LIBOR and FX benchmark manipulation enforcement measures and the legislative changes made after the crisis have been examined, this chapter will take a closer look at the key themes that will be analysed in each subsequent chapter of the book. The themes are the competition law leniency and whistleblowing regime in the UK, an evaluation of civil vs criminal penalties for benchmark manipulation, corporate criminal liability and the consideration of deferred prosecution agreements (DPAs).

3.7 Competition Law Leniency and Whistleblowing Regime in the UK

As mentioned in Chapter 2, because cartels are typically carried out in extremely secretive conditions, leniency applications and information received

183 Sidley Austin LLP, 'Key Proposals Under the UK's Landmark Completion Reforms' (Sidley, 26 April 2023) <https://www.sidley.com/en/insights/newsupdates/2023/04/key-proposals-under-the-uk-s-landmark-competition-reforms> accessed 23 July 2024.

184 Dentons, 'The Digital Markets, Competition and Consumers Act: A Watershed Moment in Consumer Protection Law' (Dentons, 5 June 2024) <https://www.dentons.com/en/insights/articles/2024/june/5/the-digital-markets-competition-and-consumers-act> accessed 23 July 2024.

185 Digital Markets, Competition and Consumers Act 2024, s.119.

186 Competition Act 1998, s.2(3).

187 Digital Markets, Competition and Consumers Act 2024, s.123.

from whistleblowers play a critical role in regulators detecting and enforcing this illegal activity.[188] This section will examine the UK's competition law leniency and competition law whistleblowing regime to assess how well it works in relation to future benchmark manipulation cartels.

A leniency protocol has been published by the CMA that relates to cartels.[189] The leniency protocol includes provision for granting reduced penalties to companies that come forward with information on cartel activity and that then cooperate fully with any subsequent investigation. The first company to apply for leniency can receive a 100% reduction in the penalty, and successive applicants may receive deductions of up to 50%, depending on the added value of the material they provide. There is a complex tiered leniency system that categorises leniency into different 'types', each of which provides different types of protection to an applicant depending on its order in the queue and whether an investigation has already commenced.[190] Individual informants may also receive a financial reward for information of up to £250,000,[191] which has recently been increased from a maximum reward of £100,000.[192]

The leniency provisions were in operation at the time of the LIBOR and FX manipulation though, but none of the traders who were involved with, or aware of, the LIBOR or FX benchmark manipulation thought to use the leniency protocol. This is likely to be because both the enforcement of competition law and the awareness of the leniency provisions for cartel members are not advertised sufficiently in the financial services sector. This is an area where reform is needed in order to bring more cartels in the financial services sector to the attention of the regulators. The competition law leniency provisions and when they should be used must be advertised in the financial services sector with a targeted approach taken to banks and traders. In 2021, the FCA launched a general whistleblowing campaign to encourage individuals working in financial services firms to report wrongdoing, but a more targeted

188 Ibid.

189 Competition and Markets Authority, 'Cartels: Come Forward and Apply for Leniency' (GOV.UK, 11 March 2019) <https://www.gov.uk/guidance/cartels-confess-and-apply-for-leniency> accessed 8 July 2024.

190 Slaughter and May, 'Spotlight: Cartel Leniency Programmes in United Kingdom' (Slaughter and May LLP, 2 March 2021) <https://www.lexology.com/library/detail.aspx?g=63f3a8fa-5b45-4b8f-9039-461036c3ba57&utm_source=Lexology+Daily+Newsfeed&utm_medium=HTML+email+-+Body+-+General+section&utm_campaign=Lexology+subscriber+daily+feed&utm_content=Lexology+Daily+Newsfeed+2021-09-13&utm_term=> accessed 17 July 2024.

191 Competition and Markets Authority, 'Cartels: Policy for Witnessing and Reporting' (GOV.UK, 31 March 2014) <https://www.gov.uk/government/publications/cartels-informant-rewards-policy> accessed 20 July 2024.

192 Competition and Markets Authority, 'Blowing the Whistle on Cartels' (GOV.UK, 6 June 2023) <https://www.gov.uk/government/news/blowing-the-whistle-on-cartels#:~:text=The%20Competition%20and%20Markets%20Authority,cartel%20activity%20they%20have%20witnessed.> accessed 20 July 2024.

approach needs to be taken to advertise the competition leniency provisions, which applies to companies such as banks, as well as to individuals.[193]

There are two further areas where reform is needed of the UK competition law leniency provisions. First, the level of financial reward must be significantly raised because it currently is not set high enough to attract a high-earning banker to blow the whistle on a lucrative cartel arrangement,[194] unlike the potential financial rewards for whistleblowers in the US, where the highest individual financial reward paid to date is $30m.[195] Second, the CMA is currently the only regulator to which leniency applications can be made. This needs to be changed so that financial services firms can apply for leniency to their own regulator, the FCA, which may make the process easier and more accessible for them. These are aspects of the competition law regime that should be addressed to ensure that the whistleblowing regime is more likely to be used for future benchmark manipulation cartels in the UK.

3.8 Criminal vs Civil Penalties

This section will look at which powers, civil or criminal, are available to regulators for benchmark manipulation in the financial services sector. It will analyse the powers and evaluate the deterrent effect of the powers available. Civil penalties, normally in the form of fines, play a key role in the regulation of financial crime, as they have the potential to act as a deterrent if imposed at a high enough level; however, they do not carry the public and reputational stigma of a criminal conviction.[196] Financial penalties when imposed on companies have a negligible impact as the fines are frequently viewed by the offending company as little more than the cost of doing business.[197] This was clear as early as 2012 when bank shares touched 18 month highs directly after the first LIBOR fines were imposed by regulators.[198] Therefore, civil penalties alone will not

193 Financial Conduct Authority, 'FCA Launches Campaign to Encourage Individuals to Report Wrongdoing' (Financial Conduct Authority, 24 March 2021) <https://www.fca.org.uk/news/press-releases/fca-launches-campaign-encourage-individuals-report-wrongdoing> accessed 17 July 2024.

194 See: efinancialcareers, 'London's Investment Banking Salaries and Bonuses' (efinancialcareers, 19 October 2023) <https://www.efinancialcareers.co.uk/news/2023/10/london-investment-bank-pay> accessed 5 July 2024.

195 US Securities and Exchange Commission, 'Whistleblower Awards over $400 Million' (Sec. Gov, 23 August 2019) <https://www.sec.gov/page/whistleblower-100million> accessed 20 May 2024.

196 N Werle, 'Prosecuting Corporate Crime When Firms Are Too Big to Jail: Investigation, Deterrence, and Judicial Review' (2019) 128 *Yale LJ* 1366.

197 R Jones, 'Unfit for Duty: The Officer and Director Bar as a Remedy for Fraud' (2014) 82 *University of Cincinnati Law Review* 444.

198 K Ridley, 'Lawsuits Cast Darker Shadow over Banks than Libor Fines' (Reuters, 21 December 2012) <https://www.reuters.com/article/banks-libor-lawsuits-idUSL5E8NH9B320121221> accessed 20 July 2024.

deter a company from repeating the offending behaviour. Regulators in the UK should be given the power to impose a range of either civil or criminal corporate penalties, depending on the seriousness of the offence committed. These powers are available to regulators when competition law used to enforce a cartel such as those seen in the LIBOR and FX benchmark manipulation scandal.

Criminal penalties are typically imposed for offences and breaches that negatively affect society as a whole, rather than just one person.[199] For offences that negatively affect the whole of the UK, such as the benchmark manipulation carried out in relation to the LIBOR and FX benchmarks, it is argued that a criminal corporate penalty is more appropriate than a civil one, such as a fine. Imposing a corporate criminal penalty is likely to result in a higher fine for a company than fine imposed pursuant to a civil penalty, and in addition to that, being in breach of a criminal law carries more weight in society, with the potential to create more reputational damage, than being in breach of a civil law.[200] This is supported by the Crown Prosecution Service which states that:

> A thorough enforcement of the criminal law against corporate offenders, where appropriate, will have a deterrent effect, protect the public and support ethical business practices. Prosecuting corporations, where appropriate, will capture the full range of criminality involved and thus lead to increased public confidence in the criminal justice system.[201]

This book argues that the financial services regulators need a corporate criminal liability offence that prosecutors can successfully use to enforce and deter financial crime such as benchmark manipulation. Financial crime typically affects a large proportion of the public, so this book argues that a criminal offence for both companies and individuals guilty of financial crime is more appropriate than relying on financial regulatory powers of enforcement alone. The facilitation of the prosecution by UK regulators of a company for a serious breach of financial crime will allow the UK to follow the lead of the US and enter into DPAs, described in Chapter 2 and below, with companies who are willing to work together with the regulator in order to commit to preventing future breaches of the law. Criminal liability for an offence sends a clearer message to companies and to the public that the offence is one that will negatively

199 Slater and Gordon, 'Difference between Criminal and Civil Law UK' (Slater + Gordon Lawyers, 11 April 2018) <https://www.slatergordon.co.uk/newsroom/criminal-vs-civil-law-understanding-the-differences/> accessed 13 July 2024.

200 G Markoff, 'Arthur Andersen and the Myth of the Corporate Death Penalty: Corporate Criminal Convictions in the Twenty-First Century' (2013) 15(3) *University of Pennsylvania Journal of Business Law* 797.

201 Crown Prosecution Service, 'Corporate Prosecutions' (CPS, 2017) <https://www.cps.gov.uk/legal-guidance/corporate-prosecutions> accessed 29 July 2024.

affect society as a whole, rather than a civil/regulatory offence that is perceived to be an offence affecting one or more people.[202]

Regulators in the UK who are able to enforce financial crime carried out by companies are the FCA, the CMA and the SFO. Between them, these regulators have the power to impose a wide assortment of civil penalties, including both behavioural and structural remedies such as commitments and directions that are available to both the FCA and CMA[203] pursuant to competition law.[204] These remedies are available for a breach of competition law, such as the Chapter I prohibition,[205] which deals with anticompetitive agreements between businesses, which would apply to the cartels seen between banks in the LIBOR and FX scandals. Civil corporate penalties could be a stronger deterrent to financial crime if regulators use the full range of powers given to them rather than relying on financial monetary penalties alone as they currently do.[206]

For cartels, the CMA is able to use its civil enforcement powers available under Chapter I Competition Act 1998.[207] Chapter I of the Competition Act 1998 prohibits agreements and concerted practices between businesses that have as their object or effect the prevention, restriction or distortion of competition within the UK. In addition to this prohibition, the Enterprise Act 2002 contains a criminal cartel offence that can be used against individuals, but not companies, involved in a cartel.[208] Other civil structural remedies exist in the Enterprise Act 2002, in which the power to break up a dominant firm guilty of serial abusive behaviour is explicitly available pursuant to a market

202 Slater and Gordon, 'Difference Between Criminal and Civil Law UK' (Slater + Gordon Lawyers, 11 April 2018) <https://www.slatergordon.co.uk/newsroom/criminal-vs-civil-law-understanding-the-differences/> accessed 13 July 2024.

203 Competition and Markets Authority, 'Guidance on Concurrent Application of Competition Law to Regulated Industries' (Competition and Markets Authority, March 2014) <https://assets.publishing.service.gov.uk/government/uploads/system/uploads/attachment_data/file/892735/Guidance_on_concurrent_application_of_competition_law_to_regulated_industries.pdf> accessed 13 July 2024.

204 Competition Act 1998, ss.31, 32.

205 Competition Act 1998, Chapter 1, s.2.

206 For instance, see the FCA's only two competition enforcement decisions: Financial Conduct Authority, 'FCA Issues Its First Decision under Competition Law' (Financial Conduct Authority, 21 February 2019) <https://www.fca.org.uk/news/press-releases/fca-issues-its-first-decision-under-competition-law> accessed 17 July 2024; and Financial Conduct Authority, 'FCA Fines Three Money Transfer Firms for Breaking Competition Law' (Financial Conduct Authority, 30 November 2023) <https://www.fca.org.uk/news/press-releases/fca-fines-three-money-transfer-firms-breaking-competition-law> accessed 2 July 2024.

207 Competition and Markets Authority, 'Annual Report and Accounts 2020 to 2021' (Competition and Markets Authority, 15 July 2021) <https://www.gov.uk/government/publications/cma-annual-report-and-accounts-2020-to-2021/annual-report-and-accounts-2020-to-2021#case-study-4-pre-cast-concrete-drainage-cartel> accessed 13 July 2024.

208 Enterprise Act 2002, s.188.

investigation reference.[209] The CMA has the ability to instigate either a market study or a market investigation into a whole sector, such as the banking sector, where it believes that particular features of the market give rise to an anticompetitive effect.[210] This was a recommended action for the banking sector in the Vickers report.[211] The report found that there were long-standing competition issues in the UK retail banking sector and one of its recommended actions was to consider whether to make a market investigation reference in the next few years if the recommendations in the report do not have sufficient impact and if the OFT (the competition regulator at the time of the Vickers report) or the Competition Commission had not already commenced an investigation by then.[212] The most recent legislative changes to the UK competition regime made by the government in the Digital Markets Act include reforms to the CMA's market investigation powers to improve the regime and to give the CMA more flexibility.[213] These new competition powers, along with the increased investigatory powers[214] and increased extraterritorial reach[215] provided in the Digital Markets Act, could assist the CMA in future investigations of companies colluding to fix prices, similar to that seen in the LIBOR and FX benchmark manipulation.

This book recommends that regulators of the financial services markets use a wider variety of enforcement options in order to create a stronger deterrent to financial crime rather than solely imposing fines on companies to enforce financial crime. For instance, the use of commitments (voluntary behavioural or structural commitments agreed between an infringing party and the FCA or CMA)[216] and directions (specific directions imposed by the regulator in an infringement decision in order to bring the infringement to an end) should be used alongside financial penalties where breaches of competition are found.

In addition, this book recommends that the power of both the CMA and FCA to disqualify directors who are in breach of competition law should be used more frequently if it can be proved that a director knew or ought to

209 Enterprise Act 2002, s161 and Schedule 8.

210 Ashurst LLP, 'The Use of Market Studies and Market Investigations in UK Competition Law' (Ashurst LLP, October 2019) <file:///Users/dianajohnson/Downloads/Quickguide%20-%20The%20use%20of%20market%20studies%20and%20market%20investigations%20in%20UK%20competition%20law.pdf> accessed 18 July 2024.

211 Independent Commission on Banking, 'Independent Commission on Banking: Final Report, Recommendations' (GOV.UK, 12 September 2011) <https://www.gov.uk/government/news/independent-commission-on-banking-final-report> accessed 10 July 2024.

212 D Harrison, *Competition Law and Financial Services* (Routledge 2014).

213 Digital Markets, Competition and Consumers Act 2024, ss.134–140.

214 Ibid, ss.121–123.

215 Ibid, s.119.

216 C Ritter, 'How Far Can the Commission Go When Imposing Remedies for Antitrust Infringements?' (2016) 7(9) *Journal of European Competition Law & Practice* 587.

have known of the actions of an employee of the company.[217] Directors in the financial services sector face an increasing risk from the power of the CMA and FCA to apply for the disqualification of directors of UK companies that have breached competition law.[218] The CMA has secured 29 disqualifications in nine anticompetitive cases in industries ranging from estate agency to pharmaceuticals.[219] In its own words, it has been 'ramping up' its use of this power and has made clear that it now assesses whether to seek disqualifications of company directors in all cases where competition law is broken.[220] This is a positive development because, until 2019, the CMA had only used its powers to disqualify one director;[221] however, currently, almost all the director disqualifications that that the CMA has instituted have been for directors of small and medium-sized companies.[222] No director disqualifications have yet taken place by the FCA, using its competition law powers. This needs to change so that much larger companies, such as the international banks that breach competition law in the UK do not feel that they are immune from competition law but, instead, realise that they need to take steps to avoid breaches of the law.[223]

3.9 Corporate Criminal Liability

As mentioned above when discussing the difference between civil and criminal penalties, there is a significant difference in the perception of society between criminal and civil penalties.[224] Criminal penalties are viewed as the more serious of the two types of penalty. It is argued that, for serious breaches of financial crime, it is more appropriate for UK regulators to impose corporate criminal liability on those companies whose employees have committed the illegal

217 Financial Conduct Authority, 'FG15/8: The FCA's Concurrent Competition Enforcement Powers for the Provision of Financial Services: A Guide to the FCA's Powers and Procedures Under the Competition Act 1998' (Financial Conduct Authority, January 2022) <https://www.fca.org.uk/publication/finalised-guidance/fg15-08.pdf> accessed 18 July 2024.

218 Company Directors Disqualification Act 1986, s.9A and s.9B.

219 Competition and Markets Authority, 'Competition and Markets Authority Cases and Projects' (GOV.UK, 2024) <https://www.gov.uk/cma-cases?case_type%5B%5D=competition-disqualification> accessed 27 July 2024.

220 Bryan Cave Leighton Paisner, 'The CMA Ramps Up Director Disqualifications for Competition Law Breaches' (Bryan Cave Leighton Paisner LLP, 25 March 2021) <https://www.bclplaw.com/en-GB/insights/the-cma-ramps-up-director-disqualifications-for-competition-law-breaches.html> accessed 17 July 2024.

221 Competition and Markets Authority, 'Competition and Markets Authority Cases and Projects' (GOV.UK, 2024) <https://www.gov.uk/cma-cases?case_type%5B%5D=competition-disqualification> accessed 27 July 2024.

222 C Chijioke-Oforji, 'Director Accountability for Breach of Competition Law: Practical Lessons from the CMA's Increased Use of Disqualification Powers' (2020) 42(1) *European Competition Law Review* 24.

223 Ibid.

224 RM White, '"It's Not a Criminal Offence"–or Is It? Thornton's Analysis of "Penal Provisions" and the Drafting of "Civil Penalties"' (2011) 32(1) *Statute Law Review* 193.

acts rather than imposing civil, administrative penalties, which are seen as less serious.[225] However, following the LIBOR and FX benchmark manipulation scandal, no criminal convictions were made against any of the banks involved by UK regulators, unlike in the US, which is discussed in Chapter 6.

As stated in Chapter 2, the main mechanism for imposing criminal corporate liability in the UK is by the identification doctrine, although there are 'failure to prevent' offences under the Bribery Act 2010, the Criminal Finance Act 2017 and the Economic Crime and Corporate Transparency Act 2023 which apply to bribery, tax evasion and fraud.[226] These offences are designed to persuade companies to devise systems to prevent offending by their employees[227] and a recent Law Commission options paper considered the case for a new offence of 'failure to prevent economic crime'.[228] The offence of corporate manslaughter has also been in existence since 2007 for cases in which a company is held responsible for deaths resulting from negligence.[229] But for crimes other than bribery, tax evasion, fraud and corporate manslaughter, the identification doctrine is the general offence used by prosecutors to assign criminal liability to a company. The identification doctrine states that, where a particular mental state is required for a criminal offence, only the mental state of a senior person in the company, such as a director, representing the company's 'directing mind and will' can be attributed to the company.[230] However, for companies with sophisticated governance structures, such as international banks, it has been especially difficult for prosecutors to attribute criminal liability using the identification doctrine.[231] The result of this is that UK companies have historically been unlikely to be prosecuted for suspected criminal behaviour, including financial crime, and if they are prosecuted, they are unlikely to be convicted.[232] However, the recent change to the identification doctrine, made in the Economic Crime and Corporate Transparency Act

225 R Lööf, 'Corporate Agency and White Collar Crime—An Experience-led Case for Causation-based Corporate Liability for Criminal Harms' (2020) 1(4) *Criminal Law Review* 275.

226 See the Bribery Act 2010, s.7, Criminal Finance Act 2017, ss. 45, 46 and the Economic Crime and Corporate Transparency Act 2023, s. 199.

227 SC Brown and B Hertstein, 'Failure to Prevent Money Laundering and the Supervisory Principle' (2022) 8 Criminal Law Review 648.

228 Law Commission, 'Corporate Criminal Liability: An Options Paper' (Law Commission, 10 June 2022) <https://lawcom.gov.uk/project/corporate-criminal-liability/> accessed 10 July 2024.

229 See the Corporate Manslaughter and Corporate Homicide Act 2007.

230 Law Commission, 'Corporate Criminal Liability: A Discussion Paper' (Law Commission, 9 June 2021) <https://www.lawcom.gov.uk/law-commission-seek-views-on-corporate-criminal-liability/> accessed 19 July 2024.

231 K Laird, 'Deferred Prosecution Agreements: The Latest Developments' (2021) 1(4) *Criminal Law Review* 283 and *Serious Fraud Office v Barclays plc and Another* [2018] EWHC 3055 (QB).

232 L Campbell, 'Corporate Liability and the Criminalisation of Failure' (2018) 12(2) *Law and Financial Markets Review* 57.

2023, has expanded the scope of people who can represent the 'directing mind and will' of a company to the company's 'senior managers'.[233] This change is a welcome one, as it will increase the chances of prosecutors of a successful corporate criminal conviction when a senior manager or above has committed a specified financial crime during the course of his or her employment.[234]

This book argues that a corporate criminal offence is needed to attribute criminal liability to companies who commit financial crime. One way of doing this would be to further reform the identification principle to make it apply to all employees of a company who carry out a crime for the benefit of the company during their employment. Another would be to introduce a new criminal liability offence for 'failure to prevent' financial crime, as recommended by the Law Commission. A further method would be to amend the cartel offence so that it can be used to attribute liability to companies whose employees have colluded with competitors for financial gain. It has been suggested by some commentators that the identification doctrine has proved disproportionately difficult to use in order to prosecute larger companies, such as banks, for financial crime committed by senior managers for the company's benefit.[235] The recent reforms to the identification doctrine in the Economic Crime and Corporate Transparency Act 2023, which have extended the identification doctrine to 'senior managers' as well as directors of a company for certain financial crimes,[236] are welcome; however, this reform could go further. Companies in the UK should be liable to criminal prosecution using the principle of vicarious liability when their employees carry out crimes during the course of their employment, either entirely or partially for the benefit of the company due to the impact that these actions have on society. Once corporate criminal liability has been established by prosecutors, enforcement tools such as DPAs can be used if companies are willing to cooperate and provide binding undertakings in relation to their future actions in order to settle the criminal action. This removes the risk of the corporate death penalty and will allow regulators to attribute criminal liability to banks without fear of catastrophic collateral damage. This is discussed further below. One of the reasons DPAs are so extensively used by the DoJ is to allow prosecutors to assign criminal liability to companies whilst minimising the likelihood of corporate death.[237] DPAs are available to UK prosecutors and could be used for the same reason if the laws relating to corporate criminal liability are reformed in the UK.

233 Economic Crime and Corporate Transparency Act 2023, s.196.

234 Ibid.

235 Law Commission, 'Corporate Criminal Liability: A Discussion Paper' (Law Commission, 9 June 2021) <https://www.lawcom.gov.uk/law-commission-seek-views-on-corporate-criminal-liability/> accessed 19 July 2024.

236 Economic Crime and Corporate Transparency Act 2023, s. 196.

237 A Palmer, 'Justice Deferred Is Justice Denied?' in N Ryder and L Pasculli (eds), *Corruption, Integrity and the Law* (Routledge 2020) 90.

Corporate criminal liability has not yet been used in the UK against large global companies in the way that has been seen in the US.[238] Although there was one successful criminal prosecution of a bank in 2021 for money laundering offences.[239] Following the LIBOR and FX crises, the FSA, then the UK's financial regulator at that time, was criticised by the Treasury Select Committee for its decision not to initiate criminal proceedings in relation to the LIBOR and FX manipulation.[240] The Committee said that 'the FSA took a narrow view of its power to initiate criminal proceedings for fraudulent conduct in this case' and recommended that the Government should clarify the FSA and its successors' power to initiate criminal proceedings when there is serious fraudulent conduct in the context of the financial markets.[241] Since the Committee published its report in 2012, two new criminal offences have been created that criminalise individuals for making false or misleading statements or giving false or misleading impressions in relation to a benchmark or investment.[242] However no new corporate criminal offence for financial crime has been introduced to hold companies responsible for the criminal actions of their employees.

As stated above, the SFO has not charged any of the banks involved in the LIBOR and FX crisis with a corporate criminal offence, despite that all the individuals involved in the LIBOR or FX benchmark manipulation cartels were employees at the time and acting to benefit the profits of their employers.[243] In 2016, David Green QC, the then director of the SFO, compared the UK and US approaches to holding banks liable for their involvement in the LIBOR crisis, stating at a symposium that:

> The operation of the identification principle meant that we could not touch the bank for which he [Tom Hayes] worked whilst manipulating Libor. That bank was held to account for Hayes' conduct in a New York courtroom, where vicarious liability made the prosecution a much simpler matter.[244]

238 J Horder and G Watts, 'The scope of Liability for Failure to Prevent Economic Crime' (2021) 10(1) *Criminal Law Review* 851.

239 See *R (FCA) v National Westminster Bank PLC* [2021] <https://www.judiciary.uk/wp-content/uploads/2022/07/FCA-v-Natwest-Sentencing-remarks-131221.pdf> accessed 25 July 2024.

240 House of Commons Treasury Committee, 'Fixing LIBOR: Some Preliminary Findings' (HC 2012-13 HC481-I) 103.

241 Ibid.

242 Financial Services Act 2012, s.91.

243 D Green, 'Report to the Cambridge Symposium on Economic Crime 2016' (Cambridge Symposium on Economic Crime, 5 September 2016) <https://www.sfo.gov.uk/2016/09/05/cambridge-symposium-2016/> accessed 30 July 2024.

244 Ibid.

It can clearly be seen that reform is needed in order for there to be a criminal corporate liability offence that can be used in situations such as the LIBOR and FX manipulation, to attribute liability to international banks when they have committed financial crime to the detriment of society.

3.10 Deferred Prosecution Agreements

Leading on from the discussion of corporate criminal liability above, it is appropriate to consider the use of DPAs in the UK. DPAs are a potential alternative to a conventional prosecution that entail a lower risk and cost for the prosecutor when a corporate criminal offence is discovered.[245] Since 2014, DPAs, described in Chapter 3, have been in use in the UK, enacted by the Crime and Courts Act 2013, for offences set out in that Act, including conspiracy to defraud.[246] The only regulators with power to issue DPAs in the UK are the SFO and the Crown Prosecution Service.[247] DPAs have an important function to play when prosecutors use a corporate criminal liability offence, as they can be used to impose a provisional cessation of litigation in exchange for compliance with its terms, which often contain behavioural commitments from the company.[248] DPAs are often seen as a way of guarding against the risk of corporate death, which from the Arthur Anderson case referred to in Chapter 2, has been seen to be catastrophic in an international company.[249] Their first use was in the case of Standard Bank in 2015, which was accused of failure to prevent bribery contrary to Section 7 of the Bribery Act 2010.[250] The DPA was granted for a three-year period, which expired in November 2018, bringing to an end the criminal charges against the bank. In exchange for dropping the criminal charges after the term of the DPA, Standard Bank had to pay a fine of $25.2m, $7m in compensation to the government of Tanzania and the sum of $330,000 to the SFO for their costs in relation to the investigation and resolution of the DPA.[251] In addition to the financial penalties, Standard Bank agreed to cooperate with the SFO and to be subject to a review of its antibribery and corruption controls. It was also required to implement recommendations made by Price Waterhouse Coopers LLP, who acted as an

245 B Hertstein, M Berry, S Brown, 'Deferred Prosecution Agreements in Jersey: Ways to Buttress the Castle. A Comparative Analysis of Regimes for Deferred Prosecution Agreements in Jersey and the UK' (2024) 3 *Journal of Economic Criminology* 100046, 1.

246 Crime and Courts Act 2013 ss.15 and 45 and Schedule 17.

247 Crime and Courts Act 2013, Schedule 17, para. 3(1).

248 RA Epstein, 'Deferred Prosecution Agreements on Trial' in A Barkow and R Barkow (eds), *Prosecutors in the Boardroom: Using Criminal Law to Regulate Corporate Conduct* (NYU Press Scholarship Online 2011).

249 Ibid.

250 C King and N Lord, 'Deferred Prosecution Agreements in England & Wales: Castles Made of Sand?' (2020) 1(1) *Public Law* 307.

251 Serious Fraud Office Case Information, 'Standard Bank PLC' (Serious Fraud Office, 3 September 2019) <https://www.sfo.gov.uk/cases/standard-bank-plc/> accessed 6 July 2024.

independent reviewer in the case.[252] It has been argued that the use of DPAs are an illustration of restorative justice in action; participating offenders such as Standard Bank work with regulators to manage their offending behaviour and are helped, as part of the DPA, to find both moral- and financial-based opportunities to repair the harm done by them to their victims.[253] Many commentators welcome the use of DPAs as a pragmatic response to corporate crime;[254] however, they are controversial, with other academics arguing that the use of DPAs deprive the right of companies of a fair trial and erode the presumption of innocence.[255]

In total, 12 DPAs have been issued to date by the SFO,[256] with one having been issued by the Crown Prosecution Service (CPS) in December 2023, in which a financial penalty of £615 was imposed on the company.[257] It is estimated that DPAs have secured over £1.7b to the public purse since they were first used in 2014, so there is every chance their use will continue.[258] Due to the well-known limitations of the identification doctrine, outlined above, DPAs have a particular significance in England and Wales; to be able to negotiate a DPA with a corporate body provides a way for prosecutors to circumvent the difficulties that may be encountered in attributing *mens rea* to the entity's directing mind and will under the identification doctrine.[259] However, until the identification doctrine is either reformed or replaced with a new corporate

252 Ibid.

253 D Mcstravick, 'Deferred Prosecution Agreements and the Restorative Justice Paradigm' in N Ryder and Pasculli (eds), *Corruption, Integrity and the Law* (Routledge 2020) 113.

254 B Hertstein, M Berry, S Brown, 'Deferred Prosecution Agreements in Jersey: Ways to Buttress the Castle. A Comparative Analysis of Regimes for Deferred Prosecution Agreements in Jersey and the UK' (2024) 3 *Journal of Economic Criminology* 100046, 11; and R Cheung, 'Deferred Prosecution Agreements: Cooperation and Confession' (2018) *Cambridge Law Journal* 77(1), 12.

255 C King and N Lord, 'Deferred Prosecution Agreements in England and Wales: Castles Made of Sand?' (2020) *Public Law* 2 307; and N Padfield, 'Deferred Prosecution Agreements' (2016) 1(7) *Criminal Law Review* 449.

256 Serious Fraud Office, 'Deferred Prosecution Agreements' (Serious Fraud Office, 2024) <https://www.sfo.gov.uk/publications/guidance-policy-and-protocols/guidance-for-corporates/deferred-prosecution-agreements/> accessed 25 July 2024.

257 Herbert Smith Freehills, 'CPS Secures Its First Deferred Prosecution Agreement' (Herbert Smith Freehills, 19 December 2023) <https://www.herbertsmithfreehills.com/notes/fsrandcorpcrime/2023-12/cps-secures-its-first-deferred-prosecution-agreement/> accessed 25 July 2024 and Crown Prosecution Service, 'First Ever CPS Deferred Prosecution Agreement for £615 million' (CPS, 5 December 2023) <https://www.cps.gov.uk/cps/news/first-ever-cps-deferred-prosecution-agreement-ps615-million> accessed 12 July 2024.

258 Serious Fraud Office, 'Annual Report and Accounts 2022-23' (Serious Fraud Office, 18 July 2023) 19 <https://www.sfo.gov.uk/2023/07/18/annual-report-accounts-2022-23/> accessed 25 July 2024.

259 B Hertstein, M Berry, S Brown, 'Deferred Prosecution Agreements in Jersey: Ways to Buttress the Castle. A Comparative Analysis of Regimes for Deferred Prosecution Agreements in Jersey and the UK' (2024) 3 *Journal of Economic Criminology* 100046, 11; and K Laird,

criminal liability offence that can be used to prosecute companies for financial crime, the use of DPAs will lag behind that of the US, when companies know that the threat of prosecution is lurking in the background.[260]

3.11 Conclusion

This chapter has considered the enforcement of the LIBOR and FX crisis in the UK through the lens of competition law. It has evaluated the benefits of using competition law in the enforcement of future benchmark manipulation and has concluded that the wide range of significant enforcement powers that a competition law enforcement action provides to the regulator have the potential to provide a strong deterrent to the crime of benchmark manipulation. This chapter recommends that the FCA and CMA use competition law, with its wide variety of enforcement options, to enforce the financial crime of benchmark manipulation rather than continuing to use regulatory fines as the sole enforcement tool against companies. Before taking direct regulatory enforcement, the FCA is now obliged to consider whether enforcement under the Competition Act is more appropriate than taking enforcement action under its own regulatory powers (the 'primacy' of competition law for regulators, as provided for by the Enterprise and Regulatory Reform Act 2013).[261] It remains to be seen, though, whether the FCA's ability to use its competition law powers will be sufficient to ensure that competition law is used in any future benchmark manipulation cartel in the financial services sector. A change in attitude, not just in law, by the financial services regulator will be needed for the FCA to use the competition enforcement powers it now has.

The sanctions imposed by the UK financial services regulator against banks for the manipulation by their employees of the LIBOR and FX benchmark interest rates were not sufficient – almost all of Tom Hayes' compatriots are still working, but there were multiple cartels and traders from multiple banks involved in the manipulation. It must be considered how a similar benchmark manipulation cartel would be identified if one was in existence now and what laws/regulation would be used to enforce it. Cartels are notoriously difficult to spot, and once identified, they are extremely difficult to prove.[262] The CMA relies on its competition law leniency provisions, referred to above, in which whistleblowers are encouraged to come forward with evidence of a cartel in return for either immunity from prosecution or a financial reward of up to

'Deferred Prosecution Agreements: The Latest Developments' (2021) 1(4) *Criminal Law Review* 283.

260 C King and N Lord, 'Deferred Prosecution Agreements in England & Wales: Castles Made of Sand?' (2020) 1(1) *Public Law* 307.

261 Enterprise and Regulatory Reform Act 2013, Schedule 14

262 H Van de Bunt, 'Walls of Secrecy and Silence: The Madoff Case and Cartels in the Construction Industry' (2010) 9(3) *Criminology and Public Policy* 435.

£250,000.[263] However, it is questionable whether the current reward for an individual whistleblower as part of the CMA's leniency policy is sufficiently high to be a realistic incentive in the financial services sector. The competition law leniency policy for cartels was in operation at the time of the LIBOR manipulation, but it was not used by a whistleblower then and there is no reason to suppose that it would be used if another cartel was in existence now or in the future. This book recommends that the FCA and CMA urgently take additional measures to bolster the cartel whistleblowing/leniency system in order to increase the likelihood of future cartels being brought to their attention. In particular, the CMA and the FCA should consider ways of increasing the profile and awareness of the carrel leniency provisions amongst banks and their staff, with the aim of increasing the likelihood of an early notification of a cartel in the future. Further, it would help to reassess and reset the financial reward offered to cartel whistleblowers, which does not appear to be set high enough at present, given the rewards a cartel will deliver to its members.

The creation of a criminal corporate offence for the FCA and/or CMA to use against companies is also recommended. As stated above, this could either be brought into being by further amendment to the identification doctrine following the US model of vicarious liability, the creation of a new 'failure to prevent financial crime' offence and/or the alteration of the cartel offence to apply to companies as well as to individuals. Any such corporate criminal liability offence could then be used in conjunction with DPAs with companies who wish to cooperate with the regulators to regulate their future behaviour. These are aspects of the competition law regime that should be addressed as a matter of urgency by the two UK competition regulators to ensure that the competition enforcement powers are more likely to be used for future benchmark manipulation cartels in the UK.

It is clear however, that without a significant change of attitude by the UK financial services regulator, competition law will not be used to enforce financial crime. The FCA is currently 'talking the talk' when referring to its motivation for using its new Competition Act powers; it is stated in the 2019 Memorandum of Understanding between the FCA and the CMA that 'The CMA and the FCA seek to use their powers to achieve more competitive outcomes in the financial services industry in the UK'.[264] However, just because the FCA now has competition powers and speaks positively in public about

263 Competition and Markets Authority, 'Blowing the Whistle on Cartels' (GOV.UK, 6 June 2023) <https://www.gov.uk/government/news/blowing-the-whistle-on-cartels#:~:text=The%20Competition%20and%20Markets%20Authority,cartel%20activity%20they%20have%20witnessed.> accessed 27 July 2024.

264 Financial Conduct Authority, Competition and Markets Authority, 'Memorandum of Understanding Between the Competition and Markets Authority and the Financial Conduct Authority – Concurrent Competition Powers' (Financial Conduct Authority, July 2019) <https://www.fca.org.uk/publication/mou/fca-cma-concurrent-competition-powers-mou.pdf> accessed 19 July 2024.

its use and intended use of them, it does not mean it will use them if future benchmark manipulation cartels come to light. As set out above, the CEO of the FCA's predecessor did not want competition law to be used in the enforcement of LIBOR manipulation in 2009 and wrote to the OFT warning of 'financial stability implications' of announcing a competition law investigation into LIBOR at that time.[265] Additionally, the Parliamentary Commission on Banking Standards stated that competition economists had expressed concern about how seriously the FCA would take its competition remit.[266] They were concerned, in particular, that the FCA would continue to use regulation rather than competition laws as its primary tool.[267] This concern appears to have materialised because the FCA has only concluded two cases since 2015, almost ten years, using its competition law powers and the fines imposed were significantly lower than the 10% of worldwide turnover maximum fine that could have been imposed. [268] In addition to this, the paucity of other competition law cases in the financial services sector is also concerning; the FCA has opened a total of eight Competition Act cases in the financial sector since gaining competition law powers; however, three were closed without a decision, and only three, commenced in September 2020, remain open.[269] So it appears that something is holding back the regulator from using its concurrent competition powers instead of its pre-existing regulatory powers, with which it is more familiar. There may be a lingering concern in the FCA about penalising banks too severely for breach of financial crimes, as enunciated in the 2013 report of the Parliamentary Committee on Banking Standards, in which it states that the Parliamentary Commission was 'warned that over-zealous action to improve banking standards would damage the competitiveness of British banks and of the UK as a financial centre' and that 'measures which

265 Financial Services Authority, 'Internal Audit Report: A Review of The Extent of Awareness Within the FSA of Inappropriate LIBOR Submissions' (Financial Services Authority, March 2013) Communication 65 (event) on pages 80-81 <https://www.fca.org.uk/publication/corporate/fsa-ia-libor.pdf> accessed 18 July 2024.

266 Parliamentary Commission on Banking Standards, 'Changing Banking for Good' (HL 2013-14 HL 27-II, HC 171-II).

267 Ibid para. 1075.

268 Financial Conduct Authority, 'FCA Issues Its First Decision under Competition Law' (Financial Conduct Authority, 21 February 2019) <https://www.fca.org.uk/news/press-releases/fca-issues-its-first-decision-under-competition-law> accessed 2 July 2024; and Financial Conduct Authority, 'FCA Fines Three Money Transfer Firms for Breaking Competition Law' (Financial Conduct Authority, 30 November 2023) <https://www.fca.org.uk/news/press-releases/fca-fines-three-money-transfer-firms-breaking-competition-law> accessed 2 July 2024.

269 Competition and Markets Authority, 'Competition Act 1998 Cases in the Regulated Sectors' (GOV.UK, 20 December 2023) <https://www.gov.uk/government/publications/competition-act-1998-cases-in-the-sectors-regulated-by-ukcn-members/competition-act-1998-cases-in-the-regulated-sectors> accessed 2 July 2024.

reduce London's attractiveness to banks could result in wider damage to the economy'.[270] However, it can be seen from the competition law enforcement that took place in the EU and US for the same manipulation of the LIBOR and FX benchmarks, that the significantly larger fines and other penalties handed out by regulators have not resulted in harm to the competitiveness of the banks or to the EU or US as financial centres, but more of a deterrent will be felt in the EU and US as a result of the stronger penalties. If these fears continue to hold back the FCA from using its competition enforcement powers, a change in attitude is urgently needed.

270 Parliamentary Commission on Banking Standards, 'Changing Banking for Good' (HL 2013-14 HL 27-II, HC 171-II).

4 EU Competition Law and Financial Crime

4.1 Introduction

The aim of this chapter is to examine the way in which the European Union (EU) enforced the instances of London Interbank Offered Rate (LIBOR) and Foreign Exchange (FX) benchmark manipulation.[1] In particular, this chapter investigates how the EU used its competition law rather than its market abuse powers to enforce the LIBOR and FX scandal.[2] This chapter critically considers the sanctions available to EU regulators when competition law is used to enforce the financial crime of market manipulation and will analyse legislative changes to the EU's market abuse regime following the LIBOR and FX scandals to determine whether competition law is likely to be the most appropriate enforcement mechanism for regulators to use to enforce future incidents of benchmark manipulation.[3]

The chapter commences by investigating how financial crime and competition law developed in the EU prior to the LIBOR and FX scandals. The EU enforcement strategies for the LIBOR and FX benchmark manipulation scandals are then examined. In particular, it will be seen that the LIBOR and the FX cases both took place whilst the 2003 Market Abuse Directive (MAD 2003)[4] was in force, but the EU used its competition law powers to enforce the market abuse of benchmark manipulation. Therefore, this chapter considers whether the 2014 (MAD 2014),[5] passed after the LIBOR and FX enforcement had taken place, will provide suitable enforcement options for regulators in individual Member States should further market manipulation offences take

1 C Lim, 'Libor, Strategy, and International Cartel Investigations' (2013) 4(1) *Journal of European Competition Law & Practice* 87.

2 B Horváth and S Szentléleky, 'Competition Law Enforcement in the Financial Markets' (2014) 59(1) *Public Finance Quarterly* (Budapest, Hungary) 28.

3 H Andersson, 'Fighting Insider Dealing at All Costs? - Due Process Aspects on The EU Market Abuse Regime' (2022) 17(2) *Capital Markets Law Journal* 196.

4 Directive 2003/6/EC of the European Parliament and of the Council of 28 January 2003 on Insider Dealing and Market Manipulation (Market Abuse) [2003] OJ 2 96/01.

5 Directive 2014/57/EU of the European Parliament and of the Council of 16 April 2014 on Criminal Sanctions for Market Abuse (Market Abuse Directive) [2014] OJ 2 173/179.

DOI: 10.4324/9781003425106-4

place in the future, or whether the competition laws are the best suited to enforce financial cartels of the sort seen in the LIBOR and FX.[6] Four separate, but linked themes will be considered in this chapter. First, the EU competition law whistleblowing and leniency regimes will be examined, as these are considered by regulators as an essential tool in cartel enforcement[7]. Then the use of criminal sanctions compared to civil sanctions will be considered and analysed in order to determine their deterrent effect, and it will be considered whether the regulators make full use of the powers they have. The chapter will conclude by looking at issues raised by corporate criminal liability and the use of deferred prosecution agreements (DPAs) as an alternative to the imposition of criminal sanctions.[8] DPAs are not currently used by the European Commission, although they are in use in some Member States. The conclusion analyses the European Commission's use of competition law in the enforcement of the LIBOR and FX scandal and draws conclusions as to its efficacy in punishing and deterring benchmark manipulation. Proposals for reforms are also made.

4.2 Development of Financial Services Regulation in the EU

The EU has a strong incentive to counter financial crime. The European Commission has stated that financial crime hampers trust in the market and undermines consumer confidence to engage in market transactions.[9] Commentators have observed that the EU's fight against financial crime appears to have departed from the internal market-based formula of the removal of obstacles from trade and, instead, ventured into the criminal law domain.[10] This demonstrates the importance the EU attaches to its fight against financial crime, as evidenced by the strong enforcement action taken by the Commission against the banks involved in the LIBOR and FX benchmark manipulation. It is impossible to quantify the cost of financial crime, although the United Nations estimates that the crime of money laundering (a type of market abuse) alone accounts for an estimated 2%–5% of global GDP

6 S Wilson, 'The New Market Abuse Regulation and Directive on Criminal Sanctions for Market Abuse: European Capital Markets Law and New Global Trends in Financial Crime Enforcement' (2015) 16(3) *ERA-Forum* 427.

7 NH Miller, 'Strategic Leniency and Cartel Enforcement' (2009) 99(3) *The American Economic Review* 750.

8 K Hardcastle, 'International Double Jeopardy and Deferred Prosecution Agreements' (2018) 12(1) *Criminal Law Review* 946.

9 C Gómez-Jara Díez and E Herlin-Karnell, 'Prosecuting EU Financial Crimes: The European Public Prosecutor's Office in Comparison to the US Federal Regime' (2018) 19(5) *German Law Journal* 1191.

10 E Herlin-Karnell and N Ryder, 'The Robustness of EU Financial Crimes Legislation: A Critical Review of the EU and UK Anti-Fraud and Money Laundering Scheme' (2017) 27(4) *European Business Law Review* 427.

or $800b–$2t.[11] This does not take into account the cost to global economies of market manipulation, another type of financial crime classified as market abuse. Ryder states that it is impossible to accurately state the extent of financial crime but points out that it has an adverse impact on the economies of countries.[12]

The World Economic Forum (WEF) states that financial crime is a trillion-dollar industry and that it takes an enormous toll on society.[13] The WEF stresses that it is imperative that public and private sector organisations, such as banks, work in partnership with each other to share data and information globally to make an impact on financial crime and the untold societal harm it can bring.[14] The high financial and societal cost of financial crime formed the context for the introduction of the market abuse enforcement strategy of the European Commission, based on two directives and one regulation. These laws are the most relevant financial legislation to the LIBOR and FX crisis and will be introduced here. The definitions of market abuse and market manipulation used in this chapter will now be outlined, the chapter then moves on to introduce the integral EU legislation and regulatory agencies for market abuse.

There is no comprehensive definition of 'market abuse', although the term is generally used as an umbrella term to cover the financial crimes of insider dealing and market manipulation.[15] This is borne out by the EU's Market Abuse Regulation (MAR 2014)[16] in which market abuse is defined as consisting of the offences of 'insider dealing, the unlawful disclosure of inside information and market manipulation'.[17] The MAD 2014 uses the same definition of market abuse[18] and explains that 'market abuse harms the integrity of financial markets and public confidence in securities, derivatives and benchmarks'.[19] Definitions of market manipulation vary. For instance, the UK's former national fraud and cybercrime reporting centre, Action Fraud, describes market manipulation as conduct that can 'mislead others into making the wrong

11 United Nations, 'Money-Laundering' (United Nations, April 2024) <https://www.unodc.org/unodc/en/money-laundering/overview.html> accessed 8 July 2024.

12 N Ryder, *Financial Crime in the 21st Century* (Edward Elgar 2011) 4; and B Unger, *The Scale and Impacts of Money Laundering* (Edward Elgar 2007).

13 D Craig, 'Why We Need to Talk About Financial Crime' (World Economic Forum, 12 January 2018) <https://www.weforum.org/agenda/2018/01/we-need-to-talk-about-financial-crime/> accessed 30 July 2024.

14 Ibid.

15 See for example B Rider, A Kern, A Stuart, and B Jeffrey, *Market Abuse and Insider Dealing* (Bloomsbury Publishing Plc, 2022) 115.

16 Regulation (EU) No 596/2014 of the European Parliament and of the Council of 16 April 2014 on Market Abuse (Market Abuse Regulation) OJ L173/1.

17 Ibid, Article 1.

18 Ibid.

19 Ibid, Preamble (1).

investment decisions'.[20] The US Securities and Exchange Commission defines market manipulation as 'intentional conduct designed to deceive investors by controlling or artificially affecting the market'.[21] Essentially these definitions describe conduct that amounts to fraud, and each refers to deception and the misleading of investors. Academics have described market manipulation as an:

> Unwarranted interference in the operation of ordinary market forces of supply and demand; an interference in the market's normal price-forming mechanism.[22]

Others agree that there is no single definition of market manipulation, and that various agencies, sectors and scholars define it differently.[23] Hamburger proposes that market manipulation should be defined as occurring when a party intentionally causes 'a price which does not reflect the market or economic forces of supply and demand operating upon the price of the particular market'.[24] These varying definitions of market manipulation and market abuse all demonstrate the harmful nature of this financial crime and the importance of enforcing sanctions against offending banks and individuals when any form of market manipulation takes place.

The MAD 2003 was introduced to harmonise the insider dealing and market manipulation laws. The Directive stated that its objective was to create a level playing field for all financial markets in the EU[25] and to encourage closer cooperation between national authorities in each Member State in the enforcement of market abuse.[26] Following the LIBOR and FX scandals, the EU reformed its market abuse regime by introducing the MAR 2014 and MAD 2014, both of which provide that it is a criminal offence to engage in market manipulation.[27] The MAR 2014 and MAD 2014 both define market

20 Action Fraud, 'Market Manipulation' (Action Fraud, 2024) <https://www.actionfraud.police.uk/a-z-of-fraud/market-manipulation> accessed 8 July 2024.

21 Securities and Exchange Commission, 'Manipulation' (US Securities and Exchange Commission, March 28 2008) <https://www.sec.gov/fast-answers/answerstmanipulhtm.html> accessed 3 July 2024.

22 E Lomnicka, 'Preventing and Controlling the Manipulation of Financial Markets: Towards a Definition of "Market Manipulation"' (2001) 8(4) *Journal of Financial Crime* 297, 297.

23 K Sergakis, *The Law of Capital Markets in the EU: Disclosure and Enforcement* (Palgrave 2018) 174; and J Hamburger, 'Crowding the Market: Is There Room for Antitrust in Market Manipulation Cases?' (2015) 21(4) *International Trade Law & Regulation* 120, 121.

24 J Hamburger, 'Crowding the Market: Is There Room for Antitrust in Market Manipulation Cases?' (2015) 21(4) *International Trade Law & Regulation* 120, 121.

25 Directive 2003/6/EC of the European Parliament and of the Council of 28 January 2003 on Insider Dealing and Market Manipulation (Market Abuse) [2003] OJ 2 96/01), Preamble 11.

26 Ibid., Preamble (36).

27 Regulation (EU) No 596/2014 of the European Parliament and of the Council of 16 April 2014 on Market Abuse (Market Abuse Regulation) [2014] OJ 2 173/1, Article 12; and Directive 2014/57/EU of the European Parliament and of the Council of 16 April 2014

manipulation as, *inter alia*, the transmitting of false or misleading information that manipulates the calculation of a benchmark.[28] This part of the definition was a new addition for MAR 2014 and MAD 2014 and did not feature in the definition of market manipulation in the EU's first market abuse Directive. The prohibition of market manipulation applies to both natural and legal persons in the MAR 2014 and MAD 2014, with natural persons who participate in the decision to carry out activities for the legal person being held responsible.[29] A key reason for the European Commission to use its competition law powers to enforce the LIBOR and FX market manipulation is likely to be that the definition of market manipulation in the MAD 2003 was not wide enough to give the regulators a strong case against the banks and brokers involved. In any event, the MAR 2003 did not carry criminal sanctions, so using the civil enforcement powers of the EU competition laws, which clearly prohibit cartels and collusive behaviour between competitors, was presumably identified by the regulator as a better fit for the benchmark manipulation.

4.3 Development of EU Competition Law and Policy

In this section, the development of EU competition law and policy will be analysed, with a particular focus on the area of competition law relevant to the enforcement of the LIBOR and FX benchmark manipulation.

The earliest competition laws for what is now the EU[30] were introduced in the Treaty of Rome in 1957, which created the European Economic Community (EEC). The Treaty of Rome established a single market between the six original members of the EEC and introduced the four freedoms of movement – of goods, services, capital and people.[31] The aim of the four freedoms and of the internal market was to eliminate Member States' barriers to trade and competition law was used to ensure that Member States would not re-erect these barriers or abuse their powers.[32] Competition law was at the heart of the EEC, with its first mention being in the Treaty of Rome, which mandated the creation of 'a system ensuring that competition in the internal market is not distorted'.[33]

on Criminal Sanctions for Market Abuse (Market Abuse Directive) [2014] OJ 2 173/179, Article 5(1).

28 Regulation (EU) No 596/2014 of the European Parliament and of the Council of 16 April 2014 on Market Abuse (Market Abuse Regulation) [2014] OJ 2 173/1, Article 12(1)(d).

29 Ibid, Article 12(4).

30 The European Union was created in the Treaty of Lisbon of 2009, taking over from the original European Economic Community and from the subsequent (from the Maastrict Treaty of 1992) European Community.

31 EM Fox and D Gerard, *EU Competition Law Cases, Texts and Context* (Edward Elgar Publishing 2017) xxv.

32 Ibid.

33 Treaty of Rome 1957, Article 3(1)(f).

The EU competition law rules govern anticompetitive agreements,[34] the abuse of a dominant market position by one or more undertakings,[35] the application of competition rules to public undertakings[36] and the prohibition of state aid to undertakings by Member States.[37] Another area of competition law is the EU Merger Regulation, which applies to concentrations between undertakings that have an EU dimension.[38] Article 101 of the Treaty for the Functioning of the EU (Article 101),[39] which governs anticompetitive agreements, is the most relevant to the enforcement of benchmark manipulation and is the primary focus of this chapter.[40] In order to establish that a breach of Article 101 has occurred, the Commission, as the principal competition regulator in the EU, must demonstrate that all three elements of Article 101 have been breached. The three elements are, first, that there must be an agreement between businesses,[41] a decision by association of undertakings[42] or a concerted practice between businesses. Second, the agreement or practice must have an effect on trade between Member States. Third, the agreement must have as its object or effect the prevention, restriction or distortion of competition within the internal market.[43] An agreement to fix prices, such as the price-fixing of benchmark interest rates seen in the LIBOR and FX benchmark manipulation cartels, is listed in Article 101(1) as an example of an agreement that would be viewed as a restriction or distortion of competition for the purposes of Article 101(1).[44] If all three criteria are met, then a breach of Article 101 will be established, thus rendering the agreement automatically void and unenforceable and the parties subject to penalties.[45] There are three 'safe harbours' that businesses who are in breach of Article 101 may be eligi-

34 Consolidated version of the Treaty on the Functioning of the European Union 2012, Article 101.
35 Ibid, Article 102.
36 Ibid, Article 106.
37 Ibid, Articles 107–109.
38 Council Regulation 139/2004 on the Control of Concentrations Between Undertakings, OJ [2004] L24/1.
39 Consolidated version of the Treaty on the Functioning of the European Union 2012, Article 101.
40 D Scheld and others, 'Managing Antitrust Risks in the Banking Industry' (2016) 12(1) *European Competition Journal* 113.
41 The word 'agreement' for the purposes of Article 101 is not limited to formal/written agreements but has been defined broadly as a 'concurrence of wills', see *Bayer v Commission* Case T-41-96 EU:T:2000:242.
42 The word 'undertaking' is used interchangeably with 'business' or 'company' in this book using the concept of an undertaking as being every entity engaged in an economic activity defined by the Court of Justice in *Hofner and Elser v Macrotron GmbH*, Case C-41/90 EU:C:1991:161, para 21.
43 Consolidated version of the Treaty on the Functioning of the European Union OJ *C 326*, Article 101(1).
44 Ibid, Article 101(1)(a).
45 Ibid, Article 101(2).

ble for, none of which were relevant to the LIBOR or FX market manipulation because price-fixing is one of the most damaging forms of behaviour to competition and price-fixing cartels are seen as 'hard-core' (the most serious) cartels, for which no exemptions apply.[46]

If all three elements of Article 101(1) are exist, the European Commission (the Commission) or any Member State Competition Authority has a range of penalties to use for breach of competition law, which include the imposition of fines of up to 10% of a company's worldwide turnover, the acceptance of behavioural or structural commitments, the imposition of directions and of interim measures.[47] These enforcement powers have changed since the first competition enforcement powers were introduced by virtue of Regulation 17/62 (Regulation 17).[48] Regulation 17 gave the Commission the power to carry out unannounced visits, known as 'dawn raids', to businesses suspected of being in breach of the competition rules, a power that is still in existence.[49] The power to make unannounced visits when the Commission suspects a breach of competition law was used in the Commission's investigation of the LIBOR benchmark manipulation.[50] It also required all businesses to prenotify the Commission if an agreement breached or might breach Article 101. However, with the increase in the number of Member States from six to 28 through the enlargement of the then EEC,[51] the Commission was overwhelmed with the large administrative burden that the prior-notification of anticompetitive agreements required by Regulation 17 had placed on it.[52] Therefore, a new regulation came into force in 2004, known as Regulation 1.[53] The changes introduced by Regulation 1 included the abolition of the

46 R Whish and D Bailey, *Competition Law* (10th edn, Oxford University Press 2021).

47 Council Regulation (EC) No 1/2003 of 16 December 2002 On the Implementation of the Rules on Competition Laid Down in Articles 81 And 82 of the Treaty [2004] OJ L 1 0001, Articles 23, 9, 7 and 8; and L Kjolbye, 'Consistent Application of EU Competition Law, The Case for Revisiting the Consistency Tool Box in Regulation 1/2003' (2020) 11(8) *Journal of European Competition Law & Practice* 456, 456.

48 EEC Council: Regulation No 17: First Regulation Implementing Articles 85 and 86 of the Treaty [1962] OJ 2 13/204.

49 EM Fox and D Gerard, *EU Competition Law Cases, Texts and Context* (Edward Elgar Publishing 2017) 9; and Council Regulation (EC) No 1/2003 of 16 December 2002 on the Implementation of the Rules on Competition Laid Down in Articles 81 and 82 of the Treaty [2004] OJ L 1 0001, Article 20.

50 See European Commission, 'AMENDED - Antitrust: Commission Fines Banks € 149 Billion for Participating in Cartels in the Interest Rate Derivatives Industry' (European Commission, 4 December 2013) <https://ec.europa.eu/commission/presscorner/detail/en/IP_13_1208> accessed 1 July 2024.

51 European Union, 'The History of the European Union' (European Union, 30 April 2020) <https://europa.eu/european-union/about-eu/history_en> accessed 13 July 2024.

52 EM Fox and D Gerard, *EU Competition Law Cases, Texts and Context* (Edward Elgar Publishing 2017) 10.

53 Council Regulation (EC) No 1/2003 of 16 December 2002 on the Implementation of the Rules on Competition Laid Down in Articles 81 and 82 of the Treaty [2004] OJ L 1 0001.

requirement for businesses across the EU to notify the Commission of all agreements that they considered to be in breach of Article 101.[54] Prior to Regulation 1, the Commission was required to carry out an analysis of each prenotified agreement and either approve it as not being in breach of Article 101 or state that it would be in breach.[55] The removal of the requirement to prenotify potentially anticompetitive agreements drastically reduced the Commission's workload, allowing it to focus on the most serious competition law breaches, including cartels, which the Commission describes as 'the most flagrant example of illegal conduct infringing Article 101'.[56] Regulation 1 also introduced a new, decentralised network of competition authorities, known as the National Competition Authorities, and national courts to assist the Commission in the enforcement of EU competition laws.[57] This change to the enforcement of EU competition law from the Commission as sole enforcer to each Member State's national competition authority being able to enforce EU competition laws alongside its national laws also resulted in the Commission having more time to spend on enforcing cartels, which, in turn, resulted in a notable increase in fines for cartels.[58]

Therefore, it can be seen that the EU has very well-established competition laws and that, following the introduction of Regulation 1, competition law has been relaunched as a key tool to restore trust in the markets.[59] The success of the EU's use of competition law to enforce the LIBOR and FX manipulation cartels, detailed below, demonstrates that competition law is a powerful tool and that it is well suited for use in financial markets, although banks and some commentators have argued for many years against the use of competition law in the financial markets to enforce the financial crime of benchmark manipulation.[60] However, the EU has made it clear that, from a competition law point of view, banks are not treated differently from other 'undertakings'.[61]

54 L Kjolbye, 'Consistent Application of EU Competition Law, The Case for Revisiting the Consistency Tool Box in Regulation 1/2003' (2020) 11(8) *Journal of European Competition Law & Practice* 456, 456.

55 Ibid.

56 N Rollings, 'Babcock and Wilcox Ltd, the "Babcock Family" and Regulation 17/62: A Business Response to New Competition Policy in The Early 1960s' (2020) 62(5) *Business History* 743.

57 BJ Rodger and A MacCulloch, *Competition Law and Policy in the EC and UK* (4th edition, Routledge Cavendish 2009) 24.

58 EM Fox and D Gerard, *EU Competition Law Cases, Texts and Context* (Edward Elgar Publishing 2017) 10.

59 S Konstantinos and M Iacovides, 'The Goals of EU Competition Law: A Comprehensive Empirical Investigation' (2022) 1(1) *Legal Studies* (Society of Legal Scholars) 1.

60 See, for example, AK Pascall, 'Tail Wagging the Dog: The Manipulation of Benchmark Rates - A Competitive Bone of Contention' (2016) 39(2) *World Competition* 161; and A Oredegbe, 'Competition and Banking Industry Stability: How Do BRICS and G7 Compare?' (2022) 21(1) *Journal of Emerging Market Finance* 7.

61 B Horvath, 'Development of the Applicability of European Competition Law on Banks As Undertakings' (2017) 38(9) *European Competition Law Review* 423; and D Harrison, *Competition Law and Financial Services* (Routledge 2014) 76.

Two EU competition law cases involving banks illustrate this message. First, in *Austrian Banks*[62] the Court of Justice of the EU (CJEU) upheld the European Commission's decision to fine eight Austrian banks €124.26m for their participation in a cartel.[63] The banks appealed the decision, stating that the banking sector should be treated differently to other market sectors due to its 'special economic context'. This argument was rejected by the European Commission, with the Competition Commissioner at the time saying that:

> The Commission is committed to making the application of the competition rules to the financial services sector one of its top priorities.[64]

The second case, *Asnef-Equifax*,[65] involved banks in Spain who were alleged to have participated in an anticompetitive exchange of information between competitor banks and reinforced the view of the European Commission that competition law should be applied in the same way in the financial sector as it is to other markets. This laid the foundations for the EU's investigation into and enforcement of competition law in the LIBOR and FX benchmark manipulation cartels.

The European Commission has used its power to fine companies involved in cartels the maximum fine of 10% of their worldwide turnover in 25 of the 461 cartel cases decided since 2011.[66] An example of this is the Daimler trucks cartel in which competitors were found to have breached Article 101 with collusive arrangements on pricing and gross price increases. The cartel members were fined €2.9b. The European Commission has fined cartels in the financial services sector a total of €3.891b since 2013.[67] For participation in the euro interest rates derivatives cartel, further details of which are set out below, fines totalling €1.3b were imposed between 2013 and 2021 by the Commission, with the FX fines amounting to €1.4b in 2019 and 2021.[68] Fines imposed by the European Commission for competition infringements are high

62 *Bank Austria Creditanstalt AG v Commission of the European Communities*, Case T-198/03.

63 B Horvath, 'Development of the Applicability of European Competition Law on Banks as Undertakings' (2017) 38(9) *European Competition Law Review* 423.

64 European Commission, 'Mario Monti European Commissioner for Competition Policy Competition Policy and Financial Services, European Banking Congress 1999 Frankfurt 19 November 1999' (European Commission, 22 November 1999) <https://ec.europa.eu/commission/presscorner/detail/en/SPEECH_99_171> accessed 24 July 2024.

65 *Asnef-Equifax, Servicios de Información sobre Solvencia y Crédito, SL v Asociación de Usuarios de Servicios Bancarios (Ausbanc)*, Case C-238/05.

66 European Commission, 'Statistics on Cartel Cases' (European Commission, 10 December 2021) <https://ec.europa.eu/competition-policy/cartels/statistics_en> accessed 21 July 2024.

67 Ibid.

68 European Commission, 'Statistics on Cartel Cases' (European Commission, 10 December 2021) <https://ec.europa.eu/competition-policy/cartels/statistics_en> accessed 21 July 2024.

by international standards.[69] When these fines are compared to those imposed by the Financial Conduct Authority (FCA) on the same banks for the same benchmark manipulation in the UK, as set out in Chapter 3, a significant disparity can be seen in favour of the EU fines. This indicates that the use of competition law to enforce benchmark manipulation can result in an increased deterrent effect when enforcement powers are used effectively and to their full extent by regulators.

Now that the development of financial regulation and competition law in the run up to the LIBOR and FX crisis has been outlined, the next section will look at the enforcement action taken in the EU in response to the benchmark manipulation cartels.

4.4 The LIBOR Scandal and Enforcement in the EU

This section of the chapter will look at the enforcement action taken following the LIBOR benchmark manipulation. The enforcement of the FX benchmark manipulation will be dealt with separately, as the Commission opened six cartel cases overall – three for the LIBOR manipulation and three for the FX manipulation.

Two international incidents of market manipulation came to light in 2012[70] and 2013[71] and involved the manipulation of the LIBOR and Euro Interbank Offered Rate (EURIBOR) benchmark interest rates in 2012 (which will be dealt with together in this section) and the FX benchmark interest rate in 2013.[72] The manipulation of the LIBOR and EURIBOR benchmark interest rates between 2005 and 2011 had a global impact, because the banks[73] who were found to be involved in making fraudulent submissions about the rate at which they would lend money to another bank all operate internationally.[74] The banks were penalised for their actions in various jurisdictions. The US, EU and also individual Member States, such as the UK, all levied fines on the banks found to have manipulated the LIBOR for their own profit. It is notable that the Commission used competition law to impose fines on the banks.[75]

69 R Alexander, 'Flogging the Wrong: EU corporate Fines Violate the Fundamental Rights of Shareholders' (2021) 12(4) *Journal of European Competition Law & Practice* 301, 302; and C Veljanovski, 'Deterrence, Recidivism, and European Cartel Fines' (2011) 7(4) *Journal of Competition Law & Economics* 871.

70 J Fouquau and PK Spieser, 'Statistical Evidence About LIBOR Manipulation: A 'Sherlock Holmes' Investigation' (2015) 50(1) *Journal of Banking and Finance* 632.

71 P Augar, 'How the Forex Scandal Happened' (*BBC News*, 20 May 2015) <https://www.bbc.co.uk/news/business-30003693> accessed 14 July 2024.

72 See Chapter 2 for brief outlines of each benchmark interest rate.

73 The banks involved in each cartel are detailed below but include Barclays, Deutsche Bank, RBS, Société Générale Crédit Agricole, HSBC and JPMorgan.

74 Ibid.

75 B Horvath, 'Development of the Applicability of European Competition Law on Banks as Undertakings' (2017) 38(9) *European Competition Law Review* 423.

As mentioned above, it is likely that the Commission considered that it had a stronger case against the banks and brokers implicated in the benchmark manipulation by using its competition law powers rather than the powers available under the market abuse regime. Under MAD 2003, the Directive in force at the time the cartels came to light, the enforcement was designed to be carried out by a 'single administrative authority' in each Member State rather than by the European Commission,[76] but the market manipulation that took place in the LIBOR and FX scandals occurred across the whole of the EU, so having a single regulator to enforce the market manipulation, as would be the case with competition law breaches that concern multiple Member States, was a more efficient way of enforcing the offences than having multiple Member States' financial authorities taking action against the same banks and brokers. This may have influenced the decision by the Commission to enforce the benchmark manipulation entirely with competition law.

The European Commission started its investigation into the alleged manipulation of the LIBOR and FX benchmarks in October 2011 by way of unannounced visits to the premises of companies suspected in participation in the cartel.[77] The Commission used its competition law powers under Article 101 of the Treaty on the Functioning of the European Union, as the basis for its enforcement action.[78] It opened a total of three cases for the manipulation of the LIBOR and EURIBOR benchmark interest rates. The European Commission established in each cartel case that there were arrangements between the banks:

> Which can either be classified as agreements or concerted practices within which the competitors knowingly substituted practical cooperation between them for the risks of competition.[79]

These arrangements consisted of online chat room messages, emails and phone contacts.[80] This conduct met the first criteria of Article 101, demon-

76 Directive 2003/6/EC of the European Parliament and of the Council of 28 January 2003 on Insider Dealing and Market Manipulation (Market Abuse) [2003] OJ 2 96/01), Article 11.

77 European Commission, 'Antitrust: Commission Confirms Inspections in Suspected Cartel in the Sector of Euro Interest Rate Derivatives' (European Commission, 19 October 2011) <https://ec.europa.eu/commission/presscorner/detail/en/MEMO_11_711> accessed 14 July 2024.

78 D Scheld and others, 'Managing Antitrust Risks in the Banking Industry' (2016) 12(1) *European Competition Journal* 113; and A Rodríguez-López and others, 'Evaluating Euribor Manipulation: Effects on Mortgage Borrowers' (2021) 40(1) *Finance Research Letters* 101795.

79 Commission Decision of 4.2.2015 Relating to Proceedings under Article 101 of the Treaty on the Functioning of the European Union and Article 53 of the EEA Agreement (AT39861 – Yen Interest Rate Derivatives) C[2015] 432 final, para. 195.

80 R Ball, 'Competition Law and LIBOR in Three Jurisdictions: US, UK and EU' in N Ryder (ed), *White Collar Crime and Risk – A Critical Reflection* (1st edn, Routledge, 2018).

strating that either agreements or concerted practices existed between the banks. The next of the three criteria of Article 101 is that there must be the potential for trade between Member States to be affected by the agreement/concerted practice. The Commission found that there was clearly an effect on trade between Member States by the behaviour of the cartels, stating that:

> The anti-competitive practices concerning these reference rates, which were described above, must have resulted, or, at the very least, were likely to result in the diversion of trade patterns from the course they would otherwise have followed.[81]

For the third criteria of Article 101, the Commission determined that, in all, the LIBOR and EURIBOR cartels the criteria was met because the bank traders' collusive behaviour had as its object or effect the restriction or distortion of competition in the relevant sector.[82] The Commission also found in its LIBOR and EURIBOR decisions that no exemptions, or 'safe-harbours', from Article 101 were met, which meant that the cartel agreements were void and the cartel members subject to penalties.[83]

In March 2013 the Commission commenced proceedings against banks and brokers suspected of involvement with cartels relating to interest rate derivatives denominated in the euro, Japanese yen and Swiss franc.[84] As outlined in Chapter 2, a cartel is a group of similar but independent companies, that typically join together to fix prices, limit production, or to share markets or customers between them for their own financial gain.[85] For the banking cartels operating in the LIBOR and EUIBOR scandal, traders and LIBOR submitters from competing banks worked together via internet chat rooms and emails to raise or lower the banks' LIBOR submissions in order to suit the traders' individual trading positions, with the aim of maximising profits from their transactions.[86] Each of the cartels involved the manipulation of either the LIBOR or EURIBOR benchmark interest rates. As stated above, the Commission opened a total of three cartel cases relating to the manipula-

81 Commission Decision of 4.2.2015 Relating to Proceedings under Article 101 of the Treaty on the Functioning of the European Union and Article 53 of the EEA Agreement (AT39861 – Yen Interest Rate Derivatives) C (2015) 432 final, para. 226.

82 Ibid, para 77.

83 For instance, see Commission Decision of 4.12.2013 Relating to a Proceeding Under Article 101 of the Treaty on the Functioning of the European Union and Article 53 of the EEA Agreement (AT39861 – Yen Interest Rate Derivatives) C (2013) 8602 final, paras 84-86.

84 A Rodríguez-López and others, 'Evaluating Euribor Manipulation: Effects on Mortgage Borrowers' (2021) 40(1) *Finance Research Letters* 101795.

85 A Lunde and others, 'Calculating the Damage of a Cartel Subject to Transition Periods: The International Uranium Cartel in the 1970s' (2019) 84(1) *Energy Economics* 104487.

86 A Jordanoska and Nicholas Lord, 'Scripting the Mechanics of the Benchmark Manipulation Corporate Scandals: The "Guardian' Paradox"' (2020) 17(1) *European Journal of Criminology* 9.

tion of the LIBOR and EURIBOR benchmark interest rates. These cases are set out below.

4.4.1 Yen LIBOR (YIRD) Cartel

The first case related to the yen LIBOR, which was manipulated by traders in order to increase the value of yen Interest Rate Derivatives. This cartel is known as the YIRD cartel.[87] 'Interest rate derivatives' is an umbrella term that covers financial instruments such as options, swaps, futures and forward rate agreements.[88] These products are used by banks to hedge against interest rate fluctuations, as a kind of insurance mechanism.[89] The collusion by the banks included discussions between traders of the participating banks on certain yen LIBOR submissions. The traders involved also exchanged commercially sensitive information relating either to their trading positions or to future yen LIBOR submissions by the bank they worked for. Here, the Commission reached an early settlement with five banks and one broker[90] who collectively agreed to pay €669.7m for their participation in the YIRD cartel.[91] UBS (one of the banks in the settlement decision) received full immunity from fines, as it revealed the existence of the cartel to the Commission, thus avoiding a fine of around €2.5b for its participation in both the YIRD and EIRD cartels.[92] One other broker was party to the cartels relating to the YIRD, but it decided not to settle with the other parties. Instead, the Commission initiated formal proceedings against this party. The missing party from the 2013 settlement decision was the interdealer broker ICAP plc, which is a holding company for ICAP Management Services Ltd and ICAP New Zealand Limited (together referred to as ICAP).

87 European Commission, 'Commission Decision of 4.2.2015 Relating to Proceedings under Article 101 of the Treaty on the Functioning of the European Union and Article 53 of the EEA Agreement (AT39861 – Yen Interest Rate Derivatives)' C(2015) 432 final, para. 1.

88 European Commission, 'Statement by Vice President Joaquín Almunia on 2 Cartel Decisions Concerning Swiss Franc Related Derivatives' (European Commission, 21 October 2014) <https://ec.europa.eu/commission/presscorner/detail/en/STATEMENT_14_330> accessed 14 July 2024.

89 Ibid.

90 The banks and broker were UBS AG and UBS Securities Japan Co., Ltd, The Royal Bank of Scotland Group plc, The Royal Bank of Scotland, Deutsche Bank Aktiengesellschaft, Citigroup Inc, Citigroup Global Markets Japan Inc., JPMorgan Chase & Co, JPMorgan Chase Bank, National Association, JP Morgan Europe Limited, RP Martin Holdings Ltd and Martin Brokers (UK) Ltd.

91 For the YIRD cartel, the fine was €669,719,000, see breakdown of fines in: European Commission, 'AMENDED - Antitrust: Commission Fines Banks € 149 Billion for Participating in Cartels in the Interest Rate Derivatives Industry' (European Commission, 4 December 2013) <https://ec.europa.eu/commission/presscorner/detail/en/IP_13_1208> accessed 12 July 2024.

92 Ibid.

In 2015 the Commission found that ICAP had facilitated discussions between banks in which each bank revealed their preferences for the direction of the yen LIBOR movements, along with commercially sensitive information. The Commission found that ICAP served as a conduit for the communications between some of the banks, and it also contacted the other panel banks for the yen LIBOR and disseminated information to the banks in order to influence their LIBOR submissions.[93] For its role in the facilitation of the yen LIBOR manipulation cartels, the Commission fined ICAP €14.9m.[94] However, in 2015 ICAP appealed this decision in the General Court[95] in Luxembourg.[96] The court ruled in ICAP's favour, partially annulling the Commission's decision of February 2015 in which it fined ICAP, stating that the European Commission had made procedural errors in its calculation of the fine for ICAP.[97] After the General Court's judgement, the European Commission decided to appeal and to take the case to the CJEU. In July 2019, the CJEU ruled that the fine levied against ICAP in 2015 was inappropriate, again citing in its judgement procedural errors by the European Commission.[98] The European Commission then readopted its decision against ICAP for its facilitation of the cartels in the yen LIBOR trading market and reduced the fine to €6.45m.[99] There was no debate in either court about the breach of competition law that ICAP had been involved in, but both cases ruled only that there had been procedural errors in the calculation of the fine. Therefore, the yen LIBOR cartel was accepted by both the General Court and the CJEU as being cartels in breach of Article 101.

The five banks and one broker mentioned above were Deutsche Bank, Royal Bank of Scotland (RBS) (both of which were involved with the EURIBOR manipulation cartels described below), Société Générale, Citigroup and RP Martin, a broker rather than a bank. Each of these parties to the cartel received

93 European Commission, 'Summary of Commission Decision of 4 February 2015 (CASE AT39861 – Yen Interest Rate Derivatives)' (European Commission, 4 February 2015) <https://ec.europa.eu/competition/antitrust/cases/dec_docs/39861/39861_4231_4.pdf> accessed 12 July 2024.

94 European Commission, 'Commission Decision of 4.2.2015 Relating to Proceedings under Article 101 of the Treaty on the Functioning of the European Union and Article 53 of the EEA Agreement (AT39861 – Yen Interest Rate Derivatives)' C(2015) 432 final, Article 2.

95 The General Court is part of the Court of Justice of the EU, see European Parliament, 'Court of Justice of the European Union' (European Parliament, November 2023) <https://www.europarl.europa.eu/factsheets/en/sheet/26/the-court-of-justice-of-the-european-union> accessed 8 July 2024.

96 *Icap plc, Icap Management Services Ltd, Icap New Zealand Ltd v European Commission* 2017 Case T-180/15.

97 Ibid.

98 *European Commission v NEX International Limited, Icap Management Services Ltd and Icap New Zealand Ltd,* Case 39/18 P.

99 European Commission, 'Daily News 28/05/2021' (European Commission, 28 May 2021) <https://ec.europa.eu/commission/presscorner/detail/fr/mex_21_2744> para 6, accessed 12 July 2024.

a reduction of their fines for their cooperation in the investigation under the Commission's leniency programme, which is described below.[100] The investment bank UBS received immunity from being fined for its participation in the cartel, as it acted as whistleblower, telling the Commission about the cartel.[101] The fines for this cartel totalled €676.1m.[102] These are significant fines imposed on international banks and a broker, which signals to the EU financial services sector that competition law applies to anticompetitive collusion and cartels in the financial markets.

4.4.2 EURIBOR (EIRDs) Cartel

The second cartel case opened by the Commission related to the manipulation of the EURIBOR benchmark interest rate, which was increased or decreased by traders in order to increase the value of euro Interest Rate Derivatives (EIRDs).[103] The cartel aimed at distorting the normal course of pricing components for these derivatives.[104] As with the yen LIBOR manipulation, traders from different banks discussed their bank's submissions for the calculation of the EURIBOR as well as their trading and pricing strategies.[105] In December 2013 the Commission reached a settlement decision with four banks, Barclays, Deutsche Bank, Société Générale and the RBS, who all admitted their participation in the EIRDs benchmark manipulation cartel and agreed to pay a total

100 European Commission, 'AMENDED - Antitrust: Commission Fines Banks € 149 Billion for Participating in Cartels in the Interest Rate Derivatives Industry' (European Commission, 4 December 2013) <https://ec.europa.eu/commission/presscorner/detail/en/IP_13_1208> accessed 12 July 2024.

101 European Commission, 'AMENDED - Antitrust: Commission Fines Banks € 149 Billion for Participating in Cartels in the Interest Rate Derivatives Industry' (European Commission, 4 December 2013) <https://ec.europa.eu/commission/presscorner/detail/en/IP_13_1208> accessed 8 July 2024.

102 See the two Commission Decisions that relate to the YIRD cartel: European Commission, 'AMENDED - Antitrust: Commission Fines Banks € 149 billion for Participating in Cartels in the Interest Rate Derivatives Industry' (European Commission, 4 December 2013) <https://ec.europa.eu/commission/presscorner/detail/en/IP_13_1208> accessed 12 July 2024; and European Commission, 'Daily News 28/05/2021' (European Commission, 28 May 2021) <https://ec.europa.eu/commission/presscorner/detail/fr/mex_21_2744> para 6, accessed 12 July 2024.

103 Commission Decision of 7.12.2016 Relating to a Proceeding under Article 101 of the Treaty on the Functioning of the European Union and Article 53 of the EEA Agreement (AT.39914 – Euro Interest Rate Derivatives (EIRD)) C(2016) 8530 final, para. 1.

104 P Zelenko and J Marthan, 'Euro Interest Rate Derivatives: Reduction of Fine in the First-Ever Appeal Against A Settlement Decision' (2016) 7(8) *Journal of European Competition Law & Practice* 525.

105 M Sousa Ferro, 'Crédit Agricole: Rejection of Attempt to (Further) Delay Publication of Commission Cartel Decision' (2019) 10(1) *Journal of European Competition Law & Practice* 22.

of €824.5m.[106] This figure includes a fine reduction for one of the parties, Société Générale, to reflect amended sales figures from Société Générale.[107] Of these banks, Barclays was not fined because it benefited from full immunity from fines under the Commission's leniency programme[108] for revealing the existence of the EIRDs cartel to the Commission.[109] Barclays, by acting as a whistleblower for this cartel avoided a fine of around €690m.[110] The European Commission's competition law leniency programme is detailed below; however, it is worth noting here that this is an example of a successful outcome for the leniency programme – without Barclays' evidence of the cartel, the European Commission may not have discovered the cartel or had sufficient evidence to enforce it, which demonstrates the value of having a leniency policy.

Three banks decided not to participate in the settlement decision made in 2013, these banks were Crédit Agricole, HSBC and JPMorgan Chase, so the Commission's investigation into their participation in the EURIBOR manipulation continued. In 2016, the Commission fined the banks €485m.[111] This decision was followed by legal action, commenced by HSBC in the General Court, seeking annulment of the Commission's 2016 decision. In 2019, the General Court largely upheld the Commission's findings that HSBC had infringed Article 101 in its manipulation of the EURIBOR benchmark interest rate. However, the Court found that the Commission had made some errors in its assessment, although these errors did not affect the validity of the finding that HSBC had breached Article 101.[112] The Court annulled the fine imposed

106 For the EIRD cartel the fine was €824,583,000, see breakdown of fines in: European Commission, 'AMENDED - Antitrust: Commission Fines Banks € 149 Billion for Participating in Cartels in the Interest Rate Derivatives Industry' (European Commission, 4 December 2013) <https://ec.europa.eu/commission/presscorner/detail/en/IP_13_1208> accessed 12 July 2024.

107 Summary of Commission Decision of 6 April 2016 Relating to a Proceeding under Article 101 of the Treaty on the Functioning of the European Union and Article 53 of the EEA Agreement (Case AT39914 — Euro Interest Rate Derivatives) OJ C 404 29.11.2017.

108 Commission Notice on Immunity from Fines and Reduction of Fines in Cartel Cases [2006] OJ C 298/17.

109 European Commission, 'AMENDED - Antitrust: Commission Fines Banks € 149 Billion for Participating in Cartels in the Interest Rate Derivatives Industry' (European Commission, 4 December 2013) <https://ec.europa.eu/commission/presscorner/detail/en/IP_13_1208> accessed 12 July 2024.

110 Ibid.

111 European Commission, 'Antitrust: Commission Fines Crédit Agricole, HSBC and JPMorgan Chase € 485 Million For Euro Interest Rate Derivatives Cartel' (European Commission, 7 December 2016) <https://ec.europa.eu/commission/presscorner/detail/en/IP_16_4304>accessed 12 July 2024.

112 Practical Law Competition, 'Advocate General Opinion on Appeal By HSBC Against General Court Judgment on Participation in Euro Interest Rate Derivatives Cartel (ECJ)' (Practical Law, 12 May 2022) <https://uk.practicallaw.thomsonreuters.com/Document/I81536f6dd1b411ec9f24ec7b211d8087/View/FullText.html?comp=pluk&transitionType

on HSBC due to inadequate reasons having been provided by the European Commission about how it had calculated the fine. The Commission then re-adopted its 2016 decision, including detailed reasons relating to how the fine was calculated.[113] HSBC went on to make a further appeal to the CJEU. The opinion of the Advocate General of the CJEU[114] found that errors were made by both the General Court and the Commission in this case; however, the Advocate General found that despite these errors, HSBC's grounds for appeal should be dismissed.[115]

Therefore, the competition law fines for each of the banks involved in the EIRD cartel total €1.3b.[116] These fines are substantial and demonstrate the successful application of competition law in the financial services sector. Despite the litigation commenced by one of the banks, HSBC, none of the European Commission's decisions in relation to there being a breach of competition law have been annulled by the courts, which is further demonstration of the success of applying competition law to the financial services markets.

4.4.3 Swiss Franc LIBOR Cartel

The third case opened by the Commission in relation to the LIBOR benchmark manipulation related to the manipulation of the Swiss franc LIBOR.[117] This decision applied to the RBS Group plc, the RBS plc, JPMorgan Chase and Co. and JPMorgan Chase Bank, National Association who were fined €94m.[118] As with each of the previous cartel cases, there was also a whistleblower for this

=Default&contextData=(sc.Default)&firstPage=true&OWSessionId=5b49b5f25f854f228e88afaa0b104b90&skipAnonymous=true> accessed 24 July 2024.

113 European Commission, 'Daily News 28/06/2021' (Ision, 28 June 2021) <https://ec.europa.eu/commission/presscorner/detail/en/mex_21_3283> accessed 24 July 2024.

114 Opinion of Advocate General Emiliou in *HSBC Holdings plc, HSBC Bank plc, HSBC Continental Europe, formerly HSBC France v European Commission* Case C-883/19 P.

115 Practical Law Competition, 'Advocate General Opinion on Appeal by HSBC Against General Court Judgment on Participation in Euro Interest Rate Derivatives Cartel (ECJ)' (Practical Law, 12 May 2022) <https://uk.practicallaw.thomsonreuters.com/Document/I81536f6dd1b411ec9f24ec7b211d8087/View/FullText.html?comp=pluk&transitionType=Default&contextData=(sc.Default)&firstPage=true&OWSessionId=5b49b5f25f854f228e88afaa0b104b90&skipAnonymous=true> accessed 24 July 2024.

116 See the two Commission Decisions that relate to the EIRD cartel: European Commission, 'AMENDED - Antitrust: Commission Fines Banks € 149 Billion for Participating in Cartels in the Interest Rate Derivatives Industry' (European Commission, 4 December 2013) <https://ec.europa.eu/commission/presscorner/detail/en/IP_13_1208> accessed 12 July 2024 and European Commission, 'Antitrust: Commission fines Crédit Agricole, HSBC and JPMorgan Chase € 485 Million for Euro Interest Rate Derivatives Cartel' (European Commission, 7 December 2016) <https://ec.europa.eu/commission/presscorner/detail/en/IP_16_4304> accessed 12 July 2024.

117 Summary of Commission Decision of 21 October 2014 (Case AT39924 — Swiss Franc Interest Rate Derivatives) (CHF LIBOR) (notified under document C (2014) 7605) [2015] OJ 1 72/7.

118 Ibid, para. 5.

cartel who provided information on the cartel to the Commission in exchange for immunity from fines for its participation. In the Swiss franc LIBOR cartel, RBS received full immunity from fines because it acted as a whistleblower, informing the Commission of the cartel.[119] The fine was, therefore, imposed solely on JPMorgan in the sum of €61.6m.[120] The competition law leniency/whistleblower provisions and their importance to the investigation and prosecution of cartels will be discussed further below.

It can be seen from the each of the above LIBOR and EURIBOR manipulation cases that the use of competition law in the enforcement of the LIBOR market manipulation was extremely successful, resulting in significant fines being imposed on the international banks involved.[121] In total, fines of €2.047b[122] were imposed by the European Commission using its competition law powers on the banks and brokers involved in the three LIBOR cartels.

The next section of this chapter will look at the parallel investigations in relation to the manipulation of the FX benchmark interest rate.

4.5 The FX Scandal and Enforcement in the EU

In this section, the European Commission's investigation into and enforcement of the three FX cartel cases will be examined. The most recent case decision in the LIBOR and FX manipulation scandal came from the Commission in December 2021 and concerned the FX cartels.[123] The FX benchmark manipulation is believed to have taken place over a ten-year period, concurrently

119 European Commission, 'Statement by Vice President Joaquín Almunia on 2 Cartel Decisions Concerning Swiss Franc Related Derivatives' (European Commission, 21 October 2014) <https://ec.europa.eu/commission/presscorner/detail/en/STATEMENT_14_330> accessed 14 July 2024.

120 A fine of €61,676,000 was imposed on JPMorgan in this decision: Summary of Commission Decision of 21 October 2014 (Case AT39924 — Swiss Franc Interest Rate Derivatives) (CHF LIBOR) (notified under document C (2014) 7605) [2015] OJ 1 72/7, para 21.

121 R Alexander, 'Flogging the Wrong: EU Corporate Fines Violate the Fundamental Rights of Shareholders' (2021) 12(4) *Journal of European Competition Law & Practice* 301, 302

122 Made up of a fine for the YIRD cartel of €676.1m, a fine for the EIRD cartel of €1.3bn and a fine for the Swiss franc LIBOR cartel of €61.6m; see European Commission, 'AMENDED - Antitrust: Commission Fines Banks € 149 Billion for Participating in Cartels in the Interest Rate Derivatives Industry' (European Commission, 4 December 2013) <https://ec.europa.eu/commission/presscorner/detail/en/IP_13_1208> accessed 12 July 2024; European Commission, 'Daily News 28/05/2021' (European Commission, 28 May 2021) <https://ec.europa.eu/commission/presscorner/detail/fr/mex_21_2744> para 6, accessed 12 July 2024; European Commission, 'Antitrust: Commission Fines Crédit Agricole, HSBC and JPMorgan Chase € 485 Million for Euro Interest Rate Derivatives Cartel' (European Commission, 7 December 2016) <https://ec.europa.eu/commission/presscorner/detail/en/IP_16_4304>accessed 12 July 2024; and Summary of Commission Decision of 21 October 2014 (Case AT39924 — Swiss Franc Interest Rate Derivatives) (CHF LIBOR) (notified under document C (2014) 7605) [2015] OJ 1 72/7, para 21.

123 C Powers, 'Filling the Regulatory Void in the FX Spot Market: How Traders Rigged the Biggest Market in the World' (2016) 42(1) *The Fordham Urban Law Journal* 167.

with, but separate from, the LIBOR manipulation.[124] The close proximity of such high-profile benchmark manipulation cases demonstrates clearly that the manipulation of benchmark interest rates by bankers is a frequent occurrence. The fact that many banks keep offending arguably demonstrates that the fines handed out are not sufficient to act as a deterrent.[125] Currently, EU regulators do not enforce or facilitate a culture change in the international banks following a finding of culpability for market manipulation, for instance via a DPA, which is used in the US and UK after a finding of corporate criminal liability. It is possible under competition law to enforce behavioural change, by imposing/agreeing commitments with the offending business, but the Commission does not use commitments to enforce cartels for policy reasons.[126] However, this could be a good tool to persuade businesses to change their behaviour in addition to the imposition of fines.

The economic impact of the FX manipulation is hard to define; however, by increasing the banks' profits, countless consumers, investors and institutions around the globe were harmed.[127] The Commission again used its competition powers, specifically Article 101, to enforce the FX manipulation cartels.[128] The three cartel cases opened by the Commission are discussed below.

4.5.1 Forex – Three Way Banana Split Cartel

The first FX benchmark manipulation cartel investigated by the Commission, known as the 'Forex – Three Way Banana Split' cartel used three Bloomberg internet chat rooms, called 'Three Way Banana Split', 'Two and a Half Men' and 'Only Marge', which were set up by traders from Barclays Bank, UBS, RBS, Citigroup and JPMorgan.[129] The traders from the competing banks were found to have exchanged commercially sensitive information and trading plans with each other using the online Bloomberg chat rooms. In 2019, the Commission imposed a total fine of€811,197,000 on Barclays, RBS, Citigroup

124 K Makortoff, 'UK Banks Fined 1 Billion Euros By EU For Rigging Foreign Exchange Market' *The Guardian* (London, 16 May 2019) <https://www.theguardian.com/money/2019/may/16/uk-banks-barclays-rbs-fined-1bn-by-eu-for-rigging-foreign-exchange-market>accessed 8 July 20224

125 S Moffatt and S Poynton, 'The Deterrent Effect of Higher Fines on Recidivism: Driving Offences' (2007) 1(106) *Crime and Justice Bulletin* 1.

126 RWhish and D Bailey, *Competition Law* (10th edn, Oxford University Press 2021) 271.

127 C Powers, 'Filling the Regulatory Void in the FX Spot Market: How Traders Rigged the Biggest Market in the World' (2016) 42(1) *The Fordham Urban Law Journal* 167.

128 European Commission, 'Antitrust: Commission Fines UBS, Barclays, RBS, HSBC and Credit Suisse €344 Million For Participating in A Foreign Exchange Spot Trading Cartel' (European Commission, 2 December 2021) <https://ec.europa.eu/commission/presscorner/detail/en/ip_21_6548> accessed 8 July 2024.

129 Summary of Commission Decision of 16 May 2019 Relating to a Proceeding under Article 101 of the Treaty on the Functioning of the European Union and Article 53 of the EEA Agreement (Case AT40135 – Forex-Three Way Banana Split) [2019] OJ 1 226/5, para 12.

and JPMorgan for their participation in this cartel. However, UBS, which was involved in the cartel, was given full immunity from fines in exchange for revealing the existence of the cartels to the Commission.[130]

4.5.2 Forex – Essex Express Cartel

The second cartel, known as the 'Forex – Essex Express' cartel, was made up of two Bloomberg chat rooms, called 'Essex Express "n" Jimmy' and 'Grumpy Semi Old Men'. The first of these chat rooms involved traders from UBS, Barclays and RBS; the second involved traders from Mitsubishi UFJ Financial Group Inc. and MUFG Bank, Ltd., Barclays and UBS.[131] The total fine imposed by the Commission on Barclays, RBS and MUFG Bank (formerly Bank of Tokyo-Mitsubishi) was €257,682,000. As with the 'Forex – Three Way Banana Split' cartel, UBS, which is an addressee of both Commission decisions, was not fined because it had revealed the existence of the cartels to the Commission.[132]

Both of the above cartels exchanged commercially sensitive information via the Bloomberg chat rooms, which enabled competing traders to coordinate with each other and to make informed decisions about whether to buy or sell the currencies they had in their portfolios.[133] Each of these traders and the banks they worked for were direct competitors, and their communication to move the foreign exchange market was in breach of EU and UK competition law. The Commission found that the traders who formed the cartels typically logged in to multilateral chat rooms on Bloomberg terminals for the whole working day, having extensive conversations about a variety of subjects, including recurring updates on their trading activities.[134] This finding demonstrates how easily these traders from different banks, who were direct competitors, slipped into illegal anticompetitive behaviour, colluding with each other and sharing commercially sensitive data. This, in turn, further demonstrates that the likelihood of this sort of cartel being formed again between traders working in competing banks is high. This will be discussed further in the final chapter, in which more recent instances of benchmark manipulation will be examined.

130 European Commission, 'Commission Fines Barclays, RBS, Citigroup, JPMorgan and MUFG E107 Billion for Participating in Foreign Exchange Spot Trading Cartel' (European Commission, 16 May 2019) <https://ec.europa.eu/commission/presscorner/detail/en/IP_19_2568> accessed 8 July 2024

131 Ibid.

132 Ibid.

133 Ibid, para 16.

134 European Commission, 'Commission Fines Barclays, RBS, Citigroup, JPMorgan and MUFG E107 Billion for Participating in Foreign Exchange Spot Trading Cartel' (European Commission, 16 May 2019) <https://ec.europa.eu/commission/presscorner/detail/en/IP_19_2568> accessed 8 July 2024.

Commissioner Margrethe Vestager said of these two cartels:

> Today we have fined Barclays, The Royal Bank of Scotland, Citigroup, JPMorgan and MUFG Bank and these cartel decisions send a clear message that the Commission will not tolerate collusive behaviour in any sector of the financial markets. The behaviour of these banks undermined the integrity of the sector at the expense of the European economy and consumers.[135]

This is a clear statement of the Commission's intention to continue to use competition law in the financial markets when cartels or other collusive behaviour are discovered to be harming competition.

4.5.3 Forex – Sterling Lads Cartel

The last decision on the FX benchmark manipulation cartels was made by the European Commission in December 2021 in relation to a third FX manipulation cartel known as the 'Forex – Sterling Lads' cartel, when a total fine of €261m was imposed on the four banks that decided to settle the case, namely UBS, Barclays, RBS and HSBC.[136] The Commission stated that this was the completion of its investigation into the FX manipulation. The Vice-President of the European Commission said of the 2021 fining decision:

> Today we complete our sixth cartel investigation in the financial sector since 2013 and conclude the third leg of our investigation into the Foreign Exchange spot trading market. Our cartel decisions to fine UBS, Barclays, RBS, HSBC and Credit Suisse send a clear message that the Commission remains committed to ensure a sound and competitive financial sector that is essential for investment and growth. The collusive behaviour of the five banks undermined the integrity of the financial sector at the expense of the European economy and consumers'[137]

Therefore, as with the LIBOR benchmark manipulation cartels, the European Commission used its competition law powers to fine the banks whose employees were members of each of the three FX benchmark manipulation cartels.[138]

135 Ibid.

136 European Commission, 'Antitrust: Commission Fines UBS, Barclays, RBS, HSBC and Credit Suisse €344 Million For Participating in a Foreign Exchange Spot Trading Cartel' (European Commission, 2 December 2021) <https://ec.europa.eu/commission/presscorner/detail/en/ip_21_6548> accessed 12 July 2024.

137 Ibid.

138 Summary of Commission Decision of 16 May 2019 Relating to a Proceeding under Article 101 of the Treaty on the Functioning of the European Union and Article 53 of the EEA Agreement (Case AT40135 – Forex-Three Way Banana Split) [2019] OJ 1 226/5, para 1.

In total, the fines imposed by the Commission on banks who participated in the FX benchmark manipulation cartels totalled €1.414b.[139] The Commission found that the way that the traders' used the online chat rooms to share commercially sensitive information and to plan their actions and trading strategies together constituted a 'concerted practice', which is the first of the three essential components of Article 101.[140] The other two elements of Article 101 were also deemed by the Commission to have been met for each cartel, as it is clear that the actions of the traders in the three FX cartels would have the potential to affect trade between Member States (Criteria 2) and that the cartel cases had as their object or effect the distortion of competition within the internal market as they were price fixing (Criteria 3).

The Commission successfully enforced the LIBOR and FX benchmark manipulation cartels in the financial services sector using its competition law powers, which allowed it to carry out unannounced inspections on the premises of suspected cartel members.[141] This investigative power is likely to have provided the Commission with evidence as to the workings of the cartels that would not otherwise have been available to it, as it is common for cartels, once discovered, to rapidly destroy incriminating evidence, making prosecutions more challenging than they otherwise would be.[142] The successful argument by the Commission that the actions of the cartel members came within the remit of Article 101 was accepted by all but one of the cartel members. ICAP, as stated above, did not accept that it was in breach of Article 101; however, after two appeals, the CJEU upheld the infringement decision of the European Commission, ruling that only that there were procedural errors in relation to the level of fine imposed.[143]

Therefore, the use by the Commission of its competition law powers to enforce the LIBOR and FX benchmark manipulation crisis was successful, and the Commission has made it clear in its statements to the press (provided

139 See two fining decisions: European Commission, 'Commission Fines Barclays, RBS, Citigroup, JPMorgan and MUFG E107 Billion for Participating in Foreign Exchange Spot Trading Cartel' (European Commission, 16 May 2019) <https://ec.europa.eu/commission/presscorner/detail/en/IP_19_2568> accessed 8 July 2024; and European Commission, 'Antitrust: Commission Fines UBS, Barclays, RBS, HSBC and Credit Suisse €344 Million For Participating in a Foreign Exchange Spot Trading Cartel' (European Commission, 2 December 2021) <https://ec.europa.eu/commission/presscorner/detail/en/ip_21_6548> accessed 12 July 2024.

140 Ibid., Article 101(1).

141 R Autio, 'Explaining Dawn Raids: A Soft Law Perspective into European Competition Authorities' Explanatory Notes on Unannounced Inspections' (2020) 11(9) *Journal of European Competition Law & Practice* 475.

142 J Polański, 'Dawn Raids and the Role of Forensic IT in Antitrust Investigations' (2020) 13(21) *Yearbook of Antitrust and Regulatory Studies* 187.

143 T Wilson, 'The ECJ's ICAP Judgment Sends a Clear Message that Procedural Rights Matter (C-39/18 P Commission v ICAP and Others)' (2020) 4(4) *European Competition and Regulatory Law Review (CoRe)* 324.

above) that it will continue to use competition law to enforce cartels in the financial markets. It is possible, however, that the changes made to the EU market abuse regime following the LIBOR and FX crisis will make the new market abuse regime more relevant and useful to regulators in future, potentially offering an alternative to the competition law that proved so successful. This will be discussed further below. The legislative changes made following the LIBOR, EURIBOR and FX cartels are set out below.

4.6 Legislation Introduced Following the LIBOR and FX Scandal

Since the LIBOR and FX scandal, a wide variety of legislation has been introduced in the EU. This section will look at the most relevant legislation to the financial crime of benchmark manipulation and will examine how this may change future enforcement of benchmark manipulation in the EU. An EU directive to protect whistleblowers (Whistleblowing Directive)[144] has been introduced, described by commentators as being 'by far the European Union's most important piece of whistleblowing legislation to date'.[145] The Whistleblowing Directive requires each Member State to have implemented the whistleblower protections contained in the Directive by 17 December 2021.[146] The Directive contains a broad definition of who can be a whistleblower, covers a wide range of policy areas and extends to both the public and private sectors.[147] All forms of retaliation against whistleblowers are prohibited and, in the case of an alleged retaliation, the burden of proof falls on the employer.[148] In the preamble to the Whistleblowing Directive, the value of whistleblower protection in the area of financial services is acknowledged, with reference being made to the whistleblowers who helped to expose serious shortcomings in the enforcement of financial rules in the aftermath of the financial crisis.[149] The importance of whistleblower and leniency regimes to the LIBOR and FX benchmark manipulation scandal is set out below, but its impact was significant, with whistleblowers providing crucial information and evidence about the benchmark manipulation cartels to regulators, enabling the infringement decisions to be made against other cartel members.

144 Directive (EU) 2019/1937 of the European Parliament and of the Council of 23 October 2019 on the Protection of Persons Who Report Breaches of Union Law, OJ L 305/17.
145 S Gerdemann and N Colneric, 'The EU Whistleblower Directive and its Transposition: Part 2' (2021) 12(3) *European Labour Law Journal* 253.
146 Directive (EU) 2019/1937 of the European Parliament and of the Council of 23 October 2019 on the Protection of Persons Who Report Breaches of Union Law, OJ L 305/17, Article 26(1).
147 V Abazi, 'The European Union Whistleblower Directive: A "Game Changer" for Whistleblowing Protection?' (2020) 49(4) *Industrial Law Journal* 640.
148 Ibid.
149 Directive (EU) 2019/1937 of the European Parliament and of the Council of 23 October 2019 on the Protection of Persons Who Report Breaches of Union Law, OJ L 305/17.

Further laws were introduced in June 2014 as a direct consequence of the LIBOR and FX manipulation, including the new and revised EU rules of 'markets in financial instruments' directive and regulation,[150] which mandate extensive record-keeping and reporting requirements with the goal of increasing the efficiency, resilience and transparency of financial markets and strengthening investor protection.[151] This directive and regulation came into force in January 2018, arguably marking the biggest regulatory change imposed on the financial services industry since the global financial crisis, which brought the global financial system to its knees.[152] These new laws are a key example of the swathe of new rules within the financial services sector that were introduced by the EU with the aim of preventing a recurrence of the financial crisis and the benchmark manipulation scandal, similar to the Dodd-Frank Act in the US discussed in Chapter 5.

Another key legislative change relating to the LIBOR and FX crisis is the change made to the market abuse regime in 2014. At the time of the LIBOR and FX scandals, the MAD 2003 was in place. Its definition of market manipulation did not refer to the manipulation of benchmark interest rates, which is likely to be one of the reasons that no prosecutions were made under the EU market abuse regime. Instead, the banks involved with the benchmark manipulation were fined by the EU using its civil competition law powers, specifically the cartel offence under Article 101.[153] Following the scandal of the LIBOR benchmark manipulation, in July 2012 the European Commission proposed the MAR 2014 and MAD 2014. The proposed legislation clearly made the manipulation of any benchmark, such as LIBOR or the EURIBOR, a criminal offence.[154] The MAR 2014 explicitly bans the manipulation of benchmark interest rates, such as LIBOR and FX.[155] The MAD 2014 includes any behaviour that manipulates the calculation of a benchmark in its definition of market manipulation, such as LIBOR and FX.[156]

150 Regulation (EU) No 600/2014 of the European Parliament and of the Council of 15 May 2014 on Markets in Financial Instruments and Amending Regulation (EU) No 648/2012 OJ L 173/8412.6.2014.

151 MW Kang, 'Rethinking Spot FX Regulation' (2019) 13(4) *Law and Financial Markets Review* 234.

152 M Smith, 'Second Markets in Financial Instruments Directive: Firms Should View the Practical Challenge of Meeting the New Record Keeping, Transaction Reporting and Best Execution Requirements Not as a Bureaucratic Nuisance but as an Opportunity' (2018) 10(4) *Journal of Securities Operations & Custody* 290.

153 R Nicholls, 'Something to Remember Him By: Commissioner Joaquín Almunia's Farewell Gift' (2014) 8(4) *Law and Financial Markets Review* 315.

154 A Kern and V Maly, 'The New EU Market Abuse Regime and the Derivatives Markets' (2015) 9(4) *Law and Financial Markets Review* 243.

155 Ibid.

156 Directive 2014/57/EU of the European Parliament and of the Council of 16 April 2014 on Criminal Sanctions for Market Abuse (Market Abuse Directive) [2014] OJ 2 173/179, Article 5.

Finally, in 2016 an EU benchmark regulation (Benchmark Regulation)[157] was adopted to complement the market abuse regime set up by the MAR 2014 and MAD 2014. The Benchmark Regulation set out a set of rules covering the use of benchmark interest rates across the whole of the EU. The new rules require, amongst other things, the supervision of key benchmarks such as the LIBOR and EURIBOR, as these rates are seen as critical to the functioning and integrity of financial markets.[158]

From the above outline of legislative measures taken by the EU since the LIBOR and FX crisis, it is apparent that the EU takes financial crime extremely seriously and has taken extensive steps to prevent a recurrence of this financial crime. There are now an increased amount of enforcement powers available to regulators, in addition to the competition law, which was used so successfully by the European Commission in its enforcement of the LIBOR and FX benchmark manipulation.

The next four sections of this chapter will take a closer look at the four themes identified in the introduction. These themes are first, how the competition law leniency and whistleblowing regime works to assist regulators in the identification and enforcement of cartels. Second, the criminal and civil powers that regulators have to enforce benchmark manipulation. Third, what powers the EU has to attribute corporate criminal liability and, finally, how the use of DPAs could work at an EU-wide level.

4.7 Competition Law Leniency and Whistleblowing Regime in the EU

The existence of a successful competition law leniency and whistleblowing regime is essential to regulators, who are able to obtain insider evidence from a whistleblower of a suspected cartel infringement and to 'pierce the cloak of secrecy in which cartels operate'.[159] Whistleblowers play a very important role in the battle against corruption and other forms of specific financial crime, including fraud and cartel activity.[160] Whistleblowers have been defined by the European Commission as:

157 Regulation (EU) 2016/1011 of the European Parliament and of the Council of 8 June 2016 on Indices Used as Benchmarks in Financial Instruments and Financial Contracts or to Measure the Performance of Investment Funds [2016] OJ 2 171/1.

158 A Kern and V Maly, 'The New EU Market Abuse Regime and the Derivatives Markets' (2015) 9(4) *Law and Financial Markets Review* 243.

159 European Commission, 'Cartels: eLeniency' (European Commission, 6 February 2020) <https://ec.europa.eu/competition/cartels/leniency/eleniency.html> accessed 8 July 2024.

160 D Hall and N Ryder, 'The Protection of Whistle-Blowers in the United Kingdom - A Critical and Comparative Commentary' in C Grasso (ed), *Whistleblowers: Voices of Justice* (Springer 2020).

> Persons who report (within the organisation concerned or to an outside authority) or disclose (to the public) information on a wrongdoing obtained in a work-related context, help preventing damage and detecting threat or harm to the public interest that may otherwise remain hidden.[161]

A whistleblower can be either a company involved in the illegal behaviour, an employee, competitor or business contact.[162]

In both the LIBOR and FX scandals, whistleblowers played an important part in notifying the Commission of cartels and illegal behaviour. The EURIBOR manipulation cartel was only discovered because of the European Commission's competition law leniency programme.[163] In the Japanese yen LIBOR cartel, UBS received total immunity from fines as it acted as whistleblower, telling the Commission about the cartels.[164] Other cartel members received a reduction of their fines for their cooperation in the investigation under the Commission's competition law leniency programme.[165] In the EURIBOR cartel, Barclays was not fined because it benefited from immunity from fines under the Commission's competition law leniency programme[166] for revealing the existence of the EIRDs cartel to the Commission.[167] Other banks, again, received a reduction in their fines in exchange for cooperation with the Commission's investigation. In the Swiss franc LIBOR cartel, in which LIBOR was manipulated by the members of the cartel in order to increase the value of Swiss franc Interest Rate Derivative products that they were trading, RBS received full immunity from fines because it acted as a whistleblower, informing the Commission of the cartel.[168] In the FX scandal, suspicious price movements were first highlighted by a whistleblower, rather

161 European Commission, 'Whistleblowers Protection' (European Commission, 23 October 2019) <https://ec.europa.euo/info/aid-development-cooperation-fundamental-rights/your-rights-eu/whistleblowers-protection_en> accessed 14 July 2024.

162 S Loosveld, 'EU Financial Supervisory Powers, Whistleblowing and Self-Reporting' 34(9) *Journal of International Banking Law and Regulation* (2019), 317.

163 D Scheld and others, 'Managing Antitrust Risks in the Banking Industry' (2016) 12(1) *European Competition Journal* 113.

164 European Commission, 'AMENDED - Antitrust: Commission Fines Banks €149 Billion for Participating in Cartels in the Interest Rate Derivatives Industry' (European Commission, 4 December 2013) <https://ec.europa.eu/commission/presscorner/detail/en/IP_13_1208> accessed 8 July 2024.

165 Ibid.

166 Commission Notice on Immunity from Fines and Reduction of Fines in Cartel Cases [2006] OJ C 298/17.

167 European Commission, 'AMENDED - Antitrust: Commission Fines Banks € 149 Billion For Participating In Cartels in the Interest Rate Derivatives Industry' (European Commission, 4 December 2013) <https://ec.europa.eu/commission/presscorner/detail/en/IP_13_1208> accessed 8 July 2024.

168 European Commission, 'Statement by Vice President Joaquín Almunia on 2 Cartel Decisions Concerning Swiss Franc Related Derivatives' (European Commission, 21 October 2014)

than from the managers who were meant to be in charge of the traders.[169] From these instances, it can be clearly seen that the encouragement and facilitation of whistleblowers had a significant impact on the ability of the Commission to identify and then to enforce the manipulation of the LIBOR and then the FX benchmarks and demonstrates the critical importance to regulators of having a competition law leniency and whistleblower programme.

The EU competition law leniency regime is well established, with the first leniency notice introduced by the Commission in 1996.[170] This first leniency notice offered reductions only in the amount of fines to a whistleblower, rather than the offer of full immunity from fines, as offered by the later Commission leniency notices in 2002 and 2006.[171] The 2002 leniency notice was generally perceived to be a success, as there was a significant increase in cartel members seeking immunity or fine reductions compared to the previous 1996 notice.[172] The 2006 leniency notice builds on the success of the 2002 notice and offers companies involved in a cartel either total immunity from fines or a reduction of fines that the Commission would otherwise have imposed on them.[173] The Commission has made it easy on its website to apply for leniency. Companies can either use the online 'eLeniency tool' or email the address provided.[174] Only the first business in a cartel to submit information to the Commission will be granted full immunity from fines, providing that the information is sufficient to either find an infringement of Article 101 by the cartel or to carry out an investigation.[175] The Commission believes that by granting full immunity to the first business submitting information, this has a deterrent effect on the formation of new cartels and also destabilises the operation of existing cartels by seeding distrust and suspicion amongst cartel members, each of whom

<https://ec.europa.eu/commission/presscorner/detail/en/STATEMENT_14_330> accessed 14 July 2024.

169 P Augar, 'How the Forex Scandal Happened' (*BBC News*, 20 May 2015) <https://www.bbc.co.uk/news/business-30003693> accessed 14 June 2024.

170 D Sharma, 'Anti-Cartel Enforcement Mechanism and Consequent Applicability of Leniency Programmes: A Comparative Study of India, the US and EU Antitrust Regimes' (2016) 37(12) *European Competition Law Review* 513.

171 Commission Notice on Immunity from Fines and Reduction of Fines in Cartel Cases [2002] OJ 1 45/03; and Commission Notice on Immunity from Fines and Reduction of Fines in Cartel Cases [2006] OJ C 298/17.

172 B Rodger, A MacCulloch, *Competition Law and Policy in the EC and UK* (4th edn., Routledge-Cavendish 2009) 264.

173 R Diogo Luz and G Spagnolo, 'Leniency, Collusion, Corruption and Whistleblowing' (2017) 13(4) *Journal of Competition Law & Economics* 729.

174 European Commission, 'Cartels: eLeniency' (European Commission, 6 February 2020) <https://ec.europa.eu/competition/cartels/leniency/eleniency.html> accessed 8 July 2024.

175 Commission Notice on Immunity from Fines and Reduction of Fines in Cartel Cases OJ [2006] C 298/17, para 8.

could become the first informant on the cartel.[176] Certain commentators agree with this analysis, stating that 'a leniency policy is designed to give members of an ongoing cartel further reason to distrust their co-conspirators'.[177] Without a competition law leniency or whistleblowing regime, the majority of cartels would be missed by regulators, so the provision of full immunity to one cartel member is a small price to pay for the uncovering of sufficient evidence of a cartel to prosecute the other members.

Under the Commission's 2006 competition law leniency notice, companies that do not qualify for immunity, by not being the first to bring information about the cartel to the Commission, may benefit from a reduction in fines if they provide evidence that represents 'significant added value' to that already in the Commission's possession and have terminated their participation in the cartel. Evidence is considered to be of 'significant added value' to the Commission when the evidence reinforces the Commission's ability to prove the infringement. The first company to meet these conditions is granted a 30%–50% reduction in fines, the second 20%–30% and subsequent companies up to 20% reduction in the fines they would otherwise receive as a cartel member.[178] These reductions in fines were used to good effect by the Commission in the LIBOR and FX scandals to encourage cooperation with the investigation by the cartel members, facilitating the Commission's role of finding evidence of cartel activity and enabling successful enforcement of the cartels. Therefore, it is clear from the success of the EU's competition law leniency and whistleblower regime that other jurisdictions should follow the EU's lead in order to detect and gain evidence to enforce cartels in the financial markets.

In addition to the Commission's competition law leniency policy, which is used as part of the Commission's competition law enforcement powers, the EU's market abuse regime includes provisions in the MAR 2014 aimed at encouraging whistleblowers in the financial services sector to come forward. In particular, Member States are able to provide financial incentives, such as a reward, for whistleblowers in some circumstances.[179] The MAR 2014 states that measures regarding whistleblowing are necessary to facilitate detection of market abuse and to ensure the protection and the respect of the rights of the whistleblower and the accused person.[180] There is also the requirement in the MAR 2014 for Member States to require financial services businesses to have in place internal procedures for their employees to be able to report infringe-

176 D Sharma, 'Anti-Cartel Enforcement Mechanism and Consequent Applicability of Leniency Programmes: A Comparative Study of India, the US and EU Antitrust Regimes' (2016) 37(12) *European Competition Law Review* 513.

177 B Rodger, A MacCulloch, *Competition Law and Policy in the EC and UK* (4th edn., Routledge-Cavendish 2009) 263.

178 Ibid.

179 Regulation (EU) No 596/2014 of the European Parliament and of the Council of 16 April 2014 on Market Abuse (Market Abuse Regulation) [2014] OJ 2 173/1, Article 32(4).

180 Ibid, Preamble 74.

ments of the market abuse laws.[181] These measures increase the likelihood of regulators finding out about potential breaches of the market abuse regime.

As mentioned above, the Whistleblowing Directive came into force in December 2021 and further bolsters the market abuse regime by providing regulators with information and evidence of market abuse.[182] These whistle-blowing powers, taken in conjunction with the wide-reaching criminal and civil powers for regulators, have created a strong framework for the EU's market abuse regime. However, there is likely to be a reluctance for regulators to use their full powers on large banks, when the use of such powers could result in a corporate death penalty, such as that seen with the prosecution of Arthur Anderson in connection with the Enron affair in the United States.[183] This is due to the collateral damage that is done when ending the life of a large company, including in Arthur Anderson's case the loss of approximately 30,000 jobs.[184] For banks, collateral damage following a removal of their licence to operate could also result in severe disruption to the global financial markets and a loss of investor confidence, which will be discussed further below.

The EU has a well-developed and well-known competition law leniency policy for cartels. It also has encouraged Member States to offer rewards to whistleblowers as part of its market abuse regime and has put in place the Whistleblowing Directive to protect the position of whistleblowers. The competition law leniency policy is aimed at cartel members, who are likely to be companies. Leniency policies have proven to be an extremely good tool for competition law enforcers when tackling cartels such as those used by banks to manipulate the LIBOR and FX benchmark interest rates.[185] The market abuse whistleblowing provisions, however, are aimed at employees of companies who may be breaching the market abuse rules,[186] so between the competition and market abuse legislative regime, both corporate and individual whistleblowers are provided for. The Whistleblowing Directive provides protection to individuals who are whistleblowers rather than to corporate whistle-blowers.[187] Corporate whistleblowers who take advantage of the Commissions

181 Ibid, Article 32(3).

182 A Vigjilenca, 'The European Union Whistleblower Directive: A "Game Changer" for Whistleblowing Protection?' (2020) 49(4) *Industrial Law Journal* (London) 640.

183 Arthur Anderson agreed to surrender its practising licence following its conviction by the US Department of Justice for obstruction of justice in 2002.

184 N Ryder, '"Too Scared to Prosecute and Too Scared to Jail?" A Critical and Comparative Analysis of Enforcement of Financial Crime Legislation Against Corporations in the USA and the UK' (2018) 82(3) *The Journal of Criminal Law* 245.

185 B Rodger, Angus MacCulloch, *Competition Law and Policy in the EC and UK* (4th edn., Routledge-Cavendish 2009) 262.

186 Regulation (EU) No 596/2014 of the European Parliament and of the Council of 16 April 2014 on Market Abuse (Market Abuse Regulation) [2014] OJ 2 173/1, Article 32.

187 Directive (EU) 2019/1937 of the European Parliament and of the Council of 23 October 2019 on the Protection of Persons Who Report Breaches of Union Law, OJ L 305/17 26/11/2019, Article 4.

2006 leniency notice are afforded limited anonymity in relation to information the Commission receives under its leniency notice as the Commission undertakes to only discuss information it receives with other Member State competition authorities pursuant to a confidentiality waiver provided by the leniency applicant.[188]

The next theme to be examined is that of criminal vs civil penalties, in which the powers available to the EU regulators will be examined and evaluated to determine which type of penalty is the most appropriate for the financial crime of benchmark manipulation.

4.8 Criminal vs Civil Penalties

As with each of the three case study chapters, the civil and criminal enforcement powers available to the EU regulators under both the market abuse and competition law regimes will be considered and analysed. One key change since the LIBOR and FX scandal was the introduction of the MAD 2014 and MAR 2014, in which criminal sanctions for market abuse were introduced in the EU. This means that the EU's market abuse regime now has criminal sanctions compared to its competition law enforcement powers, which are entirely civil.[189] In 2011, the then European Commission's Justice Commissioner set out the Commission's enforcement strategy on market abuse, stating that 'Criminal behaviour should have no place in Europe's financial markets!'[190] This signalled the Commission's enforcement strategy for market abuse, ahead of the introduction of the MAR 2014 and MAD 2014 and following the LIBOR and FX scandals. The MAD 2014, which required each Member State to transpose its provisions into its national law by 3 July 2016, introduced criminal sanctions for market abuse, detailed below.[191]

Under the MAD 2014, national competent authorities have the power to impose criminal penalties on both natural and legal persons for the offence of market manipulation. The offence of market manipulation in the MAD 2014, unlike in the MAD 2003, clearly covers the transmission of false or misleading information that manipulates the calculation of a benchmark,[192] which is exactly

188 European Commission, 'Cartels: eLeniency' (European Commission, 6 February 2020) <https://ec.europa.eu/competition/cartels/leniency/eleniency.html> accessed 8 July 2024.

189 B Silviu Gabriel, 'Trends Regarding Fines and Sanctions in Competition Law, Labor Law and Data Protection Law' (2019) X(I) *Law Review* (Romania).

190 European Commission, 'Getting Tough on Insider Dealing and Market Manipulation' (European Commission, 20 October 2011) <https://ec.europa.eu/commission/presscorner/detail/hr/IP_11_1217> accessed 26 July 2024.

191 Directive 2014/57/EU of the European Parliament and of the Council of 16 April 2014 on Criminal Sanctions for Market Abuse (Market Abuse Directive) [2014] OJ 2 173/179, Articles 3 and 5.

192 Regulation (EU) No 596/2014 of the European Parliament and of the Council of 16 April 2014 on Market Abuse (Market Abuse Regulation) [2014] OJ 2 173/1, Article 12(1)(d).

what happened in each of the LIBOR and FX scandals. However, at the time of those scandals, the current market abuse regime was not in force and competition laws, which do not have any criminal sanctions at EU level, were used in the enforcement. The MAR 2014 introduced new powers for each Member State to impose fines of up to €5m for an individual and €15m or up to 15% of annual turnover for a firm for the offences of insider dealing and market manipulation.[193] In addition to the power to impose heavy fines on banks and individual traders, regulators in each Member State now have the power to imprison natural persons for these offences for up to four years.[194] Under the MAD 2014, in addition to fines and to the power to imprison natural persons, regulators are able to sanction legal persons by, *inter alia*, temporarily or permanently disqualifying perpetrators from the practice of commercial activities, or they can order a judicial winding up or liquidation of a company or closure of establishments used for committing the offence.[195] These are significant powers and could have catastrophic collateral consequences if used against an international bank such as those involved in the LIBOR and FX benchmark manipulation cartels. These powers have all been introduced as a direct response to the LIBOR and FX market manipulation scandals. These common EU sanctions were viewed as necessary following a report produced by the European Securities and Markets Authority (ESMA),[196] the EU's securities markets regulator,[197] which showed that not all national competent authorities had a full set of enforcement powers at their disposal for use in connection with market abuse offences. In particular, not all Member States provided for fines for insider dealing and market manipulation, and the level of fines varied widely among Member States.[198]

Under the EU market abuse regime, there is one central enforcement agency (ESMA) and designated 'competent authorities' in each Member State.[199] In the UK, the designated competent authority is the FCA. EMSA is responsible

193 Ibid Article 30(2)(i)(i) and Article 30(2)(j)(i).
194 Directive 2014/57/EU of the European Parliament and of the Council of 16 April 2014 on Criminal Sanctions for Market Abuse (Market Abuse Directive) [2014] OJ 2 173/179, Article 7(2).
195 Directive 2014/57/EU of the European Parliament and of the Council of 16 April 2014 on Criminal Sanctions for Market Abuse (Market Abuse Directive) [2014] OJ 2 173/179, Article 9.
196 Ibid. Preamble (4).
197 ESMA, 'Market Abuse and Accepted Market Practices' (European Securities and Markets Authority, 26 April 2012) <https://www.esma.europa.eu/Regulation/trading/market-abuse> accessed 14 July 2024.
198 ESMA, 'Report: Actual Use of Sanctioning Powers Under MAD' (European Securities and Markets Authority, 26 April 2012) <https://www.esma.europa.eu/sites/default/files/library/2015/11/2012-270.pdf> accessed 14 July 2024.
199 Directive 2014/57/EU of the European Parliament and of the Council of 16 April 2014 on Criminal Sanctions for Market Abuse (Market Abuse Directive) [2014] OJ 2 173/179, Preamble (2) and Article 11.

for safeguarding the stability of the EU's financial system and part of its role is to ensure the uniform application of the market abuse regime across the EU. The question that must be considered is whether the new criminal powers against market abuse in each Member State will change the behaviour of international banks and prevent them from breaking the law in order to maximise their profits. Clearly, even substantial fines of millions of pounds/euros/dollars are not having a deterrent effect on banks who keep breaking the law.[200] It is possible that the criminal sanctions legislated for by the MAR 2014 and MAD 2014 will act as more of a deterrent than the competition law fines that were imposed in the wake of the LIBOR and FX scandals, although this is not certain, for the reasons discussed below.

It is argued that the new criminal powers are likely to have a significant deterrent effect if they are ever used to their full extent; however, in practice, policy reasons may prevent regulators from using these powers to withdraw banking licences or to wind up banks involved in offences such as market manipulation. This is because banks are widely perceived to be too big to fail for fear of the impact it would have on society.[201] This view is supported by previous government officials who have publicly declared that some banks have become so large that it is difficult to prosecute them.[202] In other words, governments fear a catastrophic fallout if an international bank has its operating licence removed as a sanction for illegally manipulating the market, so, in practice, this power of all EU regulators is unlikely to be used. A further demonstration of this fear of putting one or more banks out of action as a sanction for their illegal actions occurred during the LIBOR crisis, when the then UK Chancellor, George Osborne, wrote to a US official and asked for Barclays Bank not to be prosecuted too aggressively due to the risk that crippling this bank would have on the UK economy.[203]

200 For instance, see the most recent fines imposed on HSBC by the FCA: Financial Conduct Authority, 'FCA Fines HSBC Bank Plc £639 Million For Deficient Transaction Monitoring Controls' (Financial Conduct Authority, 6 May 2022) <https://www.fca.org.uk/news/press-releases/fca-fines-hsbc-bank-plc-deficient-transaction-monitoring-controls#:~:text=FCA%20fines%20HSBC%20Bank%20plc%20%C2%A363.9%20million%20for%20deficient%20transaction%20monitoring%20controls,-Press%20Releases%20First&text=The%20FCA%20has%20fined%20HSBC,to%20identify%20possible%20financial%20crime.> accessed 26 July 2024.

201 H Hillman, 'Are the Current Laws and Potential Enforcement Measures Effective in Achieving the Accountability of Bank Directors for Their Actions, or the Actions of the Banks They Manage? A Comparison of UK and US Approaches' in N Ryder and others (eds), *Fighting Financial Crime in the Global Economic Crisis* (Routledge 2016).

202 M Regmi, and others, 'Big Banks versus Agricultural Banks: Has Too-Big-To-Fail Regulation Affected Efficiency and Scale Economies Measures?' (2021) 103(3) *American Journal of Agricultural Economics* 1164.

203 Republican Staff of the Committee on Financial Services, US House of representatives, 'Too Big to Jail: Inside the Obama Justice Department's Decision Not To Hold Wall Street Accountable' (US House of representatives, 11 July 2016) <https://financialservices.house.gov/uploadedfiles/07072016_oi_tbtj_sr.pdf>accessed 8 July 2024.

Therefore, although the EU and each Member State of the EU now has the power to impose significant financial sanctions for market abuse, it is unlikely that the most powerful of these criminal sanctions will ever be used against the main perpetrators of market manipulation and, therefore, no sufficient deterrent will be imposed on the guilty parties, which will lead to further repeat offences by the banks. However, there are potential solutions to this problem, one of which is the use of deferred prosecution agreements, considered in detail below.

It is worth noting that, in addition to its powers to fine companies up to 10% of their worldwide turnover for breaches of competition law, which has been described as a power that is almost penal in nature due to the size of the fines that can be imposed,[204] the EU also uses recidivism as an aggravating factor when considering the level of fines to impose on an undertaking for breach of competition law.[205] The European Commission's objectives in the imposition of its competition law fines are to promote both general and specific deterrence as well as to reward cooperation and compliance.[206] The way the European Commission applies recidivism as an aggravating factor to fines is that if a company is a repeat offender, having breached competition once or more in the past, the basic fine for the offence can be increased by up to 100% for each infringement established.[207] Therefore, given the level of civil fines that the EU can already impose for breaches of competition law and the consistent use of those powers by the European Commission, the criminal powers introduced by the MAD and MAR 2014 may not be necessary to create a deterrent effect for financial crime in the EU.

4.9 Corporate Criminal Liability

As explained in Chapter 2, corporate criminal liability has been defined as the criminal liability of legal persons for offences.[208] This book is concerned with the different ways in which a bank or broker can be held liable for the actions of its employees, such as its traders who may be involved in benchmark manipulation cartels. In the EU, however, there is not a standard approach to corporate

204 B Rodger, A MacCulloch, *Competition Law and Policy in the EC and UK* (4th edn., Routledge-Cavendish 2009) 25.

205 C Veljanovski, 'Deterrence, Recidivism, and European Cartel Fines' (2011) 7(4) *Journal of Competition Law & Economics* 871.

206 Ibid and R Alexander, 'Flogging the Wrong: EU Corporate Fines Violate the Fundamental Rights of Shareholders' (2021) 12(4) *Journal of European Competition Law & Practice* 301, 303.

207 R Whish and D Bailey, *Competition Law* (10th edn, Oxford University Press 2021).

208 European Commission, 'Liability of Legal Persons for Offences in the EU' (European Commission, 14 February 2014) <https://op.europa.eu/en/publication-detail/-/publication/e6a11989-48d3-41a1-b4ee-8f7051d84253/language-en> accessed 8 July 2024.

criminal liability, as different Member States have different approaches, with some Member States not recognising criminal liability for legal persons.[209]

The EU's competition rules do not contain any criminal sanctions, so corporate criminal liability is not currently an option for EU competition regulators, although individual Member States are able to have criminal corporate liability laws.[210] However, debate exists as to whether the significant fines that can be imposed by the European regulator should be considered to be penal in nature.[211] Fines of up to 10% of the worldwide turnover in the preceding accounting year can be imposed by the Commission on an infringing company,[212] which, due to the significance of the level of the fine, has been described as a 'competence creep' into the sphere of penal law, which, in turn, is seen by some commentators as introducing corporate criminal sanctions through the back door and breaching the general right to a fair trial.[213] The lack of explicit corporate criminal sanctions at the EU level for competition law infringements differs from both the UK, which has individual criminal sanctions for cartels[214] and the US, in which any breach of competition (or antitrust) law carries potential criminal sanctions of up to $100m for a corporation, $1m for an individual and up to 10 years in prison.[215]

Despite not having corporate criminal sanctions for competition law infringements, the EU does recognise the concept of corporate criminal liability, and this has been incorporated into legislation for some financial crimes, such as money laundering[216] and its market abuse regime.[217] The use of criminal sanctions to penalise certain crimes is seen by some as a method for expressing values and for indicating the wrongfulness of certain behaviour.[218] However, there is a diversity of approach to corporate criminal liability amongst Member States, and the EU, therefore, uses the word 'sanctions' rather than 'penalties'

209 E Herlin-Karnell and N Ryder, *Market Manipulation and Insider Trading* (Hart, 2019) 38.

210 For instance, the UK has criminal corporate liability laws – see Chapter 3 for more detail on the identification principle.

211 B Rodger, A MacCulloch, *Competition Law and Policy in the EC and UK* (4th edn., Routledge-Cavendish 2009) 25.

212 Regulation 1/2003/EC on the Implementation of the Rules on Competition Laid Down in Articles 81 and 82 of the Treaty, OJ 2003, L1/1.

213 PA Albrecht and S Braum, 'Deficiencies in the Development of European Criminal Law' (1999) 5 *European Law Journal* 293.

214 Enterprise Act 2002, s.188.

215 Federal Trade Commission, 'The Antitrust Laws' (Federal Trade Commission, 2022) <https://www.ftc.gov/tips-advice/competition-guidance/guide-antitrust-laws/antitrust-laws> accessed 8 July 2024.

216 Directive (EU) 2018/1673 of the European Parliament and of the Council of 23 October 2018 on Combating Money Laundering by Criminal Law, OJ L 284.

217 Directive 2014/57/EU of the European Parliament and of the Council of 16 April 2014 on Criminal Sanctions for Market Abuse (Market Abuse Directive) [2014] OJ 2 173/179.

218 E Herlin-Karnell and N Ryder, *Market Manipulation and Insider Trading* (Hart, 2019) 44.

in its legislation.[219] The MAR 2014 and the MAD 2014 imposed criminal sanctions for the first time in EU law for the financial crimes of market manipulation, money laundering and the unlawful disclosure of inside information. These sanctions can be imposed by regulators against both legal and natural persons in the EU's market abuse regime.[220] Commentators state that the introduction of the criminal sanctions in the MAR 2014 and MAD 2014 'represented an attempt to solve the 2008 financial crisis and its shadows by using the criminal law to boost investor confidence'.[221]

The major weakness of the criminal sanctions given to regulators as part of the 2014 update of the EU market abuse regime is that regulators unlikely to use their powers on large banks for the reasons stated above, and banks know this. In addition to this, it has been demonstrated that fines alone, whether criminal or civil, do not work as a sufficient deterrent to punish market abuses, as many international banks are repeat offenders, presumably because they make so much money through the market abuse and collusion with their competitors.[222] However, the use of criminal sanctions against one or more of the agents, whether these are employees or directors of the company, could result in the deterrent effect hoped for by regulators. It may, therefore, be more useful to use criminal sanctions against individual employees/agents of a corporate entity rather than, or preferably as well as, against the legal person.

4.10 Deferred Prosecution Agreements

This final theme to be examined in this chapter is that of the use of DPAs to enforce corporate crime. The reluctance of regulators to impose criminal sanctions on international banks could be redressed if regulators would consider the use of DPAs in their enforcement of market abuse. According to Camilla de Silva, Joint Head of Bribery and Corruption at the Serious Fraud Office, DPAs were introduced in the UK as a way of a company avoiding prosecution for economic offences by entering into an agreement with the regulator on negotiated terms.[223] De Silva states that:

219 European Commission, 'Liability of Legal Persons for Offences in the EU' (European Commission, 14 February 2014) <https://op.europa.eu/en/publication-detail/-/publication/e6a11989-48d3-41a1-b4ee-8f7051d84253/language-en> accessed 8 July 2024.

220 Regulation (EU) No 596/2014 of the European Parliament and of the Council of 16 April 2014 on Market Abuse (Market Abuse Regulation) [2014] OJ 2 173/1, Articles 8(5), 12(4) and 10(1).

221 E Herlin-Karnell and N Ryder, *Market Manipulation and Insider Trading* (Hart, 2019) 40.

222 See, for example, Barclays, Royal Bank of Scotland and CitiBank, who were each fined by the European Commission in 2013 for their part in the LIBOR manipulation, then again in 2019 for rigging the FX.

223 C de Silva, 'Corporate Criminal Liability and DPAs' (Serious Fraud Office, 21 June 2018) <http://sfo.gov.uk/2018/06/21/corporate-criminal-liability-ai-and-dpas/> accessed 29 July 2024.

> The terms of a DPA might include a financial penalty, costs, restitution for victims and will include disgorgement of profits of wrongdoing and implementation of reforming measures.[224]

The inclusion of some form of behaviour regulation to manage the offending behaviour is a key feature of a DPA. The behaviour regulation for an offence such as benchmark manipulation could include the implementation of a compliance policy designed to avoid future benchmark manipulation, or agreeing to cooperate in the future prosecution of individuals involved in the crime.[225] The advantages for regulators of entering into a DPA with an offending institution rather than taking the business to trial are significant. One commentator summarises the advantages as being:

> DPAs provide authorities with a tool to punish and correct corporate wrongdoing and to help protect the livelihood of employees with no involvement in the wrongdoing, all while reducing the costs associated with going to trial.[226]

Will EU authorities follow the lead of US, French and UK authorities in their use of DPAs? It remains to be seen, but a commentator has noted:

> Two of the most notable developments I think in the areas of white-collar legislation and enforcement in recent years have been an extension of the concept of corporate criminal liability and the separate but linked rise of negotiated structured settlement frameworks.[227]

This statement strongly suggests that the trend in the EU is toward an increased use of DPAs in the regulation of financial crime, including the market abuse of benchmark manipulation. A further advantage of entering a DPA with an offending bank, rather than simply imposing a significant fine for the offence, is that many international banks are repeat offenders for similar financial crimes so, as commentators observe:

> Financial penalties have done little to alter the future conduct of the offending corporations. Indeed, it can be suggested that the frequency with which financial institutions are fined means that it has become

224 Ibid.

225 Serious Fraud Office, 'Deferred Prosecution Agreements' (Serious Fraud Office, 2021) <https://www.sfo.gov.uk/publications/guidance-policy-and-protocols/deferred-prosecution-agreements/> accessed 8 July 2024.

226 Dow Jones Risk & Compliance, 'Deferred Prosecution Agreements in Europe: What to Expect' (Dow Jones Risk & Compliance, 2020) <https://visit.dowjones.com/content/dpa-europe/> accessed 25 July 2024.

227 Ibid.

normal practice for them to set aside large sums of finances in order to meet their financial penalty commitments.[228]

Therefore, the use of a DPA, which will still require the payment of a significant fine by the offending financial institution, will add a new dimension to the enforcement by imposing behavioural changes as well.

Any DPA used in the EU to regulate a financial crime carrying criminal sanctions would involve an agreement being entered into between the competent authority of a Member State, or ESMA, and the bank being investigated for breach of the market abuse rules. In the DPA, the bank would be liable to pay a fine for its behaviour and could be required to make a number of changes to its internal governance procedures in exchange for the promise to drop all criminal charges against the bank at the end of the term of the DPA if it has been complied with. Ryder states that one of the purposes of a DPA is to permit the offending corporation to illustrate good conduct,[229] so the use of DPAs following a finding of market abuse by a regulator could persuade the bank in question to alter its future conduct and comply with the rules of the market for the period of the DPA.

To date, neither the European Commission nor ESMA has yet used a DPA in connection with financial crime; however, DPAs have been used by one Member State – France – and they are used in both the US and UK as well.[230] If the EU and/or each of the Member States were to consider using a DPA alongside the relatively new EU criminal market abuse powers for regulators, it could provide both the deterrent effect of criminal sanctions as well as preventative measures designed to significantly reduce the risk of reoffending by the business that is subject to the DPA. It is worth noting, though, that, for a DPA to maximise its deterrent effect, it should be used in conjunction with criminal proceedings against employees and/or agents of corporations.[231]

4.11 Conclusion

This chapter has argued that the use of the EU's competition law powers was successful in the enforcement of the market manipulation that took place in

228 A Francis and N Ryder, 'Preventing and Intervening in White Collar Crimes: The Role of Regulatory Agencies' in ML Rorie (ed), *The Handbook of White-Collar Crime* (John Wiley & Sons, Inc 2020) 275.

229 N Ryder, '"Too Scared to Prosecute and Too Scared to Jail?" A Critical and Comparative Analysis of Enforcement of Financial Crime Legislation Against Corporations in the USA and the UK' (2018) 82(3) *The Journal of Criminal Law* 245.

230 Dow Jones Risk & Compliance, 'Deferred Prosecution Agreements in Europe: What to Expect' (Dow Jones Risk & Compliance, 2020) <https://visit.dowjones.com/content/dpa-europe/> accessed 25 July 2024.

231 N Ryder, '"Too Scared to Prosecute and Too Scared to Jail?' A Critical and Comparative Analysis of Enforcement of Financial Crime Legislation Against Corporations in the USA and the UK' (2018) 82(3) *The Journal of Criminal Law* 245.

the LIBOR and FX scandals. It is notable that in using its competition powers to enforce these scandals that the EU was aligned with the US, which also used its competition (or antitrust) laws for this purpose, discussed in Chapter 5. Both the EU and US differ from the approach that the UK took to the same scandals, as the UK used financial regulation as its primary enforcement tool, along with criminal charges of conspiracy to defraud levied against some of the traders involved in the manipulation. However, since the LIBOR and FX scandals, the MAD 2014 and MAR 2014 have been introduced, and much greater powers have been given to regulators of market abuse in different Member States of the EU.[232] The criminal powers included in the MAD 2014 and MAR 2014 will have a strong deterrent effect, if used by each Member State to regulate future market manipulation. However, for policy reasons, regulators in different Member States are unlikely to use their wide-ranging powers against large banks. This is because the imposition of MAD 2014's criminal and civil sanctions by regulators, including the power to remove a bank's licence to operate, or to jail individuals in the bank's management team, could result in a corporate death penalty for the bank(s) concerned, which would have a significant effect on investor and market confidence and many innocent employees and trading partners of the banks concerned would be penalised.

In the LIBOR and FX scandals, the EU used its competition law powers to fine benchmark manipulators staggeringly large amounts.[233] The European Commission has fined a total of 25 undertakings between 9% and 10% of their worldwide turnover for cartel infringements of competition law.[234] This demonstrates that the European Commission is making full use of its extensive competition law fining powers, but is underusing some of its other powers, such as the imposition/acceptance of commitments from an offending party. As stated above, some commentators have argued that this level of fine is, in fact, penal in nature, even though it is a civil sanction.[235] If another benchmark manipulation case were to arise now, under the MAD 2014, regulators in each Member State now have the power to levy even larger fines of up to 15% of a company's turnover, so it is possible that the MAD 2014 would be used in future enforcement of market manipulation.[236] As discussed above, if individual regulators in Member States of the EU are reluctant to use the

232 P Nylén, 'Challenges in Market-Abuse Monitoring: Post MiFID' (2020) 12(4) *Journal of Securities Operations & Custody* 367.

233 For instance, the fine to Deutsche Bank for its participation in the ERIDs cartel was €465.8 million.

234 European Commission, 'Statistics on Cartel Cases' (European Commission, 10 December 2021) <https://ec.europa.eu/competition-policy/cartels/statistics_en> accessed 21 July 2024.

235 B Rodger, A MacCulloch, *Competition Law and Policy in the EC and UK* (4th edn., Routledge-Cavendish 2009) 25.

236 Regulation (EU) No 596/2014 of the European Parliament and of the Council of 16 April 2014 on Market Abuse (Market Abuse Regulation) [2014] OJ 2 173/1, Article 30(2)(j)(i).

wide-ranging criminal powers they now have to enforce market abuse, they should consider using a DPA, which offers them the opportunity to combine a large fine with the imposition of obligations on an offending bank to improve its internal corporate governance procedures and refrain from future market abuse for the term of the DPA.

Overall, in the enforcement of the LIBOR and FX benchmark manipulation cartels competition law, as used by the European Commission, has been shown to be a good tool to enforce financial crime, providing regulators with the power to issue extremely large fines that send a clear message to banks and deter them from future financial crime.

5 US Competition Law and Financial Crime

5.1 Introduction

This chapter examines the enforcement mechanisms used by United States (US) regulators[1] in relation to the London Interbank Offered Rate (LIBOR) and Foreign Exchange (FX) benchmark interest rate manipulation (benchmark manipulation). The aim of this chapter is to examine the response of the US to the LIBOR and FX scandal through the lens of competition law with the aim of adding to and updating the limited literature on this topic.[2] This chapter focuses on the roles of the different US regulators and how they interacted with each other to enforce the same benchmark manipulation offences. The difference between the enforcement approaches used by the Department of Justice (DoJ) for the LIBOR and the FX benchmark manipulation will be assessed and conclusions will be drawn as to the possible reasons for its use of competition law to enforce the FX scandal, but its limited use of competition law in the earlier LIBOR scandal.[3]

1 The US regulators involved in the LIBOR and FX benchmark manipulation enforcement were the Department of Justice, the Federal Trade Commission, the Federal Reserve, the Office of the Comptroller of the Currency, the Securities and Exchange Commission and the Commodities Futures Trading Commission.

2 See, for example, SE Foster, 'LIBOR Manipulation and Antitrust Allegations' (2013) 11(3) *DePaul Business & Commercial Law Journal* 291; SD Ledgerwood and others, 'The Intersection of Market Manipulation Law and Monopolization under the Sherman Act: Does It Make Economic Sense?' (2019) 40(1) *Energy Law Journal* 47; S Strimling, E Talley, 'Who Put the 'Lie' in LIBOR (And Who Should Take It Out)? Civil LIBOR Litigation in the US' (2014) 8(2) *Law and Financial Markets Review* 145; JK Wald, 'Antitrust Damages in Financial Markets' (2020) 16(1) *Journal of Competition Law and Economics*, 63; and J Rhee, 'Who Is Responsible for LIBOR Rate-Fixing?' (26 December 2013, The Harvard Law School Forum on Corporate Governance and Financial Regulation) <https://papers.ssrn.com/sol3/papers.cfm?abstract_id=3400237> accessed 3 July 2024.

3 SD Ledgerwood and others, 'The Intersection of Market Manipulation Law and Monopolization under the Sherman Act: Does It Make Economic Sense?' (2019) 40(1) *Energy Law Journal* 47, 84; and US Department of Justice, 'Deutsche Bank's London Subsidiary Agrees to Plead Guilty in Connection with Long-Running Manipulation of LIBOR' (US Department of

DOI: 10.4324/9781003425106-5

This chapter begins by tracing the development of US financial services regulation to provide a comprehensive background to the laws in force at the time of the LIBOR and FX scandals. The various regulators in the financial services industry will be identified and their powers and role in the benchmark manipulation scandals described. The chapter will then provide an overview of the US antitrust, or competition, law that was primarily used in the US enforcement of the FX manipulation. Competition law was also used to bring private class actions by private investors who claimed financial loss because of the benchmark manipulations carried out by the banks involved in the LIBOR and FX scandals.[4] Following the summary of the development of financial services regulation and competition law in the run up to the LIBOR and FX crisis, the enforcement measures taken by US regulators to the benchmark manipulation will then be examined and critically analysed.

The chapter moves on to look at the legislation introduced following the benchmark manipulation scandals. Following this, the four themes that run through each chapter of this book will be addressed. First, there will be an examination of the competition law leniency and whistleblowing regime in the US. The reason for this examination is that an integral part of the enforcement of cartel activity, such as the cartels seen in the LIBOR and FX manipulation, is the operation of a successful whistleblowing and leniency regime. A successful leniency and whistleblowing regime is a crucial tool for any regulator dealing with cartels because of the difficulty regulators experience in gathering sufficient evidence to prosecute a cartel without inside information.[5] The DoJ views its cartel leniency programme as a key enforcement tool, and it is heavily incentivised.[6]

The next theme to be examined will be the pros and cons of using civil and/or criminal penalties against the benchmark manipulation cartels.[7] This section of the chapter will evaluate the deterrent effects of the criminal and civil penalties. Following on from this, the third theme, the issue of corporate

---

Justice, 23 April 2015) <https://www.justice.gov/opa/pr/deutsche-banks-london-subsidiary-agrees-plead-guilty-connection-long-running-manipulation> accessed 14 July 2024.

4 Reuters, 'Law Firms Susman Godfrey, Hausfeld Seek $25 Mln From Latest LIBOR Settlement' (*Reuters,* 30 October 2023) <https://www.reuters.com/legal/transactional/law-firms-susman-godfrey-hausfeld-seek-25-mln-latest-libor-settlement-2023-10-30/> accessed 12 July 2024; Managed Care Advisory Group, 'LIBOR Manipulation Settlements' (MCAG, 2024) <https://www.mcaginc.com/post/libor> accessed 12 July 2024; and M Capodanno, 'Market Braces for Drawn-Out LIBOR Scandal' (2012) 1(1) *Total Securitization & Credit Investment* 49, 49.

5 NH Miller, 'Strategic Leniency and Cartel Enforcement' (2009) 99(3) *The American Economic Review* 750.

6 Daniel D Sokol, 'Cartels, Corporate Compliance, and What Practitioners Really Think about Enforcement' (2012) 78(1) *Antitrust Law Journal* 201.

7 P O'Loughlin, 'The Criminal Enforcement of Antitrust Law - The Importance of Building an Enforcement Culture and How to Create It' (2016) 5(1) *UCL Journal of Law and Jurisprudence* 116, 120.

liability, will be considered. Issues surrounding corporate criminal liability will be analysed in order to assess the impact of a criminal conviction on a company compared to the impact of a civil penalty.[8] The final theme to be considered is the use of deferred prosecution agreements (DPAs), available when corporate criminal liability has been established. The use of DPAs by the US regulators in the LIBOR and FX enforcement will be analysed and evaluated.

Finally, the chapter will conclude with an overview of the use of competition law by US regulatory agencies to enforce the LIBOR and FX benchmark manipulation scandal and will put forward recommendations for changes to the US regime.

5.2 Development of Financial Services Regulation in the US

In this section, the recent history of financial services regulation will be examined to set the scene for the LIBOR and FX enforcement action taken by regulators. US banking laws have been subjected to several decades of deregulation, followed by re-regulation, followed by deregulation.[9] Deregulation is always driven by a desire to increase banking efficiency, which is seen to provide benefits for the economy as a whole.[10] Conversely, deregulation has also been blamed for the emergence of shadow banking and the increasingly opaque transactions and practices that contributed to the 2008 financial crisis and the LIBOR and FX manipulation.[11]

US banks are subject to regulation at both federal and state level; each state has its own regulatory commission governing banking, and at the federal level, there are multiple regulatory authorities.[12] The key regulators of the financial services sector are the Federal Reserve (Fed), the Office of the Comptroller of the Currency (OCC), the Securities and Exchange Commission (SEC) and the Commodities Futures Trading Commission (CFTC). The key responsibilities of each regulator will be briefly summarised below.[13] The Fed is the central bank of the US and is responsible for the stability and viability of the financial system, including the regulation of banks.[14] The OCC supervises all national banks and federal savings associations as well as federal branches and

8 A Hamdani and A Klement, 'Corporate Crime and Deterrence' (2008) 61(2) *Stanford Law Review* 271.

9 K Judge, 'Regulation and Deregulation: The Baseline Challenge' (2018) 104(1) *Virginia Law Review* 101.

10 S Chava and others, 'Banking Deregulation and Innovation' (2013) 109(3) *Journal of Financial Economics* 759.

11 NL Rose, 'Regulation and Deregulation of the US Banking Industry Causes, Consequences, and Implications for the Future' (2015) 1(1) *Chicago Scholarship Online*.

12 LG Baxter, 'Capture Nuances in Financial Regulation' (2012) 47(3) *Wake Forest Law Review* 537.

13 Ibid.

14 R Grosse, 'The Global Financial Crisis—Market Misconduct and Regulation From a Behavioral View' (2017) 41(1) *Research in International Business and Finance* 387.

agencies of foreign banks. It is an independent bureau of the Department of the Treasury, and its mission is to promote and expand the banking industry, which can sometimes cause clashes with that of the Fed on financial policy and regulation.[15] Two further key US financial services regulators are the SEC and the CFTC.[16] The SEC was created by the Securities Exchange Act of 1934 in order to bring more regulation to the financial markets following the stock market collapse.[17] The SEC's primary aim is to enforce the law against market manipulation and to act as an 'economic watchdog'.[18] The CFTC regulates the US derivatives markets, including futures, swaps and certain kinds of options. Its stated aim is to promote the integrity, resilience and vibrancy of the US derivatives market through sound regulation.[19] This 'hodgepodge of regulatory structures' is often criticised by commentators as being irrational and incomprehensive.[20] Each of these federal regulators were involved with the enforcement of the LIBOR and/or the FX manipulation scandals, resulting in multiple regulatory fines and criminal actions for the banks involved, as described below.

This chapter will focus on the enforcement action adopted by the DoJ and the extent to which it used its competition law enforcement powers in the LIBOR and FX scandal. It is important to look at the development of antifraud legislation in the decades prior to the LIBOR crisis because the manipulation of the LIBOR benchmark interest rate was primarily enforced by regulators using offences in the Wire Fraud Statute 1952.[21] This statute has been described as a 'first line of defence' or 'stopgap' device to permit prosecution of new forms of fraud.[22] The fines imposed by the DoJ for the manipulation of the yen, Swiss franc, British pound, euro and US dollar LIBOR, as well as for manipulation of the Euroyen Tokyo Interbank offered Rate (TIBOR) were for wire fraud and/or conspiracy to commit wire fraud, both criminal

15 LG Baxter, 'Capture Nuances in Financial Regulation' (2012) 47(3) *Wake Forest Law Review* 537.

16 B Istemi and R Jannes, 'Regulatory Interventions in the US Oil and Gas Sector: How Do the Stock Markets Perceive the CFTC's Announcements During the 2008 Financial Crisis?' (2016) 54(1) *Energy Economics* 337.

17 A Francis and N Ryder, 'Preventing and Intervening in White Collar Crimes: The Role of Regulatory Agencies' in ML Rorie (ed) *The Handbook of White-Collar Crime* (John Wiley & Sons Inc 2020).

18 E Herlin-Karnell and N Ryder, *Market Manipulation and Insider Trading* (Hart 2019) 111.

19 D Fischer, 'Dodd-Frank's Failure to Address CFTC Oversight of Self-Regulatory Organization Rulemaking' (2015) 115(1) *Columbia Law Review* 69.

20 LG Baxter, 'Capture Nuances in Financial Regulation' (2012) 47(3) *Wake Forest Law Review* 537, 549.

21 See, for example: US Department of Justice, 'Deutsche Bank's London Subsidiary Agrees to Plead Guilty in Connection with Long-Running Manipulation of LIBOR' (Department of Justice, 23 April 2015) <https://www.justice.gov/opa/pr/deutsche-banks-london-subsidiary-agrees-plead-guilty-connection-long-running-manipulation> accessed 4 July 2024.

22 A Palmer, *Countering Economic Crime* (Routledge 2018); and A Zelcer, 'Mail and Wire Fraud' (2012) 49(2) *The American Criminal Law Review* 985, 986.

offences.[23] The Wire Fraud Statute is drafted widely, and it can be seen from the wording (provided below) that the manipulation of a financial benchmark carried out through the medium of electronic chat rooms clearly comes within its remit, which states that:

> Whoever, having devised or intending to devise any scheme or artifice to defraud, or for obtaining money or property by means of false or fraudulent pretences, representations, or promises, transmits or causes to be transmitted by means of wire, radio or television communication in interstate or foreign commerce, any writings, signs, signals, pictures or sounds for the purpose of executing such a scheme or artifice, shall be fined under this title or imprisoned.[24]

However, in January 2022 the wire fraud convictions for two Deutsche Bank traders for their participation in the LIBOR manipulation were overturned by a Second Circuit court. The court stated that the federal Mail and Wire Fraud Statutes 'are not catch-all laws designed to punish all acts of wrongdoing or dishonourable practices'.[25] This demonstrates that the use of competition law, which the DoJ used in its enforcement of the FX benchmark manipulation, is a more appropriate enforcement mechanism for the benchmark manipulation which took place in the LIBOR and FX scandal than the offence of wire fraud.

A key development in the regulation of fraud in the financial services sector was the introduction of the Sarbanes-Oxley Act in 2002.[26] This was introduced following the Enron scandal, and one of the Act's key aims was to deter fraudulent and unethical behaviour.[27] The Sarbanes-Oxley Act increased the penalties for destroying, altering or fabricating records in federal investigations, and it also imposed corporate criminal penalties for certain misconduct including fraudulent financial activity and required the SEC to create regulations concerning how public companies must comply with the law.[28] The

23 Practical Law Antitrust, 'DoJ LIBOR Manipulation Investigation Chart' (Practical Law, 31 December 2020) <https://uk.practicallaw.thomsonreuters.com/w-001-0974?transitionType=Default&contextData=(sc.Default)&firstPage=true> accessed 8 July 2024.

24 Wire Fraud Statute 1952, 18 U.S.C. s.1343.

25 Foley Hoag LLP, 'Second Circuit's Rejection of Fraud Theory in LIBOR Manipulation Case May Have Far-Reaching Implications' (Foley Hoag LLP, 8 February 2022) <https://foleyhoag.com/news-and-insights/blogs/white-collar-law-and-investigations/2022/february/second-circuit-s-rejection-of-fraud-theory-in-libor-manipulation-case-may-have-far-reaching-implicat/> accessed 29 July 2024.

26 A Palmer, *Countering Economic Crime* (Routledge 2018); and Sarbanes-Oxley Act of 2002, Pub.L. 107–204, 116 Stat.745.

27 UQ Bajra and others, 'The Impact of the Sarbanes-Oxley Act on the Integrity of Financial Reporting: Was it Meritorious?' (2023) 34(1) *Journal of Corporate Accounting and Finance* 184, 184.

28 LL Bargeron and others, 'Sarbanes-Oxley and Corporate Risk-Taking' (2010) 49(1) *Journal of Accounting & Economics* 34.

Sarbanes-Oxley Act also increased the maximum penalty for wire and mail fraud from five years to 20 years' imprisonment, and it provided prosecutors with several new weapons that can be used in fraud cases.[29] These additional powers for regulators include the codification of securities fraud as a federal crime and the criminalisation of the early destruction of corporate audit records.[30] Following the Sarbanes-Oxley Act, the Securities Fraud Statute of 2003 was introduced in order to address a number of securities frauds that had resulted in investors losing over $40b.[31] The Securities Fraud Statute had as one of its stated aims the deterrence of people from committing securities fraud by the imposition of a 25-year custodial sentence.[32] A large number of fraud statutes have been created by the US, each criminalising a different fraudulent activity. The Wire Fraud Statute mentioned above, together with the Mail Fraud Act of 1872, remain the Acts most used by prosecutors though, as demonstrated by regulators' use of the Wire Fraud Statute for the enforcement of the LIBOR crisis.[33]

The 2008 financial crisis resulted in a lingering recession and slow-down in growth across most countries.[34] In the US, the crisis produced losses of financial wealth estimated by the International Monetary Fund at more than $2.7t in the US and another $1.4t in the rest of the world.[35] This crisis led to the introduction of new regulations in the US, with the aim of preventing a similar crisis in the future.[36] At the time of the 2008 financial crisis, the US financial system was fragmented, with many different regulators, including many of those described above. This fragmentation resulted in regulators struggling to identify which of them had the authority to act in certain situations, and there was no single regulator overseeing the efforts to deal with the financial crisis.[37] Timothy Geithner, former president of the New York Fed, referred to the multiple regulators as 'the Balkanised financial regulatory system' and said that

29 K Brickey, 'White Collar Criminal Law in Comparative Perspective: The Sarbanes-Oxley Act of 2002' (2004) 8 *Buffalo Criminal Law Review* 221.

30 N Ryder, *Financial Crime in the 21st Century* (Edward Elgar 2011).

31 K Brickey, 'From Enron to Worldccom and Beyond: Life and Crime After Sarbanes-Oxley' (2003) 81 *Washington University Law Review* 357.

32 L Pazicky, 'A New Arrow in the Quiver of Federal Securities Fraud Prosecutors: Section 807 of the Sarbanes-Oxley Act of 2002' (2003) 81 *Washington University Law Quarterly* 801.

33 CJ Williams, 'What Is the Gist of the Mail Fraud Statute' (2014) 66(2) *Oklahoma Law Review* 287.

34 R Grosse, 'The Global Financial Crisis—Market Misconduct and Regulation From a Behavioral View' (2017) 41(1) *Research in International Business and Finance* 387.

35 Ibid.

36 Harvard Law Review, 'Financial Regulation – Dodd-Frank Act – FSOC Determines General Electric Subsidiary No Longer a Systemically Important Financial Institution – Financial Stability Oversight Council, Basis for the Financial Stability Oversight Council's Recession of its Determination Regarding GE Capital Global Holdings, LLC' (2017) 130(4) *Harvard Law Review* 1289.

37 BS Bernanke and others, *Firefighting: The Financial Crisis and Its Lessons* (Penguin Random House 2019) 115.

the system: 'could use reform, to reduce turf battles among redundant agencies with overlapping responsibilities'.[38] Geithner noted that the US system of financial regulation has barely been reformed, despite the many weaknesses revealed by the financial crisis, even after the regulatory changes implemented in its wake, which are described below.[39]

Following the 2008 financial crisis, the Financial Stability Oversight Council (FSOC) was created by the Dodd-Frank Wall Street Reform and Consumer Protection Act of 2010 (the Dodd-Frank Act).[40] The FSOC is headed by the Department of the Treasury, and its stated aim is to comprehensively monitor the stability of the US financial system.[41] It is a collaborative body made up of the head of each of its member agencies, which include the SEC, the Fed, the CFEC and the Department of the Treasury.[42] There are significant flaws in the structure and mandate of the FSOC, which is intended to bring US financial regulators together in order to identify and respond to threats to financial stability. The main flaw being that the FSOC is dominated by the Fed and the Department of the Treasury.[43]

As a response to the 2008 financial crisis, there was a clear drive to re-regulate the financial markets.[44] The aim of the Dodd-Frank Act was to promote the financial stability of the US by improving accountability and transparency in the financial system, to end 'too big to fail', to protect the US taxpayer by ending bailouts and to protect consumers from abusive financial services practices.[45] However the Dodd-Frank Act has failed in its aims to end 'too big to

38 Ibid, 116 and H Davies, 'Bernanke, Paulson and Geithner: Revisiting the 2008 Financial Crisis' *The Guardian* (London, 29 May 2019) <https://www.theguardian.com/business/2019/may/29/bernanke-paulson-and-geithner-revisiting-the-2008-financial-crisis> accessed 18 July 2024.

39 Ibid, 116.

40 A Francis and N Ryder, 'Preventing and Intervening in White Collar Crimes: The Role of Regulatory Agencies' in ML. Rorie (ed), *The Handbook of White Collar Crime* (John Wiley & Sons, Inc. 2020).

41 Harvard Law Review, 'Financial Regulation – Dodd-Frank Act – FSOC Determines General Electric Subsidiary No Longer a Systemically Important Financial Institution – Financial Stability Oversight Council, Basis for the Financial Stability Oversight Council's Recession of its Determination Regarding GE Capital Global Holdings, LLC' (2017) 130(4) *Harvard Law Review* 1289.

42 HJ Allen, 'Putting the "Financial Stability" in Financial Stability Oversight Council' (2015) 76(5) *Ohio State Law Journal* 1087.

43 For example, see Harvard Law Review, 'Financial Regulation – Dodd-Frank Act – FSOC Determines General Electric Subsidiary No Longer a Systemically Important Financial Institution – Financial Stability Oversight Council, Basis for the Financial Stability Oversight Council's Recession of its Determination Regarding GE Capital Global Holdings, LLC' (2017) 130(4) *Harvard Law Review* 1289; and HJ Allen, 'Putting the "Financial Stability" in Financial Stability Oversight Council' (2015) 76(5) *Ohio State Law Journal* 1087.

44 A Palmer, *Countering Economic Crime* (Routledge 2018).

45 R Chaudhuri, *The Changing Face of American Banking Deregulation, Reregulation and the Global Financial System* (Palgrave Macmillan 2014) 147.

fail' companies, demonstrated by the lack of any effort to break up large bank holding companies such as Bank of America, Citigroup, JP Morgan Chase and others.[46]

The multiplicity of regulators with overlapping jurisdiction leaves the US with many problems, some of which individual regulators have attempted to solve themselves by entering into memorandums of understanding (MoU) with each other to foster cooperation and communication between them – for example the DoJ's Antitrust Division entered into a MoU with the SEC in 2020.[47] The number of regulators causes even more problems for the banks and other financial institutions when they break the law and have to run the gauntlet of many fines and prosecutions for the same offence. It is important to note too that the double jeopardy clause of the Fifth Amendment is limited by the dual sovereignty doctrine, which holds that prosecutions under federal and state law are not prosecutions from different regulators for the same offence.[48] This means that one state can prosecute a defendant who has already been prosecuted by the federal government or another state for the same conduct – a powerful deterrent.[49] This array of different financial services regulators formed the backdrop for the LIBOR and FX manipulation, which is described below, together with the enforcement action taken by the various regulators.

The next section describes the development of competition law in the run up to the LIBOR and FX crisis.

5.3 Development of US Competition Law and Policy

As with the development of the financial services regulation prior to the LIBOR and FX crisis, this section will now review the recent development of competition law, known as antitrust law in the US. The start of US antitrust law can be traced to the Sherman Antitrust Act of 1890 (the Sherman Act),[50] which was enacted to govern the behaviour of large businesses or trusts as they were then referred to.[51] This legislation was based on two antitrust concepts: restraint of trade and monopolisation. The Sherman Act was not detailed or specific, which meant that it was largely left to the interpretation

46 R Prasch, 'The Dodd-Frank Act: Financial Reform or Business as Usual?' (2012) XLV I(2) *Journal of Economic Issues* 549, 552.

47 Securities and Exchange Commission, 'Securities and Exchange Commission and Justice Department's Antitrust Division Sign Historic Memorandum of Understanding' (US *Securities and Exchange Commission*, 22 June 2020) <https://www.sec.gov/news/press-release/2020-140> accessed 29 July 2024.

48 See *Abbate v United States*, 359 U.S. 187 (1959) and *Bartkus v Illinois*, 359 U.S. 121 (1959).

49 SS Beale, 'What Are the Rules if Everybody Wants to Play? Multiple Federal and State Prosecutors (Acting) as Regulators' in A Barkow and R Barkow (eds), *Prosecutors in the Boardroom: Using Criminal Law to Regulate Corporate Conduct* (New York University Press 2011) 281.

50 Sherman Antitrust Act, ch. 647, 26 Stat. 209 (codified as amended by 15 U.S.C. §1-7 (2018)).

51 EM Fox, 'Against Goals' (2013) 81(5) *Fordham Law Review* 2157.

of the judiciary to create the substantive content of the law.[52] Of great significance was the Supreme Court's decision in 1897 in the case of *United States v. Trans-Missouri Freight Ass'n,* which interpreted Section 1 of the Sherman Act to apply to all restraints of trade, whether those restraints were reasonable or not.[53] The heavy reliance on federal case law for the development of antitrust law has resulted in a myriad of individual judgements that can significantly deviate in both their reasoning and their conclusions.[54]

Unlike in the UK or EU, competition law has a long history of being applied in the financial services sector in the US, with the landmark case of *United States v Philadelphia National Bank* in 1963, heralding the start of competition laws being applied to bank mergers.[55] Since *Philadelphia National Bank,* competition law, mainly in the form of merger regulation by the DoJ and the FTC, has been a feature of the financial services sector.[56] However, before this case, it was not universally accepted that antitrust law should be used to regulate the financial sector.[57] The banking sector had used the argument that financial regulation alone was sufficient to protect the public interest and, therefore, antitrust jurisdiction was unnecessary. This argument, when put forward in *Philadelphia National Bank,* was rejected by the Supreme Court.[58] Since then, the DoJ has been active in enforcing antitrust in the financial sector, with cases involving credit card networks and mergers being two of the key areas of antitrust enforcement in the banking industry in recent years.[59] Deputy Assistant Attorney General Murray stated in 2020 that the Antitrust Division of the DoJ:

> Consciously has decided to play an active role in promotion of competition in the financial markets, through criminal prosecution, civil merger and conduct analysis, and partnership with the SEC.[60]

This long history of enforcement of competition law in the banking sector, dating from the *Philadelphia National Bank* case, set the scene for the use of

52 M Glick, 'Antitrust and Economic History: The Historic Failure of the Chicago School of Antitrust' (2019) 64(3) *Antitrust Bulletin* 295.

53 *United States v. Trans-Missouri Freight Ass'n,* 166 U.S. 290 (1897).

54 DJ Gerber, *Competition Law and Antitrust* (Oxford University Press 2020) 92.

55 *United States v Philadelphia National Bank* 374 U.S. 321 (1963).

56 H Hovenkamp and C Shapiro, 'Horizontal Mergers, Market Structure, and Burdens of Proof' (2018) 127(7) Yale Law Journal 1996.

57 LJ White, 'Antitrust and Financial Regulation in the Wake of Philadelphia National Bank: Complements, Not Substitutes' (2015) 80(2) *Antitrust Law Journal* 413.

58 Ibid.

59 Ibid.

60 M Murray, 'Deputy Assistant Attorney General Michael Murray Delivers Remarks at University of Michigan Law School' (US Department of Justice, 14 October 2020) <https://www.justice.gov/opa/speech/deputy-assistant-attorney-general-michael-murray-delivers-remarks-university-michigan-law> accessed 30 July 2024.

competition law in the LIBOR and FX benchmark manipulation and in the private multijurisdictional class actions that will be looked at below, based on competition law.

The goals of US competition law have changed significantly since the introduction of the Sherman Act. Before the 1970s the courts were primarily concerned with the domestic impact of antitrust law, often focusing on issues such as fairness, economic liberty and equality of opportunity amongst competitors.[61] However a significant change to competition law goals took place with the emergence of the Chicago School of Antitrust, which took over from the prevailing intellectual movement of neoliberalism. The Chicago School of Antitrust persuaded the judiciary to refocus antitrust law on the interests of consumers rather than on the interests of competing firms.[62] This resulted in the judiciary taking a very narrow view of the goals of competition law, focusing only on the efficiency of the economy and benefits to consumers.[63] Recently, competition law goals in the US changed again, with the emergence of a new antitrust movement called neo-Brandeis.[64] The neo-Brandeis school of antitrust has become known for its abhorrence of big business as anticompetitive and harmful to democracy. This ideology is known as 'the curse of bigness' and is seen as a challenger movement to the previously reigning consumer welfare establishment in antitrust law.[65] This current antitrust movement explains much of what happened in the LIBOR and FX enforcement actions taken by the DoJ and other competition enforcement agencies in the US, which took significant criminal and civil action against the international banks when they were found to have participated in the benchmark manipulation scandal.

Following the enactment of the Sherman Act, a second key antitrust statute, the Clayton Antitrust Act of 1914 (the Clayton Act),[66] extended the scope of the Sherman Act to include the regulation of mergers.[67] A third key antitrust statute is the Federal Trade Commission Act of 1914 (the FTC Act)[68] which established the FTC, described below, and prohibited unfair methods of competition and unfair or deceptive acts or practices.[69]

61 DJ Gerber, *Competition Law and Antitrust* (Oxford University Press 2020) 92.

62 KG Elzinga, DE Mills, 'Antitrust Predation and the Antitrust Paradox' (2014) 57(3) *Journal of Law and Economics* 181.

63 A Bradford and others, 'The Chicago School's Limited Influence on International Antitrust' (2020) 87(1) *University of Chicago Law Review* 297.

64 DA Crane, 'How Much Brandeis Do the Neo-Brandeisians Want?' (2019) 64(4) *Antitrust Bulletin* 531.

65 D Sokol, 'Antitrust's "Curse of Bigness" Problem' (2020) 118(1) *Michigan Law Review* 1259, 1260.

66 Clayton Antitrust Act 38 Stat. 730 (1914).

67 M Glick, 'Antitrust and Economic History: The Historic Failure of the Chicago School of Antitrust' (2019) 64(3) *Antitrust Bulletin* 295, 307.

68 Federal Trade Commission Act, 15 U.S.C..

69 M Glick, 'Antitrust and Economic History: The Historic Failure of the Chicago School of Antitrust' (2019) 64(3) Antitrust Bulletin 295, 302.

Of particular relevance to benchmark manipulation is Section 1 of the Sherman Act, which deals with agreements that unreasonably restrain trade:

> Every contract, combination in the form of trust or otherwise, or conspiracy, in restraint of trade or commerce among the several States, or with foreign nations, is declared to be illegal. Every person who shall make any contract or engage in any combination or conspiracy hereby declared to be illegal shall be deemed guilty of a felony.[70]

Therefore, in order to prove a breach of this section, the courts must, first, determine that a contract, agreement or conspiracy exists and, second, that the agreement or conspiracy is an unreasonable restraint of trade. The third and final criteria that must be established to prove a breach of Section 1 of the Sherman Act is that the agreement or conspiracy must affect trade in the states or foreign nations. The Supreme Court has defined an agreement for the purposes of antitrust law very widely as 'a unity of purpose or a common design and understanding or a meeting of the minds in an unlawful arrangement'.[71]

Once an agreement has been established, the court will consider whether it unreasonably restrains trade. Restraints of trade have been divided into two distinct categories by the courts: restraints that are conclusively presumed to be unreasonable, known as *per se* illegal,[72] and restraints analysed under a test developed by the Supreme Court called the rule of reason.[73] In relation to *per se* illegality, the US Supreme Court has stated that:

> Certain kinds of agreements will so often prove so harmful to competition and so rarely prove justified that the antitrust laws do not require proof that an agreement of that kind is, in fact, anticompetitive in the particular circumstances.[74]

The characterisation of conduct as *per se* illegal has powerful consequences in criminal prosecutions of Section 1 of the Sherman Act by the DoJ and in the litigation of private claims for treble damages, mentioned below.[75] Examples of agreements held to be *per se* illegal include agreements to fix prices or out-

70 Sherman Antitrust Act, ch. 647, 26 Stat. 209 (codified as amended by 15 U.S.C. §1-7 (2018)) section 1.

71 *Copperweld Corp v Independence Tube Corp.*, 467 US 752 (1984).

72 WE Kovacic, 'The Future Adaptation of the Per Se Rule of Illegality in US Antitrust Law' (2021) 1(1) *Columbia Business Law Review* 33.

73 GJ Werden, 'Antitrust's Rule of Reason: Only Competition Matters' (2014) 79(2) *Antitrust Law Journal* 713.

74 *NYNEX Corp. v Dixon, Inc.*, 525 US 128 (1998).

75 See *Palmer v BCG of Ga., Inc.* 498 U.S. 46, 48 (1990); and WE Kovacic, 'The Future Adaptation of the Per Se Rule of Illegality in US Antitrust Law' (2021) 1(1) *Columbia Business Law Review* 33.

put and agreements to divide territories or customers.[76] In the case of benchmark manipulation, a private multidistrict antitrust class action case brought before US courts relating to the LIBOR manipulation has alleged that the agreements between traders of competing banks to raise or lower the LIBOR or FX benchmark interest rate violated the *per se* rule against horizontal price fixing.[77] This has been a mainstay of the plaintiffs' contention that the financial crime of benchmark manipulation breached Section 1 of the Sherman Antitrust Act. The US Court of Appeal for the Second Circuit concluded that the facts alleged by the plaintiffs, namely that executives and managers for several banks were directing the suppression of LIBOR from within the US, were sufficient to establish personal jurisdiction over the banks under a conspiracy-based theory of jurisdiction.[78]

In addition to the *per se* rule, the rule of reason is a concept developed by the courts to test whether an anticompetitive practice restrains trade within the meaning of Section 1 of the Sherman Act.[79] Unlike *per se* violations of Section 1 of the Sherman Act, which are automatically prohibited, the rule of reason is applied in order to evaluate the competitive effect of agreements by analysing the facts peculiar to the business, the history of the restraint and the reasons why it was imposed.[80]

In the LIBOR and FX benchmark manipulation cartels, the *per se* rule, not the rule of reason, was relevant because the cartels involved price fixing, which is automatically prohibited by Section 1 of the Sherman Act. If the court determines that the conduct of a corporation or an individual breaches Section 1 of the Sherman Act, it could lead to civil and/or criminal penalties being imposed. For example, criminal antitrust enforcement can give rise to a fine of either up to $100m for a corporation or twice the gain from the illegal conduct, or twice the loss to the victims.[81] The DoJ increasingly seeks the latter in its cases against larger corporations.[82] Individuals, if convicted of a breach of competition law, can be fined up to $1m and may also be imprisoned for

76 JF Ponsoldt, 'Toward the Reaffirmation of the Antitrust Rule of Per Se Illegality as a Law of Rules for Horizontal Price Fixing and Territorial Allocation Agreements: A Reflection on the Palmer Case in a Renewed Era of Economic Regulation' (2009) 62(2) *SMU Law Review* 635.

77 *In re LIBOR-based Financial Instruments Antitrust Litigation*, No. 17-1569 (2d Cir. 2021).

78 Justia US law, 'In re LIBOR-based Financial Instruments Antitrust Litigation, No 17-1569 (2d Cir 2021)' (*Justia*, 30 December 2021) <https://law.justia.com/cases/federal/appellate-courts/ca2/17-1569/17-1569-2021-12-30.html> accessed 30 July 2024.

79 GJ Werden, 'Antitrust's Rule of Reason: Only Competition Matters' (2014) 79(2) *Antitrust Law Journal* 713.

80 JF Ponsoldt, 'Toward the Reaffirmation of the Antitrust Rule of Per Se Illegality as a Law of Rules for Horizontal Price Fixing and Territorial Allocation Agreements: A Reflection on the Palmer Case in a Renewed Era of Economic Regulation' (2009) 62(2) *SMU Law Review* 635.

81 JD Beretta and J Terzaken, 'The Cartels and Leniency Review: USA' (2022) 11(1) *The Cartels and Leniency Review* 294, 299.

82 Ibid.

up to ten years.[83] The fines for violation of the Sherman Act can be increased beyond the statutory maximums in appropriate cases that involve cartel-related activities pursuant to the alternative criminal fine provision of the Sentencing Reform Act.[84]

Civil sanctions for a breach of the Sherman Act include damages, injunctive orders to prevent and restrain violations of the antitrust laws and structural remedies (including dissolution and divestiture) in order to restore competition.[85] There are two federal agencies responsible for the enforcement of antitrust law: the DoJ Antitrust Division and the FTC. The DoJ is part of the executive branch of government and is subject to political control. The DoJ does not enforce antitrust law directly but is permitted to commence a lawsuit pursuing criminal and/or civil remedies. The FTC is an independent enforcement agency, although it is dependent on Congress for funding, so it is not entirely free of political influence.[86] The FTC, unlike the DoJ, enforces antitrust law directly, through fines or other orders. Because both the DoJ and FTC have jurisdiction to investigate many of the same types of antitrust offences, in practice, they often coordinate with each other before moving forward with an investigation and will refer cases to each other if one agency is better equipped to deal with a particular investigation.[87]

The DoJ, as a matter of policy, pursues criminal charges only for the most serious breaches of antitrust law.[88] These are the breaches mentioned above – breaches of the *per se* rule – which can also be categorised as 'horizontal' breaches or cartels, compared to the less serious 'vertical' breaches of competition law. Horizontal restraints of competition law are those restrictions put into place between competitors, into which category the LIBOR and FX cartels fall, which have the effect of tying up the market and reducing or eliminating competition between competitors.[89] The LIBOR and FX benchmark manipulation agreements between traders at different banks are

83 Sherman Antitrust Act, ch. 647, 26 Stat. 209 (codified as amended by 15 U.S.C. §1-7 (2018)) section 1.

84 See the case of *US v. Pilgrim's Pride Corporation*, 20-cr-00330-RM (D. Colo. Feb. 16. 2021) in which the DoJ imposed a criminal fine in excess of $100 million pursuant to 18 U.S.C. § 3751(c). Also see Sentencing Reform Act, 18 U.S.C. §3571(d).

85 Clayton Act, §11, 15 U.S.C. §21.

86 DJ Gerber, *Competition Law and Antitrust* (Oxford University Press 2020) 95.

87 Federal Trade Commission, 'The Enforcers' (Federal Trade Commission, 2021) <https://www.ftc.gov/tips-advice/competition-guidance/guide-antitrust-laws/enforcers> accessed 8 July 2024.

88 D Yeres and Others, 'Understanding and Preparing for the Convergence of US Criminal Antitrust Enforcement with Anti-Manipulation Laws Regulating Derivatives, FX, Cryptocurrency, Futures, Options and Other Commodities under the Commodity Exchange Act' (2019) 39(1) *The Journal on the Law of Investment and Risk Management Products* 5.

89 JF Ponsoldt, 'Toward the Reaffirmation of the Antitrust Rule of Per Se Illegality as a Law of Rules for Horizontal Price Fixing and Territorial Allocation Agreements: A Reflection on the Palmer Case in a Renewed Era of Economic Regulation' (2009) 62(2) *SMU Law Review* 635.

examples of horizontal agreements, which have the effect of eliminating elements of competition between the banks for the sole purpose of achieving higher profits from their trades. Because the market manipulation took place between competitors, the criminal penalties provided for in the Sherman Act were used by the DoJ to reflect the seriousness of the competition law breaches.

Above, the development of the public antitrust enforcement provisions relevant to the crime of benchmark manipulation have been presented. In addition to the public criminal powers provide to regulators, the US has the world's most established system of private antitrust enforcement, originating from provisions of the Clayton Act that authorise 'any person' injured in his 'business or property by reason of anything forbidden in the antitrust laws' to sue for treble damages.[90] Many private antitrust claims are brought as class actions, which is the case for the leading LIBOR antitrust class action.[91] Private litigants bring civil actions either as a result of their own investigations or, more commonly, following a civil or criminal action brought by a federal or state authority. When an individual or company has already been convicted of a breach of the Sherman Act, that conviction can be used by a private litigant as *prima facie* evidence against the defendant in a civil action, saving the private litigant the burden of having to prove the legal breach.[92] US antitrust laws are mature and well developed. The importance of private litigation to the US antitrust regime cannot be overstated, and it can be seen from the description below that the settlement sums payable by banks from the private LIBOR litigation are significant and comparable to the fines meted out by the federal regulators.[93]

This section has summarised some of the key developments in US competition law since its inception and has set the scene for the enforcement action taken in the LIBOR and FX benchmark manipulation crisis, which will now be examined in the following two sections.

90 J Bial, L Hibbler, 'Cartels & Leniency Laws and Regulations USA 2024' (ICLG.com, 2024) <https://iclg.com/practice-areas/cartels-and-leniency-laws-and-regulations/usa> accessed 13 July 2024 and Clayton Act, §11, 15 U.S.C. §4.

91 Reuters, 'Law Firms Susman Godfrey, Hausfeld Seek $25 Mln From Latest LIBOR Settlement' (*Reuters,* 30 October 2023) <https://www.reuters.com/legal/transactional/law-firms-susman-godfrey-hausfeld-seek-25-mln-latest-libor-settlement-2023-10-30/> accessed 2 July 2024; Managed Care Advisory Group, 'LIBOR Manipulation Settlements' (MCAG, 2024) <https://www.mcaginc.com/post/libor> accessed 12 July 2024 and *In re: Libor-based Financial Instruments Antitrust Litigation,* 327 F.R.D. 483 (S.D.N.Y. 2018).

92 Practical Law Antitrust, 'US Antitrust Laws: Overview' (*Practical Law*, 2021) <https://uk.practicallaw.thomsonreuters.com/9-204-0472?comp=pluk&transitionType=Default&contextData=(sc.Default)&firstPage=true&OWSessionId=f75eb2ed5ce44e81a0392481a9970ca7&skipAnonymous=true> accessed 8 July 2024.

93 DJ Gerber, *Competition Law and Antitrust* (Oxford University Press 2020) 97.

5.4 The LIBOR Scandal and Enforcement in the US

This section of the chapter will consider the response of US regulators to the LIBOR and FX scandal and will critically analyse the role played in that enforcement by competition law. This section will focus on the enforcement of the LIBOR benchmark manipulation, which came to light earlier than the FX benchmark manipulation. The following section will focus on the enforcement carried out in relation to the FX benchmark manipulation.

A combination of competition and noncompetition law was used to tackle the alleged instances of LIBOR benchmark manipulation. The Antitrust Division of the DoJ charged banks and traders involved in the LIBOR scandal, although it predominantly used the charge of wire fraud and conspiracy to commit wire fraud in its LIBOR benchmark manipulation enforcement. However, some competition law was used by the DoJ in relation to its LIBOR benchmark manipulation enforcement. Deutsche Bank admitted its participation in a price-fixing conspiracy with other banks, in violation of Section 1 of the Sherman Act, in relation to its manipulation of the yen LIBOR.[94] In total, the DoJ brought criminal proceedings against 14 individual bank employees and ten companies for LIBOR manipulation using the offences of wire fraud and conspiracy to commit wire fraud.[95] For the four individual bank traders who went to trial for their part in the LIBOR manipulation, they were initially convicted and imprisoned for terms ranging between one and two years.[96] However four of the individuals' trial convictions have since been overturned by the Second Circuit court.[97] The first case to be overturned was that of the two Rabobank traders, Anthony Allen and Anthony Conti, with the court ruling in 2017 that the case was tainted by their forced testimony to the Financial Conduct Authority.[98] The most recent case to have LIBOR-related wire fraud charges overturned involved two former Deutsche Bank traders, Matthew

94 US Department of Justice, 'Deutsche Bank's London Subsidiary Sentenced for Manipulation of LIBOR' (Department of Justice, 28 March 2017) <https://www.justice.gov/opa/pr/deutsche-bank-s-london-subsidiary-sentenced-manipulation-libor> accessed 8 July 2024.

95 Practical Law Competition, 'DoJ LIBOR Manipulation Investigation Chart' (Practical Law, January 2023) <https://uk.practicallaw.thomsonreuters.com/Link/Document/Blob/I02f47372a46e11e598dc8b09b4f043e0.pdf?targetType=PLC-multimedia&originationContext=document&transitionType=DocumentImage&uniqueId=89411439-d608-4c78-af0a-21ea30ca61ff&ppcid=076fbb06578f42dbb220b5b6bebad073&contextData=(sc.DocLink)&comp=pluk> accessed 13 July 2024.

96 For instance see *United States v. Anthony Allen, Anthony Conti, et al.* 160 F.Supp.3d 684 (2016).

97 Practical Law Competition, 'DoJ LIBOR Manipulation Investigation Chart' (Practical Law, January 2023) <https://uk.practicallaw.thomsonreuters.com/Link/Document/Blob/I02f47372a46e11e598dc8b09b4f043e0.pdf?targetType=PLC-multimedia&originationContext=document&transitionType=DocumentImage&uniqueId=89411439-d608-4c78-af0a-21ea30ca61ff&ppcid=076fbb06578f42dbb220b5b6bebad073&contextData=(sc.DocLink)&comp=pluk> accessed 8 July 2024.

98 *United States v. Allen*, 864 F.3d 63, 69-70 (2d Cir. 2017).

Connolly and Gavin Black, and judgement was given in January 2022, with the court stating that there are limits to the use of the wire fraud offence to police financial conduct.[99] This most recent overturning of the LIBOR trial convictions for individual bank traders means that now all the wire fraud convictions for the manipulation of LIBOR have been overturned.[100] The court pointed out in its judgement that there are limits to the use of the wire fraud offence, which is not a 'catch-all' law designed to punish all sorts of wrongdoing or dishonourable practices.[101] Commentators have observed that the use of the broadly drafted antifraud laws were not well suited to prosecute traders who operated in sophisticated markets in which standards of conduct were not always documented.[102] The problems experienced in the prosecutions using the wire fraud charges are all the more interesting when the approach taken by the DoJ of using competition law to enforce the subsequent FX benchmark manipulation cases is analysed below, as none of the competition-law-based enforcement action has yet been overturned by a court, demonstrating that competition law is more suited to the cartels seen in the LIBOR and FX manipulation scandals than a generic criminal offence such as wire fraud.[103] Also, it is worth noting that all private enforcement action brought in relation to the LIBOR benchmark manipulation was based on competition law, more detail about this is set out below.

In relation to the corporate criminal wire fraud charges, the DoJ entered into DPAs with five banks: Royal Bank of Scotland,[104] Deutsche Bank,[105]

99 *U.S. v Connolly*, No. 19-3806, (2d Cir. 2022) U.S. Court of Appeals, Second Circuit.

100 D Michaels, 'All U.S. Trial Convictions in Crisis-Era Libor Rigging Have Now Been Overturned' (*The Wall Street Journal*, 27 January 2023) <https://www.wsj.com/articles/all-u-s-trial-convictions-in-crisis-era-libor-rigging-have-now-been-overturned-11643310178> accessed 8 July 2024.

101 The Volkov Law Group, 'DOJ Loses Another Libor-Rigging Case on Appeal' (JD Supra, 8 February 2022) <https://www.jdsupra.com/legalnews/doj-loses-another-libor-rigging-case-on-3207295/> accessed 30 July 2024.

102 D Michaels, 'All U.S. Trial Convictions in Crisis-Era Libor Rigging Have Now Been Overturned' (*The Wall Street Journal*, 27 January 2023) <https://www.wsj.com/articles/all-u-s-trial-convictions-in-crisis-era-libor-rigging-have-now-been-overturned-11643310178> accessed 8 July 2024.

103 SE Foster, 'LIBOR Manipulation and Antitrust Allegations' (2013) 11(3) *DePaul Business & Commercial Law Journal* 291.

104 US Department of Justice, 'RBS Securities Japan Limited Agrees to Plead Guilty in Connection with Long-Running Manipulation of Libor Benchmark Interest Rates' (US Department of Justice, 6 February 2013) <https://www.justice.gov/opa/pr/rbs-securities-japan-limited-agrees-plead-guilty-connection-long-running-manipulation-libor> accessed 18 July 2024.

105 US Department of Justice, 'Deutsche Bank's London Subsidiary Agrees to Plead Guilty in Connection with Long-Running Manipulation of LIBOR' (US Department of Justice, 23 April 2015) <https://www.justice.gov/opa/pr/deutsche-banks-london-subsidiary-agrees-plead-guilty-connection-long-running-manipulation> accessed 24 July 2024.

UBS,[106] Barclays[107] and Rabobank[108] in relation to its enforcement of the LIBOR manipulation. These DPAs imposed significant fines on these banks, ranging from $50m to $710m,[109] as well as behavioural commitments given by the banks to the DoJ for the term of each DPA, including ongoing corporate monitoring for the term of the DPA.[110] However, the fines imposed were insignificant compared to the vast profits the traders made for the banks by manipulating the LIBOR. US Assistant Attorney General Lanny Breuer stated 'make no mistake, for UBS traders the manipulation of Libor was about getting rich', he added 'we cannot and will not tolerate misconduct on Wall Street as admitted by UBS'.[111] The fines levied on UBS by US regulators were $1.2b; however, UBS said that although the fines were likely to result in the bank recording a loss of 2–2.5b Swiss francs for the last three months of the year, UBS would still record a profit for the year as a whole.[112] This demonstrates that the fine is unlikely to have had a significant deterrent effect on the bank.

Additionally, a raft of civil cases were brought by customers of the banks involved in LIBOR who had suffered financial losses as a result of the benchmark manipulation. These actions have been brought using competition law, with the plaintiffs alleging a *per se* antitrust violation involving horizontal price

106 US Department of Justice, 'UBS Securities Japan Co Ltd to Plead Guilty to Felony Wire Fraud for Long-running Manipulation of LIBOR Benchmark Interest Rates' (US Department of Justice, 19 December 2012) <https://www.justice.gov/opa/pr/ubs-securities-japan-co-ltd-plead-guilty-felony-wire-fraud-long-running-manipulation-libor> accessed 24 July 2024.

107 US Department of Justice, 'Barclays Bank PLC Admits Misconduct Related to Submissions for the London Interbank Offered Rate and the Euro Interbank Offered Rate and Agrees to Pay $160 Million Penalty' (US Department of Justice, 27 June 2012) <https://www.justice.gov/opa/pr/barclays-bank-plc-admits-misconduct-related-submissions-london-interbank-offered-rate-and> accessed 14 July 2024.

108 US Department of Justice, 'Rabobank Admits Wrongdoing in Libor Investigation, Agrees to Pay $325 Million Criminal Penalty' (US Department of Justice, 29 October 2013) <https://www.justice.gov/opa/pr/rabobank-admits-wrongdoing-libor-investigation-agrees-pay-325-million-criminal-penalty> accessed 24 July 2024.

109 Practical Law Competition, 'DoJ LIBOR Manipulation Investigation Chart' (Practical Law, January 2023) <https://uk.practicallaw.thomsonreuters.com/Link/Document/Blob/I02f47372a46e11e598dc8b09b4f043e0.pdf?targetType=PLC-multimedia&originationContext=document&transitionType=DocumentImage&uniqueId=89411439-d608-4c78-af0a-21ea30ca61ff&ppcid=076fbb06578f42dbb220b5b6bebad073&contextData=(sc.DocLink)&comp=pluk> accessed 18 July 2024.

110 For instance, see the DPA entered with Deutsche Bank Group Services (UK) Limited – US Department of Justice, 'Deutsche Bank's London Subsidiary Agrees to Plead Guilty in Connection with Long-Running Manipulation of LIBOR' (US Department of Justice, 23 April 2015) <https://www.justice.gov/opa/pr/deutsche-banks-london-subsidiary-agrees-plead-guilty-connection-long-running-manipulation> accessed 24 July 2024.

111 BBC News, 'UBS fined $15bn for Libor Rigging' (BBC News, 19 December 2012) <https://www.bbc.co.uk/news/business-20767984> accessed 28 July 2024.

112 Ibid.

fixing, and in the 2020 judgement in the class action case of *In re: Libor-based Financial Instruments Antitrust Litigation,* Judge Naomi Buchwald of the Southern District of New York provided final approval of a $22m settlement between a class of indirect investors and five Wall Street banks accused by the plaintiff investors of manipulating LIBOR in violation of the Sherman Act.[113] Under the terms of the October 2020 settlement agreement, Citi must pay approximately $7m, HSBC must pay $4.75m, and JPMorgan and Bank of America must each pay approximately $5m.[114] This case was appealed to the US Court of Appeals by the defendant banks on issues relating to antitrust standing and based on the lack of personal jurisdiction over the defendants of some of the plaintiffs.[115] A judgement was given on 30 December 2021, which affirmed and reversed parts of the judgement and remanded part of the proceedings back to the District Court. This judgement did not affect the settlement agreed or the basis of the claim (breach of antitrust law) but related to some of the circa 40 plaintiffs from the original case.[116] The private competition law settlements for the LIBOR manipulation have resulted in significant additional payments from the banks, which, when combined with the fines from the regulators for the same offences, significantly increases the financial sanctions against each bank.

It can, therefore, be seen from the above that the US enforcement of the LIBOR benchmark manipulation predominantly involved criminal prosecutions of individuals and banks using the offence of wire fraud and/or conspiracy to commit wire fraud, with only limited use of antitrust charges.[117] As stated above, the four individual convictions secured at trial by the DoJ have now all been overturned, demonstrating that the offence of wire fraud did not adequately fit the crime of benchmark manipulation. However, the private

113 *In re Libor-Based Fin. Instruments Antitrust Litig.*, 11 MD 2262 (NRB), (S.D.N.Y. Nov. 24, 2020).

114 M Slachetka, 'Five Banks Settle LIBOR Manipulation Suit for $22 Million' (Lexology, 13 October 2020) <https://www.lexology.com/library/detail.aspx?g=88150e13-77c7-44af-8004-bb4ba337f36c> accessed 8 July 2024.

115 *In re LIBOR-based Financial Instruments Antitrust Litigation*, No. 17-1569 (2d Cir. 2021).

116 Ibid.

117 The only LIBOR antitrust charges were levied against Deutsche Bank, RBS and Tom Hayes; see US Department of Justice, 'Deutsche Bank's London Subsidiary Agrees to Plead Guilty in Connection with Long-Running Manipulation of LIBOR' (US Department of Justice, 23 April 2015) <https://www.justice.gov/opa/pr/deutsche-banks-london-subsidiary-agrees-plead-guilty-connection-long-running-manipulation> accessed 24 July 2024; US Department of Justice, 'RBS Securities Japan Limited Agrees to Plead Guilty in Connection with Long-Running Manipulation of Libor Benchmark Interest Rates' (US Department of Justice, 6 February 2013) <https://www.justice.gov/opa/pr/rbs-securities-japan-limited-agrees-plead-guilty-connection-long-running-manipulation-libor> accessed 23 July 2024; and US Department of Justice, 'UBS Securities Japan Co. Ltd. to Plead Guilty to Wire Fraud for Long-Running Manipulation of LIBOR Benchmark Interest Rates' (19 December 2012) <https://www.justice.gov/opa/pr/ubs-securities-japan-co-ltd-plead-guilty-felony-wire-fraud-long-running-manipulation-libor> accessed 23 July 2024.

enforcement action taken against the banks was based on competition law and has been successful in obtaining a settlement for the plaintiffs.[118] From this, it can be seen that competition law is better suited to the crime of benchmark manipulation than a generic fraud offence.

5.5 The FX Scandal and Enforcement in the US

This section will look at the enforcement of the FX benchmark manipulation in the US. The DoJ took a different approach for the enforcement of the FX manipulation than for the LIBOR manipulation, so these different approaches will be compared and contrasted. The FX benchmark manipulation scandal first came to light when Bloomberg News reported that currency dealers said they had been rigging the FX benchmark interest rates by colluding with their counterparts in other banks in order to maximise their own profits.[119] This behaviour had been taking place for at least a decade, and some commentators note that before the FX manipulation and bank collusion was uncovered that the FX spot market was widely perceived to be too competitive to be subject of market abusive behaviour.[120]

In contrast to the LIBOR benchmark manipulation, six banks and six individuals were prosecuted by the DoJ under Section 1 of the Sherman Act[121] for engaging in a conspiracy to fix the price of and rig bids for the euro/US dollar currency pair in the FX spot market by agreeing to eliminate competition in violation of the Sherman Antitrust Act.[122] This is an interesting difference in approach to that taken by the DoJ in the enforcement of the LIBOR manipu-

118 *In re Libor-Based Fin. Instruments Antitrust Litig.*, 11 MD 2262 (NRB), (S.D.N.Y. Nov. 24, 2020).

119 C Powers, 'Filling the Regulatory Void in the FX Spot Market: How Traders Rigged the Biggest Market in the World' (2016) 43(1) *The Fordham Urban Law Journal* 139.

120 A Stenfors, 'Bid-As Spread Determination in the FX Swap Market: Competition, Collusion or a Convention?' (2018) 54(1) *Journal of International Financial Markets, Institutions & Money* 78.

121 Sherman Antitrust Act, 15 U.S.C. §1 and see press releases for the banks prosecuted: US Department of Justice, 'Five Major Banks Agree to Parent-Level Guilty Pleas' (Department of Justice, 20 May 2015) <https://www.justice.gov/opa/pr/five-major-banks-agree-parent-level-guilty-pleas> accessed 14 July 2024; US Department of Justice, 'BNP Paribas USA Inc. Pleads Guilty to Antitrust Conspiracy' (US Department of Justice, 26 January 2018) <https://www.justice.gov/opa/pr/bnp-paribas-usa-inc-pleads-guilty-antitrust-conspiracy> accessed 23 July 2024; and see US Department of Justice, 'Former Foreign Exchange Trader Sentenced to Prison for Price Fixing and Bid Rigging' (US Department of Justice, 17 September 2020) <https://www.justice.gov/opa/pr/former-foreign-exchange-trader-sentenced-prison-price-fixing-and-bid-rigging> accessed 23 July 2024.

122 For example, see details of the charges in the Barclays Plea Agreement: United States District Court District of Connecticut, 'United States of America v Barclays PLC Plea Agreement' (United States District Court District of Connecticut, 20 May 2015) <chrome-extension://efaidnbmnnnibpcajpcglclefindmkaj/https://www.justice.gov/opa/file/485116/dl> 2,3 accessed 18 July 2024.

lation. In that case, the Antitrust Division of the DoJ did not use the Sherman Act as the primary offence with which to charge the traders from competitor banks who had colluded and conspired together to raise or lower the LIBOR benchmark interest rate. As stated above, in the LIBOR enforcement, the DoJ used the charge of 'wire fraud' rather than Section 1 of the Sherman Antitrust Act. Perhaps the use of the name 'The Cartel' by the traders in the FX benchmark manipulation scandal was too persuasive to ignore, despite the plethora of financial regulation that was available to the DoJ to prosecute the misconduct.

The DoJ used Section 1 of the Sherman Act (competition law) to impose large financial penalties on banks[123] and individual traders[124] for manipulating FX rates. As of December 2023, the DoJ has charged six companies and eight individuals with manipulating the FX spot market and has issued fines totalling over $2.7b.[125] The highest financial penalty for FX benchmark manipulation imposed under the Sherman Act was $925m, which was imposed on Citicorp in 2015 for its participation in the FX benchmark manipulation cartel.[126] This far exceeds the highest fine for the LIBOR manipulation, which was $710m.[127] As mentioned above, the primary enforcer of the cartel provisions

123 Banks include Citigroup, JPMorgan Chase, Bank of America, Barclays, Union Bank of Switzerland, HSBC and RBS; see A Akhigbe and others 'Foreign Exchange Manipulation and the Equity Returns of Global Banks' (2020) 57(2) *Journal of Financial Services Research* 207; and US Department of Justice, 'Five Major Banks Agree to Parent-Level Guilty Pleas' (Department of Justice, 20 May 2015) <https://www.justice.gov/opa/pr/five-major-banks-agree-parent-level-guilty-pleas> accessed 24 July 2024; and US Department of Justice, 'BNP Paribas USA Inc. Pleads Guilty to Antitrust Conspiracy' (US Department of Justice, 26 January 2018) <https://www.justice.gov/opa/pr/bnp-paribas-usa-inc-pleads-guilty-antitrust-conspiracy> accessed 23 July 2024.

124 See, for example: United States District Court Southern District of New York, 'United States of America v Christopher Cummins Plea Agreement' (US Department of Justice, 13 January 2017) <https://www.justice.gov/atr/case-document/file/930946/download> accessed 28 July 2024; and US Department of Justice, 'Former Foreign Exchange Trader Sentenced to Prison for Price Fixing and Bid Rigging' (US Department of Justice, 17 September 2020) <https://www.justice.gov/opa/pr/former-foreign-exchange-trader-sentenced-prison-price-fixing-and-bid-rigging> accessed 23 July 2024.

125 Practical Law Antitrust, 'DoJ FX Spot Market Manipulation Investigation Chart' (Practical Law, 31 December 2023) <https://uk.practicallaw.thomsonreuters.com/9-617-3995?comp=pluk&transitionType=Default&contextData=(sc.Default)&firstPage=true&OWSessionId=2ae7dfa62ec44b7a80cf7da23d2950d0&skipAnonymous=true> accessed 28 July 2024.

126 US Department of Justice, 'Sherman Act Violations Resulting in Criminal Fines & Penalties of $10 Million or More' (US Department of Justice, 25 January 2024) <https://www.justice.gov/atr/sherman-act-violations-yielding-corporate-fine-10-million-or-more> accessed 28 June 2024.

127 Practical Law Competition, 'DoJ LIBOR Manipulation Investigation Chart' (Practical Law, January 2023) <https://uk.practicallaw.thomsonreuters.com/Link/Document/Blob/I02f47372a46e11e598dc8b09b4f043e0.pdf?targetType=PLC-multimedia&originationContext=document&transitionType=DocumentImage&uniqueId=89411439-d608-4c78

of the Sherman Act is the Antitrust Division of the DoJ, which is empowered to bring criminal charges against both individuals and companies who engage in cartel behaviour.[128] Previous Sherman Act antitrust cases typically involve a combination of both fines and imprisonment for individuals.[129] The maximum criminal fine for a company in breach of the Sherman Act is $100m; however, the Alternative Fines Act[130] permits prosecutors to ignore this statutory maximum and fine defendants up to 'twice the gross gain or twice the gross loss' for the offence.[131] This provision has enabled the DoJ to collect extremely high fines for breach of the cartel provisions of the Sherman Act.[132] This can be seen by the fines imposed on banks for the FX benchmark manipulation, in which CitiCorp had to pay a fine of $925m, Barclays $650m, JPMorgan $550m and RBS $395m, all of which are significantly higher than the fines imposed for the LIBOR manipulation, based on the wire charge offence.[133]

Between December 2007 and January 2013, traders at four competing banks, CitiCorp, JPMorgan, Barclays and RBS, communicated with each other via different online chat rooms, one of which they called 'The Cartel'.[134] Other chat room names had less obvious connections with a breach of competition law but still suggest that the traders knew that what they were doing was against the law, as the chat room names included 'The Bandit's Club' and 'The Mafia'.[135] The traders used the online chat rooms to conspire to manipulate the price of US dollars and euros in the FX spot market. The very high level of market concentration in these chat rooms is striking; the 'Cartel' chat room alone included banks with more than 40% of the overall market share.[136] The FX benchmark manipulation continued until 2013 when US, EU and UK regulators started punishing banks for their participation in the

-af0a-21ea30ca61ff&ppcid=076fbb06578f42dbb220b5b6bebad073&contextData=(sc.DocLink)&comp=pluk> accessed 23 July 2024.

128 US Department of Justice, 'Criminal Enforcement' (US Department of Justice, 22 May 2020) <https://www.justice.gov/atr/criminal-enforcement> accessed 24 July 2024.

129 For instance, see *United States v Clark Mechanical Contractors, Inc.* 1973 Trade Cas. (CCH) 74,482 (W.D. Ky. 1973).

130 Alternative Fines Act, 18 U.S.C., s.3,571.

131 A Hemlock, 'United States: DOJ Takes Aggressive Enforcement Approach and Faces No-Poach Challenges' (Global Competition Review, 2 May 2024) <https://globalcompetitionreview.com/insight/market-reviews/cartels-2024/article/united-states-doj-takes-aggressive-enforcement-approach-and-faces-no-poach-challenges> accessed 23 July 2024.

132 MP Kerns, 'Criminal Sentencing in Antitrust Cases' (1982) 13(4) *Loyola University Chicago Law*.

133 US Department of Justice, 'Five Major Banks Agree to Parent-Level Guilty Pleas' (Department of Justice, 20 May 2015) <https://www.justice.gov/opa/pr/five-major-banks-agree-parent-level-guilty-pleas> accessed 24 July 2024.

134 Ibid.

135 C Powers, 'Filling the Regulatory Void in the FX Spot Market: How Traders Rigged the Biggest Market in the World' (2016) 43(1) *The Fordham Urban Law Journal* 139.

136 PH Verdier, *Global Banks on Trial, U.S. Prosecutions and the Remaking of International Finance* (Oxford University Press 2020) 64.

LIBOR benchmark manipulation, and banks were forced to overhaul their corporate compliance and stop all illegal behaviours. In total, regulators in the US and abroad fined five banks nearly $9b for their conduct in conspiring to manipulate the FX market.[137] The FX benchmark manipulation will have had a significant impact on the millions of people who use the FX market daily, as it is used for transactions ranging from tourists buying foreign money for their holidays to transactions made by trillion-dollar investment houses.[138] Barclays, one of the banks fined for the FX manipulation, was found by regulators to have continued to engage in misleading sales practices despite a pledge by its CEO Antony Jenkins to overhaul the bank's high-risk, high-reward culture.[139] The culture at Barclays was summed up by one trader as 'If you ain't cheating, you ain't trying'.[140] This gives an insight into the banking culture that led to the cartel set up by traders in the LIBOR and FX scandals and demonstrates the scale of the problem that the compliance programmes, which the regulators require banks to set up, must address.

As mentioned above, the charges brought by the DoJ against the banks and traders for conspiring to manipulate the FX benchmark interest rate were criminal charges under the Sherman Act, which led to, for the first time in decades, the parent of a major American financial institution pleading guilty to criminal charges.[141] Traditionally, US regulators deal with small foreign subsidiaries who have breached US laws, so bringing criminal charges against the parent company of an international bank such as Barclays or Citi was a significant departure for the authorities in this case. The change in policy was designed to deter banks from illegal actions in the future, with one analyst noting that, in relation to the FX corporate prosecutions:

> In the worst cases, U.S. prosecutors insisted that banks plead guilty, rather than settle under non-prosecution agreements (NPAs) or deferred prosecution agreements (DPAs). At least six of the world's largest banks…are now convicted felons.[142]

137 US Department of Justice, 'Five Major Banks Agree to Parent-Level Guilty Pleas' (US Department of Justice, 20 May 2015) <https://www.justice.gov/opa/pr/five-major-banks-agree-parent-level-guilty-pleas> accessed 28 July 2024.

138 C Powers, 'Filling the Regulatory Void in the FX Spot Market: How Traders Rigged the Biggest Market in the World' (2016) 43(1) *The Fordham Urban Law Journal* 139.

139 N Goodway, 'New Boss at Barclays Pledges to Change its Culture' (*The Independent*, 30 August 2012) <https://www.independent.co.uk/news/business/news/new-boss-at-barclays-pledges-to-change-its-culture-8096757.html> accessed 18 July 2024.

140 K Freifield, D Henry, S Slater, 'Global Banks Admit Guilt in Forex Probe, Fined Nearly $6 Billion' (*Reuters*, 20 May 2015) <https://www.reuters.com/article/us-banks-forex-settlement-idUSKBN0O50CQ20150520> accessed 18 July 2024.

141 PH Verdier, *Global Banks on Trial* (Oxford University Press 2020) 7, 133; and US Department of Justice, 'Five Major Banks Agree to Parent-Level Guilty Pleas' (US Department of Justice, 20 May 2015) <https://www.justice.gov/opa/pr/five-major-banks-agree-parent-level-guilty-pleas> accessed 19 July 2024.

142 PH Verdier, *Global Banks On Trial* (Oxford University Press 2020) 7.

The six banks who pleaded guilty to felony charges for their participation in the manipulation of the FX market were Citicorp, JPMorgan Chase & Co, Barclays PLC, Royal Bank of Scotland, UBS AG and BNP Paribas. In 2015 Citicorp, JPMorgan Chase & Co, Barclays PLC, Royal Bank of Scotland plc and UBS AG all pleaded guilty and agreed to pay collectively more than $2.5b in criminal fines for their participation in the manipulation of the US dollar and euro in the FX market, which breached criminal antitrust laws.[143] This was followed in 2018 by BNP Paribas, which also pleaded guilty and paid a fine of $90m for its part in the price-fixing conspiracy in the FX market.[144]

In addition to the corporate guilty pleas secured, the DoJ obtained convictions for bank employees for participating in the manipulative conduct on a concerted basis with competitors.[145] In total, the DoJ has charged five companies and six individuals for collusion in the FX market.[146] Deputy Assistant Attorney General Brent Snyder, of the DoJ's Antitrust Division, said that:

> Collusion by FX dealers for the purpose of fixing foreign currency exchange rates is no different than collusion regarding traditional products and services that the Antitrust Division routinely prosecutes.[147]

Therefore, US authorities clearly decided it was appropriate to bring criminal competition law charges against the banks for their manipulation of the FX. US Attorney General Loretta Lynch said:

> The penalty these banks will now pay is fitting considering the long-running and egregious nature of their anticompetitive conduct. It is commensurate with the pervasive harm done. And it should deter

143 US Department of Justice, 'Five Major Banks Agree to Parent-Level Guilty Pleas' (US Department of Justice, 20 May 2015) <https://www.justice.gov/opa/pr/five-major-banks-agree-parent-level-guilty-pleas> accessed 29 July 2024.

144 US Department of Justice, 'BNP Paribas USA Inc. Pleads Guilty to Antitrust Conspiracy' (US Department of Justice, 26 January 2018) <https://www.justice.gov/opa/pr/bnp-paribas-usa-inc-pleads-guilty-antitrust-conspiracy> accessed 19 July 2024.

145 D Yeres and others, 'Understanding and Preparing for the Convergence of US Criminal Antitrust Enforcement with Anti-Manipulation Laws Regulating Derivatives, FX, Cryptocurrency, Futures, Options and other Commodities under the Commodity Exchange Act' (2019) 39(1) *The Journal on the Law of Investment and Risk Management Products* 5.

146 US Department of Justice, 'Former Foreign Exchange Trader Sentenced to Prison for Price Fixing and Bid Rigging' (US Department of Justice, 17 September 2020) <https://www.justice.gov/opa/pr/former-foreign-exchange-trader-sentenced-prison-price-fixing-and-bid-rigging> accessed 18 July 2024.

147 US Department of Justice, 'Second Foreign Currency Exchange Dealer Pleads Guilty to Antitrust Conspiracy' (US Department of Justice, 12 January 2017) <https://www.justice.gov/opa/pr/second-foreign-currency-exchange-dealer-pleads-guilty-antitrust-conspiracy> accessed 18 July 2024.

competitors in the future from chasing profits without regard to fairness, to the law, or to the public welfare.[148]

This message was reinforced by the Assistant Director in Charge who added: 'these resolutions make clear that the U.S. Government will not tolerate criminal behaviour in any sector of the financial markets'.[149]

In addition to the above enforcement by the DoJ, other US regulators have also fined the banks for the attempted manipulation of the global FX benchmark interest rates for their own benefit or the benefit of their individual traders. For example, the CFTC fined the five banks involved a combined total of over $1.4b for their participation in the attempted manipulation of the FX benchmark interest rate.[150] Furthermore, the Fed also fined the five banks involved with the manipulation of the FX rates more than $1.6b and Barclays settled related claims with the New York State Department of Financial Services.[151] The OCC also fined Bank of America, Citibank and JPMorgan a total of $950m for FX trading improprieties.[152] Barclays has now been the subject of three CFTC enforcement actions for benchmark manipulation, involving the ISDAFIX,[153] LIBOR[154] and FX[155] benchmark interest rates. It has been fined by numerous regulators in the US as well as others in the rest of the world. The CFTC alone has fined Barclays $175m for its role in the

148 US Department of Justice, 'Five Major Banks Agree to Parent-Level Guilty Pleas' (US Department of Justice, 20 May 2015) <https://www.justice.gov/opa/pr/five-major-banks-agree-parent-level-guilty-pleas> accessed 24 July 2024.

149 Ibid.

150 Commodity Futures Trading Commission, 'CFTC Orders Five Banks to Pay over $14 Billion in Penalties for Attempted Manipulation of Foreign Exchange Benchmark Rates' (Commodity Futures Trading Commission, 12 November 2014) <https://cftc.gov/PressRoom/PressReleases/7056-14> accessed 18 July 2024.

151 US Department of Justice, 'Five Major Banks Agree to Parent-Level Guilty Pleas' (US Department of Justice, 20 May 2015) <https://www.justice.gov/opa/pr/five-major-banks-agree-parent-level-guilty-pleas> accessed 24 July 2024.

152 Office of the Comptroller of the Currency, 'OCC Fines Three Banks $950 Million for FX Trading Improprieties' (Office of the Comptroller of the Currency, 12 November 2014) <https://www2.occ.gov/news-issuances/news-releases/2014/nr-occ-2014-157.html> accessed 28 July 2024.

153 Commodity Futures Trading Commission, 'CFTC Orders Barclays to Pay $115 Million Penalty for Attempted Manipulation of and False Reporting of U.S. Dollar ISDAFIX Benchmark Swap Rates' (Commodity Futures Trading Commission, 20 May 2015) <https://www.cftc.gov/PressRoom/PressReleases/7180-15> accessed 23 July 2024.

154 Commodity Futures Trading Commission, 'CFTC Orders Barclays to Pay $200 Million Penalty for Attempted Manipulation of and False Reporting Concerning Libor and Euribor Benchmark Interest Rates' (Commodity Futures Trading Commission, 27 June 2012) <https://www.cftc.gov/PressRoom/PressReleases/6289-12> accessed 24 July 2024.

155 Commodity Futures Trading Commission, 'Barclays to Pay $400 Million Penalty to Settle CFTC Charges of Attempted Manipulation and False Reporting of Foreign Exchange Benchmark Rates' (Commodity Futures Trading Commission, 20 May 2015) <https://www.cftc.gov/PressRoom/PressReleases/7181-15> accessed 28 July 2024.

manipulation of these benchmark interest rates and has required the bank to cease and desist from further violations and to take specific steps to implement and strengthen its internal compliance procedures.[156]

When the above multiplicity of fines imposed by US regulators is compared to the other jurisdictions studied, it can be seen that in each of the EU and the UK there was just one central authority that imposed fines and sanctions on the banks involved in the FX benchmark manipulation; the European Commission in the EU and the Financial Services Authority, then the Financial Conduct Authority, in the UK. The involvement of such a plethora of financial regulators in the US may result in more fines and more uncertainty to the offending banks, but it may also result in confusion and a lack of coherent oversight by the financial regulators.[157] This may result in some double or triple counting when fines are imposed on banks for the same misconduct, and it may slow down investigations, with some regulators missing key information held by other regulators.[158] For these reasons, it is suggested that having one overall financial authority, with oversight over the information gathered by the different regulators, would result in a more coherent approach by US financial regulators.

An FX benchmark manipulation class action lawsuit based on competition law began in 2015 on behalf of private investors who claimed that 16 major banks colluded to fix and manipulate the FX benchmark interest rate in order to align pricing and to eliminate competition between themselves.[159] The investors numbered nearly 1,300.[160] The 15 defendants are Bank of America, Bank of Tokyo-Mitsubishi, Barclays, BNP Paribas, Citigroup, Deutsche Bank, Goldman Sachs, HSBC, JPMorgan Chase, Morgan Stanley, RBC Capital Markets, Royal Bank of Scotland, Société Generale, Standard Chartered and UBS, which, together, controlled 90% of the FX market.[161] To date, the lawsuit

156 Commodity Futures Trading Commission, 'Barclays to Pay $400 Million Penalty to Settle CFTC Charges of Attempted Manipulation and False Reporting of Foreign Exchange Benchmark Rates' (Commodity Futures Trading Commission, 20 May 2015) <https://www.cftc.gov/PressRoom/PressReleases/7181-15> accessed 24 July 2024.

157 BS Bernanke and others, *Firefighting the Financial Crisis and Its Lessons* (Penguin Random House 2019).

158 A Francis and N Ryder, 'Preventing and Intervening in White Collar Crimes: The Role of Regulatory Agencies' in ML Rorie (ed), *The Handbook of White-Collar Crime* (John Wiley & Sons Inc 2020).

159 *In re Foreign Exchange Benchmark Rates Antitrust Litigation*, 74 F.Supp.3d 581 (2015).

160 A Stenfors, 'Bid-As Spread Determination in the FX Swap Market: Competition, Collusion or a Convention?' (2018) 54(1) *Journal of International Financial Markets, Institutions & Money* 78.

161 EPIQ, 'Foreign Exchange Antitrust Litigation U.S. District Court for the Southern District of New York Case No. 13-cv-7789-LGS' <http://www.fxantitrustsettlement.com/index> accessed 25 July 2024 and A Shome, 'US Court Approves FX-Rigging Lawsuit Against 15 Big Banks' (Finance Magnates, 29 May 2020) <https://www.financemagnates.com/institutional-forex/exchanges/us-court-approves-fx-rigging-lawsuit-against-15-big-banks/> accessed 6 July 2024.

has resulted in more than $2.3b in settlements for US investors.[162] Citi, for instance, settled its class action for $394m.[163] Fifteen settlements received final approval from the US District Court for the Southern District of New York,[164] and the last class action lawsuit brought by currency investors in 2013 against Credit Swisse was dismissed by the court in October 2022; however, the bank had settled with some investors, including BlackRock Inc. and Allianz SE's Pimco who had opted-out of the class litigation, in July 2022.[165]

The class action alleged that the 15 major banks conspired to fix prices in the FX market in violation of the competition law's price-fixing provisions in Sections 1 and 3 of the Sherman Antitrust Act.[166] The action also alleges that the defendants' manipulation of the FX benchmark interest rate was in breach of the Commodity Exchange Act.[167] District Judge Lorna Schofield of the US District for the Southern District of New York said when granting permission to continue the lawsuit: 'This is an injury of the type the antitrust laws were intended to prevent'.[168] Therefore, competition law was deemed an appropriate legal basis for the class lawsuit, despite the fact that the subject matter of the action was the manipulation of a financial benchmark, and competition law proved a successful enforcement tool for the plaintiffs.

Another private FX benchmark manipulation enforcement case that must be discussed is *United States v Usher*.[169] In May 2018, a New York federal court affirmed that the DoJ's indictment of three former currency traders in connection with the FX cartel investigation was correct.[170] The three traders had attempted to argue that the criminal charge of price fixing in connection with the FX cartel investigation was inappropriate because they did not

162 EPIQ, 'Foreign Exchange Antitrust Litigation U.S. District Court for the Southern District of New York Case No. 13-cv-7789-LGS' (EPIQ, 2024) <http://www.fxantitrustsettlement.com/index> accessed 6 July 2024.

163 Citigroup Inc, 'Citigroup Announces Foreign Exchange Settlements with the US Department of Justice and the Federal Reserve' (Citi, 20 May 2015) <https://www.citigroup.com/citi/news/2015/150520a.htm> accessed 8 July 2024.

164 EPIQ, 'Foreign Exchange Antitrust Litigation US District Court for the Southern District of New York Case No 13-cv-7789-LGS' (EPIQ, 2024) <http://www.fxantitrustsettlement.com/index> accessed 18 July 2024.

165 J Godoy, 'U.S. Jury Finds Credit Swisse Did Not Rig Forex Market' (*Reuters*, 20 October 2022) <https://www.reuters.com/markets/us/us-jury-finds-credit-suisse-did-not-rig-forex-market-2022-10-20/> accessed 10 July 2024.

166 EPIQ, 'Foreign Exchange Antitrust Litigation US District Court for the Southern District of New York Case No 13-cv-7789-LGS' (EPIQ, 2024) <http://www.fxantitrustsettlement.com/index> accessed 18 July 2024.

167 Commodity Exchange Act, 7 U.S.C. §§1.

168 A Shome, 'US Court Approves FX-Rigging Lawsuit Against 15 Big Banks' (Finance Magnates, 29 May 2020) <https://www.financemagnates.com/institutional-forex/exchanges/us-court-approves-fx-rigging-lawsuit-against-15-big-banks/> accessed 18 July 2024.

169 *United States v Usher*, No. 1:17-cr-00019 (Southern District of New York 4 May 2018).

170 D Yeres and others, 'Understanding and Preparing for the Convergence of US Criminal Antitrust Enforcement with Anti-Manipulation Laws Regulating Derivatives, FX, Cryptocurrency, Futures, Options and other Commodities under the Commodity Exchange Act' (2019) 39(1) *The Journal on the Law of Investment and Risk Management Products* 6.

compete on the same side of the FX spot market as they were sometimes buyers of the currency, sometimes sellers of it.[171] They argued that their actions were sometimes horizontal and sometimes vertical, so they should not be charged with a *per se* violation of the Sherman Act, which relates just to the most serious of horizontal competition breaches.[172] However, the New York District Court disagreed, finding that they were competitors for price of the EUR-USD currency pairs, and this meant that they were horizontally positioned to one another, and, therefore, the criminal charges brought by the DoJ against them were appropriate.[173]

Therefore, the use of competition law to enforce the FX benchmark manipulation was successful, as seen by the significant fines issued on companies and the criminal charges imposed on individual traders. When this is compared with the enforcement strategy followed by the DoJ for the LIBOR manipulation, which was to predominantly use wire fraud and conspiracy to commit wire fraud charges, competition law was more successful because the cases that went to trial relating to the conviction of individual traders for the wire fraud offence have since been successfully appealed. This has not happened to any of the cases based on competition law. Therefore, it has been demonstrated that competition law is well suited to use in the enforcement of the financial crime of benchmark manipulation. The next section of this chapter will look at legislative changes made since the LIBOR and FX scandal to see whether anything significant has changed and whether future enforcement action for benchmark manipulation will use competition law again, given its success in the enforcement of the FX benchmark manipulation discussed above.

5.6 Legislation Introduced Following the LIBOR and FX Scandal

Following the LIBOR and FX scandal, there was a perceived need for increased regulation of the financial markets. For example, Sandy Weill, former chief executive and chairman of Citigroup, stated in 2012 that commercial and investment banks should be split up and that the regulation brought in by the Glass-Steagall Act of 1933 should be brought back, citing the half a century free of financial crisis after the Glass-Steagall Act as the rationale for his argument.[174] Then, in 2015, US Deputy Attorney General Sally Yates announced a shift in the DoJ's policy about the prosecution of companies when she said that all corporate prosecutions would hold responsible those individuals within

171 Ibid.
172 Ibid.
173 Ibid.
174 S Denning, 'Rethinking Capitalism: Sandy Weill Says Bring Back Glass-Steagall' *Forbes* (New Jersey, 25 July 2012) <https://www.forbes.com/sites/stevedenning/2012/07/25/rethinking-capitalism-sandy-weill-says-bring-back-glass-steagall/?sh=3588ad3937d5> accessed 26 July 2024.

the company who had misbehaved.[175] This policy was a radical departure from the one held until that point, which was the 'Holder Doctrine'. The Holder Doctrine argued that companies were 'too big to jail' and that the collateral consequences of a corporate conviction had to be considered before bringing any conviction.[176] The result of the Holder Doctrine was the imposition of huge fines on companies, but no corporate criminal liability imposed for financial misconduct. This doctrine held no disincentive for banks or other financial services companies to follow the rules, as the absence of individual or corporate criminal liability for any crimes meant that the fines imposed for misconduct could be viewed by banks as a cost of business rather than a disincentive for breaking the rules. Following the policy change in 2015, which aimed to prosecute the individuals within a company who had broken the law, the DoJ brought its first case in 2015 against two individuals, former Rabobank traders, both of whom were found guilty of wire fraud for their role in rigging LIBOR.[177] However, as mentioned above, both convictions were overturned by the court in 2017 due to evidential difficulties in connection with the use of the wire fraud charge.[178]

A further change that has been made since the LIBOR scandal is that the benchmark itself has now been phased out. It has been replaced by a new benchmark interest rate called the Secured Overnight Financing Rate (SOFR).[179] The SOFR uses rates that investors offer for bank securities, instead of relying on bank quotes based on the rates for interbank loans, which is the basis of the LIBOR. The SOFR is viewed by many in the financial industry as being less open to manipulation than LIBOR because it is based entirely on transactions in the Department of the Treasury repurchase market, in which banks and investors borrow or lend Treasuries overnight. This differs from the calculation of the LIBOR benchmark interest rate because LIBOR is based partially on market data 'expert judgement' and is also based on a seven day average, unlike the SOFR, which is a daily rate based entirely on Treasuries.[180]

This section has looked at key changes made as a result of the LIBOR and FX scandal in the US. Now the chapter will move on to consider the four

175 WD Cohan, 'Justice Dept Shift on White-Collar Crime Is Long Overdue' *The New York Times* (New York, 11 September 2015) <https://www.nytimes.com/2015/09/12/business/dealbook/justice-dept-shift-on-white-collar-crime-is-long-overdue.html> accessed 26 July 2024.

176 BL Garrett, *Too Big to Jail: How Prosecutors Compromise with Corporations* (Harvard University Press 2014) 252, 253.

177 A Youngblood, 'Aftermath of the LIBOR Scandal' (2016) 35(1) *Review of Banking and Financial Law* 57.

178 *United States v. Allen*, 864 F.3d 63, 69-70 (2d Cir. 2017).

179 AP Fassas, 'Price Discovery in US Money Market Benchmarks: LIBOR vs SOFR' (2021) 204(1) *Economics Letters* 109882.

180 Morgan Stanley, 'Transitioning LIBOR: What It Means for Investors' (Morgan Stanley, 29 October 2019) <https://www.morganstanley.com/ideas/libor-its-end-transition-to-sofr> accessed 25 July 2024.

themes that run through each chapter of this book. The first theme is the role that the leniency and whistleblowing regime plays in the identification and enforcement of cartels in the US.

5.7 Leniency and Whistleblowing Regime in the US

This section examines how the competition law whistleblowing and leniency regimes operates in the financial services sector of the US. Corporate and individual leniency programmes are the primary means by which the Antitrust Division of the DoJ uncovers potential cartel agreements such as those seen in the LIBOR and FX manipulation scandal.[181] The Antitrust Division of the DoJ describes its leniency programme as its most important investigative tool for detecting cartel activity,[182] which demonstrates the importance the DoJ places on the programme, which has been in existence since 1993.[183] The DoJ's leniency programme is designed to create an incentive for individual cartel members to be the first to disclose the cartel to authorities in order to receive immunity from prosecution, as well as a limitation on the damages that may be recovered against cartel members by private plaintiffs in subsequent litigation.[184] The DoJ grants only one leniency application per conspiracy. Subsequent cooperators are not immune from criminal prosecution, but they will generally receive smaller fines and expose fewer of their executives to indictment than do non-cooperators.[185] The leniency regime worked well in the FX benchmark manipulation, in which UBS claimed immunity from fines for its participation in the cartel in exchange for being the first to tell the DoJ about the cartel.[186]

Competition law leniency and whistleblowing regimes are important tools to help detect many different types of wrongdoing such as cartels, which are notoriously difficult for regulators to find and to prosecute due to the extreme secrecy in which they operate.[187] Whistleblowing does not have a common

181 JD Beretta and J Terzaken, 'The Cartels and Leniency Review: USA' (2022) 1(1) *The Cartels and Leniency Review* 294, 299.

182 US Department of Justice, 'Leniency Program' (US Department of Justice, 6 December 2023) <https://www.justice.gov/atr/leniency-program> accessed 23 July 2024.

183 NH Miller, 'Strategic Leniency and Cartel Enforcement' (2009) 99(3) *The American Economic Review* 750.

184 NH Miller, 'Strategic Leniency and Cartel Enforcement' (2009) 99(3) *The American Economic Review* 750.

185 JD Beretta and John Terzaken, 'The Cartels and Leniency Review: USA' (2022) 1(1) *The Cartels and Leniency Review* 294, 299.

186 J McGeever, 'Exclusive: UBS Seeks First-Mover Immunity in U.S. Currency Probe' (*Reuters*, 7 February 2014) <https://www.reuters.com/article/idUSBREA161UN/> accessed 26 July 2024.

187 Ibid.

legal definition amongst academics,[188] but a good starting point is the definition of whistleblowing used by the International Labour Organisation, which describes whistleblowing as 'the reporting by employees or former employees of illegal, irregular, dangerous or unethical practices by employers'.[189] The Leniency Programme of the DoJ's Antitrust Division has been successful. Leniency applicants have led to the majority of the DoJ's international cartel prosecutions, resulting in substantial fines, prison sentences and opportunities for recovery for victims in recent years.[190] The competition law leniency programme allows both individuals and corporations to report their participation in an antitrust crime, such as a cartel, directly to the DoJ. In doing so, the first individual or corporation to confess will receive full immunity from prosecution for the antitrust violation, provided the conditions of the programme are met. The key requirements of the leniency programme are that (a) the DoJ has not found out about the breach of antitrust law (Type A leniency) or does not yet have enough information to pursue a conviction for the breach (Type B leniency); and (b) the corporation or individual reports the misconduct fully and cooperates with the DoJ's investigation.[191]

Deputy Assistant Attorney General Richard Powers described the antitrust leniency programme as 'our most important prosecutorial tool over the last 26 years'.[192] The success of the leniency programme is demonstrated by the fact that more than 90% of fines that the Division has collected for Sherman Act violations since 1996 have derived from investigations involving leniency applicants.[193] Powers states that trust is an important component of any successful leniency programme, stating that:

188 C Auberta and others, 'The Impact of Leniency and Whistle-Blowing Programs on Cartels' (2006) 24(6) *International Journal of Industrial Organisation* 1241.

189 G20 Anti-Corruption Working Group, 'Study on Whistleblower Protection Frameworks, Compendium of Best Practices and Guiding Principles for Legislation' (OECD, 2012) <https://www.oecd.org/corruption/48972967.pdf> accessed 15 July 2024.

190 A Hemlock, 'United States: DOJ Takes Aggressive Enforcement Approach and Faces No-Poach Challenges' (Global Competition Review, 2 May 2024) <https://globalcompetitionreview.com/insight/market-reviews/cartels-2024/article/united-states-doj-takes-aggressive-enforcement-approach-and-faces-no-poach-challenges> accessed 13 July 2024.

191 US Department of Justice, 'Leniency Program' (US Department of Justice, 6 December 2023) <https://www.justice.gov/atr/leniency-program> accessed 28 July 2024; and A Hemlock, 'United States: DOJ Takes Aggressive Enforcement Approach and Faces No-Poach Challenges' (Global Competition Review, 2 May 2024) <https://globalcompetitionreview.com/insight/market-reviews/cartels-2024/article/united-states-doj-takes-aggressive-enforcement-approach-and-faces-no-poach-challenges> accessed 23 July 2024.

192 RA Powers, 'A Matter of Trust: Enduring Leniency Lessons for the Future of Cartel Enforcement' (US Department of Justice, 19 February 2020) <https://www.justice.gov/opa/speech/deputy-assistant-attorney-general-richard-powers-delivers-remarks-13th-international> accessed 23 July 2024.

193 RB Bell, 'DOJ Antitrust Division Announces Changes to Corporate Leniency Program' (Hughes Hubbard and Reed LLP, 17 July 2019) <https://www.hugheshubbard.com/news

> For leniency to work, trust must go both ways – applicant and enforcer alike must honor their commitments in order to reap the significant benefits of the leniency bargain.[194]

He also highlighted the importance of having the threat of severe and significant sanctions to the success of a leniency programme. Sanctions for participation in a criminal cartel can range from:

> Criminal fines to civil treble damages and other collateral consequences, and engulf the entire company, its employees and shareholders in expensive investigations, and protracted litigation and cause real damage to its reputation and standing with its customers.[195]

That threat, combined with a heightened fear of detection and transparent and predictable enforcement policies, are the cornerstones on which the antitrust leniency programme has been built.[196] In the LIBOR crisis, UBS, which was involved in the LIBOR benchmark manipulation, was the first of the banks to report the misconduct to US regulators.[197] As a result, its fine for its role in the LIBOR manipulation was lower than expected. However, UBS still had to pay a fine for its part in the manipulation of the FX benchmark interest rate which came to light later, despite being the first to report the misconduct and pleading guilty because its conduct involved the breach of its prior DPA with the DoJ for the LIBOR manipulation.[198]

Alongside the competition law leniency programme, the SEC has a (non-competition law) whistleblowing programme that rewards whistleblowers who provide information about financial misconduct to regulators, originating

---

/doj-antitrust-division-announces-changes-to-corporate-leniency-program> accessed 11 July 2024.

194 RA Powers, 'A Matter of Trust: Enduring Leniency Lessons for the Future of Cartel Enforcement' (US Department of Justice, 19 February 2020) <https://www.justice.gov/opa/speech/deputy-assistant-attorney-general-richard-powers-delivers-remarks-13th-international> accessed 15 July 2024.

195 M Delrahim, 'Wind of Change: A New Model for Incentivizing Antitrust Compliance Programs' (*US Department of Justice*, 11 July 2019) <https://www.justice.gov/opa/speech/assistant-attorney-general-makan-delrahim-delivers-remarks-new-york-university-school-l-0> accessed 27 July 2024.

196 RA Powers, 'A Matter of Trust: Enduring Leniency Lessons for the Future of Cartel Enforcement' (US Department of Justice, 19 February 2020) <https://www.justice.gov/opa/speech/deputy-assistant-attorney-general-richard-powers-delivers-remarks-13th-international> accessed 12 July 2024.

197 US Department of Justice, 'Deferred Prosecution Agreement: US v UBS AG' (Department of Justice, 18 December 2012) <https://www.justice.gov/iso/opa/resources/1392012121911745845757.pdf> accessed 21 July 2024.

198 K Freifield, D Henry, S Slater, 'Global Banks Admit Guilt in Forex Probe, Fined Nearly $6 Billion' (*Reuters*, 20 May 2015) <https://www.reuters.com/article/us-banks-forex-settlement-idUSKBN0O50CQ20150520> accessed 24 July 2024.

from the Dodd-Frank Act of 2012; so in contrast to the DoJ, the SEC's whistleblowing programme is of very recent origin.[199] The SEC's whistleblowing programme differs from the DoJ's leniency programme in some key ways. The SEC is authorised to provide a financial incentive of between 10% and 30% of the money collected from the infringing parties. The monetary award will only be provided to individuals who come forward with high-quality, original information that leads to an SEC enforcement action in which more than $1m in sanctions is ordered.[200] In order to manage and administer the SEC's whistleblower programme, the Office of the Whistleblower was set up and is the point of contact for all would-be whistleblowers. A recent example of monetary awards issued by the SEC to whistleblowers is the award in May 2023 of its largest ever award, the sum of nearly $279m to one individual who provided information and assistance that led to a successful enforcement action.[201] The Director of the SEC's Division of Enforcement said of this award:

> The size of today's award – the highest in our program's history – not only incentivizes whistleblowers to come forward with accurate information about potential securities law violations, but also reflects the tremendous success of our whistleblower program[202]

This demonstrates the importance of the information provided by whistleblowers to the regulator and the high monetary awards act as an incentive to other people considering providing information to the SEC to do so. In its 2023 Annual Report to Congress on the Whistleblower Program, the SEC reports that:

> In FY 2023, the Commission awarded nearly $600 million—the highest annual total by dollar value in the Program's history—to 68 individual whistleblowers. These totals include a single award for almost $279 million—the largest in the history of the Program. The SEC has now

199 D Hall and N Ryder, 'The Protection of Whistle-Blowers in the United Kingdom – A Critical and Comparative Commentary' in C Grasso (ed), *Whistleblowers: Voices of Justice Springer* (Springer 2020).

200 LH Rubin and AM Selin, 'Self-Disclosing to the SEC in the Age of the Whistleblower' (2016) 23(4) *The Investment Lawyer* 3.

201 US Securities and Exchange Commission, 'SEC Issues Largest-Ever Whistleblower Award' (US SEC, 5 May 2023) <https://www.sec.gov/news/press-release/2023-89#:~:text=The%20Securities%20and%20Exchange%20Commission,of%20SEC%20and%20related%20actions.> accessed 24 July 2024.

202 US Securities and Exchange Commission, 'SEC Issues Largest-Ever Whistleblower Award' (US SEC, 5 May 2023) <https://www.sec.gov/news/press-release/2023-89#:~:text=The%20Securities%20and%20Exchange%20Commission,of%20SEC%20and%20related%20actions.> accessed 24 July 2024.

awarded more than $1.9 billion to 397 individual whistleblowers since the beginning of the Program in 2011.[203]

This shows that the whistleblower programme is of great importance to the SEC's enforcement efforts and assists in protecting investors and markets from financial crime. A recent example of a SEC whistleblower award is the sum of $279m, paid in May 2023, which is the largest ever whistleblower award paid by the SEC in exchange for information.[204]

The extensive competition law leniency programme and the SEC whistleblower provisions demonstrate that the US relies heavily on both leniency programmes and whistleblowing incentives to destabilise and deter cartels such as those involved in the LIBOR and FX manipulation scandal.[205] The DoJ's competition law leniency programme was instrumental in the detection and enforcement of the benchmark manipulation cartels; without the information provided from the first bank to 'confess' to each cartel, it is doubtful whether enough evidence to prosecute the cartels would have come to the regulator's attention.[206] The leniency and whistleblowing regimes fill the gap that any failure in deterrence leaves by proving incentives to encourage individuals to act in the interest of the common good and companies to act in the interest of reducing fines and criminal prosecutions.[207] What is certain is the value the DoJ places on its leniency programme and the part the programme played in the detection and enforcement of the LIBOR and FX cartels.[208]

5.8 Criminal vs Civil Penalties

This section of the chapter will consider whether civil or criminal sanctions are best suited for the enforcement of the financial crime of benchmark manipulation. This question has been referred to as 'the eternal debate' by commentators

203 US Securities and Exchange Commission, 'Securities and Exchange Commission Office of the Whistleblower, Annual Report to Congress for Fiscal Year 2023' (SEC, 14 November 2023) 1 <https://www.sec.gov/files/fy23-annual-report.pdf> accessed 20 July 2024.

204 Reuters, 'SEC Issues Largest Ever Whistleblower Award of $279 Million' *Reuters* (US, 5 May 2023) <https://www.reuters.com/world/us/us-sec-issues-largest-ever-whistleblower-award-279-mln-2023-05-05/> accessed 20 July 2024.

205 NH Miller, 'Strategic Leniency and Cartel Enforcement' (2009) 99(3) *The American Economic Review* 750.

206 JA Batten, 'Financial Market Manipulation, Whistleblowing, and the Common Good: Evidence from the LIBOR Scandal' (2022) 58(1) *ABACUS* 1.

207 For example, see JA Batten, 'Financial Market Manipulation, Whistleblowing, and the Common Good: Evidence from the LIBOR Scandal' (2022) 58(1) *ABACUS* 1

N Feltovich and Y Hamaguchi, 'The Effect of Whistle-Blowing Incentives on Collusion: An Experimental Study of Leniency Programs' (2018) 84(4) *Southern Economic Journal* 1024.

208 A Hemlock, 'United States: DOJ Takes Aggressive Enforcement Approach and Faces No-Poach Challenges' (Global Competition Review, 2 May 2024) <https://globalcompetitionreview.com/insight/market-reviews/cartels-2024/article/united-states-doj-takes-aggressive-enforcement-approach-and-faces-no-poach-challenges> accessed 23 July 2024.

who highlight the sometimes blurred line between civil or 'administrative' fines and criminal fines, pointing to jurisdictions such as the EU where the extremely high civil fines for competition law breaches can appear 'quasi-penal'.[209] The enforcement powers available to the US regulators for cartels, such as those found in the LIBOR and FX manipulation scandal, will now be considered and critically analysed.

US regulators have a selection of both civil and criminal penalties available to them to impose for breaches of financial and of competition law, detailed below.[210] This gives the regulators more choice when it comes to sending a message to the perpetrators and the public at large about the seriousness of their offence. The penalties available to regulators for breach of competition law comprise civil and criminal penalties for breach of the Sherman Act, the Clayton Act or the FTC Act. Cartels are enforced under Section 1 of the Sherman Act, which outlaws all agreements between competitors to fix prices, which covers the benchmark manipulation seen in the LIBOR and FX benchmark manipulation.[211] Therefore, the DoJ has the ability to use its criminal law enforcement powers when there is a breach of Section 1 of the Sherman Act. These powers were outlined above and include penalties of up to $100m, which can be imposed on companies, or fines of up to $1m, which can be imposed on individuals, along with criminal penalties of up to ten years in imprisonment for individuals. Criminal prosecutions are more likely to be imposed when violations of the Sherman Act are intentional and clear, such as when competitors fix prices, as they did in the LIBOR and FX benchmark manipulations, or rig bids.[212] The FTC Act allows the FTC to bring cases under the FTC Act against the same kind of breaches of competition law that breach the Sherman Act; however, the DoJ is recognised as the main regulator for breaches of competition law under the Sherman Act.[213]

Additional civil powers for regulators in relation to competition law crimes come from the Clayton Act, which addresses specific practices that the Sherman Act does not clearly ban, such as the setting of discriminatory prices, services and allowances in dealings between businesses. It is particularly relevant for practices such as mergers and acquisitions, which may lead to a substantial

209 E Herlin-Karnell, N Ryder, *Market Manipulation and Insider Trading* (Hart Publishing 2019) 45, 46.

210 D Yeres and others, 'Understanding and Preparing for the Convergence of US Criminal Antitrust Enforcement with Anti-Manipulation Laws Regulating Derivatives, FX, Crypto-currency, Futures, Options and other Commodities under the Commodity Exchange Act' (2019) 39(1) *The Journal on the Law of Investment and Risk Management Products* 2.

211 Ibid.

212 BA Howell, 'Sentencing of Antitrust Offenders: What Does the Data Show?' (US Sentencing Commission, 2007) <https://www.ussc.gov/sites/default/files/pdf/about/commissioners/selected-articles/Howell_Review_of_Antitrust_Sentencing_Data.pdf> accessed 31 July 2024.

213 A Palmer, *Countering Economic Crime* (Routledge 2018) and A Zelcer, 'Mail and Wire Fraud' (2012) 49(2) *The American Criminal Law Review* 985.

lessening of competition or lead to a monopoly. If the Clayton Act has been breached, it authorises private parties to sue the offending businesses for triple damages when they have been harmed by conduct that violates either the Sherman or the Clayton Act.[214] Private parties are also enabled, by the Clayton Act, to obtain a court order prohibiting the anticompetitive practice being carried out again in the future.[215] So, it can be seen that there are substantial civil and criminal penalties available to regulators for competition breaches of the Sherman Act and that private actions brought by injured parties can involve significant sums of money as well, if triple damages are awarded by a court, as allowed by the Clayton Act.

Penalties available to regulators for breach of financial regulations, as for competition law, also consist of both civil and criminal powers. The Sentencing Reform Act 1984, which was introduced as part of the Comprehensive Crime Control Act of 1984,[216] granted both law enforcement and regulatory agencies additional powers to tackle corporate economic crime. The Sentencing Reform Act is the most frequently used enforcement power against companies in the US and is regularly used in association with a DPA. A further relevant statute used by regulators of financial crime in the US is the Financial Institutions Reform, Recovery and Enforcement Act 1989 (Financial Institutions Reform Act).[217] This was introduced in the aftermath of the Savings and Loans crisis[218] in the 1980s and permits law enforcement and financial regulatory agencies to instigate civil proceedings against companies for a wide range of financial crimes.[219] The civil penalties under the Financial Institutions Reform Act have been used by the DoJ many times to enforce corporate financial crime and has generated billions of dollars in financial penalties as well as compensation for victims when they have been identifiable.[220]

A further key statute that confers civil enforcement powers on regulators is the Commodity Exchange Act 1936.[221] which prohibits the manipulation of prices in a vast array of product markets, including products such as financial

214 D Yeres and others, 'Understanding and Preparing for the Convergence of US Criminal Antitrust Enforcement with Anti-Manipulation Laws Regulating Derivatives, FX, Cryptocurrency, Futures, Options and other Commodities under the Commodity Exchange Act' (2019) 39(1) *The Journal on the Law of Investment and Risk Management Products* 24.

215 BA Howell, 'Sentencing of Antitrust Offenders: What Does the Data Show?' (US Sentencing Commission, 2007) <https://www.ussc.gov/sites/default/files/pdf/about/commissioners/selected-articles/Howell_Review_of_Antitrust_Sentencing_Data.pdf> accessed 31 July 2024.

216 Comprehensive Crime Control Act 1984, Public Law 98–473.

217 Financial Institutions Reform, Recovery and Enforcement Act 1989, Public Law 101-73.

218 WK Black, *The Best Way to Rob a Bank Is to Own One* (University of Texas Press 2005) 26, 27.

219 Ibid.

220 E Herlin-Karnell, N Ryder *Market Manipulation and Insider Trading* (Hart Publishing 2019) 120.

221 Commodity Exchange Act, 7 U.S.C.A. §1.

instruments and currencies. The regulator of the Commodity Exchange Act is the CFTC, which has civil enforcement powers to target conduct that manipulates price in any of the regulated markets. In the past decade, some of the CFTC's most high-profile market manipulation cases, including those brought in connection with the LIBOR and FX benchmark manipulation, have been brought at the same time as the DoJ's criminal cartel investigations, in which the Antitrust Division secured corporate guilty pleas and imprisonment for employees guilty of participating in the benchmark manipulation cartels.[222]

US regulators, when they have a choice between the imposition of civil or criminal penalties, must consider what the difference in impact is between civil and criminal penalties when imposed on companies rather than individuals. There is a clear difference between civil and criminal penalties when an individual faces imprisonment from criminal charges, but a company cannot be sent to prison, so the difference between civil and criminal penalties is less apparent for corporations, with larger fines and the stigma of being branded a criminal being the main distinguishing factors between civil and criminal penalties for companies. The imposition of criminal penalties, whether on a company or on an individual, signifies that the offence is more serious than those offences imposed for civil breaches of the law.[223]

The most significant differences between a criminal investigation and civil enforcement are that a criminal case stigmatises more, it decides more and it requires more of the firm or individual.[224] The DoJ has an enhanced ability to gather information in criminal investigations with the ability to use grand jury subpoenas to obtain almost any nonprivileged information in the US and abroad.[225] The power to subpoena for information is much more limited in civil cases. There is a difference in the rights of the parties under investigation and in the applicable standard of proof. The standard of proof in criminal cases is beyond a reasonable doubt. In civil enforcement the standard of proof is much lower; the DoJ will just have to prove that it is 'more likely than not' that the individual or company engaged in the wrongful conduct. Either

222 D Yeres and others, 'Understanding and Preparing for the Convergence of US Criminal Antitrust Enforcement with Anti-Manipulation Laws Regulating Derivatives, FX, Cryptocurrency, Futures, Options and other Commodities under the Commodity Exchange Act' (2019) 39(1) *The Journal on the Law of Investment and Risk Management Products* 2.

223 P O'Loughlin, 'The Criminal Enforcement of Antitrust Law - The Importance of Building an Enforcement Culture and How to Create It' (2016) 5(1) *UCL Journal of Law and Jurisprudence* 116, 116.

224 SW Buell, 'Potentially Perverse Effects of Corporate Civil Liability' in A Barkow and R Barkow (eds), *Prosecutors in the Boardroom: Using Criminal Law to Regulate Corporate Conduct* (New York University Press 2011) 87.

225 P O'Loughlin, 'The Criminal Enforcement of Antitrust Law - The Importance of Building an Enforcement Culture and How to Create It' (2016) 5(1) *UCL Journal of Law and Jurisprudence* 116.

civil or criminal cases may result in a trial, but civil cases are not jury trials.[226] Criminal cases against companies rarely end up at a trial, more commonly being resolved with a criminal settlement with the DoJ, known as a DPA – this will be discussed below. Finally, the sanctions that can be imposed are a key differentiator between civil and criminal cases.[227] A criminal conviction can result in a prison sentence for individuals and dissolution and stigma for a company.[228] Even though fines imposed for civil and criminal offences may appear to be similar, it can be seen from the above that there are other, significant differences between civil and criminal investigations.[229]

For cartels, known as 'the supreme evil' of antitrust, criminal enforcement appears to be the most appropriate choice for regulators, as it sends a clear message that the activity is harmful to society and worthy of punishment.[230] It is, therefore, strange that the LIBOR benchmark manipulation cartels were not enforced by the DoJ using its competition law powers. The effect of criminal enforcement on companies is looked at below, as there are public policy issues as well as much academic debate focused on criminal corporate liability. It can, therefore, be seen from the above that for the most serious financial crime offences, such as the LIBOR and FX benchmark manipulation cartels, regulators should use criminal law powers against companies.

5.9 Corporate Criminal Liability

This section will consider the third theme, corporate criminal liability, and will look at how corporate criminal liability was used by regulators in the LIBOR and FX benchmark manipulation scandal. In the US, all the enforcement action taken by the DoJ against the LIBOR and FX cartel participants was taken using criminal law, using first the offence of wire fraud or conspiracy to commit wire fraud, then the offence of breach of Section 1 of the Sherman Act. The enforcement taken was brought against both individuals and companies, so it is relevant for this research to look at the notoriously controversial doctrine of corporate criminal liability. [231] In particular, when criminal law is enforced against systemically important corporate bodies, such as the interna-

226 BA Howell, 'Sentencing of Antitrust Offenders: What Does the Data Show?' (US Sentencing Commission, 2007) <https://www.ussc.gov/sites/default/files/pdf/about/commissioners/selected-articles/Howell_Review_of_Antitrust_Sentencing_Data.pdf> accessed 31 July 2024.

227 Ibid.

228 M Kerns, 'Criminal Sentencing in Antitrust Cases' (1982) 13(4) *Loyola University Chicago Law Journal* 985.

229 Ibid.

230 P O'Loughlin, 'The Criminal Enforcement of Antitrust Law - The Importance of Building an Enforcement Culture and How to Create It' (2016) 5(1) *UCL Journal of Law and Jurisprudence* 116.

231 A Hamdani and A Klement, 'Corporate Crime and Deterrence' (2008) 61(2) *Stanford Law Review* 271.

tional banks involved in the LIBOR and FX manipulation, policy issues must be considered by regulators, which may affect their enforcement strategies.

As mentioned in Chapter 2, the most infamous criminal conviction of a company in recent times is that of Arthur Andersen in 2002.[232] In that case, the prosecutor successfully argued that the company should receive the maximum criminal penalty of a $500,000 fine and five years of probation, saying that:

> Andersen's conduct in obstructing the Securities and Exchange Commission investigation of Enron, we submit, contributed to – contributed to significantly – the historic shaking of the foundations of our markets.[233]

In the case, US District Judge Melinda Harmon sided with prosecutors and the SEC, who wanted her to make an example of the firm. In a corporate criminal conviction, a federal judge has to start by looking at the US Sentencing Guidelines.[234] The fine given to Arthur Andersen was the maximum fine listed for obstruction of justice because the company had not accepted responsibility and was still proclaiming its innocence; it had also violated a prior SEC consent decree.[235]

The Enron scandal, with the subsequent demise of Arthur Andersen, demonstrated to regulators the significant fall out that could occur following a successful corporate criminal prosecution. One commentator states that:

> A single prosecution of a company…can have enormous repercussions in the U.S. and the global economy, particularly since other industry actors will be watching and nervous about whether they might be next.[236]

The Enron scandal resulted in the bankruptcy of the Enron Corporation itself but also the dissolution of Arthur Andersen, then one of the five largest audit and accountancy firms in the world, who were found guilty of illegally destroying documents relevant to the SEC's investigation of Enron. The United States District Court for the Southern District of Texas found Arthur

232 E Herlin-Karnell, N Ryder, *Market Manipulation and Insider Trading* (Hart Publishing 2019) 54–56.

233 M Flood and T Fowler, 'Andersen Gets the Maximum Sentence' (*Houston Chronicle* Houston,16 October 2002) <https://www.chron.com/business/enron/article/Andersen-gets-the-maximum-sentence-2115792.php> accessed 14 July 2024.

234 MKerns, 'Criminal Sentencing in Antitrust Cases' (1982) 13(4) *Loyola University Chicago Law Journal* 985; and United States Sentencing Commission, (Guidelines Manual, November 2018).

235 BL Garrett, *Too Big to Jail: How Prosecutors Compromise with Corporations* (Harvard University Press 2014) 148.

236 Ibid, 7.

Andersen guilty of obstructing an official proceeding of the SEC, and because federal regulations do not allow felons to audit public companies, Arthur Andersen was forced to surrender its licence to audit public companies, which ended the company's operation entirely.[237] This has become known as the corporate death penalty, which refers not just to the end of a company's 'life' but to the terrible collateral consequences that can result from it.[238]

The judgement against Arthur Andersen was eventually overturned by the US Supreme Court in 2005 due to the inaccurate instructions provided to the jury, which the court stated in its judgement were flawed in important respects.[239] However, by then, Arthur Andersen had lost most of its customers and had ended its operations. The corporate death penalty has been written about by many commentators, and the prevailing view is that prosecuting companies can lead to massive social and economic collateral harm, which reaches far wider than the company itself or of its employees, directors and shareholders.[240] It is important to note that the DoJ did not attempt to enter into a DPA with Arthur Anderson in lieu of the trial.[241] Following the Arthur Anderson trial, described as 'the corporate trial of the century'[242] prosecutors from that point markedly changed their approach to corporate criminal enforcement, and there was a significant increase in the use of DPAs by the DoJ,[243] discussed in more detail below.

The US approach toward imposing criminal sanctions on companies can be traced back to the decision in 1909 of the Supreme Court in *New York*

237 Justia US Law, 'United States of America, Plaintiff-Appellee, v Arthur Andersen, LLP, Defendant-appellant, 374 F3d 281 (5th Cir 2004)' (Justia US Law, 16 June 2004) <https://law.justia.com/cases/federal/appellate-courts/F3/374/281/505799/> accessed 8 July 2024.

238 G Markoff, 'Arthur Andersen and the Myth of the Corporate Death Penalty: Corporate Criminal Convictions in the Twenty-First Century' (2013) 15(3) *University of Pennsylvania Journal of Business Law* 797.

239 *Arthur Andersen LLP v United States,* 544 U.S. 696 (2005).

240 For example, see N Werle, 'Prosecuting Corporate Crime When Firms Are Too Big to Jail: Investigation, Deterrence, and Judicial Review' (2019) 128 *Yale L J* 1366; G Markoff, 'Arthur Andersen and the Myth of the Corporate Death Penalty: Corporate Criminal Convictions in the Twenty-First Century' (2013) 15(3) *University of Pennsylvania Journal of Business Law* 797; and N Ryder, '"Too Scared to Prosecute and Too Scared to Jail?" A Critical and Comparative Analysis of Enforcement of Financial Crime legislation against Corporations in the USA and the UK' (2018) 82(3) *The Journal of Criminal Law* 245.

241 N Ryder, '"Too Scared to Prosecute and Too Scared to Jail?" A Critical and Comparative Analysis of Enforcement of Financial Crime Legislation against Corporations in the USA and the UK' (2018) 82(3) *Journal of Criminal Law* 245.

242 BL. Garrett, *Too Big to Jail: How Prosecutors Compromise with Corporations* (The Belknap Press of Harvard University Press 2014) 12.

243 N Ryder, '"Too Scared to Prosecute and Too Scared to Jail?" A Critical and Comparative Analysis of Enforcement of Financial Crime legislation against Corporations in the USA and the UK' (2018) 82(3) *The Journal of Criminal Law* 245.

Central & Hudson River Railroad Company v US.[244] In this case the Supreme Court held that a corporation could be constitutionally prosecuted for a federal crime based on the criminal conduct of a single employee. The decision was based on the US rule called the master–servant rule or *respondeat superior,* which means 'let the master answer' in Latin. The rule has the effect of making the master responsible for the servant's acts. In the above case, the Supreme Court held that the corporation was in the position of 'master' and that, as an employer, it was responsible for the employee's wrongs, provided that those wrongs were committed during their employment and could be said to at least partially have been for the benefit the employer.[245] The judgement in this case marked a turning point from previous case law, which had been based on the doctrine that a corporation cannot commit a crime, which in the *New York Central* case, the Supreme Court held was no longer appropriate.[246] Since this decision, this rule has been expanded by the courts to include the actions of agents of corporations who are acting without authority or who are breaching specific directions.[247] Commentators have noted that this means a company can be held liable for the conduct even of 'low level employees who acted contrary to the corporate policy and to the compliance program of its firm'.[248]

For many years, US prosecutors were not successful in obtaining more than modest sentences for companies and, therefore, often took the view that it was not worth prosecuting them.[249] However, in the past decade or so, the size and importance of federal prosecutions of companies has increased, although the number of cases being brought has not increased significantly.[250] The US Sentencing Commission, convened by Congress, published the first sentencing guidelines for companies in 1991, and these became law the same year.[251] Since this point, the size of corporate fines increased until the Enron scandal shook the US in 2001, which resulted in the DoJ forming an Enron Task Force and later a Corporate Fraud Task Force. The Corporate Task Force

244 *New York Central & Hudson River Railroad Company v US* 212 US 481 (1909).

245 BL Garrett, *Too Big to Jail: How Prosecutors Compromise with Corporations* (The Belknap Press of Harvard University Press 2014) 4.

246 E Herlin-Karnell, N Ryder *Market Manipulation and Insider Trading* (Hart Publishing 2019) 52.

247 *United States v Hilton Hotels Corp.*, 467 F.2d 1000, 1004 (9th Cir. 1972).

248 E Lederman, 'Corporate Criminal Liability: The Second Generation' (2016) 46 *Stetson Law Review* 74; and N Ryder, '"Too Scared to Prosecute and Too Scared to Jail?" A Critical and Comparative Analysis of Enforcement of Financial Crime legislation against Corporations in the USA and the UK' (2018) 82(3) *The Journal of Criminal Law* 245.

249 MA Cohen, 'Theories of Punishment and Empirical Trends in Corporate Criminal Sanctions' (1996) 17 *Managerial and Decision Economics* 401.

250 BL Garrett, *Too Big to Jail: How Prosecutors Compromise with Corporations* (The Belknap Press of Harvard University Press 2014) 6.

251 IH Nagel and WM Swenson, 'The Federal Sentencing Guidelines for Corporations: Their Development, Theoretical Underpinnings, and Some Thoughts About Their Future' (1993) 71(2) *Washington University Law Review* 205.

was set up in 2002 and lasted until 2009 when President Obama replaced it with the Financial Fraud Enforcement Task Force (FFETF), which still exists today.[252] It has been claimed that the creation of the FFETF illustrated the importance of the investigation and prosecution of financial and investment fraud to the US government.[253] Since then, in 2018, President Trump set up a further task force to fight financial crime, called the Task Force on Market Integrity and Consumer Fraud, which is part of a government-wide initiative to combat fraud against consumers and corporate fraud.[254] These various initiatives over the past 20 years demonstrate the intent of the US government to fight corporate financial crime, including fraud and market manipulation. This intent is behind the DoJ's approach to corporate prosecutions; however, this intent has to be balanced with mitigating the impact of the corporate death penalty, seen in the Enron scandal with the subsequent demise of Arthur Andersen.

The above consideration of the way in which the US imposed corporate criminal liability on such immense companies as the international banks involved in the LIBOR and FX manipulation provides an important point of comparison with the other two jurisdictions studied, the UK and EU. The EU does not impose any corporate criminal liability, using entirely civil sanctions for breaches of competition law. However, the UK can impose corporate criminal liability, although the existing identification doctrine is flawed as discussed in Chapter 3. The approach of the US in imposing criminal liability on international companies such as Arthur Andersen and then international banks such as HSBC, Barclays, Citi, JPMorgan and others is a crucial comparator for this book.

5.10 Deferred Prosecution Agreements

The final theme considered in this chapter builds on the above discussion of corporate criminal liability. When corporate criminal liability is considered, the way which US regulators have found to avoid the corporate death penalty, seen to have catastrophic consequences in the Arthur Andersen case mentioned above, is to enter DPAs with the offending company.[255] This section

252 US Department of Justice, 'Attorney General Eric Holder Speaks at the Financial Fraud Enforcement Task Force Press Conference' (US Department of Justice, 17 November 2009) <https://www.justice.gov/opa/speech/attorney-general-eric-holder-speaks-financial-fraud-enforcement-task-force-press> accessed 15 July 2024.

253 E Herlin-Karnell, N Ryder *Market Manipulation and Insider Trading* (Hart Publishing 2019) 117.

254 US Department of Justice, 'Task Force on Market Integrity and Consumer Fraud' (Department of Justice, 11 July 2018) <https://www.justice.gov/archives/fraudtaskforce> accessed 8 July 2024.

255 RA Epstein, 'Deferred Prosecution Agreements on Trial' in A Barkow and R Barkow (eds), *Prosecutors in the Boardroom: Using Criminal Law to Regulate Corporate Conduct* (New York University Press 2011) 87.

will consider the advantages and disadvantages of this approach, as DPAs have their detractors as well as proponents amongst academic commentators.

Some academics have argued that DPAs do not have the deterrent effect of a criminal prosecution,[256] that there is a lack of judicial oversight[257] and that DPAs risk a trend of 'insufficient deterrence' of repeat behaviour;[258] however, others note that after more than 20 years of their use in the US legal system, they have proved to be a successful legal enforcement tool.[259] According to Deputy Assistant Attorney General Richard Powers, DPAs have an important role to play in the enforcement of cartels such as those seen in the LIBOR and FX benchmark manipulation. Their use by the DoJ is a recent policy change and is designed to incentivise companies to have suitable compliance programmes. Powers explains the difference between the leniency programme and DPAs as being:

> Leniency's exclusive benefits include complete immunity from criminal prosecution for the company and its covered cooperating employees, as well as detrebling[260] and other benefits available under the Antitrust Criminal Penalty Enhancement and Reform Act. A DPA provides none of these extraordinary benefits.[261]

Powers goes on to emphasise that obtaining leniency in the DoJ's antitrust leniency programme for participation in a cartel is the best option for any cartel member; however, entering into a DPA is a good consolation prize for companies who have missed the 'first past the post' application for leniency.[262] When considering whether a company is eligible for a DPA instead of a criminal prosecution, prosecutors will consider the adequacy of the company's

256 For example, see DM Uhlmann, 'Deferred Prosecution and Non-Prosecution Agreements and the Erosion of Corporate Criminal Liability' (2013) 72(4) *Maryland Law Review* 1295; and O'Sullivan, 'How Prosecutors Apply the"'Federal Prosecutions of Corporations" Charging Policy in the Era of Deferred Prosecutions' (2014) 51 *American Criminal Law Review* 30.

257 A Palmer, 'Justice Deferred is Justice Denied?' in N Ryder and L Pasculli (eds), *Corruption, Integrity and the Law* (Routledge 2020) 89, 90.

258 Ibid, 90.

259 For example see C Grasso, 'Peaks and Troughs of the English Deferred Prosecution Agreement: The Lesson Learned from the DPA between the SFO and ICBC SB Plc' (2016) 1(5) *Journal of Business Law* 388–408; and D Mcstravick, 'Deferred Prosecution Agreements and the Restorative Justice Paradigm' in N Ryder and L Pasculli (eds), *Corruption, Integrity and the Law* (Routledge 2020) 113, 116.

260 'Detrebling' refers to the reduction of treble damages (damages increased using a multiplier of three) to single damages.

261 RA Powers, 'A Matter of Trust: Enduring Leniency Lessons for the Future of Cartel Enforcement' (US Department of Justice, 19 February 2020) <https://www.justice.gov/opa/speech/deputy-assistant-attorney-general-richard-powers-delivers-remarks-13th-international> accessed 27 July 2024.

262 Ibid.

compliance programme, as well as factors such as prompt self-reporting of the wrongdoing, cooperation and remedial action taken by the company.[263] It can be seen from the above that corporate compliance programmes play an important role in qualifying cartel members for a DPA.

The DoJ used DPAs to settle most of the corporate criminal charges against the banks involved in the LIBOR and FX market manipulation. One of the last DPAs for the FX manipulation to be agreed was with HSBC, which agreed to pay a $101.5m penalty including a $63.1m fine and $38.4m in restitution as part of the settlement with the DoJ.[264] In addition to agreeing to the financial penalty, HSBC agreed in the DPA to take additional steps to enhance its existing compliance programme and to improve internal controls in its investment banking unit. This is one of the key areas where DPAs add value, as obliging banks to overhaul or improve their compliance programmes is designed to focus on the prevention of further breaches of the law rather than just punishing the breach that has just taken place.[265] It has already been noted that financial penalties imposed on banks may not have the deterrent effect the authorities wish because the fines often appear to be simply viewed as a cost of business and absorbed into the bank's operating costs. Whereas if a bank is obliged in a DPA to improve its compliance programme, the possibility of avoiding future breaches of the law, when combined with a punishment for past breaches, is a more powerful enforcement tool than simply imposing a financial penalty.[266]

Then next issue to consider in relation to how well DPAs operate as an enforcement tool is what happens when a bank breaches a current DPA; what are the consequences, if any? During the FX scandal, two banks were found to have breached their DPAs, and each received additional criminal fines from the DoJ as a result. The first bank was Barclays, who agreed that its FX collusive conduct constituted federal crimes that violated a principal term of its June 2012 nonprosecution agreement for its part in the manipulation of the LIBOR benchmark interest rate. Barclays was ordered to pay an additional $60m criminal penalty as a result of this violation of its DPA.[267] The other

263 RA Epstein, 'Deferred Prosecution Agreements on Trial' in A Barkow and R Barkow (eds), *Prosecutors in the Boardroom: Using Criminal Law to Regulate Corporate Conduct* (New York University Press 2011).

264 HSBC, 'HSBC Settles Foreign Exchange Investigation with the US Department of Justice' (HSBC, 18 January 2018) <file:///Users/dianajohnson/Downloads/sea-180118-hsbc-fx-doj-settlement.pdf> accessed 22 July 2024.

265 C Grasso, 'Peaks and Troughs of the English Deferred Prosecution Agreement: The Lesson Learned from the DPA between the SFO and ICBC SB Plc' (2016) 1(5) *Journal of Business Law* 388.

266 D Mcstravick, 'Deferred Prosecution Agreements and the Restorative Justice Paradigm' in N Ryder and L Pasculli (eds), *Corruption, Integrity and the Law* (Routledge 2020) 113, 123.

267 US Department of Justice, 'Five Major Banks Agree to Parent-Level Guilty Pleas' (US Department of Justice, 20 May 2015) <https://www.justice.gov/opa/pr/five-major-banks-agree-parent-level-guilty-pleas> accessed 23 July 2024.

bank that was also deemed to have breached an existing DPA was UBS. The DoJ decided that UBS's deceptive currency trading and its collusive conduct in certain FX markets also violated its December 2012 nonprosecution agreement that had, like the one for Barclays, also been put into place to resolve the LIBOR investigation. UBS has been fined an additional criminal penalty of $203m for the breach of its DPA.[268] It can be seen from the significant fines imposed on the two banks for breaching an existing DPA that the US regulator takes the breach seriously. In addition to the fines for breaching the DPAs, Barclays and UBS, together with the other three banks involved with the manipulation of the FX benchmark interest rate, were each required to agree to a three-year period of corporate probation, to be overseen by the court.[269] The probation involves the cessation of all criminal activity together with regular reporting to authorities and cooperation with any ongoing criminal investigations into their conduct and that of any of their employees. The banks were all required to inform their customers and counterparties of their misconduct and the penalties imposed on them for it, which provides a strong deterrent from committing future financial crime.

This chapter argues that the most successful way to combat corporate crime without invoking the corporate death penalty is to prosecute both the individuals who committed the crime and the company involved, using a DPA to impose sanctions and ongoing corporate monitoring on the company.[270] The use of DPAs, although some commentators express concerns about them, has the advantage of imposing criminal liability on a company, with the social stigma that a criminal conviction brings.[271] DPAs are often used by regulators to institute structural changes to a company, to increase accountability of chief officers and to invite an external compliance monitor to assess compliance programming.[272] Some of these provisions were featured in the DPA entered into between the DoJ and Barclays to settle the FX manipulation charges, in which Barclays agreed to implement and continue to implement a compliance programme designed to prevent and detect the benchmark manipulation to which it had pleaded guilty.[273] Barclays also agreed to report annually to the dedicated probation officer and the DoJ on its progress in implementing the compliance programme. It can be seen that, if used in conjunction

268 Ibid.

269 Ibid.

270 DM Uhlmann, 'Deferred Prosecution and Non-Prosecution Agreements and the Erosion of Corporate Criminal Liability' (2013) 72(4) *Maryland Law Review* 1295.

271 A Hamdani and A Klement, 'Corporate Crime and Deterrence' (2008) 61(2) *Stanford Law Review* 271.

272 S Hamann, 'Effective Corporate Compliance: A Holistic Approach for the SEC and the DOJ' (2019) 94(2) *Washington Law Review* 851.

273 United States District Court District of Connecticut, 'United States of America v Barclays PLC Plea Agreement' (United States District Court District of Connecticut, 20 May 2015) <https://www.justice.gov/file/440481/download> accessed 23 July 2024.

with significant financial penalties, civil litigation and the prosecution of the offending employees, DPAs can both be a deterrent to further financial crime and encourage companies to adopt and comply with compliance programmes, designed to deter further financial crime such as benchmark manipulation.[274]

5.11 Conclusion

This chapter has considered the different approaches that have been taken by US regulators to the enforcement of the LIBOR and the FX benchmark manipulation scandals of 2012–2014. In the LIBOR manipulation, the enforcement agencies used generic financial services laws, such as the offence of wire fraud under the Wire Fraud Statute 1952, to prosecute the banks involved.[275] It was, however, then particularly notable that in the subsequent FX scandal the DoJ took a different approach and prosecuted the perpetrators under Section 1 of the Sherman Antitrust Act and, therefore, using competition law to enforce what is a crime committed in the financial services sector.[276] The successful use of competition law to prosecute financial crime can also be seen in the LIBOR private class action brought in the US, which was brought on the basis of a breach of competition law and resulted in a settlement of nearly $22m for the plaintiffs.[277]

It has been noted above that there was a change of approach by the DoJ in its enforcement action for benchmark manipulation from the use of the wire fraud criminal offence as its primary method of enforcement in the LIBOR prosecutions to the use of the criminal competition law offence in the FX prosecutions, in relation to a materially identical crime. This change could be explained by the DoJ observing the use by the European Commission of its

274 D Mcstravick, 'Deferred Prosecution Agreements and the Restorative Justice Paradigm' in N Ryder and L Pasculli (eds), *Corruption, Integrity and the Law* (Routledge 2020) 113,124.

275 Practical Law Antitrust, 'DoJ LIBOR Manipulation Investigation Chart' (Practical Law, 31 December 2020) <https://uk.practicallaw.thomsonreuters.com/w-001-0974?transitionType=Default&contextData=(sc.Default)&firstPage=true> accessed 26 July 2024.

276 SE Foster, 'LIBOR Manipulation and Antitrust Allegations' (2013) 11(3) *DePaul Business & Commercial Law Journal* 291; US Department of Justice, 'Five Major Banks Agree to Parent-Level Guilty Pleas' (Department of Justice, 20 May 2015) <https://www.justice.gov/opa/pr/five-major-banks-agree-parent-level-guilty-pleas> accessed 24 July 2024; US Department of Justice, 'BNP Paribas USA Inc. Pleads Guilty to Antitrust Conspiracy' (US Department of Justice, 26 January 2018) <https://www.justice.gov/opa/pr/bnp-paribas-usa-inc-pleads-guilty-antitrust-conspiracy> accessed 23 July 2024; and see US Department of Justice, 'Former Foreign Exchange Trader Sentenced to Prison for Price Fixing and Bid Rigging' (US Department of Justice, 17 September 2020) <https://www.justice.gov/opa/pr/former-foreign-exchange-trader-sentenced-prison-price-fixing-and-bid-rigging> accessed 23 July 2024.

277 JD Supra, 'Five Banks Settle LIBOR Manipulation Suit for $22 Million' (JD Supra, 13 October 2020) <https://www.jdsupra.com/legalnews/five-banks-settle-libor-manipulation-70879/> accessed 22 July 2024.

competition law rules to enforce the LIBOR scandal and the decisions made by the Commission in which cartel activity was clearly identified by them in the manipulation of the benchmark interest rate.[278] The change of approach to using competition law powers by the DoJ can also be attributed to the names given to the bank traders' chat rooms; they themselves called one of their chat rooms 'The Cartel', which is something that cannot have escaped the notice of the US's principal competition law regulator, the DoJ.[279]

Whatever the reason for the notable change in enforcement policy by the DoJ between the LIBOR and the FX scandals, it can be seen that for many years after the Commodity Exchange Act was enacted in 1936 to deal with price manipulation or any other disruptions to market integrity, the DoJ did not pursue any antitrust actions in the financial services sector, leaving the enforcement of market manipulation and other financial crimes to the CFTC.[280] However, following the LIBOR and FX cartel cases, which had such wide-reaching ramifications across the financial markets, the Antitrust Division of the DoJ changed its policy and started to prosecute individuals and companies for breaches of competition law in the financial services sector.[281] The DoJ's Antitrust Division is now committed to pursuing antitrust cases in the financial markets in conjunction with the CFTC and the SEC.[282] Andrew Finch, Principal Deputy Assistant Attorney-General, responsible for overseeing the Antitrust Division's criminal enforcement programme, stated that:

> Today, I think we all recognise that, when it comes to antitrust enforcement, the financial services industry is in many ways no different than any other industry.[283]

278 See European Commission, 'Antitrust: Commission Fines UBS, Barclays, RBS, HSBC, Credit Swisse E344 Million for Participating in a Foreign Exchange Spot Trading Cartel' (European Commission, 2 December 2021) <https://ec.europa.eu/commission/presscorner/detail/en/ip_21_6548> accessed 23 July 2024.

279 D Yeres and others, 'Understanding and Preparing for the Convergence of US Criminal Antitrust Enforcement with Anti-Manipulation Laws Regulating Derivatives, FX, Cryptocurrency, Futures, Options and other Commodities under the Commodity Exchange Act' (2019) 39(1) *The Journal on the Law of Investment and Risk Management Products* 9.

280 Ibid.

281 Ibid.

282 US Department of Justice, 'Director Emma Burnham of the Antitrust Division's Criminal Enforcement Section Delivers Remarks to the New York State Bar Association' (The US Department of Justice, 18 October 2023) <https://www.justice.gov/opa/speech/director-emma-burnham-antitrust-divisions-criminal-enforcement-section-delivers-remarks> accessed 26 July 2024.

283 US Department of Justice, 'Principal Deputy Assistant Attorney General Andrew Finch Delivers Remarks at "Antitrust in the Financial Sector: Hot Issues & Global Perspectives"' (US Department of Justice, 2 May 2018) <https://www.justice.gov/opa/speech/princi-

It is notable that the DoJ puts great store on its competition law leniency programme, described above, which was used by UBS during the FX investigation[284] and that the DoJ says is its most important investigative tool for detecting cartel activity.[285] The DoJ has had a competition law leniency programme, in one form or another, since 1978.[286] This is an area of which the competition regulators in the UK should take note, as the UK cartel leniency programme should be advertised more widely in the financial services sector by either the main UK competition authority, the Competition and Markets Authority, or the sectoral competition authority, the Financial Conduct Authority. Interestingly, out of the three jurisdictions examined in this book, only the UK offers a financial reward to whistleblowers who report cartels – it offers a payment of up to £100,000 for cartel informers, whereas neither the DoJ leniency programme nor the EU cartel leniency regime offer financial rewards in return for information on cartels. However, the SEC does offer significant financial incentives to whistleblowers in relation to financial crime of between 10% and 30% of the money collected from the infringing parties.[287] The EU leniency programme does not offer a financial reward to whistleblowers, although like the US and UK versions of leniency, it offers complete protection from penalties to the first cartel member who provides sufficient information to the investigation.[288]

One area where the EU and UK should look to the US in the enforcement of benchmark manipulation with competition law is the area of follow-on antitrust class actions. Many private antitrust claims have been brought as class actions following the LIBOR and FX benchmark manipulation scandals in the US. In particular, the class action judgement given in October 2020 approved a nearly $22m settlement between a class of indirect investors and five Wall Street banks accused by the plaintiff investors of manipulating

---

pal-deputy-assistant-attorney-general-andrew-finch-delivers-remarks-antitrust> accessed 26 July 2024.

284 K Freifield, D Henry, S Slater, 'Global Banks Admit Guilt in Forex Probe, Fined Nearly $6 Billion' (*Reuters*, 20 May 2015) <https://www.reuters.com/article/us-banks-forex-settlement-idUSKBN0O50CQ20150520> accessed 22 July 2024.

285 N Feltovich and Y Hamaguchi, 'The Effect of Whistle-Blowing Incentives on Collusion: An Experimental Study of Leniency Programs' (2018) 84(4) *Southern Economic Journal* 1024.

286 Ibid.

287 Reuters, 'SEC Issues Largest Ever Whistleblower Award of $279 Million' *Reuters* (US, 5 May 2023) <https://www.reuters.com/world/us/us-sec-issues-largest-ever-whistleblower-award-279-mln-2023-05-05/> accessed 20 July 2024 and LH Rubin and AM Selin, 'Self-Disclosing to the SEC in the Age of the Whistleblower' (2016) 23(4) *The Investment Lawyer* 3.

288 European Commission, 'Cartels: eLeniency' (European Commission, 6 February 2020) <https://ec.europa.eu/competition/cartels/leniency/eleniency.html> accessed 21 July 2024.

LIBOR in violation of the Sherman Act.[289] Class actions such as this, based on an alleged breach of competition law, significantly increase the financial penalties imposed on banks for breach of the Sherman Act and can act as a further deterrent to illegal cartel activity. Such follow-on actions are common in the US, as when an individual or company has already been convicted of a breach of the Sherman Act, that conviction can be used by a private litigant as *prima facie* evidence against the defendant in a civil action, saving the private litigant the burden of having to prove the legal breach.[290] The facilitation of follow-on class actions such as those seen in the US following the LIBOR and FX scandals is something that the UK and, to a lesser extent, the EU should consider, in order to increase the deterrent effect of the financial misconduct and also to encourage victims of the benchmark manipulation to seek compensation for their losses.[291]

Another key area in which the UK and EU could learn from the US enforcement approach to the LIBOR and FX scandals is the use of DPAs as an enforcement tool. DPAs can be used only if a criminal offence has been committed, which breach of Section 1 of the Sherman Antitrust Act provides for cartels. The advantages to regulators of entering into a DPA with an offending company in lieu of a criminal prosecution is that DPAs usually contain commitments by the offending company to comply with all relevant laws for a set time and can include regular reporting obligations to the regulator, which is a good way to prevent the reoccurrence of the same or a similar crime for a set period of time.[292]

Areas in which the US could learn from other jurisdictions who have also tackled the LIBOR and FX benchmark manipulation, include having a more streamlined regulatory approach to both the investigation and enforcement of offences. The US approach to enforcement of the benchmark manipulation in 2012–2014 involved multiple regulators, apparently acting independently, although under the oversight of the umbrella organisation the FSOC.[293] In total there were four federal US regulators – the DoJ, the CFTC, the OCC and the Fed – all of whom fined the same banks for the same financial

289 JD Supra, 'Five Banks Settle LIBOR Manipulation Suit for $22 Million' (JD Supra, 13 October 2020) <https://www.jdsupra.com/legalnews/five-banks-settle-libor-manipulation-70879/> accessed 22 July 2024.

290 Practical Law Antitrust, 'US Antitrust Laws: Overview' (Practical Law, 2021) <https://uk.practicallaw.thomsonreuters.com/9-204-0472?comp=pluk&transitionType=Default&contextData=(sc.Default)&firstPage=true&OWSessionId=f75eb2ed5ce44e81a039248 1a9970ca7&skipAnonymous=true> accessed 23 July 2024.

291 LS Simard, 'A View From within the Fortune 500: An Empirical Study of Negative Value Class Actions and Deterrence' (2014) 47(3) *Indiana Law Review* 739.

292 A Palmer, 'Justice Deferred is Justice Denied?' in N Ryder and L Pasculli (eds), *Corruption, Integrity and the Law* (Routledge 2020) 89, 94.

293 LG Baxter, 'Capture Nuances in Financial Regulation' [2012] 47(3) *Wake Forest Law Review* 537.

misconduct.[294] This multiplicity of regulators can lead to inefficiencies at every stage of the investigation and enforcement process and may also result in confusion and a lack of coherent oversight by the financial regulators.[295]

294 For instance, see Commodity Futures Trading Commission, 'CFTC Orders Five Banks to Pay over $14 Billion in Penalties for Attempted Manipulation of Foreign Exchange Benchmark Rates' (Commodity Futures Trading Commission, 12 November 2014) <https://cftc.gov/PressRoom/PressReleases/7056-14> accessed 28 July 2024; Office of the Comptroller of the Currency, 'OCC Fines Three Banks $950 Million for FX Trading Improprieties' (Office of the Comptroller of the Currency, 12 November 2014) <https://www2.occ.gov/news-issuances/news-releases/2014/nr-occ-2014-157.html> accessed 28 July 2024; and Commodity Futures Trading Commission, 'Barclays to Pay $400 Million Penalty to Settle CFTC Charges of Attempted Manipulation and False Reporting of Foreign Exchange Benchmark Rates' (Commodity Futures Trading Commission, 20 May 2015) <https://www.cftc.gov/PressRoom/PressReleases/7181-15> accessed 28 July 2024.

295 A Francis and N Ryder, 'Preventing and Intervening in White Collar Crimes: The Role of Regulatory Agencies' in ML Rorie (ed), *The Handbook of White-Collar Crime* (John Wiley & Sons Inc 2020).

6 UK, EU and US Comparison

6.1 Introduction

This chapter compares the use of competition law in the enforcement of the London Interbank Offered Rate (LIBOR) and Foreign Exchange (FX) benchmark interest rate manipulation (benchmark manipulation) in the three jurisdictions examined in this book. The aim of this comparison is to demonstrate the advantages of using competition law to enforce the financial crime of benchmark manipulation. The United States (US) has a long history of using antitrust, or competition, law to penalise companies for participating in banking cartels, such as those seen in the LIBOR and FX benchmark manipulation scandal.[1] As stated in Chapter 5, it continues to be the avowed aim of the Department of Justice (DoJ) to use antitrust law in the financial markets. Deputy Assistant Attorney General Michael Murrey recently stated that 'the first component of our muscular role is aggressive enforcement of the antitrust laws to police the financial markets'.[2]

It is notable that the European Union (EU) also used its competition laws to enforce these two instances of benchmark manipulation. However, in the United Kingdom (UK), the banks involved were sanctioned using civil financial regulations and individual traders were prosecuted with the offence of conspiracy to defraud rather than using competition law specifically designed for cartels.[3] As a result, lower fines and limited criminal convictions for the LIBOR and FX financial crimes have been achieved in the UK when compared to the EU and US. Changes have since been made to compel the Financial

1 US Department of Justice, 'Sherman Act Violations Resulting in Criminal Fines & Penalties of $10 Million or More' (US Department of Justice, 25 January 2024) <https://www.justice.gov/atr/sherman-act-violations-yielding-corporate-fine-10-million-or-more> accessed 24 July 2024.

2 US Department of Justice, 'The Muscular Role for Antitrust in Fintech, Financial Markets and Banking: The Antitrust Division's Decision to Lean In' (US Department of Justice, 14 October 2020) <https://www.justice.gov/opa/speech/deputy-assistant-attorney-general-michael-murray-delivers-remarks-university-michigan-law> accessed 16 July 2024.

3 Enterprise Act 2002, s.88.

DOI: 10.4324/9781003425106-6

Conduct Authority (FCA) to use its competition law powers. This new legislation was examined in Chapter 3, and its use to date will be considered below.

This chapter will compare the enforcement mechanisms used in the UK, EU and the US in relation to the LIBOR and FX benchmark manipulation. These benchmark manipulation scandals affected each jurisdiction and provide a good comparative study of the enforcement strategies used by each jurisdiction for the same financial crimes. The chapter commences by comparing the enforcement tools used in the UK, EU and US for the LIBOR and FX benchmark manipulation. It then moves on to compare and contrast these regulatory approaches and to identify improvements that can be made to the enforcement strategy of the UK, EU and/or US regulators for the enforcement of future benchmark manipulation.

The use of competition law to enforce benchmark manipulation is examined in detail in this chapter with the aim of drawing conclusions and formulating proposals for future enforcement approaches to the financial crime of benchmark manipulation using competition law. The wide range of enforcement tools available under competition law in the UK will be examined in detail, and the use by the FCA of its competition enforcement tools to date will be considered. Following this analysis, the first theme will be introduced, which is the comparison of the competition law whistleblowing and/or leniency regimes in each of the US, EU and UK, with a view to identify how each operates and to identify key differences between the three jurisdictions. The second theme, the significance of the imposition of civil as opposed to criminal penalties on both companies and individuals for benchmark manipulation, will then be considered. The chapter will then move on to the third theme examined in each of the case study chapters of this book, which is an analysis benefits of having a corporate criminal offence that can be used against banks involved in benchmark manipulation cartels, such as those seen in the LIBOR and FX cases. One benefit of regulators being able to impose corporate criminal liability for benchmark manipulation cartels is that it opens the potential use of Deferred Prosecution Agreements (DPAs) as an additional enforcement tool for regulators in the enforcement of corporate financial crime, which is the fourth theme to be considered. The merits of the use of DPAs as an alternative to the imposition of criminal penalties on a company will be analysed and the level of deterrence that DPAs have will be examined. The chapter will conclude the comparison of the US, EU and UK enforcement approaches to the LIBOR and FX manipulation cartels by identifying areas that the UK regulator and legislators could adopt to improve the enforcement of financial crime in the UK.

6.2 Comparison of the UK, EU and US Approaches to the LIBOR and FX Scandals

This section will examine the differences in approach taken by the UK, EU and US, each of which adopted different enforcement approaches and used different laws for the same financial crime of benchmark manipulation. The background to the LIBOR and FX scandals was set out for each jurisdiction in Chapter 2, which looked at the laws in operation in each jurisdiction at the time of the benchmark manipulation. These differences in approach have been examined in detail in each of the case study chapters, Chapters 3, 4 and 5, and are summarised and compared below.

The US used a combination of competition (antitrust) and nonantitrust law to prosecute and fine banks and brokers involved with the LIBOR and FX benchmark manipulation. The Antitrust Division of the DoJ charged banks and traders involved in the LIBOR and FX scandal, although for the earlier LIBOR enforcement action, it predominantly used the charge of wire fraud and conspiracy to commit wire fraud rather than the antitrust provisions of the Sherman Antitrust Act.[4] This approach changed in the enforcement of the FX benchmark manipulation, in which antitrust laws were used.[5] The DoJ brought criminal proceedings against individual bank employees for LIBOR related offences. These proceedings involved jury trials and resulted in imprisonment for terms ranging between 12 and 24 months.[6] However, four of the individuals' trial convictions have since been overturned by the Second Circuit court.[7] The DoJ entered DPAs with five banks in which significant fines and behavioural commitments were given by the banks for the term of each DPA.[8] In the FX benchmark manipulation, the DoJ used criminal antitrust law to levy high fines against banks and convicted individual traders for breach of the

4 Although Deutsche Bank was also charged with breach of the Sherman Antitrust Act of 1890, Section 1, see US Department of Justice, 'Deutsche Bank's London Subsidiary Sentenced for Manipulation of LIBOR' (Department of Justice, 28 March 2017) <https://www.justice.gov/opa/pr/deutsche-bank-s-london-subsidiary-sentenced-manipulation-libor> accessed 15 July 2024.

5 See US Department of Justice, 'Five Major Banks Agree to Parent-Level Guilty Pleas' (Department of Justice, 20 May 2015) <https://www.justice.gov/opa/pr/five-major-banks-agree-parent-level-guilty-pleas> accessed 15 July 2024 and US Department of Justice, 'BNP Paribas USA Inc. Pleads Guilty to Antitrust Conspiracy' (US Department of Justice, 26 January 2018) <https://www.justice.gov/opa/pr/bnp-paribas-usa-inc-pleads-guilty-antitrust-conspiracy> accessed 15 July 2024; and see US Department of Justice, 'Former Foreign Exchange Trader Sentenced to Prison for Price Fixing and Bid Rigging' (US Department of Justice, 17 September 2020) <https://www.justice.gov/opa/pr/former-foreign-exchange-trader-sentenced-prison-price-fixing-and-bid-rigging> accessed 15 July 2024.

6 For instance, see *United States v. Allen*, 864 F.3d 63, 69-70 (2d Cir. 2017).

7 Practical Law Competition, 'DoJ LIBOR Manipulation Investigation Chart' (Practical Law, January 2023) <https://uk.practicallaw.thomsonreuters.com/Link/Document/Blob/I02f47372a46e11e598dc8b09b4f043e0.pdf?targetType=PLC-multimedia&originationContext=document&transitionType=DocumentImage&uniqueId=89411439-d608-4c78-af0a-21ea30ca61ff&ppcid=076fbb06578f42dbb220b5b6bebad073&contextData=(sc.DocLink)&comp=pluk> accessed 18 July 2024.

8 For example, see the DPA entered into with Deutsche Bank, which included a fine of $775 million: US Department of Justice, 'Closed Criminal Division Cases' (US Department of Justice, 8 May 2018) <https://www.justice.gov/criminal-fraud/case/dbgroupservices-n-deutsche-bankag> accessed 24 July 2024.

cartel provisions in the Sherman Act.[9] The highest fine ever levied against a company for a criminal Sherman Act violation is $925m, which was imposed in 2017 on CitiCorp for its participation in the FX benchmark manipulation cartel.[10]

Additionally, there were civil cases brought in the US by customers of the banks involved in the LIBOR benchmark manipulation who had suffered financial losses because of the benchmark manipulation. These actions, described in Chapter 5, were brought using competition law and resulted in the banks being ordered to pay multiple millions of dollars being to investors.[11] The competition law settlements imposed on the banks involved in the LIBOR and FX benchmark manipulation by both regulators and the courts are significant. However, some commentators argue that fines are seen as just a 'cost of doing business' for banks, whose annual profits exceed the fines imposed.[12] Although the size of the fines issued by the US sent a clear message that this financial crime will be in breach of the criminal provisions of antitrust law and will not be tolerated. The Antitrust Division of the DoJ has made it clear that it intends to continue to use its antitrust laws to regulate the financial sector, stating that 'the primary antitrust laws by their terms do not limit their purview to certain regulatory sectors'.[13] This is a clear message that the DoJ believes that the US antitrust laws are well suited to the regulation of financial markets, a view that was shared by the EU Commission when it used competition law to regulate the LIBOR and FX scandals. Only the UK did not use its competition powers in these scandals, which will be discussed further below.

9 US Department of Justice, 'Five Major Banks Agree to Parent-Level Guilty Pleas' (Department of Justice, 20 May 2015) <https://www.justice.gov/opa/pr/five-major-banks-agree-parent-level-guilty-pleas> accessed 24 July 2024 and US Department of Justice, 'BNP Paribas USA Inc. Pleads Guilty to Antitrust Conspiracy' (US Department of Justice, 26 January 2018) <https://www.justice.gov/opa/pr/bnp-paribas-usa-inc-pleads-guilty-antitrust-conspiracy> accessed 23 July 2024 and see US Department of Justice, 'Former Foreign Exchange Trader Sentenced to Prison for Price Fixing and Bid Rigging' (US Department of Justice, 17 September 2020) <https://www.justice.gov/opa/pr/former-foreign-exchange-trader-sentenced-prison-price-fixing-and-bid-rigging> accessed 23 July 2024.

10 US Department of Justice, 'Sherman Act Violations Resulting in Criminal Fines & Penalties of $10 Million or More' (US Department of Justice, 25 January 2024) <https://www.justice.gov/atr/sherman-act-violations-yielding-corporate-fine-10-million-or-more> accessed 18 July 2024.

11 M Slachetka, 'Five Banks Settle LIBOR Manipulation Suit for $22 Million' (Lexology, 2020) <https://www.lexology.com/library/detail.aspx?g=88150e13-77c7-44af-8004-bb4ba337f36c> 8 July 2024.

12 See, for example: DS Lund and N Sarin, 'The Cost of Doing Business: Corporate Crime and Punishment Post-Crisis' (2020) *Faculty Scholarship at Penn Law* <https://scholarship.law.upenn.edu/faculty_scholarship/2147> accessed 28 July 2024.

13 US Department of Justice, 'The Muscular Role for Antitrust in Fintech, Financial Markets and Banking: The Antitrust Division's Decision to Lean In' (US Department of Justice, 14 October 2020) <https://www.justice.gov/opa/speech/deputy-assistant-attorney-general-michael-murray-delivers-remarks-university-michigan-law> accessed 28 July 2024.

The EU used competition law to enforce all instances of LIBOR, Euro Interbank Offered Rate (EURIBOR) and FX benchmark manipulation. The fines imposed on banks in relation to the LIBOR manipulation totalled €2.047b,[14] and the fines imposed on banks involved in the FX benchmark manipulation cartels totalled €1.414b.[15] EU competition law fines are the highest of any EU civil fines,[16] and some commentators view the level of the fines in EU competition law as penal in nature.[17] Fines of up to 10% of a company's worldwide turnover in the preceding business year can be imposed for breaches of competition law.[18] The European Commission used its competition law powers from the outset of its investigation into the market manipulation of the LIBOR and FX benchmark interest rates. Between the US and EU, some of the world's biggest banks have been fined more than $11b for their part in manipulating the LIBOR and FX benchmark interest rates.[19] The EU's decision to use its competition law powers to enforce the LIBOR and EURIBOR cartels was successful. It resulted in substantial fines being levied against the banks involved, which will have a deterrent effect on the banks. The competition law enforcement by the European Commission of these

14 Made up of a fine for the YIRD cartel of €676.1m, a fine for the EIRD cartel of €1.3b and a fine for the Swiss franc LIBOR cartel of €61.6m, see European Commission, 'AMENDED - Antitrust: Commission Fines Banks € 149 Billion for Participating in Cartels in the Interest Rate Derivatives Industry' (European Commission, 4 December 2013) <https://ec.europa.eu/commission/presscorner/detail/en/IP_13_1208> accessed 12 July 2024; European Commission, 'Daily News 28/05/ 2021' (European Commission, 28 May 2021) <https://ec.europa.eu/commission/presscorner/detail/fr/mex_21_2744> para 6, accessed 22 July 2024; European Commission, 'Antitrust: Commission Fines Crédit Agricole, HSBC and JPMorgan Chase € 485 Million for Euro Interest Rate Derivatives Cartel' (European Commission, 7 December 2016) <https://ec.europa.eu/commission/presscorner/detail/en/IP_16_4304>accessed 22 July 2024; and European Commission, 'Summary of Commission Decision of 21 October 2014 (Case AT39924 — Swiss Franc Interest Rate Derivatives) (CHF LIBOR) (notified under document C (2014) 7605)' [2015] OJ 1 72/7, para 21.

15 See two fining decisions: European Commission, 'Commission Fines Barclays, RBS, Citigroup, JPMorgan and MUFG E107 Billion for Participating in Foreign Exchange Spot Trading Cartel' (European Commission, 16 May 2019) <https://ec.europa.eu/commission/presscorner/detail/en/IP_19_2568> accessed 16 July 2024; and European Commission, 'Antitrust: Commission Fines UBS, Barclays, RBS, HSBC and Credit Suisse € 344 Million for Participating in a Foreign Exchange Spot Trading Cartel' (European Commission, 2 December 2021) <https://ec.europa.eu/commission/presscorner/detail/en/ip_21_6548> accessed 22 July 2024.

16 R Alexander, 'Flogging the Wrong: EU Corporate Fines Violate the Fundamental Rights of Shareholders' (2021) 12(4) *Journal of European Competition Law & Practice* 301.

17 Ibid.

18 Council Regulation (EC) No 1/2003 of 16 December 2002 on the Implementation of the Rules in Competition Laid Down in Articles 81 and 82 of the Treaty [2003] OJ 2 1/1, Article 23(2)(c).

19 European Commission, 'Antitrust: Commission Fines UBS, Barclays, RBS, HSBC and Credit Suisse € 344 Million for Participating in a Foreign Exchange Spot Trading Cartel' (European Commission, 2 December 2021) <https://ec.europa.eu/commission/presscorner/detail/en/IP_21_6548> accessed 21 July 2024.

benchmark manipulation cartels also demonstrated the value of the EU's competition law leniency regime. The leniency regime, which is discussed further below, assisted the Commission in each of the cartel cases by providing vital information and evidence about the cartel and its members.

In contrast to the above, in the UK, the banks and individuals involved with LIBOR and FX benchmark manipulation were not penalised as heavily as when they were prosecuted under the combination of antitrust and non-antitrust law by US regulators[20] or when competition law was used by the European Commission. Six banks and two brokers were fined by the FCA's predecessor, the Financial Services Authority (FSA) and by the FCA between 2012 and 2015 for breaches to the FSA and FCA's 'Principles for Businesses' in relation to LIBOR benchmark manipulation.[21] Fines ranged from £59m for Barclays[22] to £227m for Deutsche Bank,[23] totalling £976m for the six banks

20 R Ball, 'Competition Law and LIBOR in Three Jurisdictions: US, UK and EU' in N Ryder (Ed), *White Collar Crime and Risk – A Critical Reflection* (Routledge 2018).

21 Financial Services Authority, 'Final Notice to Barclays Bank Plc' (Financial Services Authority, 27 June 2012) <https://www.fca.org.uk/publication/final-notices/barclays-jun12.pdf> accessed 8 July 2024; Financial Services Authority, 'Final Notice to UBS AG' (Financial Services Authority, 19 December 2012) <https://www.fca.org.uk/publication/final-notices/ubs.pdf> accessed 24 July 2024;

Financial Services Authority, 'Final Notice to The Royal Bank of Scotland plc' (Financial Services Authority, 6 February 2013) <https://www.fca.org.uk/publication/final-notices/rbs.pdf> accessed 8 July 2024; Financial Conduct Authority, 'ICAP Europe Limited Fined £14 million for Significant Failings in Relation to LIBOR' (Financial Services Authority, (25 September 2013) <https://www.fca.org.uk/news/press-releases/icap-europe-limited-fined-%C2%A314-million-significant-failings-relation-libor> accessed 8 July 2024; Financial Conduct Authority, 'The FCA Fines Rabobank £105 Million for Serious LIBOR-Related Misconduct' (Financial Services Authority, 29 October 2013) <https://www.fca.org.uk/news/press-releases/fca-fines-rabobank-%C2%A3105-million-serious-libor-related-misconduct> accessed 8 July 2024; Financial Conduct Authority 'Martin Brokers (UK) Limited Fined £630,000 for Significant Failings in Relation to LIBOR' (Financial Services Authority, 15 May 2014) <https://www.fca.org.uk/news/press-releases/martin-brokers-uk-limited-fined-%C2%A3630000-significant-failings-relation-libor> accessed 8 July 2024; Financial Conduct Authority, 'The Financial Conduct Authority (FCA) Has Fined Lloyds Bank plc (Lloyds) and Bank of Scotland plc (BoS), Both Part of Lloyds Banking Group (LBG) £105 Million for Serious Misconduct Relating to the Special Liquidity Scheme (SLS), the Repo Rate Benchmark and the London Interbank Offered Rate (LIBOR)', (Financial Services Authority, 28 July 2014) <https://www.fca.org.uk/news/press-releases/lloyds-banking-group-fined-%C2%A3105m-serious-libor-and-other-benchmark-failings> accessed 8 June 2024; and Financial Conduct Authority, 'Deutsche Bank Fined £227 Million by Financial Conduct Authority for LIBOR and EURIBOR Failings and for Misleading the Regulator' (Financial Services Authority, 23 April 2015) <https://www.fca.org.uk/news/press-releases/deutsche-bank-fined-%C2%A3227-million-financial-conduct-authority-libor-and-euribor> accessed 8 July 2024.

22 Financial Services Authority, 'Final Notice to Barclays Bank Plc' (Financial Services Authority, 27 June 2012) <https://www.fca.org.uk/publication/final-notices/barclays-jun12.pdf> accessed 16 July 2024.

23 Financial Conduct Authority, 'Deutsche Bank Fined £227 Million by Financial Conduct Authority for LIBOR and EURIBOR Failings and for Misleading the Regulator' (Financial

and two brokers.[24] However, these fines were significantly smaller than those imposed for the same misconduct in the US, where fines totalling $2.519b were made.[25]

As an example of the discrepancy in fines between the UK, EU and US, the fine of £227m (or $340m) imposed by the FCA on Deutsche Bank was the largest of any LIBOR related fines in the UK and was more than double than any other fines imposed by either the FSA or FCA for LIBOR manipulation.[26] However, this fine is dwarfed when compared with the fines levied on Deutsche Bank by both the EU and the US regulators. US regulators imposed fines totalling $2.1b on Deutsche Bank, in addition to entering into a DPA with the bank and ordering the dismissal of seven of its employees, six of whom were based in London.[27] In the EU, Deutsche Bank was fined €725.4m (or $8.6m) by the European Commission for participating in the illegal cartel to rig the rate of the LIBOR and EURIBOR benchmark interest rates.[28] It is clear from the level of these fines that a bank that breaks the law in the UK will not be penalised as severely as if it breaks the same law in the US or EU. If the UK had used its competition law powers, which were available at the time of the LIBOR and FX enforcement actions, fines of up to 10% of the worldwide turnover of the bank calculated on the preceding business year, could have been imposed.[29] It is, therefore, clear that, in the future, the UK should follow the lead of both the US and EU and use the powers it has under the Competition Act 1998 to impose fines of up to 10% of a company's turnover in order to create a strong deterrent. However, the Office of Fair Trading (OFT), the competition regulator at that time, was told not to take any action

Services Authority, 23 April 2015) <https://www.fca.org.uk/news/press-releases/deutsche-bank-fined-%C2%A3227-million-financial-conduct-authority-libor-and-euribor> accessed 16 July 2024.

24 A Jordanoska and N Lord, 'Scripting the Mechanics of the Benchmark Manipulation Corporate Scandals: The "Guardian" Paradox' (2020) 17(1) *European Journal of Criminology* 9.

25 US Department of Justice, 'Deutsche Bank's London Subsidiary Sentenced for Manipulation of LIBOR' (US Department of Justice, 28 March 2017) <https://www.justice.gov/opa/pr/deutsche-bank-s-london-subsidiary-sentenced-manipulation-libor> accessed 4 July 2024.

26 Financial Conduct Authority, 'Deutsche Bank Fined £227 Million by Financial Conduct Authority for LIBOR and EURIBOR Failings and for Misleading the Regulator' (Financial Services Authority, 23 April 2015) <https://www.fca.org.uk/news/press-releases/deutsche-bank-fined-%C2%A3227-million-financial-conduct-authority-libor-and-euribor> accessed 25 July 2024.

27 J Treanor, 'Deutsche Bank Hit By Record $2.5bn Libor-Rigging Fine' *The Guardian* (London, 23 April 2015) <https://www.theguardian.com/business/2015/apr/23/deutsche-bank-hit-by-record-25bn-libor-rigging-fine> accessed 8 July 2024.

28 M Thompson, 'EU Fines Banks Record $2.3b over Libor' (CNN Business, 4 December 2013) <https://money.cnn.com/2013/12/04/news/companies/libor-europe-fines/?iid=EL> accessed 11 July 2024.

29 Competition Act 1998 s.36(8).

in the UK in relation to the LIBOR benchmark manipulation.[30] In retrospect, this is clearly an error, and legislators have attempted to correct this for future financial crime by giving competition law enforcement powers to the FCA and obliging the FCA to consider using its competition law powers before taking any action.[31] These legislative changes are discussed below.

Overall, the differences in UK, EU and US enforcement of the LIBOR and FX market manipulation – the same offence – demonstrates that using competition law to enforce benchmark manipulation can result in wider and stronger powers for the regulators and an increased deterrent for this financial crime.

The next section will examine the key changes (if any) that were made in the UK, EU and US following the LIBOR and FX benchmark manipulation crisis.

6.3 Key Legislative Changes Made Following the LIBOR and FX Scandals

No legislation was introduced in the US as a direct response to either the LIBOR or the FX scandals; however, there were some policy changes made to address the perceived need for increased regulation of the financial markets. Following the LIBOR scandal, there were calls by academics, regulators and even industry insiders for increased regulation of the financial markets. In 2015, US Deputy Attorney General Sally Yates announced a shift in the DoJ's policy toward the prosecution of corporations when she said that all corporate prosecutions would hold responsible those individuals within the company who had misbehaved.[32] Following the policy change toward corporate criminal prosecutions, the DoJ brought its first case in 2015 against two corporate individuals, former Rabobank traders, both of whom were found guilty of wire fraud for their role in rigging LIBOR.[33] The lack of new legislation as a reaction to the LIBOR and FX benchmark manipulation scandals may well indicate that the US regulators were happy with the enforcement powers they had available to them during the enforcement period. The various regulators involved, including the Commodity Futures Trading Commission (CFTC), the DoJ and the Securities and Exchange Commission (SEC) used a variety of criminal laws to enforce the LIBOR manipulation but then used antitrust laws

30 Financial Services Authority, 'Internal Audit Report: A Review of the Extent of Awareness Within the FSA of Inappropriate LIBOR Submissions' (Financial Services Authority, March 2013) <https://www.fca.org.uk/publication/corporate/fsa-ia-libor.pdf> accessed 12 July 2024.

31 Financial Services Act 2012, s.1B(3)(c).

32 WD Cohan, 'Justice Dept Shift on White-Collar Crime Is Long Overdue' *The New York Times* (New York, 11 September 2015) <https://www.nytimes.com/2015/09/12/business/dealbook/justice-dept-shift-on-white-collar-crime-is-long-overdue.html> accessed 26 July 2024.

33 A Youngblood, 'Aftermath of the LIBOR Scandal' (2016) 35(1) *Review of Banking and Financial Law* 57.

to enforce the FX manipulation, which appears to have worked very well, with the DoJ now stating that it intends to continue using antitrust law to regulate the financial markets.[34]

Following the scandal of the LIBOR and FX benchmark manipulation, in July 2012, the European Commission proposed new laws; the Market Abuse Regulation 2014 (MAR 2014) and the Market Abuse Directive 2014 (MAD 2014). The proposed legislation clearly made the manipulation of any benchmark interest rate, such as LIBOR or EURIBOR, a criminal offence.[35] The MAR 2014 explicitly bans the manipulation of benchmark interest rates,[36] such as LIBOR and FX. The MAD 2014 includes any behaviour that manipulates the calculation of a benchmark interest rate in its definition of market manipulation,[37] thus criminalising this action. This new legislation may mark a change in the way that the EU intends to prosecute financial crime in the future, perhaps as an alternative to using its civil competition law powers and, instead, using the criminal powers written expressly for the crime of benchmark manipulation in the MAD 2014. However, *the power to* enforce the MAD 2014 and MAR 2014 is devolved *by the EU* to each Member State, so there is no central regulator for these criminal enforcement powers, as there is for competition law.

Further legislation was introduced in 2016 when an EU Benchmark Regulation[38] (Benchmark Regulation) was adopted to complement the market abuse regime set up by the MAR 2014 and MAD 2014. The Benchmark Regulation established a set of rules covering the use of benchmark interest rates across the whole of the EU. The new rules require, amongst other things, the supervision of key benchmarks such as the LIBOR and EURIBOR, as these rates are seen as critical to the functioning and integrity of financial markets.[39] Other complementary legislation brought in by the EU following the LIBOR and FX scandals to boost confidence in the financial markets is

34 US Department of Justice, 'The Muscular Role for Antitrust in Fintech, Financial Markets and Banking: The Antitrust Division's Decision to Lean In' (US Department of Justice, 14 October 2020) <https://www.justice.gov/opa/speech/deputy-assistant-attorney-general-michael-murray-delivers-remarks-university-michigan-law> accessed 12 July 2024.

35 European Commission, 'Libor Scandal: Commission Proposes EU-Wide Action to Fight Rate-Fixing' (European Commission, 25 July 2012) <https://ec.europa.eu/commission/presscorner/detail/en/IP_12_846> accessed 12 July 2024.

36 Regulation (EU) No 596/2014 of the European Parliament and of the Council of 16 April 2014 on Market Abuse (Market Abuse Regulation) [2014] OJ 2 173/1, Article 12(1)(d).

37 Directive 2014/57/EU of the European Parliament and of the Council of 16 April 2014 on Criminal Sanctions for Market Abuse (Market Abuse Directive) [2014] OJ 2 173/179, Article 5.

38 Regulation (EU) 2016/1011 of The European Parliament and of the Council of 8 June 2016 on Indices Used As Benchmarks in Financial Instruments and Financial Contracts or to Measure the Performance of Investment Funds [2016] OJ 2 171/1.

39 Ibid, Preamble (1).

the new Markets in Financial Instruments Directive,[40] which aims to ensure a level playing field for regulated markets and strengthen the supervisory powers of competent authorities in each Member State, who are themselves supervised by European Securities and Markets Authority (ESMA).[41] The legislative changes made in the EU since the LIBOR and FX crisis demonstrate that the EU wanted a stronger criminal offence to tackle the offence of benchmark manipulation in the future. The competition laws that the EU used to enforce the LIBOR and FX manipulation cartels are entirely civil, unlike the criminal antitrust laws used in the US or the combination of civil and criminal competition law powers available (but not used) in the UK. These new criminal laws may be used by individual Member States as well as, or instead of, a centralised EU enforcement of benchmark manipulation using competition law in the future.

Significant changes were made to legislation and regulation in the UK after the LIBOR and FX scandal, including a change of regulator from the FSA to the FCA. The FCA has three operational objectives: consumer protection, protecting the integrity of the UK's financial markets and promoting competition in financial markets.[42] The FCA's new competition objective was supported by three acts relating to the use of competition law in the financial services sector, which were passed by the UK government immediately following the LIBOR and FX crisis.[43] These acts are discussed in Chapter 3. The new legislation marked a significant change of direction and policy, especially given that no competition law had been used in the enforcement of any of the LIBOR or FX benchmark manipulation. The FCA's new competition powers can be used concurrently with those of the previously sole competition regulator in the UK, which was the OFT at the time of the LIBOR and FX crisis and is now the Competition and Markets Authority (CMA).[44] One key change in UK law compels the FCA to consider the use of competition law[45] in all future cases of financial crime and, if relevant, to justify its lack of use of competition law if it, instead, relies on enforcing financial crime, such as benchmark manipulation, using financial regulations, as it did in the aftermath

40 Directive 2014/65/EU of the European Parliament and of the Council of 15 May 2014 on Markets in Financial Instruments and Amending Directive 2002/92/EC and Directive 2011/61/EU, OJ L 173, 12.6.2014.

41 E Herlin-Karnell and N Ryder, *Market Manipulation and Insider Trading* (Hart 2019).

42 Financial Services and Markets Act 2000, as amended by the Financial Services Act 2012, sections 1B-1E.

43 Financial Services (Banking Reform) Act 2013, Financial Services Act 2012 and Enterprise and Regulatory Reform Act 2013.

44 Financial Services Authority, 'How We Use Our Competition Powers' (Financial Services Authority, 22 May 2019) <https://www.fca.org.uk/about/promoting-competition/powers> accessed 13 July 2024.

45 Financial Services (Banking Reform) Act 2013, s.234K.

of the LIBOR and FX crisis.[46] This legislation appears to be trying to bring the UK regulation of financial crime into line with the US and EU, each of which used competition/antitrust powers to enforce the benchmark manipulation of the LIBOR and FX benchmark interest rates. However, since the date of the Financial Services (Banking Reform) Act 2013, the FCA has only entered into two decisions in the financial sector using its competition law powers[47] and has not used its new competition law enforcement powers to the full extent possible in those decisions.[48] The lack of use of its new competition law powers appears to demonstrate a reluctance by the financial services regulator to use its competition law powers to their full extent and shows that there is a gap between legislating and changing the policy of regulators. This gap needs to be tackled to provide better regulation and enforcement of benchmark manipulation in the future.

In summary, of the three jurisdictions studied in this book, only the US appears to have had sufficient powers to tackle the LIBOR and FX benchmark manipulation cartels, as its regulators used a combination of the criminal offence of wire fraud for the LIBOR manipulation and criminal antitrust laws for the FX manipulation. These powers enabled US regulators to sanction both companies and individuals, unlike the EU, where the only sanctions imposed were on companies – banks and brokers – rather than individuals. The EU used its civil competition laws for the LIBOR and FX enforcement, which allowed it to impose substantial corporate fines. The most significant legislative changes after the LIBOR and FX scandals were seen in the UK, which changed its financial services and competition regulators, as well as giving competition powers to the new FCA, together with an obligation to consider using its competition powers before any other regulatory powers in the future. The UK also created further benchmark manipulation offences,

46 Financial Conduct Authority, 'Our Approach to Competition' (Financial Conduct Authority, 21 March 2024) <https://www.fca.org.uk/publications/corporate-documents/our-approach-competition> accessed 13 July 2024.

47 Financial Conduct Authority, 'FCA Issues Its First Decision under Competition Law' (Financial Conduct Authority, 21 February 2019) <https://www.fca.org.uk/news/press-releases/fca-issues-its-first-decision-under-competition-law> accessed 22 July 2024; and Financial Conduct Authority, 'FCA Fines Three Money Transfer Firms For Breaking Competition Law' (Financial Conduct Authority, 30 November 2023) <https://www.fca.org.uk/news/press-releases/fca-fines-three-money-transfer-firms-breaking-competition-law> accessed 22 July 2024.

48 Cleary Gottlieb, 'FCA Issues First Penalties for Competition Infringements' (Cleary Gottlieb, 26 February 2019) <https://www.clearygottlieb.com/-/media/files/alert-memos-2019/fca-issues-first-penalties-for-competition-infringements.pdf> accessed 22 July 2024; and see the size of the fines in the second case, which range from £3,600 for one of the businesses to £139,500: Financial Conduct Authority, 'FCA Fines Three Money Transfer Firms For Breaking Competition Law' (Financial Conduct Authority, 30 November 2023) <https://www.fca.org.uk/news/press-releases/fca-fines-three-money-transfer-firms-breaking-competition-law> accessed 15 July 2024.

which are criminal offences for individuals, but a corporate criminal offence for benchmark manipulation is still lacking in the UK, compared to the those available for benchmark manipulation/market abuse in the US and the EU, although the recent changes made to the identification doctrine, outlined in Chapters 2 and 3, may assist UK regulators to attribute corporate criminal liability for benchmark manipulation in the future.[49]

This section has summarised and compared the key legislative changes made in the UK, EU and US in the immediate aftermath of the LIBOR and FX benchmark manipulation scandal. The next section will examine in detail the competition law sanctions available in each of these jurisdictions to establish what enforcement powers regulators will have if they utilise their competition law powers to enforce future instances benchmark manipulation.

6.4 Competition Law Sanctions for Financial Crime

This section will examine the extent of the criminal and civil sanctions available pursuant to the competition law provisions in each of the UK, EU and US, and the sanctions available will be compared, building on the detail from each of the case study chapters.

The key competition legislation in the US is the Sherman Act 1890,[50] outlined in Chapter 5, which allows regulators to pursue either civil or criminal sanctions against infringing individuals and companies. Criminal sanctions available to regulators for a breach of antitrust law include a fine of up to $100m for a company or up to $1m for individuals. Individuals, if convicted, may also be imprisoned for up to ten years.[51] The fines for violation of the Sherman Act can be increased beyond the statutory maximums in appropriate cases that involve cartel-related activities pursuant to the alternative criminal fine provision of the Sentencing Reform Act.[52] Civil sanctions for a breach of the Sherman Act include treble damages, injunctive orders to prevent and restrain violations of the antitrust laws and structural remedies (including dissolution and divestiture) in order to restore competition.[53] These are extremely significant sanctions, more so than those available to enforce either the UK or EU competition laws.

In addition to the above public enforcement powers, private enforcement plays a greater role in the US system than in either the EU or UK, where victims of anticompetitive behaviour can be awarded damages of up to treble the amount of the actual damage suffered.[54] Provisions of the Clayton

49 Economic Crime and Corporate Transparency Act 2023, s.196.

50 Sherman Antitrust Act, ch. 647, 26 Stat. 209 (codified as amended by 15 U.S.C. §1-7 (2018)).

51 Ibid, section 1.

52 Sentencing Reform Act, 18 U.S.C. §3571(d).

53 Clayton Act, §11, 15 U.S.C. §21.

54 European Parliament Research Service, 'EU and US Competition Policies: Similar Objectives, Different Approaches' (European Parliament Research Service, 27 March 2014)

Act,[55] another of the main competition laws in the US, authorises 'any person' injured in 'business or property by reason of anything forbidden in the antitrust laws' to sue for treble damages.[56] Many private antitrust claims are brought as class actions, which is the case for the leading LIBOR antitrust class action, discussed in Chapter 5.[57] The US competition laws are the most significant and powerful of each of the three jurisdictions considered in this book. They give regulators the option to pursue either civil or criminal penalties against infringing parties, powers that can be used against individuals and/or companies. These wide-ranging powers are greater than the civil, regulatory competition laws of the EU and greater than the predominantly civil competition laws of the UK. The UK does have a criminal cartel offence, which can be used against individuals, but neither the EU nor UK competition regulators have the option of imposing corporate criminal liability, which carries with it the most significant deterrent to companies from committing breaches of competition law. This is something that needs to change in order to increase the deterrent effect for a bank's participation in benchmark manipulation cartels.

The EU's substantive competition law rules[58] govern anticompetitive agreements and the abuse of a dominant market position by one or more businesses. Of these different competition laws, Article 101, which governs anticompetitive agreements, is the most relevant to the enforcement of benchmark manipulation. The European Commission gains its competition law enforcement powers from Regulation 1.[59] Regulation 1 gives the regulator extensive powers to investigate suspected breaches of Articles 101 and 102 and the power to impose penalties for any breaches found. Penalties include the imposition of fines of up to 10% of the infringing undertaking's worldwide turnover in the market in the preceding business year.[60] Other enforcement actions, such as the imposition of decisions, the agreement to accept behavioural or structural commitments in settlement of an infringement action or the imposition of interim measures, are also available to the regulator.[61] These enforcement powers give the EU Commission a wide range of options when a finding has been made of a competition law infringement. The fines are the

<https://www.europarl.europa.eu/RegData/bibliotheque/briefing/2014/140779/LDM_BRI(2014)140779_REV1_EN.pdf> accessed 14 July 2024.

55 Clayton Antitrust Act, 38 Stat. 730 (1914) (codified as amended at 15 U.S.C. §12-27 (2018); 29 U.S.C. §52-53 (2018)).

56 J Bial, L Hibbler, 'Cartels & Leniency Laws and Regulations USA 2024' (ICLG.com, 2024) <https://iclg.com/practice-areas/cartels-and-leniency-laws-and-regulations/usa> accessed 23 July and Clayton Act, §11, 15 U.S.C. §4.

57 *In re: Libor-based Financial Instruments Antitrust Litigation,* 327 F.R.D. 483 (S.D.N.Y. 2018).

58 Treaty on the Functioning of the European Union, Articles 101 and 102.

59 Council Regulation (EC) No 1/2003 of 16 December 2002 on the Implementation of the Rules on Competition Laid down in Articles 81 and 82 of the Treaty [2004] OJ L 1 0001.

60 Ibid, Article 23(2).

61 Ibid.

most significant of the penalties, with the Commission having imposed the maximum fines on several occasions over the past decade.[62]

The UK's competition law is based on EU competition law, as a consequence of its 47 year membership in the EU, which ended in December 2020.[63] However, one key difference between EU and UK competition law is that, since 2002, the UK competition regulator has had the power to pursue custodial sentences of up to five years against individuals who have set up and maintained a hard-core cartel, described in Chapter 2.[64] The regulator can also pursue financial penalties pursuant to the criminal cartel offence, although both criminal penalties have to be imposed by a court.[65] Despite this criminal cartel power having existed for a number of years, there have been only five criminal prosecutions of the cartel offence, not all of them resulting in imprisonment of the individuals prosecuted.[66] None of these cartel offence cases have been in the financial services sector and none of the cartel prosecutions were contested.[67] There is clearly a need to reform the cartel offence to make it of more use to UK regulators. The CMA proposed changes to the cartel offences in 2019, one of which was that the Serious Fraud Office (SFO) should be the sole regulator to bring criminal prosecutions under the cartel offence; however, the government has not yet responded to these proposals.[68]

Other competition law powers that could be of use in the future to the UK financial services regulator include the power for the FCA to make competition disqualification orders or to take competition undertakings from directors.[69] This power can be used for any serious breach of competition law and will prohibit the director from being involved in the management of a company for up to 15 years.[70] The FCA has not yet used this power. The power to disqualify

62 R Whish and D Bailey, *Competition Law* (10th edition, Oxford University Press 2021).

63 J Tomlinson and L Lovdahl Gormsen, 'Stumbling Towards the UK's New Administrative Settlement: A Study of Competition Law Enforcement After Brexit' (2018) 20(1) *Cambridge Yearbook of European Legal Studies* 233; and European Union (Withdrawal) Act 2018.

64 Enterprise Act 2002, s.190.

65 Enterprise Act 2002, s190.

66 Competition and Markets Authority, 'Competition and Markets Authority Cases' (Competition and Markets Authority, 2024) <https://www.gov.uk/cma-cases?case_type%5B%5D=criminal-cartels> accessed 10 July 2024; and R Whish and D Bailey, *Competition Law* (10th edn, Oxford University Press 2021).

67 Norton Rose Fulbright, 'The Future of the Criminal Cartel Offence in the UK' (Norton Rose Fulbright, January 2021) <https://www.nortonrosefulbright.com/en/knowledge/publications/51dd9da8/the-future-of-the-criminal-cartel-offence-in-the-uk> accessed 25 July 2024.

68 Competition and Markets Authority, 'Letter from Andrew Tyrie to the Secretary of State for Business, Energy and Industrial Strategy' (GOV.UK, 25 February 2019) <https://www.gov.uk/government/publications/letter-from-andrew-tyrie-to-the-secretary-of-state-for-business-energy-and-industrial-strategy> accessed 25 July 2024.

69 Company Directors Disqualification Act 1986, ss.9A, 9B and 9E(2)(h).

70 Pinsent Masons, 'Individual Liability for UK Competition Law Infringements' (Pinsent Masons, 5 September 2018) <https://www.pinsentmasons.com/out-law/guides/individuals-liability-uk-competition-law-infringements> accessed 28 July 2024.

a director could be used by either the CMA or FCA against a culpable bank director if he or she was involved in a competition crime such as benchmark manipulation and would act as a significant deterrent to other bank directors if the regulator used the power for this purpose. Another competition law power that could be of use to the UK financial services regulator in future market manipulation instances is the power to accept commitments from the infringing banks.[71] Commitments, which can be behavioural or structural, are similar in some ways to DPAs in that they may involve the bank being investigated making legally binding commitments to the regulator as to their future behaviour to end the investigation. If the bank was to breach its commitments, the competition regulator may apply to the court for an order to enforce compliance.[72] This is a tool that could be used in the regulation of financial crime, as commitments can be used to enforce good behaviour and to prevent further breaches of financial regulation, although it is worth noting that commitments are not, except in exceptional cases, used for hard-core competition breaches, which would include cartels.[73] In the case of hard-core competition breaches, an additional competition law enforcement tool – directions – could be used.[74] Directions enable the competition regulator to give directions to bring a breach of competition law to an end, and directions can include provisions such as positive action and reporting obligations, similar to DPAs.[75] Under competition law, sectoral regulators such as the FCA also have the power to fine companies up to 10% of their worldwide turnover.[76] The fact that the fine is based on turnover, rather than profit, also increases the potential maximum amount that can be levied by a regulator, which has a corresponding effect on the deterrent effect of this penalty. The CMA has imposed the maximum possible fine in several cases,[77] although the FCA has only issued two decisions in the financial sector using its competition law powers,[78] and the fines issued were only equivalent to 1% of the turnover of the three asset management

71 Competition Act 1998, s.31A.

72 R Whish and D Bailey, *Competition Law* (10th edn., Oxford University Press 2021).

73 S Cardell, 'Sarah Cardell Speaks About the CMA's Enforcement Priorities and Approach' (IBC UK Competition Law Conference, London, 23 February 2016) <https://www.gov.uk/government/speeches/sarah-cardell-speaks-about-the-cmas-enforcement-priorities-and-approach> accessed 11 July 2024.

74 Competition Act 1998, s.31.

75 R Whish and D Bailey, *Competition Law* (10th edn., Oxford University Press 2021).

76 Competition Act 1998, s.36.

77 R Whish and D Bailey, *Competition Law* (10th edn., Oxford University Press 2021).

78 Financial Conduct Authority, 'FCA Issues Its First Decision under Competition Law' (Financial Conduct Authority, 21 February 2019) <https://www.fca.org.uk/news/press-releases/fca-issues-its-first-decision-under-competition-law> accessed 22 July 2024; and Financial Conduct Authority, 'FCA Fines Three Money Transfer Firms For Breaking Competition Law' (Financial Conduct Authority, 30 November 2023) <https://www.fca.org.uk/news/press-releases/fca-fines-three-money-transfer-firms-breaking-competition-law> accessed 22 July 2024.

firms involved in the first case.[79] The FCA would send a much clearer signal to the financial services sector if it were to use its new competition law enforcement powers to a much greater extent and with more frequency.

As can be seen from the above, significant competition law sanctions exist in each jurisdiction studied and did so at the time of the LIBOR and FX benchmark manipulation; however, only the EU and US used their competition laws to enforce the benchmark manipulation seen in the LIBOR and FX scandal. The UK did not use its competition law enforcement powers then and has not made any significant use of them since. This is clearly an area where reform is needed if the UK is to apply its extensive competition law powers in the enforcement of future benchmark manipulation cartels.

6.5 Competition Law Leniency and Whistleblowing Regimes in the UK, EU and US

This section analyses how the competition law whistleblowing and leniency regimes operate in the financial services sector in the UK, EU and US. Each jurisdiction recognises that there is a clear need for a successful whistleblowing and/or leniency regime for any regulator operating in the financial services market and investigating a banking or other cartel. Cartels are notoriously difficult for regulators to gain sufficient evidence to prosecute because they are typically extremely secretive, with cartel members aware that they are breaking the law. The existence of a successful whistleblowing or leniency regime is, therefore, of tremendous benefit to regulators of financial crime, allowing them to obtain insider evidence from a whistleblower of a suspected cartel infringement and to 'pierce the cloak of secrecy in which cartels operate'.[80]

Whistleblowing and/or leniency regimes exist as part of the competition law/antitrust law in each of the jurisdictions examined in this book, with regulators from each jurisdiction stating how critical these regimes are to their investigations of competition law breaches. Lord Tyrie, Chair of the CMA from 2018 to 2020, said that 'information from whistleblowers is essential to the CMA's work' and that 'the knowledge that people might "blow the whistle" is itself a deterrent to wrongdoing by companies'.[81] The Antitrust Division of the DoJ describes its leniency programme as its most important

79 Cleary Gottlieb, 'FCA Issues First Penalties for Competition Infringements' (Cleary Gottlieb, 26 February 2019) <https://www.clearygottlieb.com/-/media/files/alert-memos-2019/fca-issues-first-penalties-for-competition-infringements.pdf> accessed 11 July 2024.

80 European Commission, 'Cartels: eLeniency' (European Commission, 6 February 2020) <https://ec.europa.eu/competition/cartels/leniency/eleniency.html> accessed 12 July 2024.

81 Competition and Markets Authority, 'Letter from Andrew Tyrie to the Secretary of State for Business, Energy and Industrial Strategy' (GOV.UK, 25 February 2019) <https://www.gov.uk/government/publications/letter-from-andrew-tyrie-to-the-secretary-of-state-for-business-energy-and-industrial-strategy> accessed 15 July 2024.

investigative tool for detecting cartel activity.[82] The Leniency Programme of the DoJ's Antitrust Division has been dramatically successful. Leniency applicants have played a key part in a huge number of cases in recent decades, providing information used by the DoJ to bring successful prosecutions.[83] The leniency programme allows both individuals and corporations to report their participation in an antitrust crime, such as a cartel, directly to the DoJ.[84] Details of the leniency programme are set out in Chapter 5. This antitrust leniency programme, combined with severe consequences of being involved in a criminal cartel work together to ensure that there is a strong deterrent from participating in a cartel in the US. The threat of criminal sanctions for cartel participants, combined with a heightened fear of detection enhanced by the leniency programme are the cornerstones on which the antitrust leniency programme has been built.[85]

In both the LIBOR and FX scandals, whistleblowers played an important part in notifying the European Commission of cartels and illegal behaviour. For example, in the Japanese yen LIBOR cartel, UBS received total immunity from fines, as it acted as whistleblower, telling the Commission about the cartels.[86] Other cartel members received a reduction of their fines for their cooperation in the investigation under the Commission's competition law leniency programme.[87] The EU's competition law leniency regime for competition law offers companies involved in a cartel either total immunity from fines or a reduction of fines that the Commission otherwise would have imposed on them.[88] The option for cartel members to obtain reductions in fines was used to good effect by the Commission in the LIBOR and FX scandals to encour-

82 US Department of Justice, 'Leniency Programme' (US Department of Justice, 20 February 2020) <https://www.justice.gov/atr/leniency-program> accessed 25 July 2024.

83 J Bial, L Hibbler, 'Cartels & Leniency Laws and Regulations USA 2024' (ICLG.com, 2024) <https://iclg.com/practice-areas/cartels-and-leniency-laws-and-regulations/usa> accessed 23 July

84 US Department of Justice, 'Leniency Programme' (US Department of Justice, 20 February 2020) <https://www.justice.gov/atr/leniency-program> accessed 25 July 2024.

85 RA. Powers, 'A Matter of Trust: Enduring Leniency Lessons for the Future of Cartel Enforcement' (US Department of Justice, 19 February 2020) <https://www.justice.gov/opa/speech/deputy-assistant-attorney-general-richard-powers-delivers-remarks-13th-international> accessed 23 July 2024.

86 European Commission, 'AMENDED - Antitrust: Commission Fines Banks €149 Billion for Participating in Cartels in the Interest Rate Derivatives Industry' (European Commission, 4 December 2013) <https://ec.europa.eu/commission/presscorner/detail/en/IP_13_1208> accessed 23 July 2024.

87 European Commission, 'AMENDED - Antitrust: Commission Fines Banks €149 Billion for Participating in Cartels in the Interest Rate Derivatives Industry' (European Commission, 4 December 2013) <https://ec.europa.eu/commission/presscorner/detail/en/IP_13_1208> accessed 23 July 2024.

88 European Commission, 'Cartels: eLeniency' (European Commission, 6 February 2020) <https://ec.europa.eu/competition/cartels/leniency/eleniency.html> accessed 23 July 2024.

age cooperation with the investigation, facilitating the Commission's role of finding evidence of cartel activity and enabling successful enforcement of the cartels.

In addition to the Commission's competition law leniency policy, which is used as part of the Commission's competition law enforcement powers, the EU's market abuse regime includes provisions in the MAR 2014 aimed at encouraging whistleblowers to come forward. Member States can provide financial incentives, such as a reward, for whistleblowers in some circumstances.[89] An EU directive to protect whistleblowers (Whistleblowing Directive)[90] came into force in December 2021 and further bolsters the market abuse regime by providing regulators with information and evidence of market abuse.

The EU has a well-developed and well-known competition law leniency policy for cartels and also has a whistleblower tool to make it easier for individuals to report anticompetitive behaviour.[91] The leniency policy is aimed at cartel members, who are likely to be companies. The market abuse whistleblowing provisions in the MAR 2014, however, are aimed at employees of companies who may be breaching the market abuse rules;[92] so between the competition and market abuse legislative regime, both corporate and individual whistleblowers are provided for. The Whistleblowing Directive provides additional protection to individuals who are whistleblowers.[93]

Like the US and the EU, the UK has a competition law leniency policy that relates to cartels.[94] The competition law leniency protocol includes provision for granting reduced penalties to companies who come forward with information on cartel activity and who then cooperate fully with any subsequent investigation. Similar to the EU's competition law leniency regime, the first company to apply for leniency can receive a 100% reduction in the penalty, and successive applicants may receive deductions of up to 50%, depending on the added value of the material they provide. Individual informants may also

89 Regulation (EU) No 596/2014 of the European Parliament and of the Council of 16 April 2014 on Market Abuse (Market Abuse Regulation) [2014] OJ 2 173/1, Article 32(4).

90 Directive (EU) 2019/1937 of the European Parliament and of the Council of 23 October 2019 on the Protection of Persons Who Report Breaches of Union Law, OJ L 305/17 26/11/2019 p 17-56.

91 European Commission, 'Whistleblowers and Informants' (European Commission, 2024) <https://competition-policy.ec.europa.eu/index/whistleblower_en> accessed 12 July 2024.

92 Regulation (EU) No 596/2014 of the European Parliament and of the Council of 16 April 2014 on Market Abuse (Market Abuse Regulation) [2014] OJ 2 173/1, Article 32.

93 Directive (EU) 2019/1937 of the European Parliament and of the Council of 23 October 2019 on the Protection of Persons Who Report Breaches of Union Law, OJ L 305/17 26/11/2019, Article 4.

94 Competition and Markets Authority, 'Guidance: Cartels: Come Forward and Apply for Leniency' (GOV.UK, 11 March 2019) <https://www.gov.uk/guidance/cartels-confess-and-apply-for-leniency> accessed 18 July 2024.

receive a financial reward for information of up to £250,000.[95] As cartels can be extremely hard to detect, competition law leniency applications play an important role in uncovering this illegal activity.[96] However, there are two key problems with the UK's competition law leniency and whistleblower provisions. First, awareness of the rewards available at both an individual and a corporate level need to be advertised widely in the financial markets sector. Without widespread knowledge of how to report a cartel to the relevant authority (in this case, either the CMA or the FCA) and knowledge of what the advantages for the first cartel member to come forward are, the authorities will miss out on valuable information that could lead to the discovery and prosecution of future benchmark manipulation cartels. Second, Lord Tyrie, ex-chair of the CMA, has previously argued that the individual financial reward offered to whistleblowers is far too low. He has stated that the level of reward is 'unlikely even to cover the loss that a typical whistleblower would incur from losing his or her job'.[97] At the time of Lord Tyrie's speech in 2019, the maximum reward for whistleblowers was £100,000.[98] It was raised in 2023 to the current maximum of £250,000, which is still arguably too low to cover the loss of salary, commission/bonuses and of future earning power of a banker in a top bank.[99] When compared with the rewards offered to whistleblowers in the US,[100] it is clear that rewarding whistleblowers is taken more seriously in the US than in the UK. This is an area that should be addressed as soon as possible by the CMA and FCA to encourage whistleblowers to come forward in the future.

This section has demonstrated the critical role that a competition law leniency and whistleblower regime has in the detection and enforcement of cartels, with some similarities being observed between the three jurisdictions.

95 Competition and Markets Authority, 'Blowing the Whistle on Cartels' (GOV.UK, 6 June 2023) <https://www.gov.uk/government/news/blowing-the-whistle-on-cartels#:~:text=The%20Competition%20and%20Markets%20Authority,cartel%20activity%20they%20have%20witnessed.> accessed 27 July 2024.

96 Competition and Markets Authority, 'Guidance: Cartels: Come Forward and Apply for Leniency' (GOV.UK, 11 March 2019) <https://www.gov.uk/guidance/cartels-confess-and-apply-for-leniency> accessed 4 July 2024.

97 Competition and Markets Authority, 'Letter from Andrew Tyrie to the Secretary of State for Business, Energy and Industrial Strategy' (GOV.UK, 25 February 2019) <https://www.gov.uk/government/publications/letter-from-andrew-tyrie-to-the-secretary-of-state-for-business-energy-and-industrial-strategy> accessed 15 July 2024.

98 Competition and Markets Authority, 'Blowing the Whistle on Cartels' (GOV.UK, 6 June 2023) <https://www.gov.uk/government/news/blowing-the-whistle-on-cartels#:~:text=The%20Competition%20and%20Markets%20Authority,cartel%20activity%20they%20have%20witnessed.> accessed 27 July 2024.

99 efinancialcareers, 'London's Investment Banking Salaries and Bonuses' (efinancialcareers, 19 October 2023) <https://www.efinancialcareers.co.uk/news/2023/10/london-investment-bank-pay> accessed 15 July 2024.

100 For example, see: US Securities and Exchange Commission, 'Whistleblower Awards over $400 Million' (Sec.Gov, 23 August 2019) <https://www.sec.gov/page/whistleblower-100million> accessed 25 July 2024.

There are also some clear areas where the UK, EU and US could learn from each other in order to improve their existing regimes.

6.6 Criminal vs Civil Penalties

This section of the chapter considers which type of penalty, criminal or civil, is the best suited to the enforcement of the financial crime of benchmark manipulation. As stated above, the US used both civil and criminal powers to enforce the LIBOR and FX crisis. It first used the criminal offence of wire fraud and/or conspiracy to commit wire fraud[101] against many banks and individual traders following the LIBOR manipulation.[102] In the FX crisis, the criminal competition laws were used to impose extremely high fines on banks and individuals and to enter DPAs with banks to regulate their future behaviour and to ensure reforms were made to prevent further offences of a similar type. The EU used its civil competition law enforcement powers, which include extremely high, almost criminal in nature, fines. However, even though the fines were comparable to those imposed for a criminal corporate offence, it is not possible to enter into a DPA with the offending companies without having a criminal offence with which to prosecute the offending companies. Since the LIBOR and FX scandals though, all Member States in the EU now have criminal powers in MAD 2014 against individuals and companies.[103]

In the UK, since the LIBOR and FX enforcement, the Financial Services Act 2012 created a new criminal offence for individuals who knowingly or deliberately make false or misleading statements relating to benchmark-setting.[104] This new criminal offence, in addition to the existing criminal cartel offence in the Enterprise Act 2002, gives the FCA two alternative options for criminal prosecutions and presumably will at least increase the regulator's chances of securing criminal convictions in any future benchmark manipulation cartel.

It appears from the abovementioned addition of new criminal offences for individuals by both the EU and UK that there is a consensus that the financial crime of benchmark manipulation is one that harms society as a whole and is, therefore, suitable to be punished as a criminal offence. This follows the lead of the US, which first used the criminal offence of wire fraud and then its criminal competition laws to punish both individuals and companies involved with the LIBOR and FX scandals. The use of criminal offences to prosecute this type of financial crime has multiple advantages over civil regulatory penalties. First,

101 Wire Fraud Statute 1952, 18 U.S.C. § 1343.

102 See, for example: US Department of Justice, 'Deutsche Bank's London Subsidiary Agrees to Plead Guilty in Connection with Long-Running Manipulation of LIBOR' (Department of Justice, 23 April 2015) <https://www.justice.gov/opa/pr/deutsche-banks-london-subsidiary-agrees-plead-guilty-connection-long-running-manipulation> accessed 23 July 2024.

103 Directive 2014/57/EU of the European Parliament and of the Council of 16 April 2014 on Criminal Sanctions for Market Abuse (Market Abuse Directive) [2014] OJ 2 173/179, Articles 3 and 5.

104 Financial Services Act 2012, s 91 and 92.

it sends a clear message to society that a severe wrong has been committed by the offenders and is being punished accordingly. Second, there is an associated deterrent effect of being found guilty of a criminal, rather than a civil offence, which comes with associated reputational damage. Third, when a company is prosecuted for a criminal offence, as seen in the US following the LIBOR and FX corporate convictions, it gives the regulator the option of entering into a DPA with the guilty company in order to regulate its future behaviour as well as to impose significant fines.[105] So on balance, the offence of benchmark manipulation, which causes significant harm to society at large, damaging trust in the financial markets, should be prosecuted as a criminal offence against both companies and individuals in order to produce a greater deterrent effect. In the UK and US, criminal competition laws can do this (although these only apply to individuals in the UK), and in the EU, the civil competition laws enable the Commission to impose such high fines on businesses that they are comparable to fines that could be imposed for a criminal offence.

6.7 Corporate Criminal Liability

Each of the jurisdictions studied has a different approach to corporate criminal liability in relation to financial crime and competition law. The US is the most frequent enforcer of corporate criminal liability in recent years, using this as a step toward the entry into a DPA with the offending company. In the US, the principle of *respondeat superior* underlies federal corporate criminal liability laws.[106] This has been applied broadly by courts and means that a business is responsible for all its employees' actions undertaken in the course and scope of their employment and, at least in part, for the benefit of the business.[107] *Respondeat superior* is a variation of the vicarious liability doctrine, allowing the imposition of criminal liability on employers for the actions of their employees.[108] This principle enables prosecutors to assign criminal liability to companies with relative ease, even when employees act contrary to corporate policy or even instructions.[109]

105 See, for example, the DPA with RBS – US Department of Justice, 'Deferred Prosecution Agreement: US v The Royal Bank of Scotland Plc' (US Department of Justice, 9 July 2020) <https://www.justice.gov/atr/case-document/deferred-prosecution-agreement> accessed 4 July 2024.

106 *Perdue v. Mitchell*, 373 So. 2d 650 (1979).

107 Bryan Cave, 'Corporate Criminal Liability – Perspectives from the US, UK and France' (Bryan Cave Leighton Paisner LLP, 13 April 2018) <https://www.lexology.com/library/detail.aspx?g=a87d8ace-7b5e-482b-a907-9a69e20f02cd>accessed 26 July 2024.

108 N Ryder, '"Too Scared to Prosecute and too Scared to Jail?" A Critical and Comparative Analysis of Enforcement of Financial Crime Legislation against Corporations in the United States of America and the United Kingdom' (2018) 82(3) *The Journal of Criminal Law* 245.

109 ME Roszkowski and CL Roszkowski, 'Making Sense of Respondent Superior: An Integrated Approach for Both Negligent and Intentional Conduct' (2005) 14(2) *Southern California Review of Law and Women's Studies* 235.

In the EU, however, there is not a standard approach to corporate criminal liability, as different Member States have different approaches to it, with some Member States not recognising criminal liability for legal persons.[110] However, as has been previously stated, debate exists as to whether the significant fines that can be imposed on companies for breach of competition law by the European Commission are arguably penal in nature.[111] Fines of up to 10% of the turnover in the preceding accounting year can be imposed by the Commission on an infringing company,[112] which, due to the significance of the level of the fine, has been described as a kind of 'competence creep' into the sphere of penal law, which, in turn, is seen by some commentators as introducing criminal sanctions through the back door and breaching the general right to a fair trial.[113] In the MAR 2014 and the MAD 2014, criminal sanctions are imposed for the first time in EU law for the financial crimes of market manipulation, money laundering and the unlawful disclosure of inside information. These sanctions can be imposed by regulators against both legal and natural persons in the EU's market abuse regime.[114]

In the UK, there appears to be a reluctance by regulators to make companies criminally liable for crimes they have committed. This is at least in part because prosecutors in the UK have a harder job on their hands to assign liability to companies. There are two primary methods of establishing corporate criminal liability: vicarious and nonvicarious liability.[115] Vicarious liability has only limited application for criminal law in areas such as health and safety and environmental offences.[116] Therefore, prosecutors for financial crime offences must look to nonvicarious liability to establish corporate liability for a crime. The main way of doing this in the UK has, for many years, been the 'identification principle', as described in Chapters 2 and 3. The identification principle requires identifying the most senior officers who represent the 'directing mind and will' of the company and then proving corporate criminal liability through his/her conduct and state of mind.[117] For many years, the courts interpreted the 'directing mind and will' to mean the actions of a director, but a recent change to the law has expanded the identification doctrine so that the actions of 'senior managers' can now attribute criminal liability to a company for cer-

110 E Herlin-Karnell and N Ryder, *Market Manipulation and Insider Trading* (Hart, 2019).

111 B Rodger, A MacCulloch, *Competition Law and Policy in the EC and UK* (4th edn., Routledge-Cavendish 2009).

112 Regulation 1/2003/EC on the Implementation of the Rules on Competition Laid Down in Articles 81 and 82 of the Treaty, OJ 2003, L1/1.

113 PA Albrecht and S Braum, 'Deficiencies in the Development of European Criminal law' (1999) 5 *European Law Journal* 293.

114 3

115 Crown Prosecution Service, 'Corporate Prosecutions' (Crown Prosecution Service, 1 May 2019) <https://www.cps.gov.uk/legal-guidance/corporate-prosecutions> accessed 29 July 2024.

116 Ibid.

117 *Tesco Supermarkets Ltd v Nattrass* [1972] AC 153.

tain specified economic crimes.[118] Before this expansion of the identification doctrine, it had proved difficult for prosecutors to attribute criminal liability to a company from an evidential point of view, with few corporate prosecutions being successful historically in the UK.[119] It now remains to be seen whether the recent changes to the identification doctrine will result in more corporate prosecutions for financial crime.

The differences in approach to corporate criminal liability in the UK, EU and US show that the US makes companies criminally liable regularly. However, since the case of Arthur Anderson, this has not had significant adverse effects on the companies subject to criminal prosecution.[120] This is due to the increased use of DPAs in the US as a settlement tool for corporate criminal prosecutions, the pros and cons of which will be discussed below. The UK and EU should learn from this approach and prosecute more companies to create a stronger deterrent to committing crime. Leading on from the above discussion about prosecuting companies, the next section will explore one method of enforcing corporate criminal liability, in lieu of a criminal trial.

6.8 Deferred Prosecution Agreements

Earlier chapters have examined in detail how DPAs have been used to regulate corporate financial crime both immediately after the LIBOR and FX crisis and in the years since then. This section will look at how, or if, DPAs have been used in each of the US, EU and UK in order to assess the use of DPAs as a settlement tool in a proposed criminal action against a banking cartel. It will also compare DPAs with commitments, a competition law enforcement tool available to regulators in the EU and UK.

Settlement tools such as Corporate Non-Prosecution Agreements and DPAs were first used in the US in the early 1990s following the *1994 Prudential Securities* trial,[121] which saw the first DPA involving a public company.[122] DPAs, which are entered into between the company or companies under investigation and the relevant regulator, operate by allowing companies to escape criminal liability if they agree to pay a fine instead of facing criminal

118 Economic Crime and Corporate Transparency Act 2023 s.196.

119 B Cave, 'Corporate Criminal Liability – Perspectives from the US, UK and France' (Bryan Cave Leighton Paisner LLP, 13 April 2018) <https://www.lexology.com/library/detail.aspx?g=a87d8ace-7b5e-482b-a907-9a69e20f02cd> accessed 13 July 2024.

120 G Markoff, 'Arthur Andersen and the Myth of the Corporate Death Penalty: Corporate Criminal Convictions in the Twenty-First Century' (2013) 15(3) *University of Pennsylvania Journal of Business Law* 797.

121 *In re Prudential Securities Inc.*, 158 F.R.D. 562 (1994).

122 CR Alexander and MA Cohen, 'The Evolution of Corporate Criminal Settlements: An Empirical Perspective on Non-Prosecution, Deferred Prosecution, and Plea Agreements' (2015) 52(1) *The American Criminal Law Review* 537.

prosecution.[123] DPAs often also involve some form of behaviour regulation of the company to manage the offending behaviour such as the regulator requiring the company to undertake to co-operate in the future prosecution of individuals, the company paying compensation to victims and agreeing to regular monitoring by a regulator or third party to ensure compliance with the terms of the DPA.[124] There has been a marked increase of use of DPAs in the US since 2003.[125] In a speech on July 2021, the Acting Assistant Attorney General defended the use of DPAs by the Antitrust Division, noting that: '[a] deferred prosecution agreement is much closer to a guilty plea than leniency, which has unmatched benefits'.[126]

To date, neither the European Commission nor ESMA, the EU regulator for MAR 2014, has used a DPA in connection with financial crime; however, DPAs have been used by one Member State – France – and they are used in both the US and UK as well.[127] If the EU and/or each of the Member States were to consider using a DPA alongside the relatively new EU criminal market abuse powers for regulators, it could provide both the deterrent effect of criminal sanctions as well as preventative measures designed to significantly reduce the risk of reoffending by the business that is subject to the DPA. It is worth noting though that, for a DPA to maximise its deterrent effect, it should be used in conjunction with criminal proceedings against employees and/or agents of companies.[128]

123 Gibson Dunn & Crutcher LLP, '2014 Year-End Update on Corporate Non-Prosecution Agreements and Deferred Prosecution Agreements' (Gibson, Dunn & Crutcher LLP, 6 January 2015) <https://www.gibsondunn.com/2014-year-end-update-on-corporate-non-prosecution-agreements-npas-and-deferred-prosecution-agreements-dpas/> accessed 14 July 2024.

124 B Hertstein, M Berry, S Brown, 'Deferred Prosecution Agreements in Jersey: Ways to Buttress the Castle. A Comparative Analysis of Regimes for Deferred Prosecution Agreements in Jersey and the UK' (2024) 3 *Journal of Economic Criminology* 100046, 1; and Serious Fraud Office, 'Deferred Prosecution Agreements' (Serious Fraud Office, 2021) <https://www.sfo.gov.uk/publications/guidance-policy-and-protocols/deferred-prosecution-agreements/> accessed 3 July 2024.

125 CR Alexander and MA Cohen, 'The Evolution of Corporate Criminal Settlements: An Empirical Perspective on Non-Prosecution, Deferred Prosecution, and Plea Agreements' (2015) 52(1) *The American Criminal Law Review* 537.

126 RA Powers, 'Acting Assistant Attorney General Richard A Powers Delivers Remarks at the Symposium on Corporate Enforcement and Individual Accountability Hosted by the University of Southern California Gould School of Law' (US Department of Justice, 21 July 2021) <https://www.justice.gov/opa/speech/acting-assistant-attorney-general-richard-powers-delivers-remarks-symposium-corporate> accessed 12 July 2024.

127 Dow Jones Risk & Compliance, 'Deferred Prosecution Agreements in Europe: What to Expect' (Dow Jones Risk & Compliance, 2020) <https://visit.dowjones.com/content/dpa-europe/> accessed 12 July 2024.

128 N Ryder, '"Too Scared to Prosecute and Too Scared to Jail?" A Critical and Comparative Analysis of Enforcement of Financial Crime Legislation against Corporations in the USA and the UK' (2018) 82(3) *The Journal of Criminal Law* 263.

Since 2014, DPAs have been in use in the UK, enacted by the Crime and Courts Act 2013,[129] for offences set out in that Act, including conspiracy to defraud.[130] The only regulators with power to issue DPAs in the UK are the SFO and the Crown Prosecution Service (CPS).[131] To date, 12 DPAs have been entered into by the SFO[132] and one with the CPS,[133] none of which relate to market manipulation. It is argued in this book that legislative changes need to be made to enable the financial services and competition regulators to be able to enter DPAs with companies under investigation for criminal offences such as benchmark manipulation.

The use of criminal sanctions against banks combined with DPAs would deter banks from committing financial crime; however, whether the use of DPAs, which only apply to companies,[134] will deter individual traders from breaking the law, which they do to make huge personal and corporate profits, is more questionable. Often the profits made over a period of years until discovery by the authorities will dwarf any fine ultimately imposed, so even for the bank itself, the risk of receiving just a fine is not considered to be prohibitive.[135] This, again, supports the argument for UK regulators to use the criminal cartel sanctions against individuals in future cases of market manipulation as well as taking strong enforcement action against the banks in order to deter future benchmark manipulation.

6.9 Conclusion

This chapter has compared the approaches taken by the UK, EU and US to the enforcement of the LIBOR and FX benchmark manipulation scandals. These three jurisdictions have been selected because each has similar competition laws and each experienced the same benchmark manipulation in the LIBOR and FX crisis, thereby providing a good basis for comparison. The US has successfully used its criminal competition law against both companies and individual traders involved with the FX cartels and has recently stated its intent to continue to use its competition law powers in the financial services

129 Crime Courts Act 2013 s.45 and Schedule 17.

130 Ibid, s.15 and Schedule 17.

131 Crime and Courts Act 2013, Schedule 17, paragraph 3(1).

132 Serious Fraud Office, 'Deferred Prosecution Agreements' (Serious Fraud Office, 2024) <https://www.sfo.gov.uk/publications/guidance-policy-and-protocols/guidance-for-corporates/deferred-prosecution-agreements/> accessed 12 July 2024.

133 Crown Prosecution Service, 'First Ever CPS Deferred Prosecution Agreement for £615 Million' (CPS, 5 December 2023) <https://www.cps.gov.uk/cps/news/first-ever-cps-deferred-prosecution-agreement-ps615-million> accessed 12 July 2024.

134 Serious Fraud Office, 'Deferred Prosecution Agreements' (Serious Fraud Office, 2020) <https://www.sfo.gov.uk/publications/guidance-policy-and-protocols/guidance-for-corporates/deferred-prosecution-agreements/> accessed 12 July 2024.

135 H Hillman, 'Current Laws and Potential Enforcement Measures' in N Ryder, U Turksen and S Hassler (Eds) *Fighting Financial Crime in the Global Economic Crisis* (Routledge 2015).

sector.[136] The EU also used its competition law enforcement powers against the companies involved in the cartels to impose extremely high fines, although no enforcement action was taken against the individuals involved. The UK was the only jurisdiction not to use its competition law powers at all in either the LIBOR or FX scandals. It used its financial regulatory enforcement powers to impose fines on companies, and it attempted the prosecution of individual traders using the 'conspiracy to defraud' offence, with limited success.[137] Therefore, it can be seen that the UK is the odd one out of the three jurisdictions by not using its competition law powers, and it is clear that the EU and US enforcement action for the LIBOR and FX benchmark manipulation cartels was greater than that of the UK, therefore providing a greater deterrent against future financial crime in the EU and US than was seen in the UK. In addition, comparison of the competition law leniency and whistleblowing regimes of each jurisdiction has shown the importance of both having a competition law leniency and/or whistleblower regime as well as making sure that it is well advertised. In the UK, it is imperative that the competition law whistleblowing and leniency competition law provisions, both for individuals and companies, are advertised in the financial services industry, as any information provided by a whistleblower about a future benchmark manipulation cartel will help the regulators to investigate and enforce this financial crime.

Overall, the merits of regulators using competition law to enforce the financial crime of benchmark manipulation can be seen by the use in the US of a combination of criminal and civil enforcement powers for the same crime. The US uses a wider variety of enforcement measures, namely the imposition of fines and the entry into DPAs with offending institutions, than the UK has done in the past for financial crime. The EU uses extremely high competition law fines as its sole enforcement tool against banking cartels. In the LIBOR and FX benchmark manipulation scandal, the UK relied on its financial regulatory powers alone to punish the banks involved in the benchmark manipulation cartels. However, the financial services regulators would have had a wider range of enforcement powers to use had they used competition law enforcement powers against the infringing banks, including the acceptance of commitments and director disqualification orders. Use of competition law by the UK financial services regulator in the LIBOR and FX crisis would have opened

136 US Department of Justice, 'The Muscular Role for Antitrust in Fintech, Financial Markets and Banking: The Antitrust Division's Decision to Lean In' (US Department of Justice, 14 October 2020) <https://www.justice.gov/opa/speech/deputy-assistant-attorney-general-michael-murray-delivers-remarks-university-michigan-law> accessed 18 July 2024.

137 In total, the SFO prosecuted 13 individuals, eight of whom have now been acquitted, four were found guilty and one entered a guilty plea – B Rose, 'Challenging the LIBOR/EURIBOR Convictions' (Hickman Rose, 21 December 2022) <https://www.hickmanandrose.co.uk/blog-challenging-the-libor-euribor-convictions/#:~:text=When%20the%20LIBOR%20investigation%20closed,whom%20just%20four%20were%20convicted.> accessed 12 July 2024.

a raft of alternative enforcement tools, including those referred to below, the use of which are likely to act as more of a deterrent to a bank than a fine alone, which can be absorbed into its operating costs and/or set against the huge profits the illegal benchmark manipulation generated for the bank.

Some of the main advantages for a financial services regulator of using competition law in the enforcement of corporate financial crime are first, the maximum fines the regulator can impose are much larger than those imposed using financial regulation alone in the UK following the LIBOR and FX crises. Competition law authorises regulators to impose fines of up to 10% of company's worldwide turnover,[138] which, for an international bank such as HSBC or Barclays, could result in a significant fine, far higher than those imposed by the FSA for banks' participation in the LIBOR and FX benchmark manipulation. Regulators will, of course, have to balance the size of the fine levied against a particular bank with the risk of the bank not being able to pay the fine, which could result in the corporate death penalty, as seen in the case of Arthur Anderson in 2002.[139] However, making banks aware of the potential for regulators to levy such a large fine should help to deter banks from illegal benchmark manipulation. Second, when there is a cartel operated between employees of different banks (as happened in the LIBOR and FX crisis), criminal sanctions are available to the UK competition regulator.[140] Since the removal of the dishonesty element in 2014,[141] prosecutors may find it easier in the future to use the criminal cartel offence than the offence used against the traders involved with the LIBOR and FX manipulation, or there is also now the option for regulators to use the new criminal offence of making misleading statements in relation to benchmark-setting.[142] In the US, breach of competition law is a criminal offence,[143] enabling regulators to enter into a DPA with companies, including banks, who have breached competition law. If this option were open to UK regulators, they would have the option of either pursuing the case in a criminal court against one/more of the infringing banks, or to enter a DPA with the bank(s), which would have the advantage of compelling those banks to comply with the law for the period of the DPA, as well as paying a substantial fine. This could then drive cultural change and increase compliance in the financial sector over time. Another advantage of using competition law in the enforcement of corporate financial crime is that it provides access to a wider range of enforcement tools than a financial services regulator would otherwise have. Such alternative competition law

138 Competition Act 1998, s.36.

139 A Groves, 'The Collapse of Arthur Andersen' (CorpComms, 1 May 2012) <https://www.corpcommsmagazine.co.uk/features-and-analysis/view/the-collapse-of-arthur-andersen> accessed 14 July 2024.

140 Enterprise Act 2002, s.188.

141 Enterprise and Regulatory Reform Act 2013, s.47.

142 Financial Services Act 2012, s.91.

143 Sherman Antitrust Act 1890, s.1.

enforcement tools include the use of commitments,[144] whereby a regulator can require the infringing company to make structural changes, or the regulator could give directions to the infringing bank to bring the infringement to an end.[145] Additionally, director disqualification orders can be imposed for breaches of competition law,[146] and these could be used against directors of banks who are found to have been involved with or to have had oversight or awareness of the infringing behaviour of the cartel members. These powers would have the effect of persuading directors and companies to take action to prevent employees from entering into benchmark manipulation cartels in the future.

Using a combination of different enforcement tools, as well as drawing from different areas of law for appropriate offences to charge offending financial institutions with, would provide the UK financial services regulators with a wider range of powers that should, in turn, result in a more substantial deterrent effect than the use of a fine alone against a bank that has been involved in financial crime. It appears, however, that legislators and regulators in the UK seem more inclined to focus criminal penalties on individuals rather than companies (for instance, the misleading statements in relation to benchmark-setting offence and the cartel offence are both aimed at individuals and do not apply to companies),[147] but if there was a suitable criminal offence that could be used against banks that benefited from employees' market manipulation in the future, it would allow the use of DPAs by UK regulators, as has been done in the US. The risk of reputational damage for committing a criminal offence is likely to provide more of a deterrent effect for banks than just civil fines alone and a significant advantage of DPAs is that banks will be required to commit to increased compliance checks.

As has been said above, the civil fines imposed by the UK financial services regulators following the LIBOR and FX scandals do not seem to deter banks from committing financial crime. Something else is needed for the UK regulators to use against corporate bodies. Either a new corporate criminal offence to sanction a bank's involvement in a cartel, or an amendment to the existing cartel offence to enable it to apply to corporations as well as to individuals, is needed. Such a corporate criminal offence will invoke the risk of reputational damage to a bank as well as large fines and will assist regulators in the future regulation of corporate financial crime, together with the use of the extensive competition law enforcement powers already in existence. There appears to be a cultural difference between the US, EU and UK, with US and EU regulators being happy to levy high fines and to cause reputational damage to companies, unlike UK regulators, who seem reluctant to use their competition law

144 Competition Act 1998, s.31A.
145 Competition Act 1998, ss.32 and 33.
146 Enterprise Act 2002, s.204.
147 Financial Services Act 2012, s 91 and 92 and Enterprise Act 2002, s.188(1).

powers to impose significant fines or other structural or behavioural sanctions on banks. UK regulators appear to prefer to prosecute individuals, but a combination of imposing criminal and civil sanctions on companies as well as on individuals would provide a better deterrent effect, following the approach of the US. Using competition law powers to enforce financial crime in the UK will enhance the variety of enforcement tools available to either the FCA or the CMA and, if the FCA is prepared to use its competition law powers, it can impose significantly higher fines on companies, following the lead of both the US and EU, to create a more substantial deterrent effect to prevent future financial crime.

The next chapter will set out the conclusions of this book, together with recommendations for reform applicable to each of the UK, EU and US based on this research.

7 Conclusion and Recommendations

7.1 Introduction

This book aimed to undertake a critical and comparative analysis of how competition law can and has been used to enforce financial crime in the United Kingdom (UK), the European Union (EU) and the United States (US). The starting point for this comparison was the London Interbank Offered Rate (LIBOR) and Foreign Exchange (FX) benchmark manipulation crisis and the laws employed by each of the jurisdictions to enforce the crime of benchmark manipulation. This comparison has established that different laws were used in the three jurisdictions to enforce the same financial crime. In the US, the criminal charge of wire fraud was predominantly utilised to enforce the LIBOR manipulation, yet competition law was used to enforce the FX manipulation. The EU employed competition law to enforce the manipulation of both the LIBOR and FX benchmark manipulation. However, the UK was alone in not utilising competition law to enforce either the LIBOR or the FX benchmark manipulation. This book has demonstrated that competition law can be used successfully by regulators to tackle the financial crime of benchmark manipulation. When competition law was used in the US[1] and EU,[2] it resulted in significantly higher fines against corporate bodies than the use of financial regulation and criminal law, the approach adopted in the UK.[3]

1 For example, see US Department of Justice, 'Sherman Act Violations Resulting in Criminal Fines & Penalties of $10 Million or More' (*US Department of Justice*, 25 January 2024) <https://www.justice.gov/atr/sherman-act-violations-yielding-corporate-fine-10-million-or-more> accessed 28 July 2024.

2 For example, see European Commission, 'Commission Fines Barclays, RBS, Citigroup, JPMorgan and MUFG E107 Billion for Participating in Foreign Exchange Spot Trading Cartel' (European Commission, 16 May 2019) <https://ec.europa.eu/commission/presscorner/detail/en/IP_19_2568> accessed 29 July 2024.

3 For example, see Financial Conduct Authority, 'FCA Fines Barclays £284,432,000 for Forex Failings' (Financial Conduct Authority, 19 May 2015) <https://www.fca.org.uk/news/press-releases/fca-fines-barclays-%C2%A3284432000-forex-failings#:~:text=The%20Financial%20Conduct%20Authority%20(FCA,(FX)%20business%20in%20London.> accessed 8 July 2024.

DOI: 10.4324/9781003425106-7

This book contributes to the existing body of knowledge in three ways. First, it adds to and updates the existing literature on the LIBOR and FX benchmark manipulation crisis by comparing the latest enforcement actions from the UK,[4] the EU[5] and the US.[6] Second, this book undertakes, for the first time, a critical and comparative analysis of the approach taken to the enforcement of the LIBOR and FX benchmark manipulation crisis by the UK, the EU and the US and examines the extent to which each jurisdiction used its competition law powers in this enforcement. Finally, this book formulates proposals for ways in which the UK can improve its enforcement of financial crime by better utilising its existing competition law powers and recommending ways in which these powers can be enhanced.

This book has highlighted that UK regulators were reluctant to use their competition law powers, which were available at the time of the LIBOR and FX benchmark manipulation, to enforce that financial crime. It has been noted that the then competition law regulator, the Office of Fair Trading (OFT), raised competition concerns about LIBOR benchmark manipulation with the then financial regulator, the Financial Services Authority (FSA), but these concerns were ignored.[7] Chapters 3 and 6 demonstrate that the UK financial regulator is *still* reluctant to use its competition powers to enforce financial crime, as demonstrated by the low level of competition law fines[8] imposed since

4 The latest UK Court of Appeal decision was given on 27 March 2024; see *R v Tom Hayes and Carlo Palombo* [2024] EWCA Crim 304 and B Castro, 'Former Traders Tom Hayes and Carlo Palombo's Convictions Upheld by Court of Appeal' *The Law Society Gazette* (London, 27 March 2024) <https://www.lawgazette.co.uk/news/former-traders-convictions-upheld-by-court-of-appeal/5119208.article> accessed 20 July 2024.

5 For example, the latest decision of the European Commission on the FX benchmark manipulation cartels was in December 2021; see European Commission, 'Antitrust: Commission Fines UBS, Barclays, RBS, HSBC and Credit Suisse €344 Million for Participating in a Foreign Exchange Spot Trading Cartel' (European Commission, 2 December 2021) <https://ec.europa.eu/commission/presscorner/detail/en/ip_21_6548> accessed 28 July 2024.

6 The latest US court decisions on the LIBOR rate fixing cartels were given in December 2021; see J Stempel, 'US Appeals Court Revives Libor-Rigging Claims against Banks' (*Reuters*, 30 December 2021) <https://www.reuters.com/markets/europe/us-appeals-court-revives-libor-rigging-claims-against-banks-2021-12-30/> accessed 20 July 2024 and January 2022; see D Michaels, 'All US Trial Convictions in Crisis-Era Libor Rigging Have Now Been Overturned' *Wall Street Journal* (New York, 27 January 2022) <https://www.wsj.com/articles/all-u-s-trial-convictions-in-crisis-era-libor-rigging-have-now-been-overturned-11643310178> accessed 26 July 2024; with the latest decision on the FX benchmark manipulation cartels given in July 2021, see K Ridley, 'US Regulator Drops Case against Two London Forex Traders' (*Reuters*, 9 July 2021) <https://www.reuters.com/business/us-regulator-drops-case-against-two-london-forex-traders-2021-07-08/> accessed 26 July 2024.

7 Financial Services Authority, 'Internal Audit Report A Review of the Extent of Awareness within the FSA of Inappropriate LIBOR Submissions' (Financial Conduct Authority, March 2013) <https://www.fca.org.uk/publication/corporate/fsa-ia-libor.pdf> accessed 28 July 2024.

8 This is small when compared with the maximum fines allowed under competition law of 10% of worldwide turnover for each undertaking.

competition law powers were bestowed on the Financial Conduct Authority (FCA).[9] This book has highlighted the wide range of enforcement tools available to UK regulators under competition law, including director disqualification, interim orders and behavioural and structural powers, and it has also looked at the whistleblower/leniency provisions available in each jurisdiction. The book has formulated a series of recommendations, set out below, to UK legislators and financial services regulators for improvements to the enforcement of the financial crime of market manipulation in the future.

The next section of this chapter will set out the findings of this book, after which five key recommendations for reform will be made.

7.2 Key Findings

The key findings of this book are set out below, following the order of the themes examined in each of the three case study chapters (Chapters 3, 4 and 5). First, the findings of the comparison of the whistleblowing and leniency regimes of the three jurisdictions are set out. Then the findings from the examination of the final three themes related to an evaluation of civil vs criminal sanctions, corporate criminal liability and deferred prosecution agreements (DPAs) will be reviewed.

7.2.1 Competition Law Leniency and Whistleblowing Regimes

Each of the case study chapters of this book examined how well the competition law whistleblowing/leniency regimes operate in the financial services sector of each of the UK, EU and US. As explained in Chapter 2, the reason for the inclusion of this examination is the critical role that competition law whistleblowing and leniency regimes play in the detection and enforcement of cartels, which are, by their very nature, extremely secretive and hard to detect.[10]

The UK cartel leniency regime was outlined and analysed in Chapter 3. Key weaknesses in the UK cartel leniency provisions were identified; in particular, the leniency regime for the reporting of cartels to the regulator is a relatively new concept in the financial services market, with the FCA first advertising its new competition powers, along with the CMA's leniency regime in 2015.[11] For

9 Financial Conduct Authority, 'FCA Issues Its First Decision under Competition Law' (Financial Conduct Authority, 21 February 2019) <https://www.fca.org.uk/news/press-releases/fca-issues-its-first-decision-under-competition-law> accessed 27 July 2024.

10 S Takuo and W Alexander, 'Maintaining Privacy in Cartels' (2018) 126(6) *Journal of Political Economy* 2569, 2571; and J Terzaken and P Huizing, 'How Much Is Too Much? A Call for Global Principles to Guide the Punishment of International Cartels' (2013) 27(2) *Antitrust* 53, 54.

11 See Financial Conduct Authority, 'FG15/8 - FCA's Powers and Procedures under the Competition Act 1998' (Financial Conduct Authority, 3 May 2022) paras. 6.1–6.8 <https://

the leniency regime to work successfully in the UK, it needs to be made much more visible to all business in the financial services sector. A further observation made in Chapter 6, when the three leniency/whistleblower regimes were compared, was that the UK incentives to individual employees to 'blow the whistle' and report potential cartels, or other breaches of competition law, were not set at an appropriate level to encourage high earners such as bankers to come forward with evidence to the authorities. The reward for informants of an illegal cartel was raised in 2023 from £100,000 to £250,000,[12] but this reward is not well publicised and needs to be much higher to tempt whistleblowers in the financial services sector to inform on a future banking cartel.

Chapter 4 examined the EU competition law leniency regime, which offers either a total immunity from fines or a reduction in fines for businesses that report illegal cartels or other anticompetitive behaviour to the regulator. Unlike either the UK or the US though, the EU leniency regime does not offer a financial reward to individual whistleblowers, but individual Member States are allowed to and many offer financial incentives for individual informants.

Chapter 5 looked at the US competition law leniency system, which is the most attractive of the three competition law whistleblowing/leniency regimes, and the Department of Justice (DoJ) is extremely supportive of it. The system allows both individuals and companies to report their participation in or observation of a competition law breach, including cartels, to the DoJ in exchange for full immunity from antitrust prosecution. The US Securities and Exchange Commission (SEC) also has a whistleblower programme that rewards whistleblowers who come forward with information about financial misconduct to regulators. This programme allows whistleblowers to be paid between 10% and 30% of the money collected from infringing parties, provided that the information provided was high-quality, original information. The highest ever award to one individual whistleblower by the SEC was awarded in May 2023, in which the sum of nearly $279m was paid to one individual who provided information and assistance that led to a successful enforcement action.[13]

Chapter 6 then compared the three competition law whistleblowing/leniency regimes and analysed their respective strengths and weaknesses. From

www.fca.org.uk/publications/finalised-guidance/fg15-8-fcas-powers-and-procedures-under-competition-act-1998> accessed 28 July 2024; and Financial Conduct Authority, 'Competition Law' (Financial Conduct Authority, 21 April 2016) <https://www.fca.org.uk/about/promoting-competition/powers> accessed 20 July 2024.

12 Raised from £100,000 in June 2023; see Competition and Markets Authority, 'Blowing the Whistle on Cartels' (GOV.UK, 6 June 2023) <https://www.gov.uk/government/news/blowing-the-whistle-on-cartels#:~:text=The%20Competition%20and%20Markets%20Authority,cartel%20activity%20they%20have%20witnessed.> accessed 27 July 2024.

13 US Securities and Exchange Commission, 'SEC Issues Largest-Ever Whistleblower Award' (US SEC, 5 May 2023) <https://www.sec.gov/news/press-release/2023-89#:~:text=The%20Securities%20and%20Exchange%20Commission,of%20SEC%20and%20related%20actions.> accessed 24 July 2024.

the analysis carried out in this book, it can be seen that the US system, which rewards whistleblowing companies with total/partial immunity from fines for breach of competition law and whistleblowing individuals with a share of the money collected from the infringing parties as a financial reward for the information, is an extremely successful one. This conclusion is reflected in the fourth recommendation below for the UK to improve its whistleblowing/leniency regime to catch more anticompetitive behaviour such as collusion between competitors and cartels, as seen in the LIBOR and FX benchmark manipulation cartels.

7.2.2 Civil vs Criminal Sanctions

Each of the case studies of the UK, EU and US considered the types of enforcement mechanisms used by regulators for the LIBOR and FX cartels and a mixed picture emerged. The EU was alone in using solely civil powers; however, commentators have argued that the level of fines imposed by the EU are penal in nature,[14] including the power to impose fines of up to 10% of a company's worldwide turnover. In the US, criminal penalties were imposed for both individuals and banks, using a mixture of competition law penalties and other criminal penalties; however, many of the noncompetition law charges have now been overturned.[15] In the UK, there was no use of civil or criminal competition law; instead, civil regulatory enforcement action was taken against the banks based on breaches of FCA Principle 2 (due skill, care and diligence) and Principle 3 (management and control),[16] resulting in the lowest fines imposed in the three jurisdictions. Additionally, in the UK, criminal action was taken against 13 individual traders, using the charge of 'conspiracy to defraud'. Many of these convictions have since been retried with numerous acquittals.[17] This book has argued that being able to impose a combination of civil and criminal penalties on both individual and corporate bodies is essential

14 For instance, see V Franssen, 'The EU's Fight against Corporate Financial Crime: State of Affairs and Future Potential' (2018) 19(5) *German Law Journal* 1221, 1244 and A Garzaro, 'Limitations of EU Competition Law and Their Influence on Recidivism and Deterrence: Analysis of the Convenience of a Penal Approach to Cartels' (2014) 4(1) *Challenges of the Knowledge Society* 247, 258.

15 PA Media, 'Ex-Deutsche Bank Traders' Libor-Rigging Convictions Overturned by US Court' *The Guardian* (London, 28 January 2022) <https://www.theguardian.com/business/2022/jan/28/ex-deutsche-bank-traders-libor-rigging-convictions-overturned-by-us-court> accessed 26 July 2024.

16 C Burnett and others, 'FCA and PRA Enforcement Themes and Trends' (A&O Shearman, 20 February 2024) <https://www.aoshearman.com/en/insights/fca-and-pra-enforcement-themes-and-trends-2023-a-shake-up> accessed 26 July 2024; and Financial Conduct Authority, 'PRIN 21 the Principles' (Financial Conduct Authority, 3 January 2018) <https://www.handbook.fca.org.uk/handbook/PRIN/2/1.html> accessed 26 July 2024.

17 Serious Fraud Office, 'Libor' (Serious Fraud Office, 9 November 2020) <https://www.sfo.gov.uk/cases/libor-landing/> accessed 26 July 2024.

for regulators; however, it has been noted that the UK does not have either a generic criminal corporate offence of 'failure to prevent economic crime' or a criminal cartel offence that applies to companies – these are both recommendations arising from this research and are discussed further below.

7.2.3 Corporate Criminal Liability

The third theme considered in each of the case study chapters of this book is that of corporate criminal liability and whether it is an effective sanction and deterrent against the financial crime of benchmark manipulation.

In Chapter 5, it was seen that US competition law provides antitrust regulators with the ability to impose criminal sanctions on both corporate bodies and individuals. As the Deputy Assistant Attorney General of the Antitrust Division of the Department of Justice (DoJ) stated in 2020:

> Neither the financial sector nor complex financial instruments are beyond the reach of the antitrust laws. And the results speak for themselves: to date, the Division's...investigations have resulted in over forty convictions and substantial corporate criminal fines and penalties.[18]

This has been the accepted view in the US since 1963 when the Supreme Court stated that banking certainly constituted 'commerce' within the meaning of the Sherman and Clayton Acts.[19] In *Philadelphia National Bank*, the court stated that 'the fact that banking is a highly regulated industry critical to the Nation's welfare makes the play of competition not less important but more so'.[20] This view taken by US courts and regulators that the banking industry is subject to competition law explains the robust approach taken when criminal competition law was used to enforce the FX benchmark manipulation.

The US differs from both the UK and EU in its approach toward the prosecutions of companies. The EU does not have the ability to impose corporate criminal liability for breaches of competition law, as its competition law powers are entirely civil. However, criminal sanctions can be imposed on corporate entities at an EU level for the financial crimes of market manipulation, money laundering and the unlawful disclosure of inside information under the 2014 Market Abuse Regulation (MAR 2014) and the 2014 Market Abuse Directive (MAD 2014).[21]

18 RA Powers, 'Criminal Antitrust Enforcement: Recent Highlights, Policy Initiatives and What's to Come' (2020) 30(1) *Journal of the Antitrust, UCL and Privacy Section of the California Lawyers Association* 82, 85.

19 Ibid.

20 *United States v Philadelphia National Bank*, 374 U.S. 321. 337 n.12 (1963).

21 Regulation (EU) No 596/2014 of the European Parliament and of the Council of 16 April 2014 on Market Abuse (Market Abuse Regulation) [2014] OJ 2 173/1, Articles 8(5), 12(4) and 10(1).

In the UK, as noted in Chapter 6, there appears to be a reluctance by regulators to impose criminal liability on large international companies, particularly upon banks, although the FCA secured its first corporate criminal prosecution of a bank under the Money Laundering Regulations[22] in 2021.[23] It was noted in Chapter 3 that the law relating to corporate criminal liability has changed recently in the UK. First, the identification doctrine has been broadened to allow 'senior managers' as well as directors to attribute criminal liability to the company in certain circumstances for financial crimes.[24] And second, a new 'failure to prevent' corporate criminal liability offence has been introduced for fraud.[25] These changes to the law relating to corporate criminal liability in the UK are welcome, as they make it easier for prosecutors to achieve a successful outcome when prosecuting a large international company for a financial crime. However, further changes are needed to give prosecutors the power to successfully convict banks and other large international companies who break criminal law by forming a cartel to manipulate the financial markets, as seen in the LIBOR and FX benchmark manipulation crisis. This is reflected in the second recommendation below.

7.2.4 Deferred Prosecution Agreements

Once corporate criminal liability has been established, the consequences of a guilty plea must be assessed. In particular, the collateral consequences of the corporate death penalty, seen in the Arthur Andersen case,[26] must be considered, together with the 'too big to fail' argument put forward by commentators when discussing the criminal prosecution of companies integral to a country's economy.[27] At this point, it becomes relevant to discuss the fourth theme looked at throughout this book, which is the entry into a DPA between the regulator and the guilty company as an alternative to an expensive and lengthy criminal trial. A DPA will normally ensure that the company pays a large fine, sometimes it will require the company to compensate victims of its

22 Money Laundering Regulations 2007, SI 2007/2157.

23 See *R (FCA) v National Westminster Bank PLC* [2021] <https://www.judiciary.uk/wp-content/uploads/2022/07/FCA-v-Natwest-Sentencing-remarks-131221.pdf> accessed 25 July 2024 and Financial Conduct Authority, 'NatWest Fined £264.8 Million for Anti-Money Laundering Failures' (Financial Conduct Authority, 13 December 2021) <https://www.fca.org.uk/news/press-releases/natwest-fined-264.8million-anti-money-laundering-failures> accessed 27 July 2024.

24 Economic Crime and Corporate Transparency Act 2023, s.196.

25 Economic Crime and Corporate Transparency Act 2023, s. 199.

26 N Ryder, '"Too Scared to Prosecute and Too Scared to Jail?" A Critical and Comparative Analysis of Enforcement of Financial Crime Legislation against Corporations in the USA and the UK' (2018) 82(3) *Journal of Criminal Law* 245, 251.

27 FM Scherer, 'A Perplexed Economist Confronts "Too Big to Fail"' (Harvard Kennedy School, March 2010) 2 <https://dash.harvard.edu/bitstream/handle/1/4454151/Scherer_PerplexedEconomist.pdf> accessed 26 July 2024.

crime and often the regulator will require the implementation of a compliance programme and the setting up of monitoring visits for the period of the DPA to prevent a recurrence of the crime. It is worth noting, though, that DPAs should be used in conjunction with criminal proceedings against employees and/or agents of companies to maximise the deterrent effect of the enforcement action taken.[28] The entry into DPAs following criminal prosecutions of banks for breach of the antitrust laws was used by US regulators following the LIBOR and FX cartels,[29] and this book argues that it is an approach that should be made available to the FCA and CMA to increase the deterrent effect of financial crime. This is discussed further in the third recommendation below.

To date neither the European Commission nor the European Securities and Markets Authority (ESMA), the EU regulator for MAR 2014, has yet to use a DPA in connection with financial crime. However, the UK has had the power to enter into DPAs since 2013[30] and has so far entered into 13 DPAs.[31] At present, however, only the Crown Prosecution Service and the Serious Fraud Office (SFO) have the ability to issue a DPA, but if DPAs are to be used more widely for corporate criminal liability in future, which this book recommends, then the competition law and financial regulators should also have the power to issue DPAs. This is discussed further in the third recommendation below.

7.3 Recommendations

This book makes several recommendations for the UK based on its findings, which, if implemented, could improve the ability of regulators to enforce and prevent financial crime. These recommendations are based on the legislative measures adopted following the LIBOR and FX crisis that gave the FCA competition law enforcement powers. More recent changes to the law, such as the Economic Crime and Corporate Transparency Act 2023 and the Digital Markets, Competition and Consumer Act 2024, are also taken into account in these recommendations.

28 N Ryder, '"Too Scared to Prosecute and Too Scared to Jail?" A Critical and Comparative Analysis of Enforcement of Financial Crime Legislation against Corporations in the USA and the UK' (2018) 82(3) *The Journal of Criminal Law* 263.

29 For example, see US Department of Justice, 'Five Major Banks Agree to Parent-Level Guilty Pleas' (US Department of Justice, 20 May 2015) <https://www.justice.gov/opa/pr/five-major-banks-agree-parent-level-guilty-pleas> accessed 28 July 2024.

30 Crime Courts Act 2013 s.45 and Schedule 17.

31 Serious Fraud Office, 'Deferred Prosecution Agreements' (Serious Fraud Office, 2024) <https://www.sfo.gov.uk/publications/guidance-policy-and-protocols/guidance-for-corporates/deferred-prosecution-agreements/> accessed 12 July 2024; and Crown Prosecution Service, 'First Ever CPS Deferred Prosecution Agreement for £615 million' (CPS, 5 December 2023) <https://www.cps.gov.uk/cps/news/first-ever-cps-deferred-prosecution-agreement-ps615-million> accessed 12 July 2024.

7.3.1 First Recommendation

The overriding recommendation is for the FCA to use its existing competition law powers more frequently and to a fuller extent.

The reason for this recommendation is that, if the FCA had allowed the UK's competition regulator of the time, the OFT, to use its competition powers to investigate the LIBOR and FX benchmark manipulation as a possible breach of the Chapter I prohibition,[32] the banks responsible could have been fined up to 10% of their worldwide turnover. For a bank such as Barclays, that would have been up to £1.919b because, in the year ending 31 December 2012, Barclays' worldwide turnover was £19.199b.[33] Compared to the fine of £59.5m that Barclays received from the FSA, there is a significant difference. In the US, the fine given to Barclays dwarfed the UK fine, as Barclays was fined a total of $360m by US regulators,[34] which is six times as much as the UK fine, despite a reduction for cooperation with the authorities.

Chapter 3 demonstrated that the FCA has hardly used its extensive competition law powers in the financial services sector, with just two decisions taken using competition law. The first case in 2019,[35] the FCA used competition law to impose fines on two businesses that amounted to just 1% of their turnover. This is an extremely low fine when the maximum fine available to the regulator was 10% of each undertaking's turnover.[36] The second case decided by the FCA using competition law was in November 2023 and, again, involved modest fines (just £150,000 in total for the three businesses found to have colluded).[37] Since the FCA gained its competition law powers in 2014, it has launched eight investigations into the financial services sector, with only two of these resulting in a decision.[38] This demonstrates that the FCA, in the ten

32 Competition Act 1998, Chapter I.

33 Barclays Bank, 'Annual Report 2012' (Barclays Bank, 3 March 2013) <https://home.barclays/content/dam/home-barclays/documents/investor-relations/annualreports/ar2012/2012-barclays-bank-plc-annual-report.pdf> accessed 24 July 2024.

34 Commodity Futures Trading Commission, 'CFTC Orders Barclays to Pay $200 Million Penalty for Attempted Manipulation of and False Reporting Concerning LIBOR and Euribor Benchmark Interest Rates' (Commodity Futures Trading Commission, 27 June 2012) <https://www.cftc.gov/PressRoom/PressReleases/pr6289-12> accessed 16 July 2024.

35 Financial Conduct Authority, 'FCA Issues Its First Decision under Competition Law' (Financial Conduct Authority, 21 February 2019) <https://www.fca.org.uk/news/press-releases/fca-issues-its-first-decision-under-competition-law> accessed 27 July 2024.

36 Competition Act 1998, s.36(8).

37 E Radcliffe, G Dowell, 'Details of the FCA's Second Competition Act Infringement Decision Made Public' (Macfarlanes, 1 May 2024) <https://www.macfarlanes.com/what-we-think/2024/details-of-the-fca-s-second-competition-act-infringement-decision-made-public/> accessed 20 July 2024; and FCA, 'Competition Act 1998 Decision: International Money Remittance' (FCA, 4 April 2024) <https://www.fca.org.uk/firms/case-study-competition-act-1998-decision> accessed 20 July 2024.

38 Competition and Markets Authority, 'Competition Act 1998 Cases in the Regulated Sectors' (GOV.UK, 30 April 2024) <https://www.gov.uk/government/publications/competition

years that it has had competition law enforcement powers, has not embraced its competition law powers but, rather, is continuing to rely on its financial regulation powers to enforce financial crime. This is a lost opportunity for the FCA because using its competition law powers would enable it to impose larger fines, as mentioned above, as well as to take other enforcement action including the imposition of structural and behavioural remedies, mentioned below.

If the UK uses competition law to enforce future banking benchmark manipulation cartels, it will also be possible for regulators to prosecute the individuals involved using the criminal cartel offence, an offence specifically designed for the crimes committed, unlike the offence of conspiracy to defraud, which was used against the cartel members in the LIBOR and FX benchmark manipulation cartels and resulted in numerous acquittals.

Additional methods of enforcement for any future market manipulation similar to the LIBOR or FX benchmark manipulation would be for the FCA and CMA to use their competition law powers to disqualify bank directors for competition law breaches and to accept commitments from banks. If commitments are to be used in future by the FCA or CMA to resolve banking cartel cases, then these can act as an equivalent to a DPA but for civil enforcement actions.[39] Like a DPA, commitments, if breached, can be enforced in courts if broken.[40]

If some or all of the above competition law powers are used alongside financial regulation, it will broaden the reach of the regulators' powers. This is particularly true if, as was the case in the LIBOR and FX crisis, the fines issued to banks involved in market manipulation may not be larger than the profits made from the financial crime. If fines of up to 10% of a bank's worldwide turnover are combined with the disqualification of directors of the banks involved and the criminal prosecution of the bank employees involved in the cartel, perhaps settled with behavioural undertakings or commitments given to the regulator by the bank, there would be a significant deterrent effect for future benchmark manipulation cartels.

7.3.2 Second Recommendation

The second recommendation is that banks should be held criminally responsible for financial crimes such as benchmark manipulation, which are committed by their employees during their employment. Should banks be found criminally liable for the actions of their employees, they are likely to take greater care to avoid breaches of financial crime in the future. One way in which banks

-act-1998-cases-in-the-sectors-regulated-by-ukcn-members/competition-act-1998-cases-in-the-regulated-sectors#financial-services> accessed 27 July 2024.

39 Competition Act 1998, ss. 31A to 31E.

40 Ibid, s. 31E.

could avoid breaches of financial crime is by implementing better supervision and training of their employees, which will, in turn, lead to a reduction of the type of financial crime examined in this book. To make it possible for UK regulators to prosecute banks in conjunction with individuals, certain legislative changes could be made.

This book recommends that an amendment is made to the cartel offence,[41] to make it applicable to corporate bodies as well as to individuals. This would open the possibility for banks to be prosecuted based on vicarious liability principles for the criminal actions of their employees in the case of future benchmark manipulation cartels. Furthermore, the current defences to the cartel offence for individuals should be amended or removed to facilitate prosecution of individuals when their participation in an illegal criminal cartel has been proved.[42] This, combined with giving powers to the CMA and FCA (see the third recommendation below) to enter into DPAs with corporate bodies, should ensure both an appropriate deterrent effect to other banks and increased compliance procedures, with regular checks by the regulators, to create more focus on compliance and a closer working relationship with the regulators.

In addition to amending the cartel offence to make it applicable to companies as well as individuals, it is recommended that a new corporate criminal offence of 'failure to prevent economic crime' is created to give regulators an alternative offence with which to prosecute banks involved in future benchmark manipulation offences. Having a choice of corporate criminal offence suitable for future instances of benchmark manipulation will increase the prospects of regulators being able to successfully find banks liable for their participation in a cartel, which could then lead to the entry into a DPA with those banks in lieu of prosecution.

7.3.3 Third Recommendation

The third recommendation is that the FCA and CMA be given the power to enter into DPAs with companies found to be in breach of competition law.[43] Currently, the Director of Public Prosecutions and the Director of the SFO are the only designated prosecutors with the power to enter into a DPA.[44] This will involve amending Schedule 17 of the Crime and Courts Act 2013 to add the FCA and CMA to the list of designated prosecutors. Providing the FCA and CMA with the power to enter into a DPA with an infringing bank would have the advantage of combining the imposition of a fine with regulation of

41 Enterprise Act 2002, s.188(1).

42 Enterprise Act 2002, s.188B.

43 The only regulators with power to issue DPAs in the UK are the Serious Fraud Office and the Crown Prosecution Service; see Crime and Courts Act 2013, Schedule 17, para. 3(1).

44 Crime and Courts Act 2013, Schedule 17, s.3(1) and 3(2).

the bank's future behaviour, which would have the effect of both penalising and deterring future financial misconduct. The DPA could be combined with action taken against the individuals responsible for the crimes, including the competition director disqualification orders[45] and civil prohibition orders made by the FCA against individual traders involved with market manipulation to bar them from carrying on regulated activities for a set period.[46]

Giving the FCA and CMA this power should contribute to the reduction and deterrence of financial crime in the financial services sector and encourage banks to work harder to ensure that their employees do not break the law by colluding with competitors to improve their trading positions.

7.3.4 Fourth Recommendation

The fourth recommendation is that the UK improves the existing competition law whistleblowing/leniency regime for competition law breaches and institutes a high-profile campaign in the financial services sector to ensure that banks and their employees know about the competition law leniency and whistleblowing regime and how to report breaches of the law, together with knowledge of the financial rewards on offer. Currently, it is not easy to find information about the financial reward offered to whistleblowers for reporting a breach of competition law – the only mention of it is at the bottom of the CMA's cartel campaign webpage.[47] This information needs to be given much more prominence in the cartel webpages of both the FCA and CMA to give regulators a greater chance of catching and prosecuting cartels in the financial services sector in the UK.

As part of the improvement to the competition law whistleblowing regime, it is essential that the UK increases the amount of money offered as a reward to whistleblowers because, for an individual working in an international bank, the maximum reward of £250,000 (recently increased by the CMA from £100,000)[48] will not adequately compensate them for informing on their employer and, in all likelihood, losing their job. UK regulators should look to the US leniency programme and the individual whistleblower awards, including the recent payment of $279m by the SEC to an individual whistleblower,[49]

45 Company Directors Disqualification Act 1986, s.9A.

46 Financial Services and Markets Act 2000, s.56.

47 Competition and Markets Authority, 'Cheating or Competing? It's Your Business to Know the Difference' (GOV.UK, 2024) <https://cheatingorcompeting.campaign.gov.uk/> accessed 26 July 2024.

48 Competition and Markets Authority, 'Blowing the Whistle on Cartels' (GOV.UK, 6 June 2023) <https://www.gov.uk/government/news/blowing-the-whistle-on-cartels#:~:text=The%20Competition%20and%20Markets%20Authority,cartel%20activity%20they%20have%20witnessed.> accessed 20 July 2024.

49 Reuters, 'SEC Issues Largest Ever Whistleblower Award of $279 Million' *Reuters* (US, 5 May 2023) <https://www.reuters.com/world/us/us-sec-issues-largest-ever-whistleblower-award-279-mln-2023-05-05/> accessed 20 July 2024.

for an appropriate level of compensation to make the leniency/whistleblower programme attractive to individuals in the banking sector.

In addition to increasing the awards offered and made to whistleblowers in the UK, further protection for whistleblowers needs to be introduced, and information about competition law and competition law breaches should be provided to potential whistleblowers in the financial services industry. It should be made possible for financial services whistleblowers to report breaches of competition law directly to the FCA, the regulator they are most familiar with, rather than (as is currently the position) solely to the CMA. This should be done by adding a prominent location on the FCA's website for whistleblowers to access if they suspect a breach of competition law at the place of their employment. These changes will encourage informers to provide evidence of future or current cartels in the financial services sector, which will enable regulators to take earlier action to stop harmful breaches of financial crime, which, in turn, will protect the UK economy and citizens.

7.3.5 Fifth Recommendation

Finally, this book recommends a greater use of the power to instigate competition law market studies and investigations in the financial services sector. The CMA has the ability to commence either a market study or a market investigation into an entire market sector, such as the banking sector, when they believe that particular features of the market give rise to an anticompetitive effect.[50] A market investigation into the banking sector was called for in 2012 by Clive Maxwell, the then Executive Director of the OFT, who identified that 'competition in the banking sector was not functioning well and has not for some time'.[51] Maxwell went on to hold open the possibility of a reference of the banking sector to the Competition Commission, with behavioural and structural remedies available, including requiring the break-up of banks if reforms were not implemented.[52] The CMA has carried out one market investigation into the retail banking sector when it investigated the supply of personal current accounts and of banking services to small- and medium-sized enterprises.[53] As a result of this 2016 investigation, a Retail Banking

50 Enterprise Act 2002, s. 130A and s131, Enterprise and Regulatory Reform Act 2013, Schedule 11 and Competition and Markets Authority, 'Market Studies and Market Investigations: Supplemental Guidance on the CMA's Approach' (GOV.UK, July 2017) 20 <https://assets.publishing.service.gov.uk/media/65cdfc4f130549000c867a9f/A._cma3-markets-supplemental-guidance-updated-june-2017.pdf> accessed 20 July 2024.

51 D Harrison, *Competition Law and Financial Services* (Routledge 2014), 61.

52 D Harrison, *Competition Law and Financial Services* (Routledge 2014), 61.

53 Competition and Markets Authority, 'Retail Banking Market Investigation' (GOV.UK, 19 October 2023) <https://www.gov.uk/cma-cases/review-of-banking-for-small-and-medium-sized-businesses-smes-in-the-uk#:~:text=Retail%20Banking%20Market%20Investigation%20Order%202017,-This%20order%20was&text=The%20order%20sets%20out%20the,to%20publish%20service%20quality%20statistics.> accessed 20 July 2024.

Market Investigation Order was passed, which contained remedies to the competition problems identified in the investigation.[54] Since then, the CMA has been granted a new and enhanced range of market investigation powers in the Digital Markets, Competition and Consumers Act 2024. These new powers include greater flexibility to define the scope and process of a market investigation and the ability to accept binding commitments from market participants at any point in the investigation. It is anticipated that these changes will lead to an increase in market investigations, particularly in concentrated markets such as banking.[55]

It is recommended that the CMA instigates a further market investigation into anticompetitive behaviour in the commercial banking sector, such as the banking collusion seen in the LIBOR and FX benchmark manipulation cartels, with appropriate behavioural and/or structural reforms being suggested following the investigation in order to ensure that no further acts of collusion between competitor banks takes place to the detriment of both the financial services sector and to individuals in each country affected.

Should the above recommendations be implemented, then larger companies, such as international banks, that breach competition law by forming illegal cartels will no longer feel that they are immune from UK competition law but, instead, will realise that they need to take steps to avoid breaches of competition law in the financial services sector, which will, in turn, reduce financial crime in the UK.

7.4 Further Research

Whilst this book has endeavoured to provide a comprehensive comparison, there are additional areas that will benefit from further research. One such area involves widening the current research to different countries to examine how they use competition law to enforce financial crime to identify further areas of best practice that can then be formulated into recommendations for UK regulators. The decision not to include more jurisdictions into this comparative research was based on the closeness of the links between the UK, EU and US competition laws, which provide a level playing field for the consideration of the approaches to the financial crime of benchmark manipulation. Widening this research into other countries will build on the research undertaken in this book.

Countries that would provide useful comparisons for future research are the large financial centres of Japan, Singapore and Australia. In particular,

54 Ibid.

55 Sidley Austin LLP, 'The Digital Markets, Competition and Consumers Act Is Approved: Key Things to Know about the UK's New Competition and Consumer Powers' (Sidley Austin LLP, 28 May 2024) <https://datamatters.sidley.com/2024/05/28/the-digital-markets-competition-and-consumers-act-is-approved-key-things-to-know-about-the-uks-new-competition-and-consumer-powers/> accessed 29 July 2024.

Australia has had criminal penalties for participation in a cartel since 2010,[56] and since then, the Australian Competition and Consumer Commission has concluded three successful criminal prosecutions over the past decade, with fines approaching A$60m and one eight month suspended sentence. Criminal charges have been laid in five further matters.[57] Australia recently signed the Multilateral Mutual Assistance and Cooperation Framework for Competition Authorities (MMAC), whose other signatories include the DoJ, US Federal Trade Commission, the CMA, the Competition Bureau of Canada and the New Zealand Commerce Commission.[58] The MMAC came into effect on 2 September 2020 and demonstrates a growing appetite amongst regulators for cross-jurisdictional cooperation in the investigation of anticompetitive behaviour by large multinational companies such as international banks. Australia brought criminal cartel charges against Citigroup Inc, Deutsche Bank AG, Australia and New Zealand Banking Group Ltd and six current and former staff for colluding during a share issue in 2020.[59] This case was ultimately unsuccessful for prosecutors, as four years later, the case was dropped, with lack of evidence cited by prosecutors as the reason.[60] Therefore, it appears that there is a need to look closely at how criminal cartel investigations and prosecutions are carried out in order to provide guidance to regulators about how to successfully gather sufficient evidence to prosecute cartels in the financial services sector.

Further research might also be warranted in order to examine and understand how the use of competition law could assist in tackling other financial crimes that involve bank collusion or the abuse of a dominant market position by one or more banks. Whilst this book has focused on the financial crime of benchmark manipulation, which has clearly been identified as collusion in breach of competition law by EU and US regulators, there are other types of

56 L Campbell, 'Trying Corporations: Why Not Prosecute?' (2019) 31(2) *Current Issues in Criminal Justice* 269.

57 International Competition Network, 'Trends and Development in Cartel Enforcement 2010-2020' (International Competition Network, 2021) <https://www.internationalcompetitionnetwork.org/wp-content/uploads/2022/01/CWGReportonTrendsSurvey_2021.pdf> accessed 22 July 2024.

58 Australian Competition and Consumer Commission, 'Multilateral Mutual Assistance and Cooperation Framework for Competition Authorities; Memorandum of Understanding' (Australian Competition and Consumer Commission, 2 September 2020) <https://www.accc.gov.au/system/files/MMAC%20-%20FINAL%20English%20-%202%20September%202020%2811501052.1%29.pdf> accessed 24 July 2024.

59 Reuters, 'Citi, Deutsche Bank, ANZ Committed for Trial In Australian Criminal Cartel Case' (*Reuters*, 8 December 2020) <https://www.reuters.com/article/us-australia-banks-cartel-idUSKBN28I0BN> accessed 1 July 2024.

60 B Kaye and S Murdoch, 'Australia Drops Landmark Criminal Cartel Case Against Citi, Deutsche' (Reuters, 11 February 2022) <https://www.reuters.com/business/finance/australian-prosecutors-drop-cartel-charges-against-citi-deutsche-bank-2022-02-11/> accessed 21 July 2024.

bank collusion that may breach Part 1 or Part 2 of the Competition Act 1998 and ought to be taken into consideration in future research.

7.5 Conclusion

Financial crime, including market manipulation, poses a significant problem for the UK, costing billions of pounds each year.[61] Financial crimes, such as banking cartels, have incredibly wide-reaching consequences for the economy of each country affected by them,[62] and banking cartels are regularly formed due to the tempting financial gains made by the individual bankers and banks.[63] Every citizen of the UK who had a mortgage, car loan or personal or commercial loan was negatively impacted by the artificial movements of the LIBOR by the banking cartels to which the majority of all financial instruments were pegged at the time.[64] This wide-reaching effect of the financial crime in question demonstrates the need for effective enforcement tools by the regulators. Both the US and EU regulators have made it clear that competition law applies to the banking sector and that it can be used with significant effect; the European Commission states that 'competition rules apply to capital markets in the same way as to any other industrial or services sector',[65] and the Commission pursued all benchmark manipulation cases with its competition law powers. Likewise, in recent remarks, Deputy Assistant Attorney General Michael Murray announced that the DoJ was ramping up its focus on antitrust enforcement in the financial services sector.[66] However, despite the raft of legislation that has bestowed competition powers on sectoral regulators,[67] the UK financial services regulator appears to be reluctant to use

61 House of Commons Library, 'Economic Crime in the UK: A Multi-Billion Pound Problem' (UK Parliament, 6 April 2022) <https://commonslibrary.parliament.uk/research-briefings/cbp-9013/> accessed 22 July 2024.

62 P Whelan, *The Criminalization of European Cartel Enforcement* (Oxford University Press 2014) 321.

63 For example, see the recent banking cartel uncovered by the European Commission: European Commission, 'Antitrust: Commission Sends Statement of Objections in US Dollar Supra Sovereign, Sovereign and Agency Bond Trading Cartel' (European Commission, 20 December 2018) <https://ec.europa.eu/commission/presscorner/detail/en/IP_18_6895> accessed 24 July 2024.

64 R Abrantes-Metz et al., 'Libor Manipulation?' (2012) 36(1) *Journal of Banking and Finance* 136.

65 European Commission, 'Capital Markets' (European Commission, 2 June 2021) <https://ec.europa.eu/competition-policy/sectors/financial-services/capital-markets_en> accessed 16 July 2024.

66 US Department of Justice, 'The Muscular Role for Antitrust in Fintech, Financial Markets, and Banking: The Antitrust Division's Decision to Lean In' (US Department of Justice, 14 October 2020) <https://www.justice.gov/opa/speech/deputy-assistant-attorney-general-michael-murray-delivers-remarks-university-michigan-law> accessed 22 July 2024.

67 See the Financial Services Act 2012, the Financial Services (Banking Reform) Act 2013 and Enterprise and Regulatory Reform Act 2013.

competition law to enforce financial crime, relying instead on its more familiar financial regulatory powers, as shown by the very low number of investigations and cases brought in the financial services sector by either the CMA or FCA since 2013.[68] However, simply using regulatory fines alone is insufficient when companies can absorb fines as part of their operating costs.[69] The FCA must change its attitude to regulation and use the wide range of its competition law enforcement powers for future benchmark manipulation. As banking is a sector vulnerable to breaches of competition law,[70] the financial services regulators must be prepared and well equipped to deal with a future instance of benchmark manipulation. By using competition law enforcement powers, with the changes recommended in this study, UK regulators will have a wider range of enforcement powers to use against both companies and individuals who have committed financial crimes.

68 Competition and Markets Authority, 'Competition Act 1998 Cases in the Regulated Sectors' (GOV.UK, 30 April 2024) <https://www.gov.uk/government/publications/competition-act-1998-cases-in-the-sectors-regulated-by-ukcn-members/competition-act-1998-cases-in-the-regulated-sectors#financial-services> accessed 17 July 2024.

69 H Macartney and P Calcagno, 'All Bark And No Bite: The Political Economy of Bank Fines in Anglo-America' (2019) 26(4) *Review of International Political Economy*.

70 M Dong, S Huangfu, H Sun and C Zhou 'A Macroeconomic Theory of Banking Oligopoly' (2021) 138 *European Economic Review* 103864.

Index

FSC
www.fsc.org
MIX
Papier | Fördert gute Waldnutzung
FSC® C083411

Kolibri 360 GmbH
Ferdinand-Jühlke-Straße 7
99095 Erfurt, Deutschland
produktsicherheit@kolibri360.de